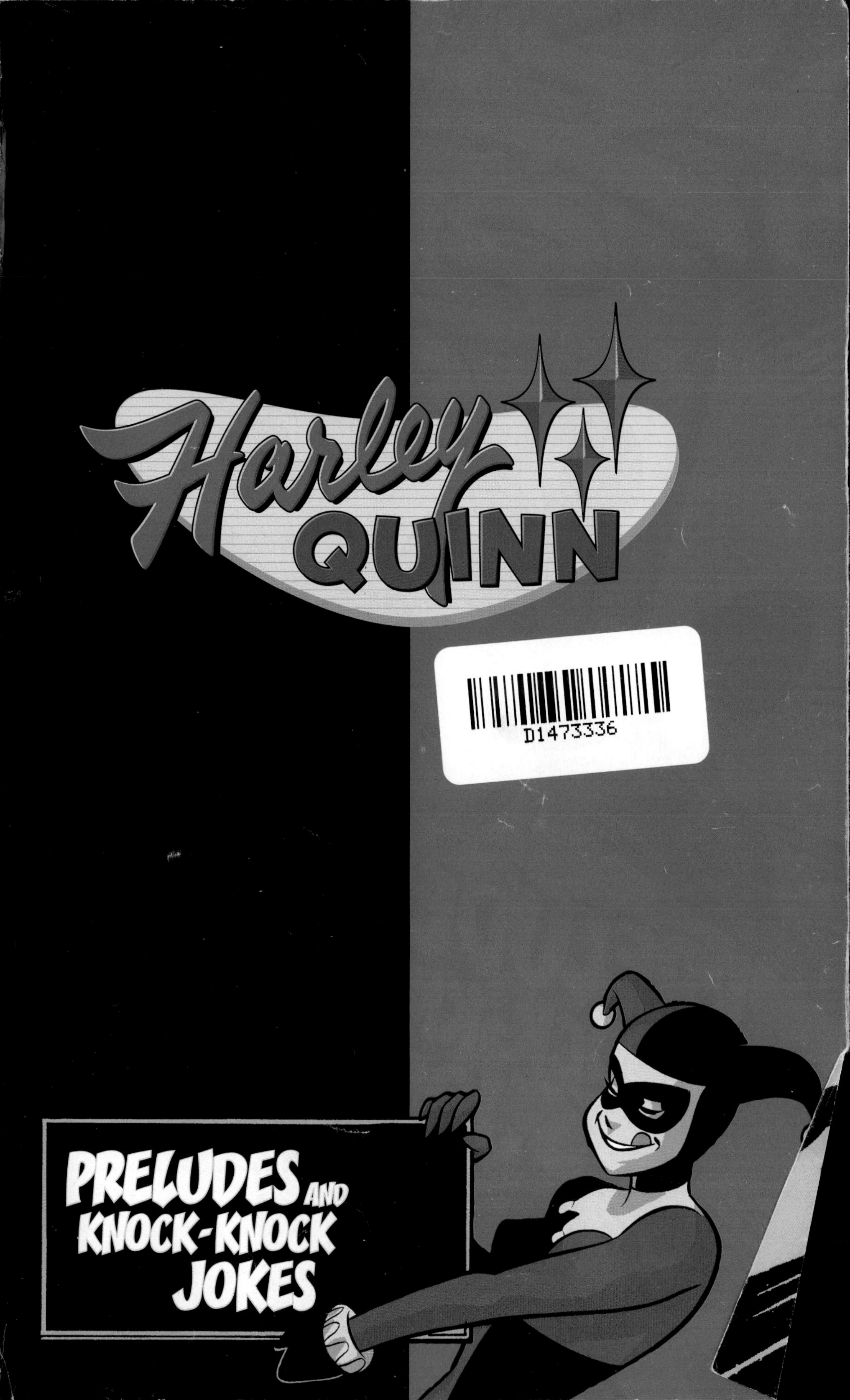
Harley
QUINN
PRELUDES AND
KNOCK-KNOCK
JOKES

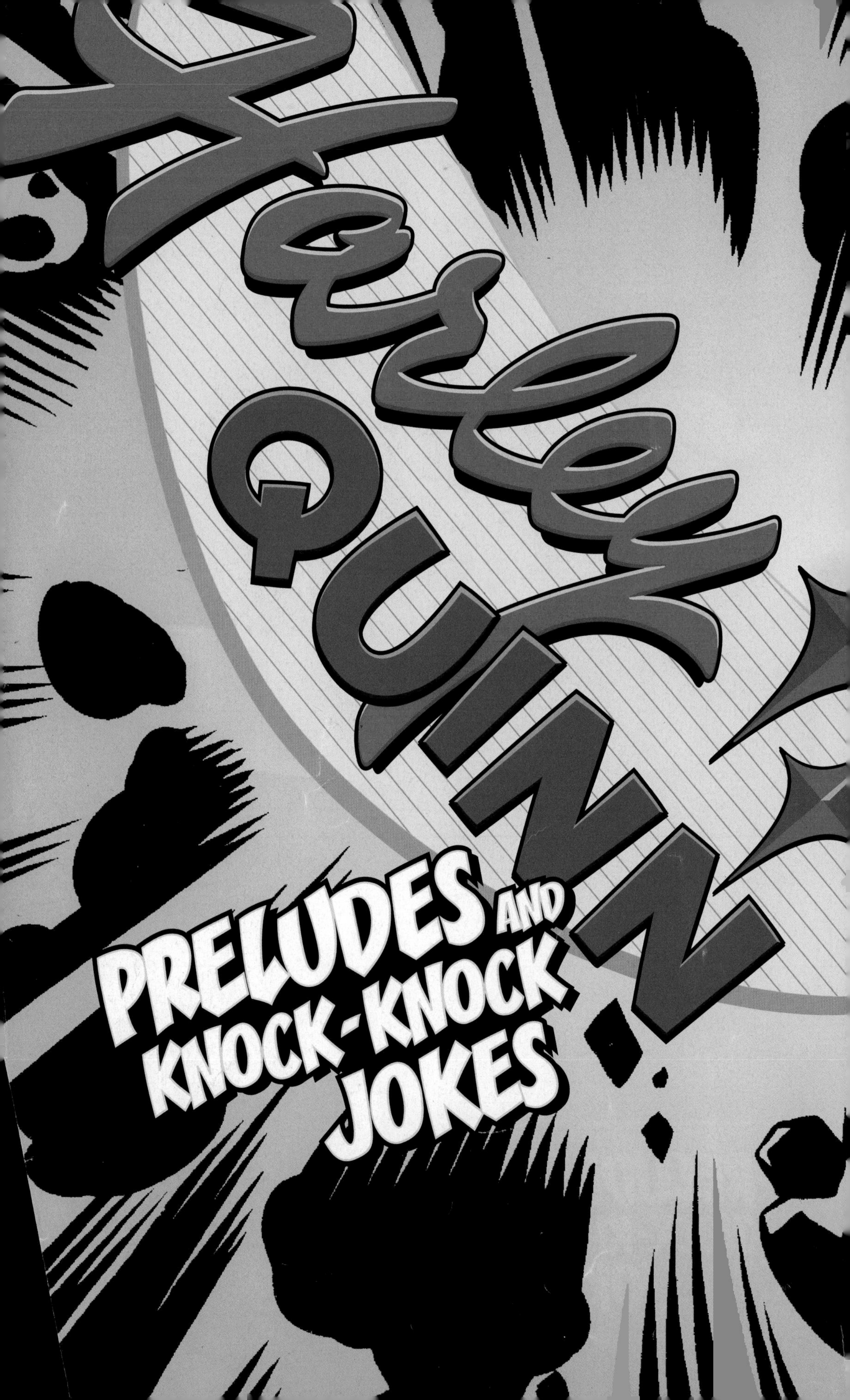
Harley
QUINN
PRELUDES AND
KNOCK-KNOCK
JOKES

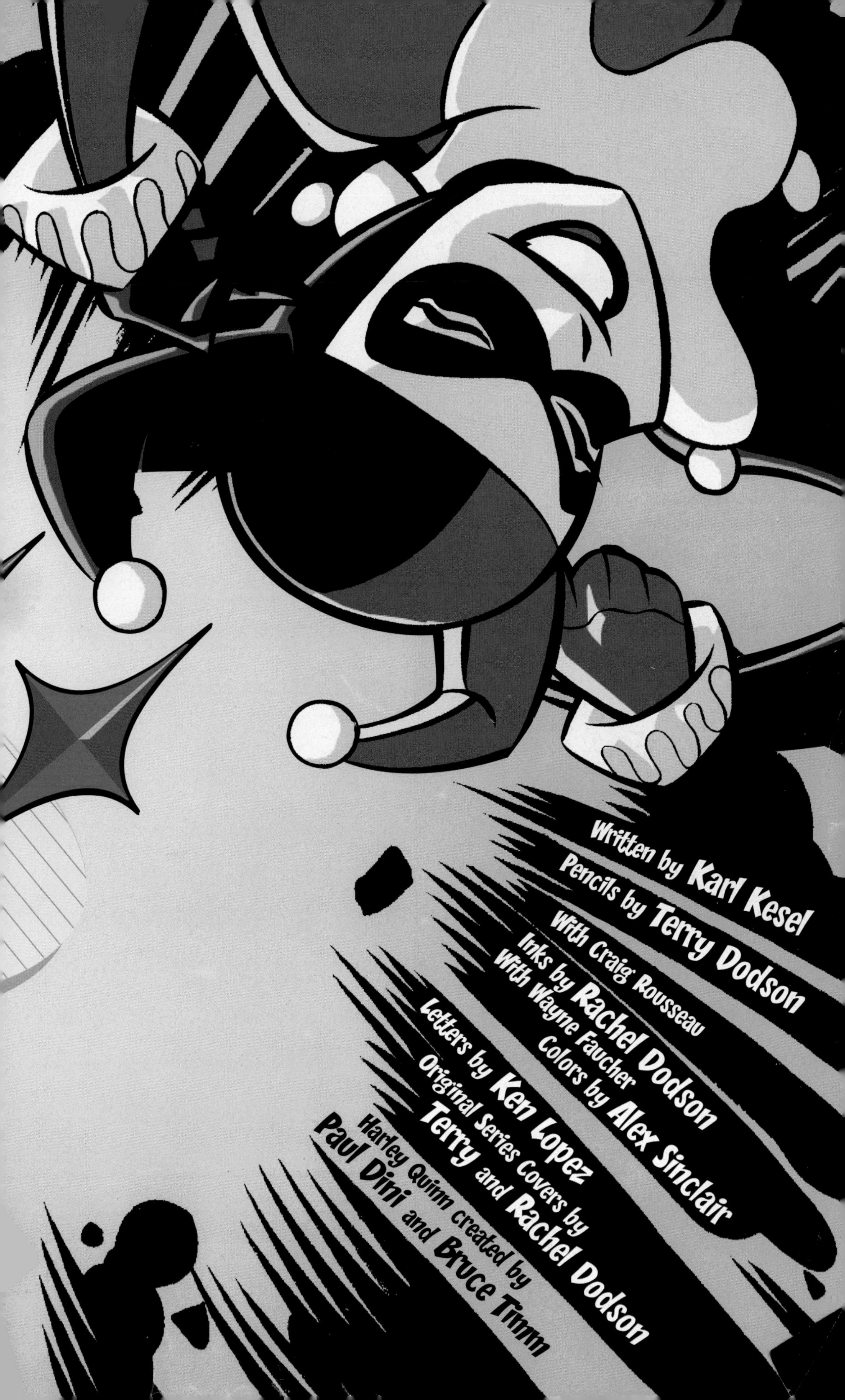
Written by Karl Kesel
Pencils by Terry Dodson
With Craig Rousseau
Inks by Rachel Dodson
With Wayne Faucher
Colors by Alex Sinclair
Letters by Ken Lopez
Original Series Covers by
Terry and Rachel Dodson
Harley Quinn created by
Paul Dini and Bruce Timm

Matt Idelson	Editor – Original Series
Frank Berrios	Assistant Editor – Original Series
Michael Wright	Associate Editor – Original Series
Robbin Brosterman	Design Director – Books
Louis Prandi	Publication Design
Bob Harras	Senior VP – Editor-in-Chief, DC Comics
Diane Nelson	President
Dan DiDio and Jim Lee	Co-Publishers
Geoff Johns	Chief Creative Officer
Amit Desai	Senior VP – Marketing and Franchise Management
Amy Genkins	Senior VP – Business and Legal Affairs
Nairi Gardiner	Senior VP – Finance
Jeff Boison	VP – Publishing Planning
Mark Chiarello	VP – Art Direction and Design
John Cunningham	VP – Marketing
Terri Cunningham	VP – Editorial Administration
Larry Ganem	VP – Talent Relations and Services
Alison Gill	Senior VP – Manufacturing and Operations
Hank Kanalz	Senior VP – Vertigo and Integrated Publishing
Jay Kogan	VP – Business and Legal Affairs, Publishing
Jack Mahan	VP – Business Affairs, Talent
Nick Napolitano	VP – Manufacturing Administration
Sue Pohja	VP – Book Sales
Fred Ruiz	VP – Manufacturing Operations
Courtney Simmons	Senior VP – Publicity
Bob Wayne	Senior VP – Sales

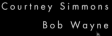

Cover by Terry Dodson and Rachel Dodson.
Logo by Chris Gardner.

HARLEY QUINN:
PRELUDES AND KNOCK-KNOCK JOKES
Published by DC Comics. Cover and compilation Copyright ©
2007 DC Comics. All Rights Reserved. Originally published
in single magazine form in HARLEY QUINN 1-7. Copyright ©
2000, 2001 DC Comics. All Rights Reserved. All characters,
their distinctive likenesses and related elements featured in this
publication are trademarks of DC Comics. The stories, characters
and incidents featured in this publication are entirely fictional.
DC Comics does not read or accept unsolicited submissions of
ideas, stories or artwork.
DC Comics, 1700 Broadway, New York, NY 10019
A Warner Bros. Entertainment Company
Printed by RR Donnelley, Salem, VA, USA. 8/21/15.
Sixth Printing.
ISBN#: 978-1-4012-1657-3

SUSTAINABLE
FORESTRY
INITIATIVE
Certified Chain of Custody
20% Certified Forest Content,
80% Certified Sourcing
www.sfiprogram.org
SFI-01042
APPLIES TO TEXT STOCK ONLY

Library of Congress Cataloging-in-Publication Data

Kesel, Karl, author.
    Harley Quinn : preludes and knock-knock jokes/ Karl Kesel,
Terry Dodson, Craig Rousseau.
      pages cm
  " Originally published in single magazine form in Harley Quinn
1-7."
  ISBN 978-1-4012-1657-3
  I. Dodson, Terry, illustrator. II. Title. III. Title: preludes and knock-
knock jokes.
  PN6727.K47 H37 2007
  741.5'973 —dc23
                                                    2009277626

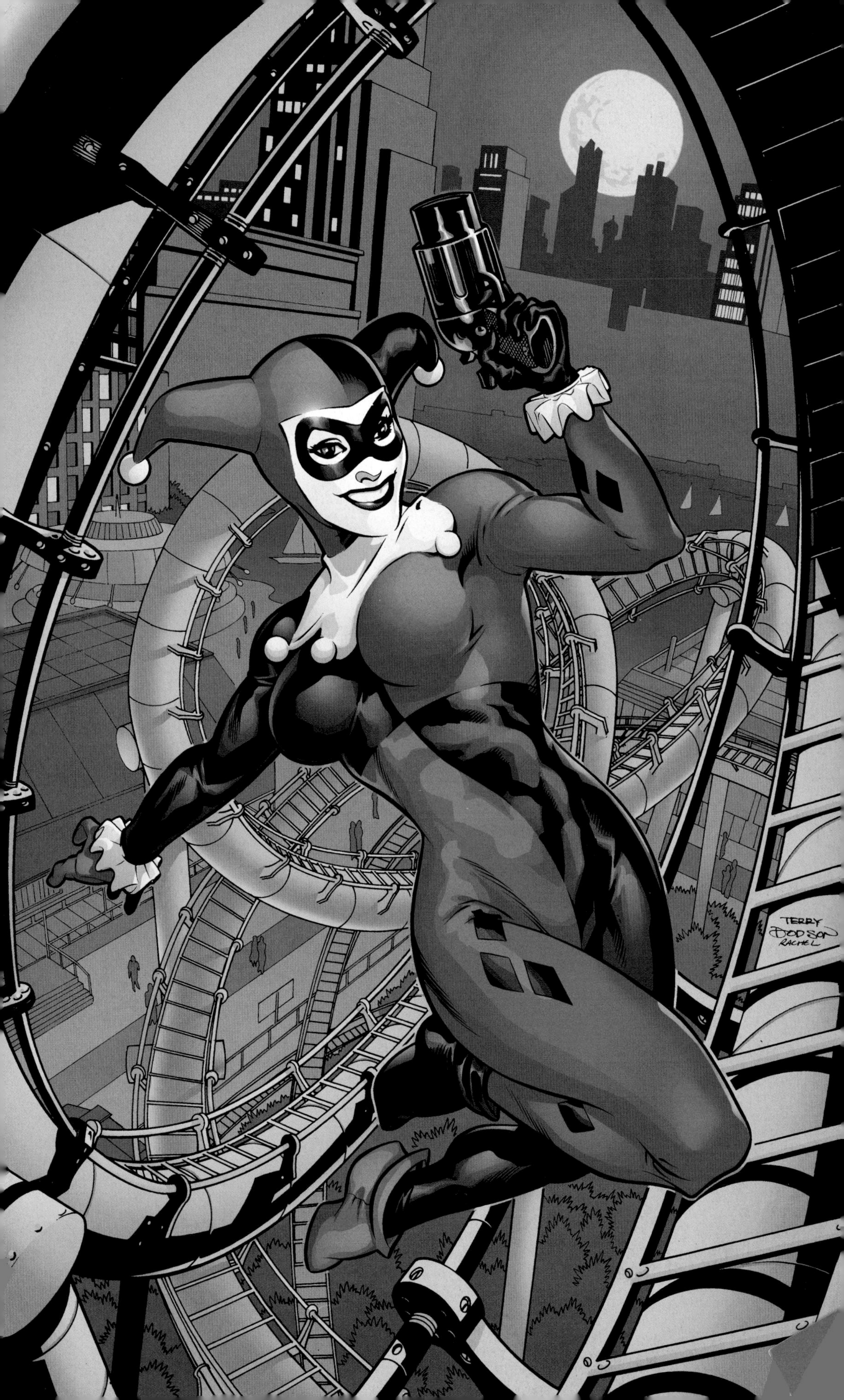
TERRY
DODSON
RACHEL

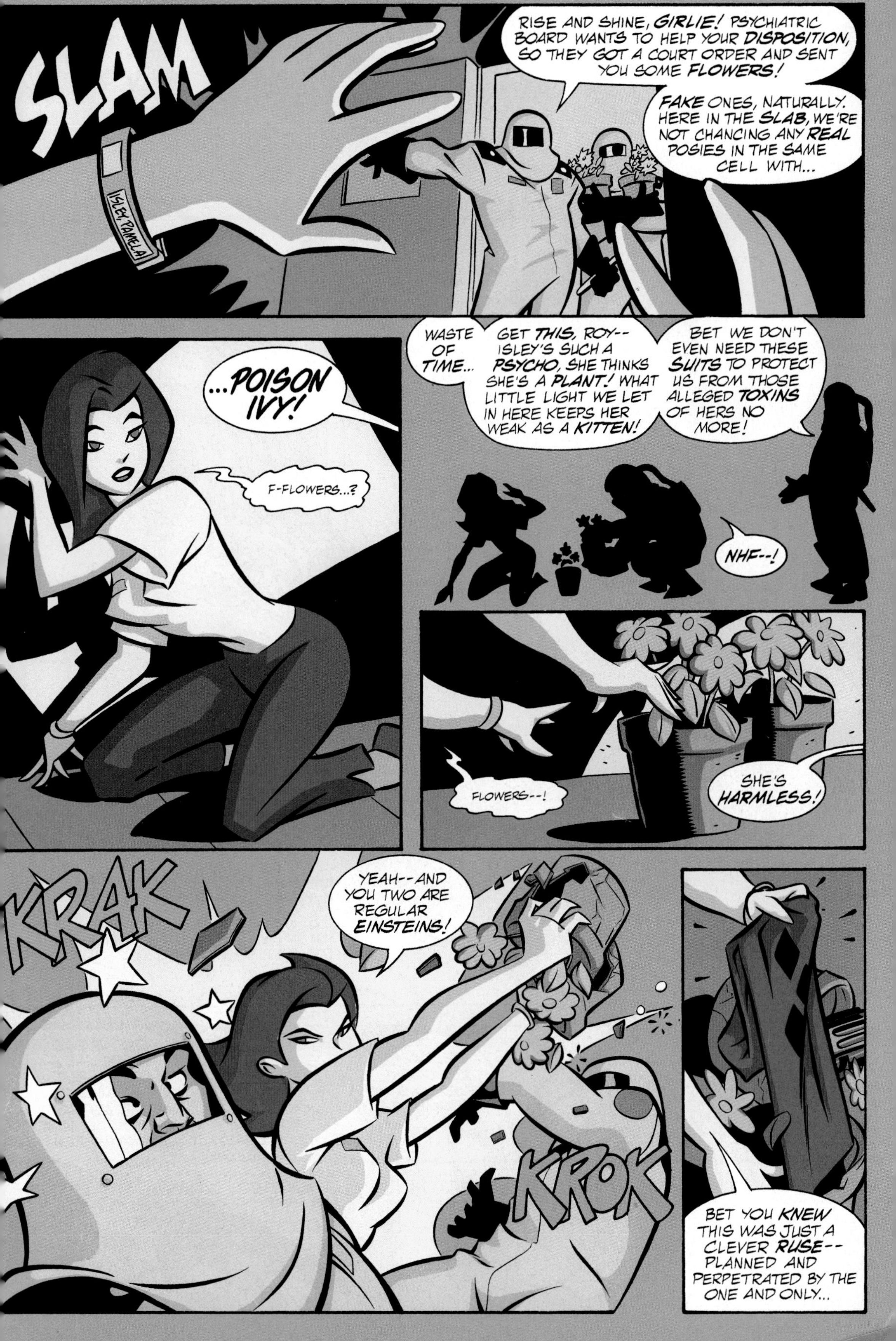
SLAM
ISLEY, PAMELA
RISE AND SHINE, GIRLIE! PSYCHIATRIC BOARD WANTS TO HELP YOUR DISPOSITION, SO THEY GOT A COURT ORDER AND SENT YOU SOME FLOWERS!
FAKE ONES, NATURALLY. HERE IN THE SLAB, WE'RE NOT CHANCING ANY REAL POSIES IN THE SAME CELL WITH...
...POISON IVY!
F-FLOWERS...?
WASTE OF TIME...
GET THIS, ROY-- ISLEY'S SUCH A PSYCHO, SHE THINKS SHE'S A PLANT! WHAT LITTLE LIGHT WE LET IN HERE KEEPS HER WEAK AS A KITTEN!
BET WE DON'T EVEN NEED THESE SUITS TO PROTECT US FROM THOSE ALLEGED TOXINS OF HERS NO MORE!
NHF--!
FLOWERS--!
SHE'S HARMLESS!
KRAK
YEAH--AND YOU TWO ARE REGULAR EINSTEINS!
KROK
BET YOU KNEW THIS WAS JUST A CLEVER RUSE-- PLANNED AND PERPETRATED BY THE ONE AND ONLY...

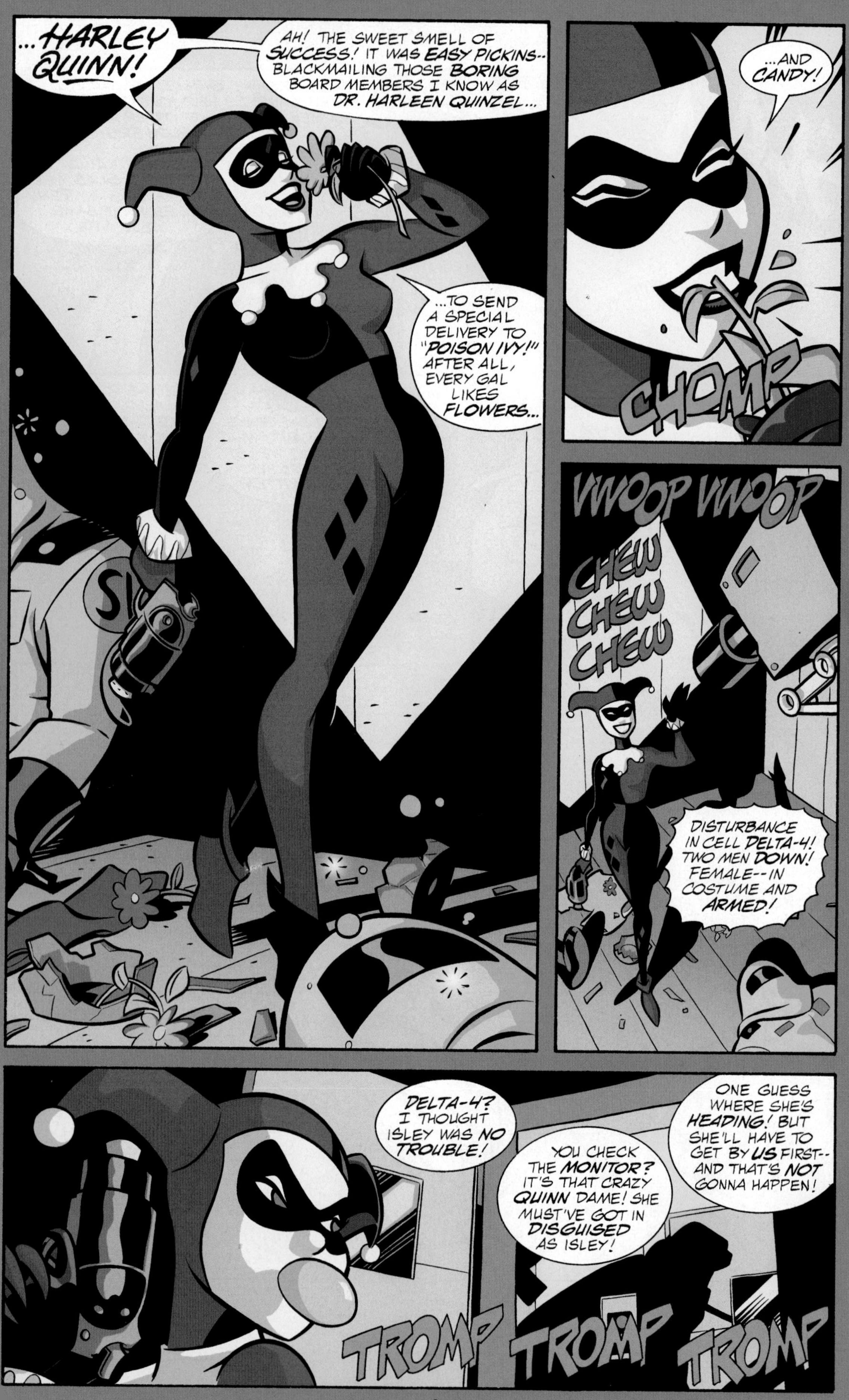

...HARLEY QUINN!
AH! THE SWEET SMELL OF SUCCESS! IT WAS EASY PICKINS-- BLACKMAILING THOSE BORING BOARD MEMBERS I KNOW AS DR. HARLEEN QUINZEL...
...TO SEND A SPECIAL DELIVERY TO "POISON IVY!" AFTER ALL, EVERY GAL LIKES FLOWERS...
...AND CANDY!
CHOMP
VWOOP VWOOP
CHEW CHEW CHEW
DISTURBANCE IN CELL DELTA-4! TWO MEN DOWN! FEMALE--IN COSTUME AND ARMED!
DELTA-4? I THOUGHT ISLEY WAS NO TROUBLE!
YOU CHECK THE MONITOR? IT'S THAT CRAZY QUINN DAME! SHE MUST'VE GOT IN DISGUISED AS ISLEY!
ONE GUESS WHERE SHE'S HEADING! BUT SHE'LL HAVE TO GET BY US FIRST-- AND THAT'S NOT GONNA HAPPEN!
TROMP TROMP TROMP

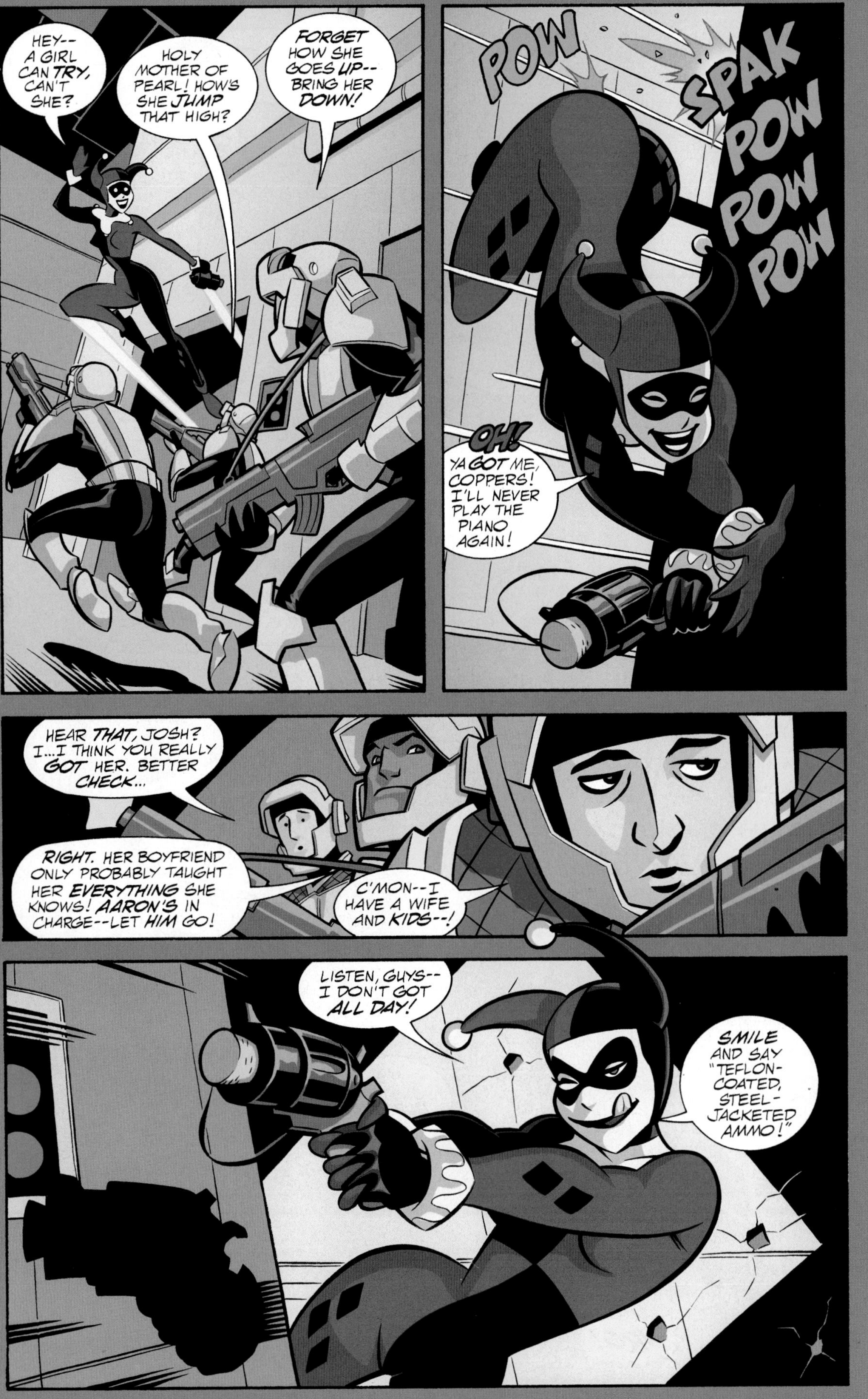
HEY-- A GIRL CAN TRY, CAN'T SHE?
HOLY MOTHER OF PEARL! HOW'S SHE JUMP THAT HIGH?
FORGET HOW SHE GOES UP-- BRING HER DOWN!
POW
SPAK
POW
POW
POW
OH!
YA GOT ME, COPPERS! I'LL NEVER PLAY THE PIANO AGAIN!
HEAR THAT, JOSH? I...I THINK YOU REALLY GOT HER. BETTER CHECK...
RIGHT. HER BOYFRIEND ONLY PROBABLY TAUGHT HER EVERYTHING SHE KNOWS! AARON'S IN CHARGE--LET HIM GO!
C'MON--I HAVE A WIFE AND KIDS--!
LISTEN, GUYS-- I DON'T GOT ALL DAY!
SMILE AND SAY "TEFLON-COATED, STEEL-JACKETED AMMO!"

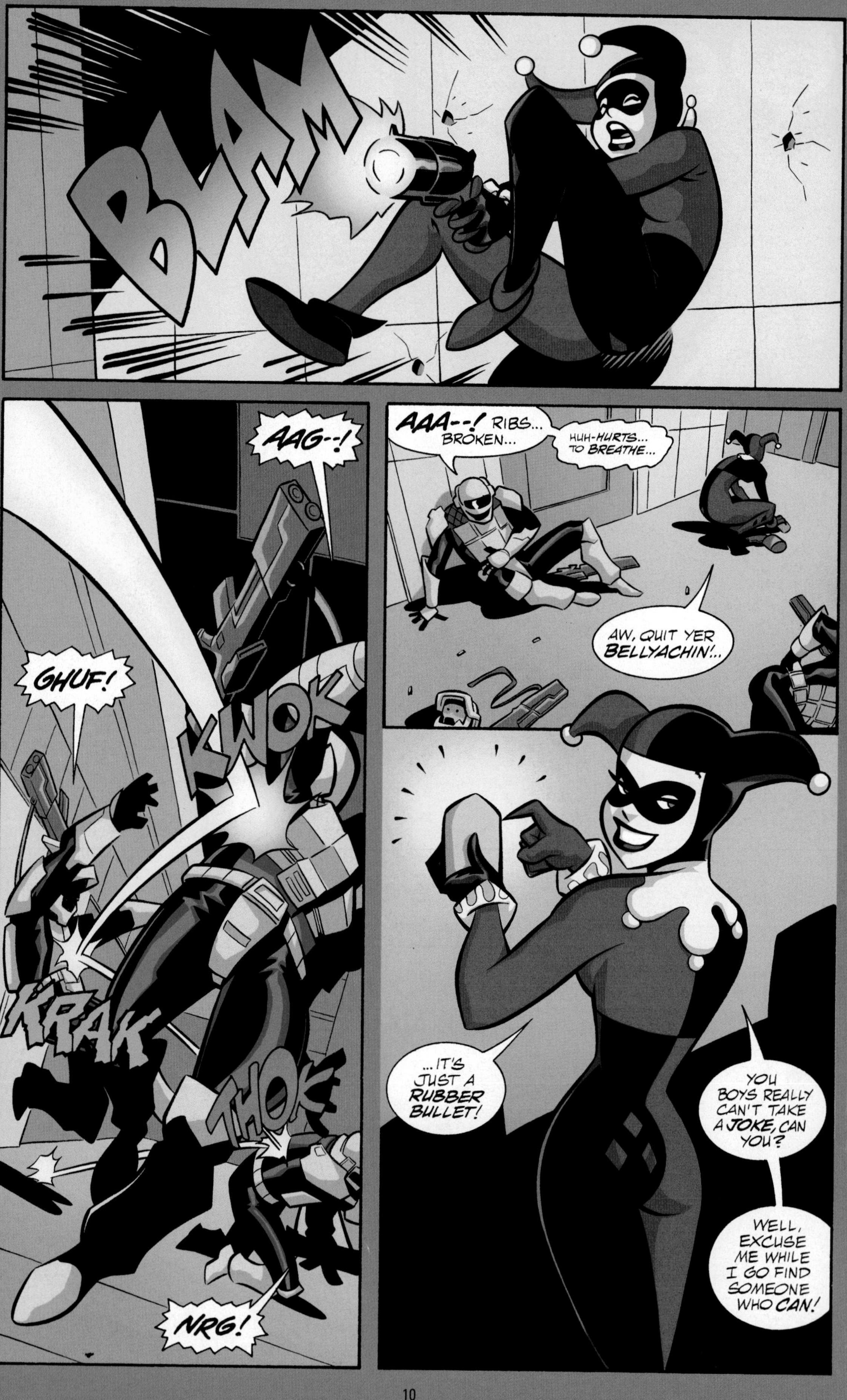

BLAM
AAG--!
GHUF!
KWOK
KRAK
THOK
NRG!
AAA--! RIBS... BROKEN...
HUH-HURTS... TO BREATHE...
AW, QUIT YER BELLYACHIN'!..
...IT'S JUST A RUBBER BULLET!
YOU BOYS REALLY CAN'T TAKE A JOKE, CAN YOU?
WELL, EXCUSE ME WHILE I GO FIND SOMEONE WHO CAN!

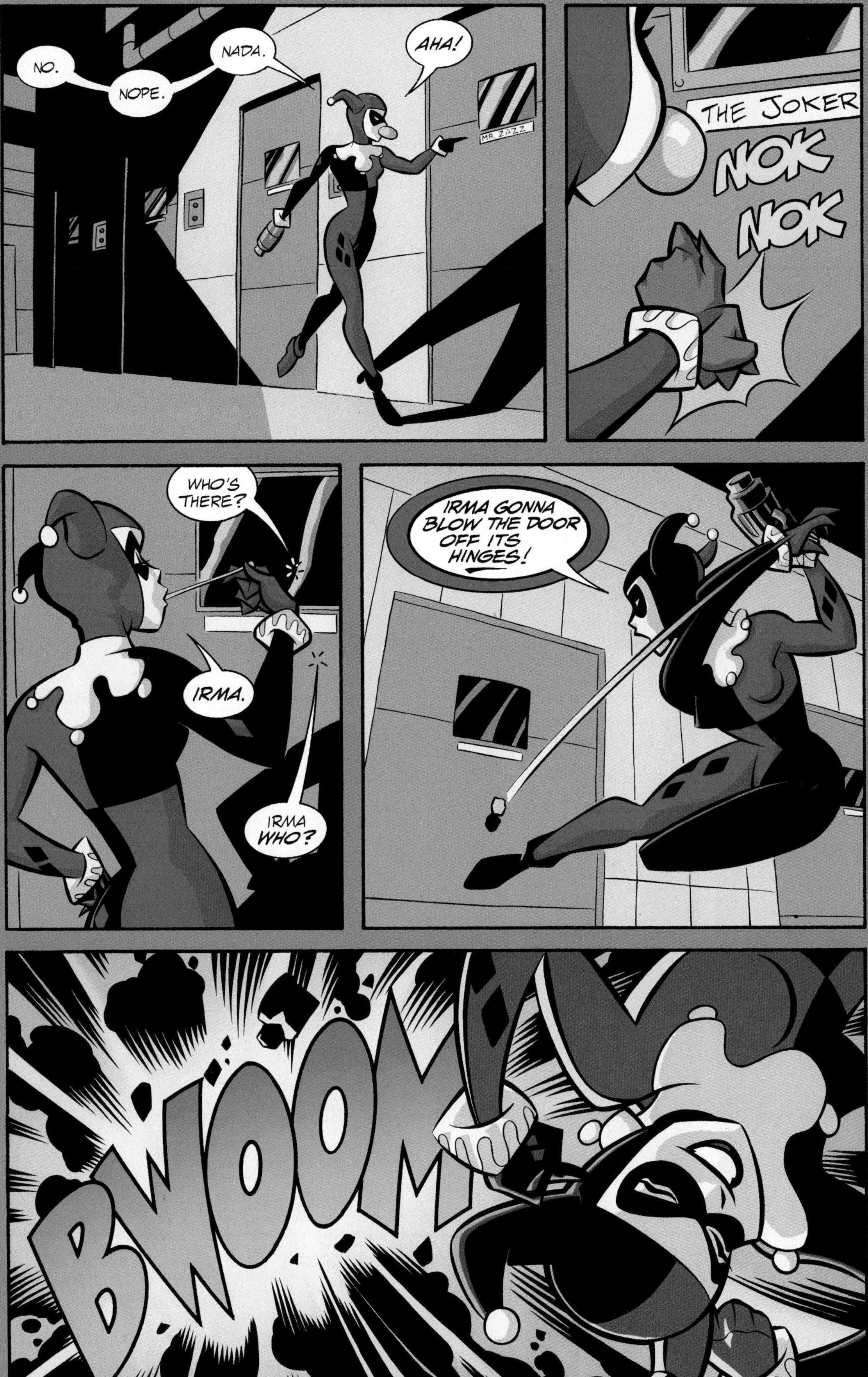
NO.
NOPE.
NADA.
AHA!
MR ZAZZ
THE JOKER
NOK
NOK
WHO'S THERE?
IRMA.
IRMA WHO?
IRMA GONNA BLOW THE DOOR OFF ITS HINGES!
BWOOM

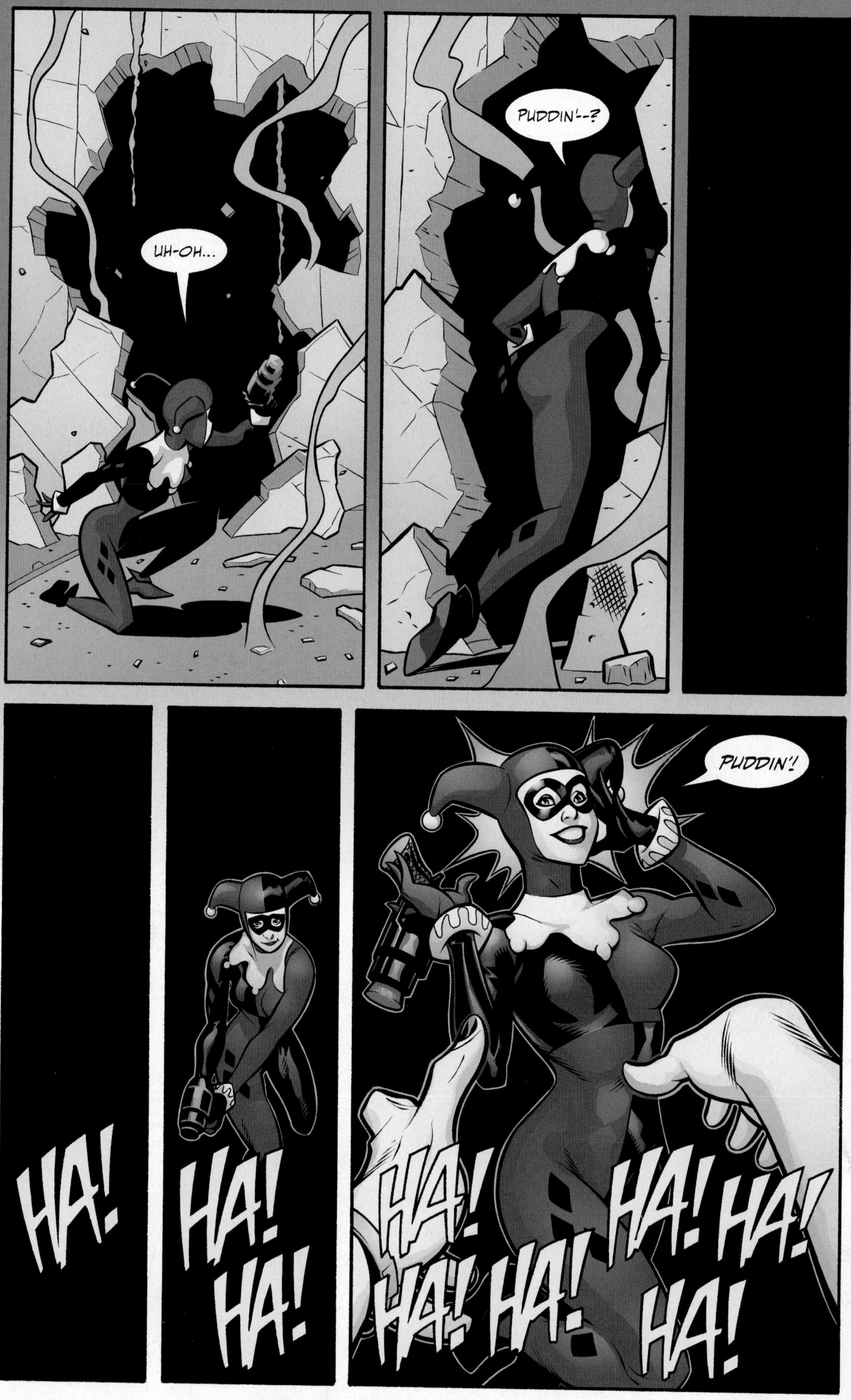
UH-OH...
PUDDIN'--?
PUDDIN'!
HA!
HA!
HA!
HA!
HA!
HA!
HA!
HA!
HA!
HA!

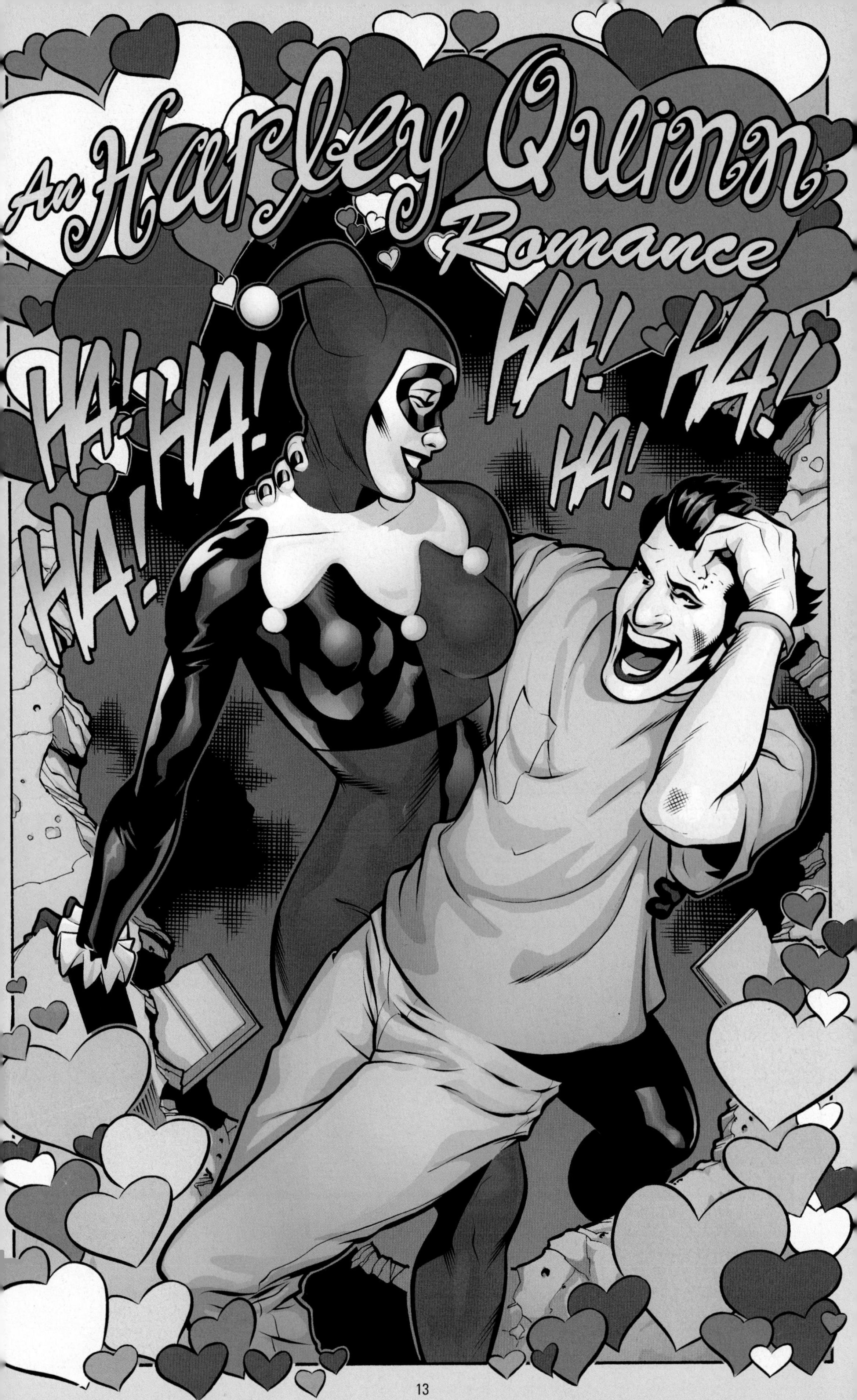
An Harley Quinn Romance
HA! HA! HA!
HA! HA! HA!

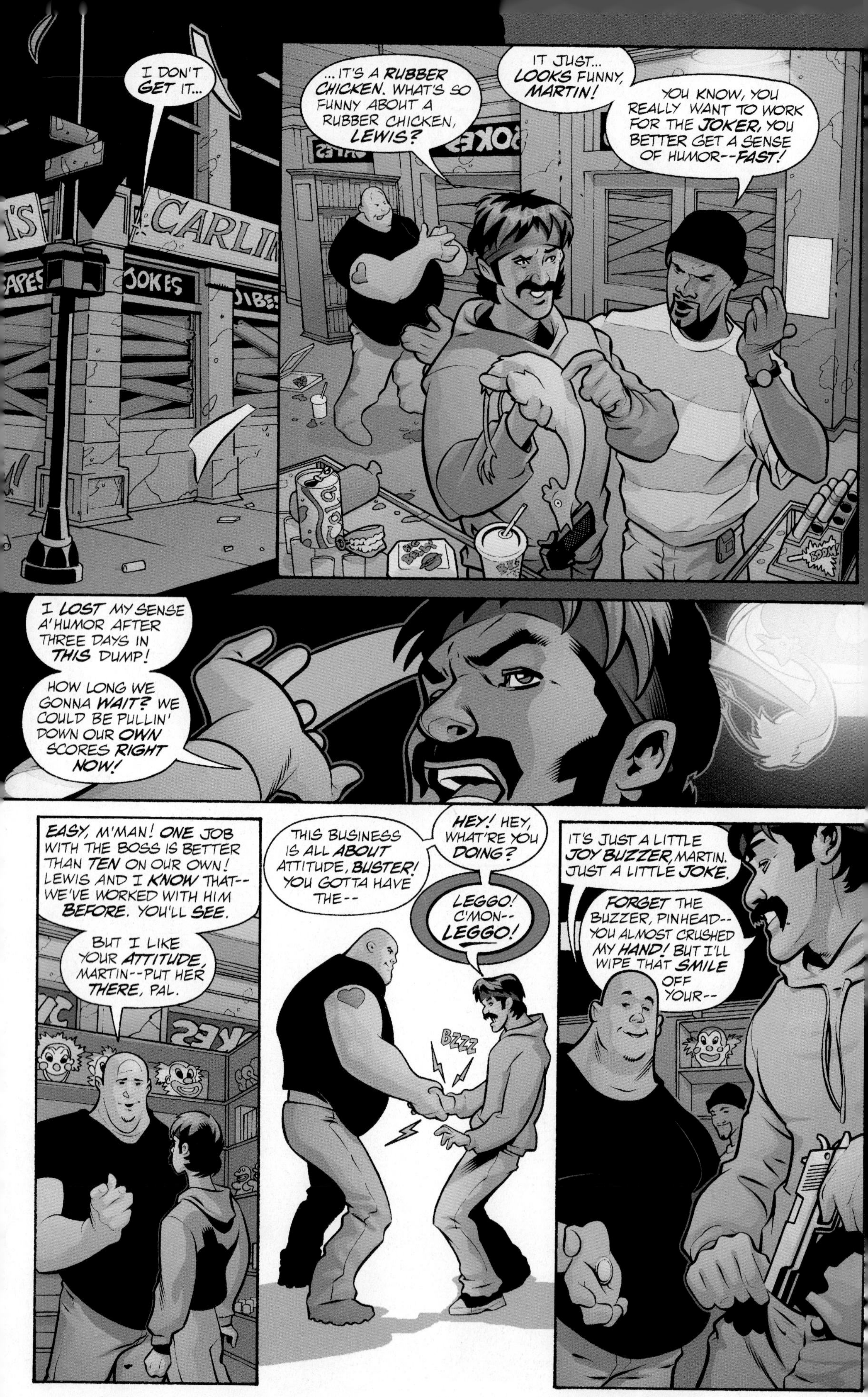

I DON'T GET IT...
CARLIN
APES
JOKES
JIBES
...IT'S A RUBBER CHICKEN. WHAT'S SO FUNNY ABOUT A RUBBER CHICKEN, LEWIS?
IT JUST... LOOKS FUNNY, MARTIN!
YOU KNOW, YOU REALLY WANT TO WORK FOR THE JOKER, YOU BETTER GET A SENSE OF HUMOR--FAST!
BOOM!
I LOST MY SENSE A'HUMOR AFTER THREE DAYS IN THIS DUMP!
HOW LONG WE GONNA WAIT? WE COULD BE PULLIN' DOWN OUR OWN SCORES RIGHT NOW!
EASY, M'MAN! ONE JOB WITH THE BOSS IS BETTER THAN TEN ON OUR OWN! LEWIS AND I KNOW THAT--WE'VE WORKED WITH HIM BEFORE. YOU'LL SEE.
BUT I LIKE YOUR ATTITUDE, MARTIN--PUT HER THERE, PAL.
THIS BUSINESS IS ALL ABOUT ATTITUDE, BUSTER! YOU GOTTA HAVE THE--
HEY! HEY, WHAT'RE YOU DOING?
LEGGO! C'MON--LEGGO!
BZZZ
IT'S JUST A LITTLE JOY BUZZER, MARTIN. JUST A LITTLE JOKE.
FORGET THE BUZZER, PINHEAD--YOU ALMOST CRUSHED MY HAND! BUT I'LL WIPE THAT SMILE OFF YOUR--

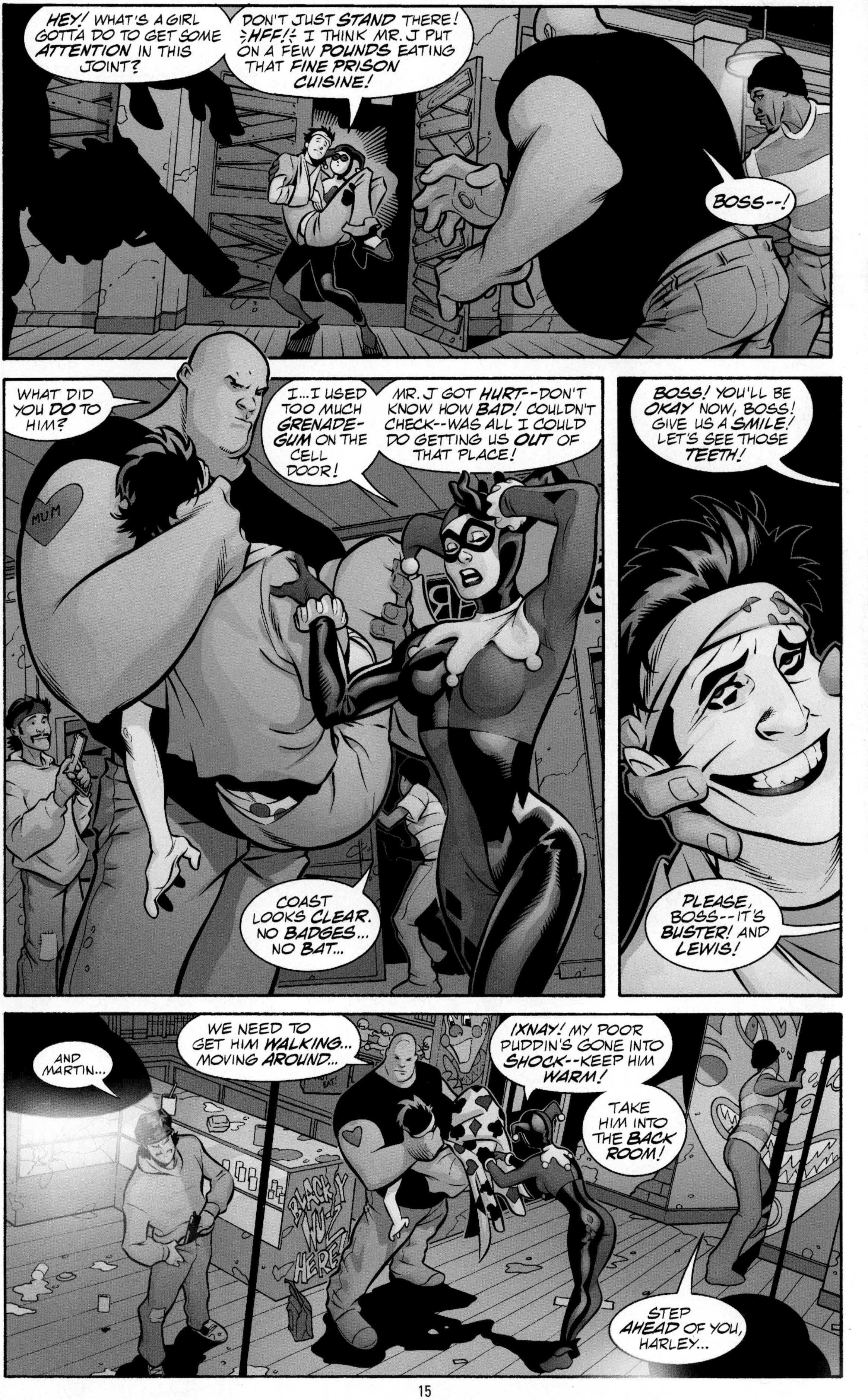
HEY! WHAT'S A GIRL GOTTA DO TO GET SOME ATTENTION IN THIS JOINT?
DON'T JUST STAND THERE! HFF! I THINK MR. J PUT ON A FEW POUNDS EATING THAT FINE PRISON CUISINE!
BOSS--!
WHAT DID YOU DO TO HIM?
I...I USED TOO MUCH GRENADE-GUM ON THE CELL DOOR!
MR. J GOT HURT--DON'T KNOW HOW BAD! COULDN'T CHECK--WAS ALL I COULD DO GETTING US OUT OF THAT PLACE!
MUM
COAST LOOKS CLEAR. NO BADGES... NO BAT...
BOSS! YOU'LL BE OKAY NOW, BOSS! GIVE US A SMILE! LET'S SEE THOSE TEETH!
PLEASE, BOSS--IT'S BUSTER! AND LEWIS!
AND MARTIN...
WE NEED TO GET HIM WALKING... MOVING AROUND...
IXNAY! MY POOR PUDDIN'S GONE INTO SHOCK--KEEP HIM WARM!
TAKE HIM INTO THE BACK ROOM!
BLACKY WUZ HERE!
STEP AHEAD OF YOU, HARLEY...

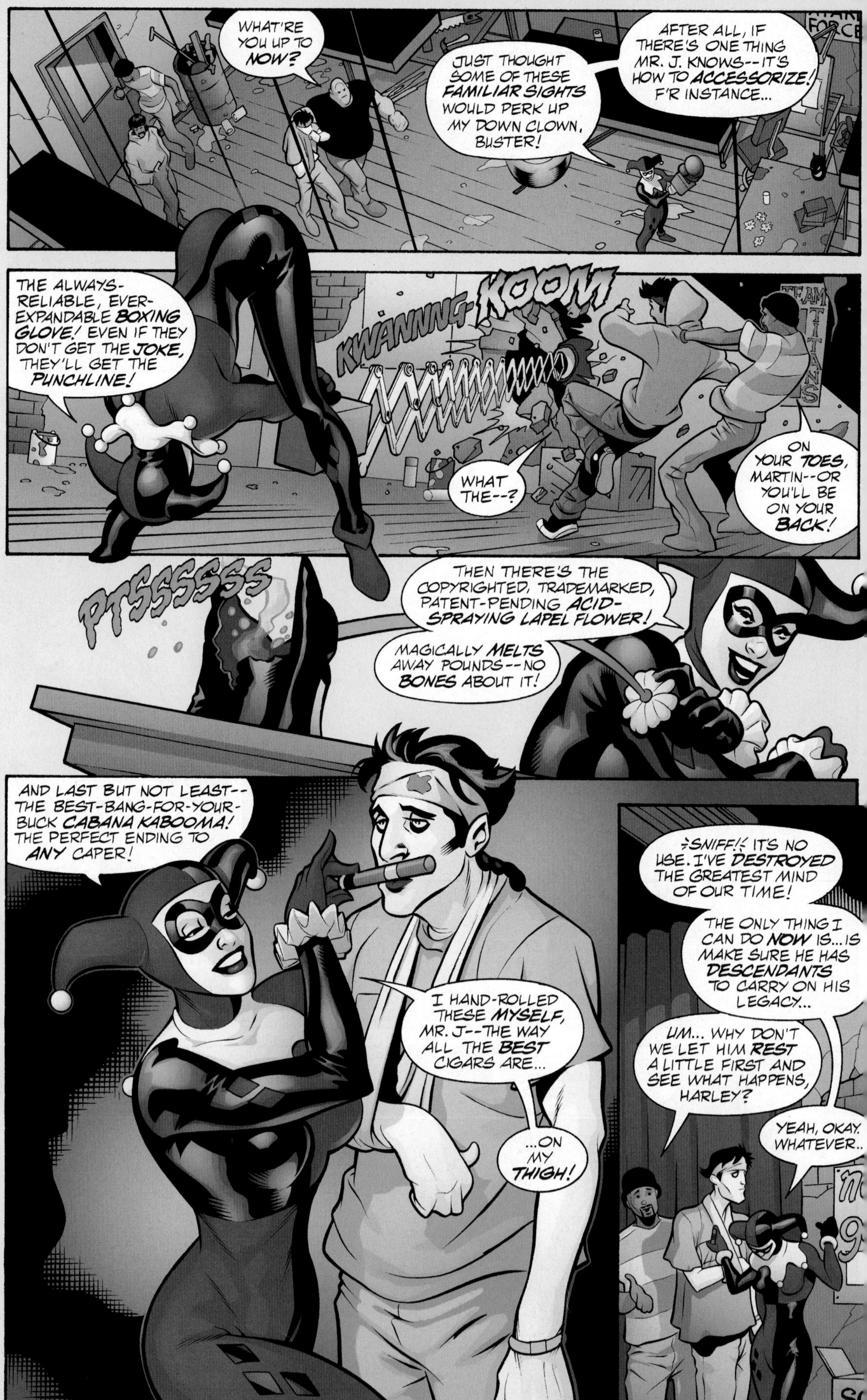
WHAT'RE YOU UP TO NOW?
JUST THOUGHT SOME OF THESE FAMILIAR SIGHTS WOULD PERK UP MY DOWN CLOWN, BUSTER!
AFTER ALL, IF THERE'S ONE THING MR. J. KNOWS--IT'S HOW TO ACCESSORIZE! F'R INSTANCE...
THE ALWAYS-RELIABLE, EVER-EXPANDABLE BOXING GLOVE! EVEN IF THEY DON'T GET THE JOKE, THEY'LL GET THE PUNCHLINE!
KWANNNG-KOOM
WHAT THE--?
ON YOUR TOES, MARTIN--OR YOU'LL BE ON YOUR BACK!
PTSSSSSS
THEN THERE'S THE COPYRIGHTED, TRADEMARKED, PATENT-PENDING ACID-SPRAYING LAPEL FLOWER!
MAGICALLY MELTS AWAY POUNDS--NO BONES ABOUT IT!
AND LAST BUT NOT LEAST--THE BEST-BANG-FOR-YOUR-BUCK CABANA KABOOMA! THE PERFECT ENDING TO ANY CAPER!
I HAND-ROLLED THESE MYSELF, MR. J--THE WAY ALL THE BEST CIGARS ARE...
...ON MY THIGH!
>SNIFF!< IT'S NO USE. I'VE DESTROYED THE GREATEST MIND OF OUR TIME!
THE ONLY THING I CAN DO NOW IS...IS MAKE SURE HE HAS DESCENDANTS TO CARRY ON HIS LEGACY...
UM... WHY DON'T WE LET HIM REST A LITTLE FIRST AND SEE WHAT HAPPENS, HARLEY?
YEAH, OKAY. WHATEVER...

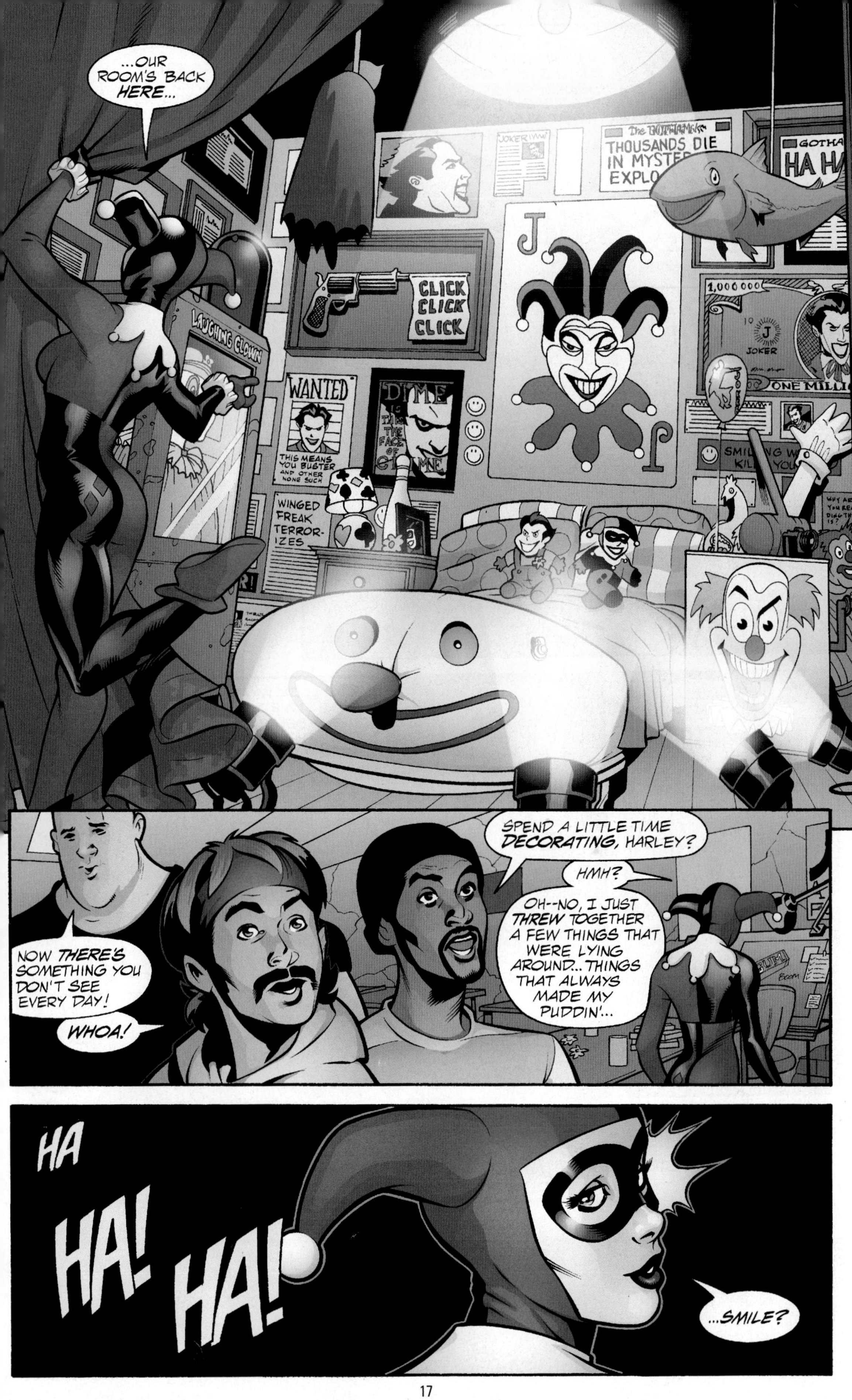
...OUR ROOM'S BACK *HERE*...
CLICK CLICK CLICK
LAUGHING CLOWN
WANTED
THIS MEANS YOU BUSTER AND OTHER NONE SUCH
WINGED FREAK TERRORIZES
JOKER
NOW *THERE'S* SOMETHING YOU DON'T SEE EVERY DAY!
WHOA!
SPEND A LITTLE TIME *DECORATING*, HARLEY?
HMH?
OH--NO, I JUST *THREW* TOGETHER A FEW THINGS THAT WERE LYING AROUND... THINGS THAT ALWAYS MADE MY PUDDIN'...
HA HA! HA!
...SMILE?

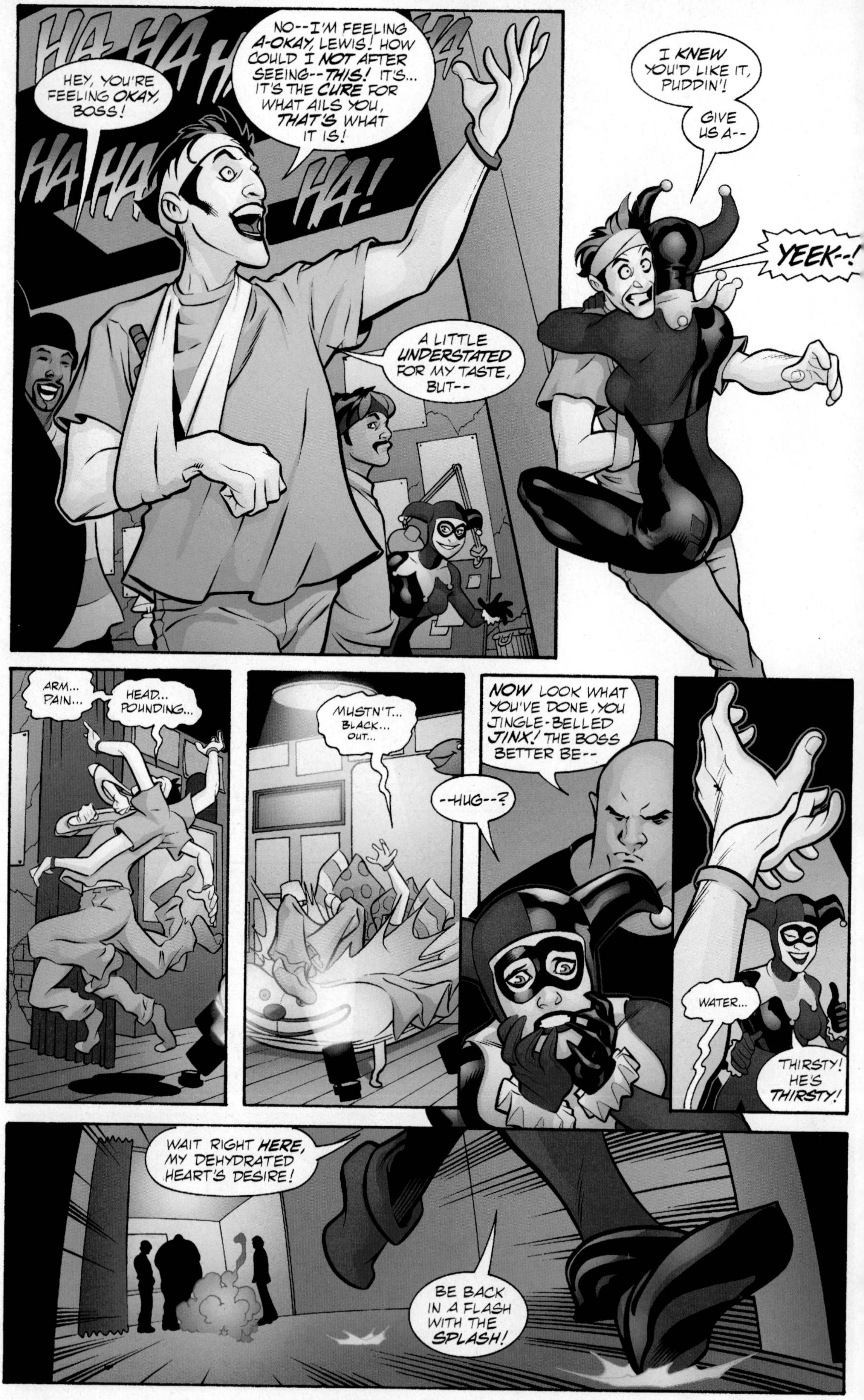
HA HA HA HA
HEY, YOU'RE FEELING OKAY, BOSS!
NO--I'M FEELING A-OKAY, LEWIS! HOW COULD I NOT AFTER SEEING--THIS! IT'S... IT'S THE CURE FOR WHAT AILS YOU, THAT'S WHAT IT IS!
HA HA HA!
A LITTLE UNDERSTATED FOR MY TASTE, BUT--
I KNEW YOU'D LIKE IT, PUDDIN'!
GIVE US A--
YEEK--!
ARM... PAIN...
HEAD... POUNDING...
MUSTN'T... BLACK... OUT...
--HUG--?
NOW LOOK WHAT YOU'VE DONE, YOU JINGLE-BELLED JINX! THE BOSS BETTER BE--
WATER...
THIRSTY! HE'S THIRSTY!
WAIT RIGHT HERE, MY DEHYDRATED HEART'S DESIRE!
BE BACK IN A FLASH WITH THE SPLASH!

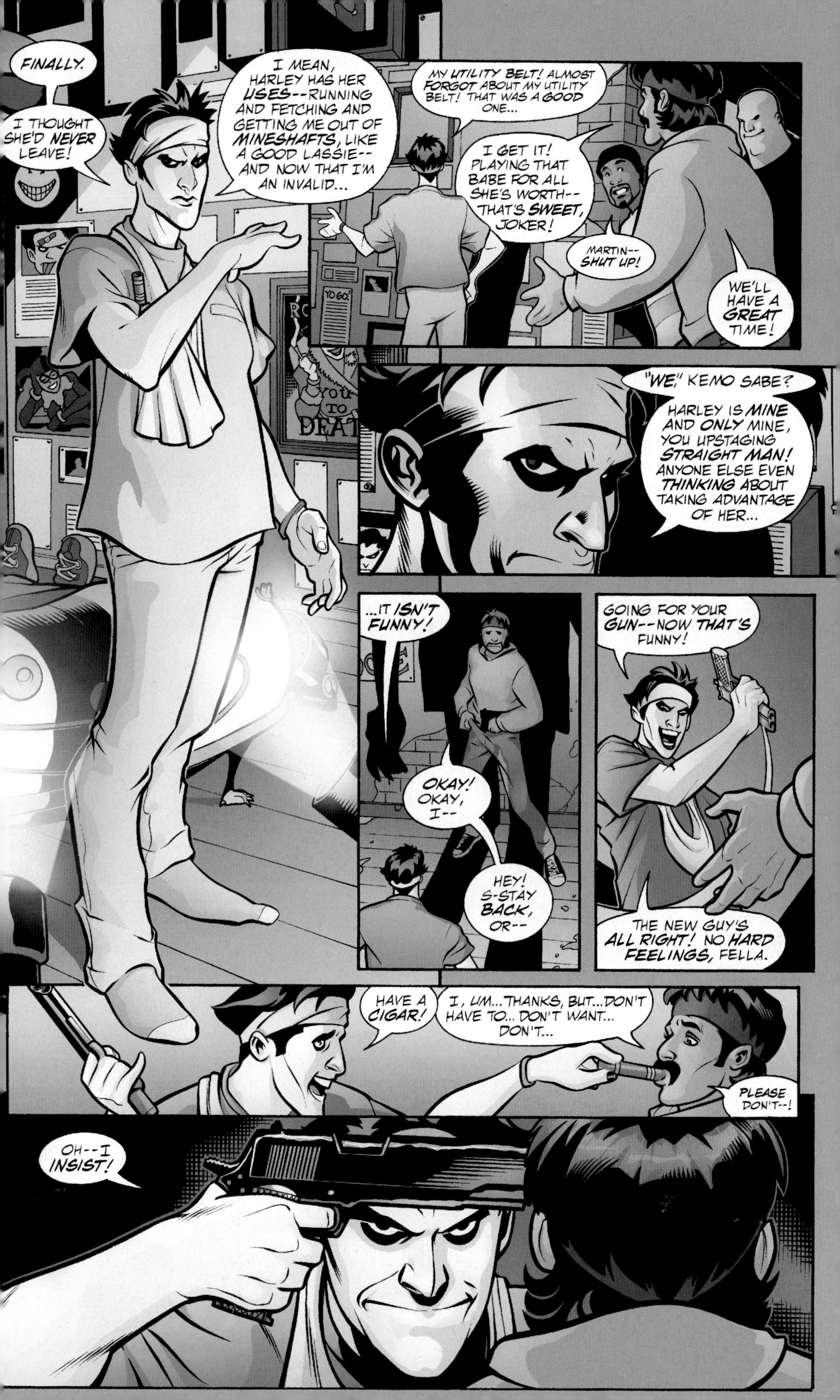
FINALLY.
I THOUGHT SHE'D NEVER LEAVE!
I MEAN, HARLEY HAS HER USES--RUNNING AND FETCHING AND GETTING ME OUT OF MINESHAFTS, LIKE A GOOD LASSIE--AND NOW THAT I'M AN INVALID...
MY UTILITY BELT! ALMOST FORGOT ABOUT MY UTILITY BELT! THAT WAS A GOOD ONE...
I GET IT! PLAYING THAT BABE FOR ALL SHE'S WORTH--THAT'S SWEET, JOKER!
MARTIN--SHUT UP!
WE'LL HAVE A GREAT TIME!
"WE," KEMO SABE?
HARLEY IS MINE AND ONLY MINE, YOU UPSTAGING STRAIGHT MAN! ANYONE ELSE EVEN THINKING ABOUT TAKING ADVANTAGE OF HER...
...IT ISN'T FUNNY!
OKAY! OKAY, I--
HEY! S-STAY BACK, OR--
GOING FOR YOUR GUN--NOW THAT'S FUNNY!
THE NEW GUY'S ALL RIGHT! NO HARD FEELINGS, FELLA.
HAVE A CIGAR!
I, UM...THANKS, BUT...DON'T HAVE TO... DON'T WANT... DON'T...
PLEASE DON'T--!
OH--I INSIST!

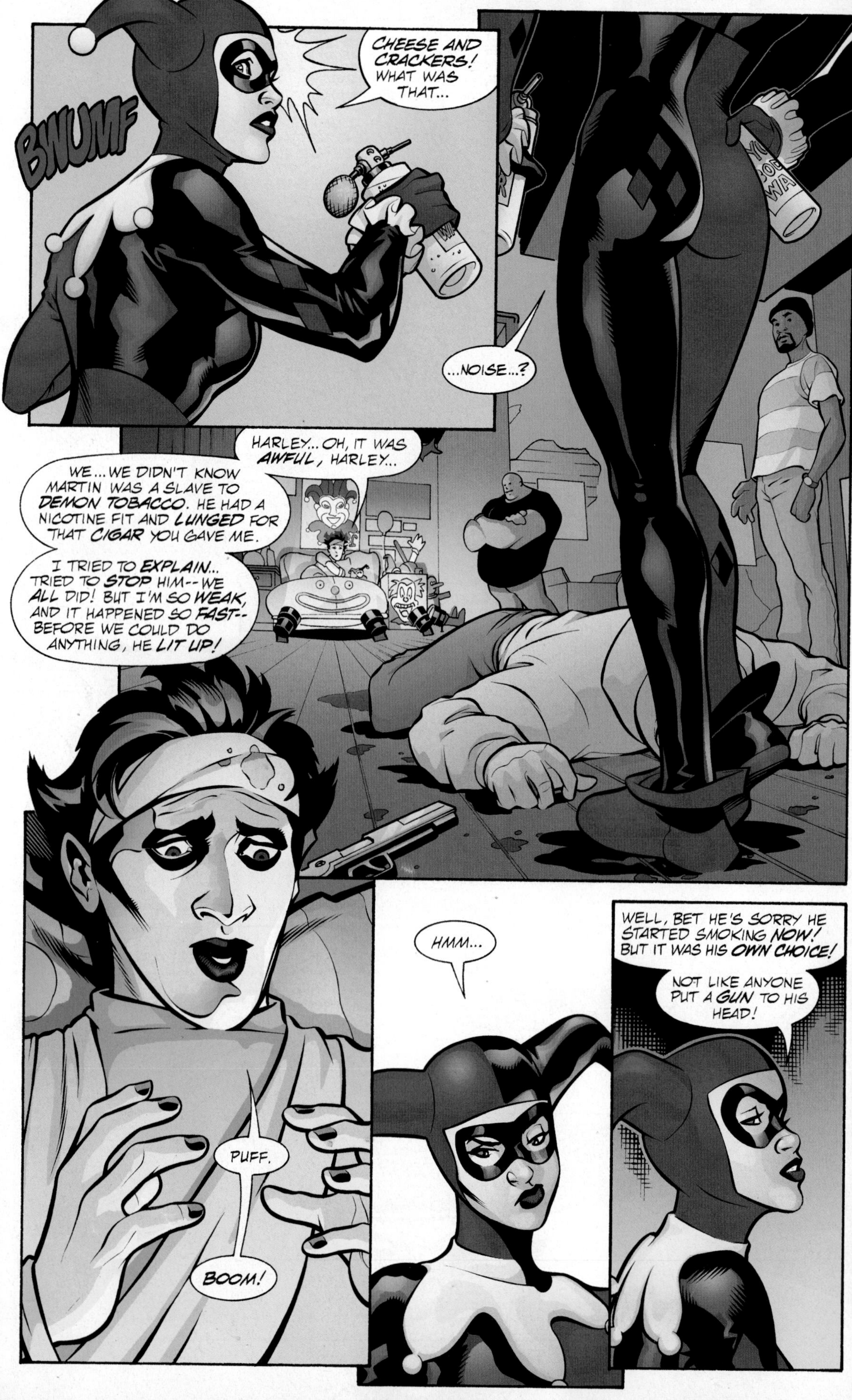
BWUMF
CHEESE AND CRACKERS! WHAT WAS THAT...
...NOISE...?
HARLEY... OH, IT WAS AWFUL, HARLEY...
WE... WE DIDN'T KNOW MARTIN WAS A SLAVE TO DEMON TOBACCO. HE HAD A NICOTINE FIT AND LUNGED FOR THAT CIGAR YOU GAVE ME.
I TRIED TO EXPLAIN... TRIED TO STOP HIM--WE ALL DID! BUT I'M SO WEAK, AND IT HAPPENED SO FAST-- BEFORE WE COULD DO ANYTHING, HE LIT UP!
PUFF.
BOOM!
HMM...
WELL, BET HE'S SORRY HE STARTED SMOKING NOW! BUT IT WAS HIS OWN CHOICE!
NOT LIKE ANYONE PUT A GUN TO HIS HEAD!

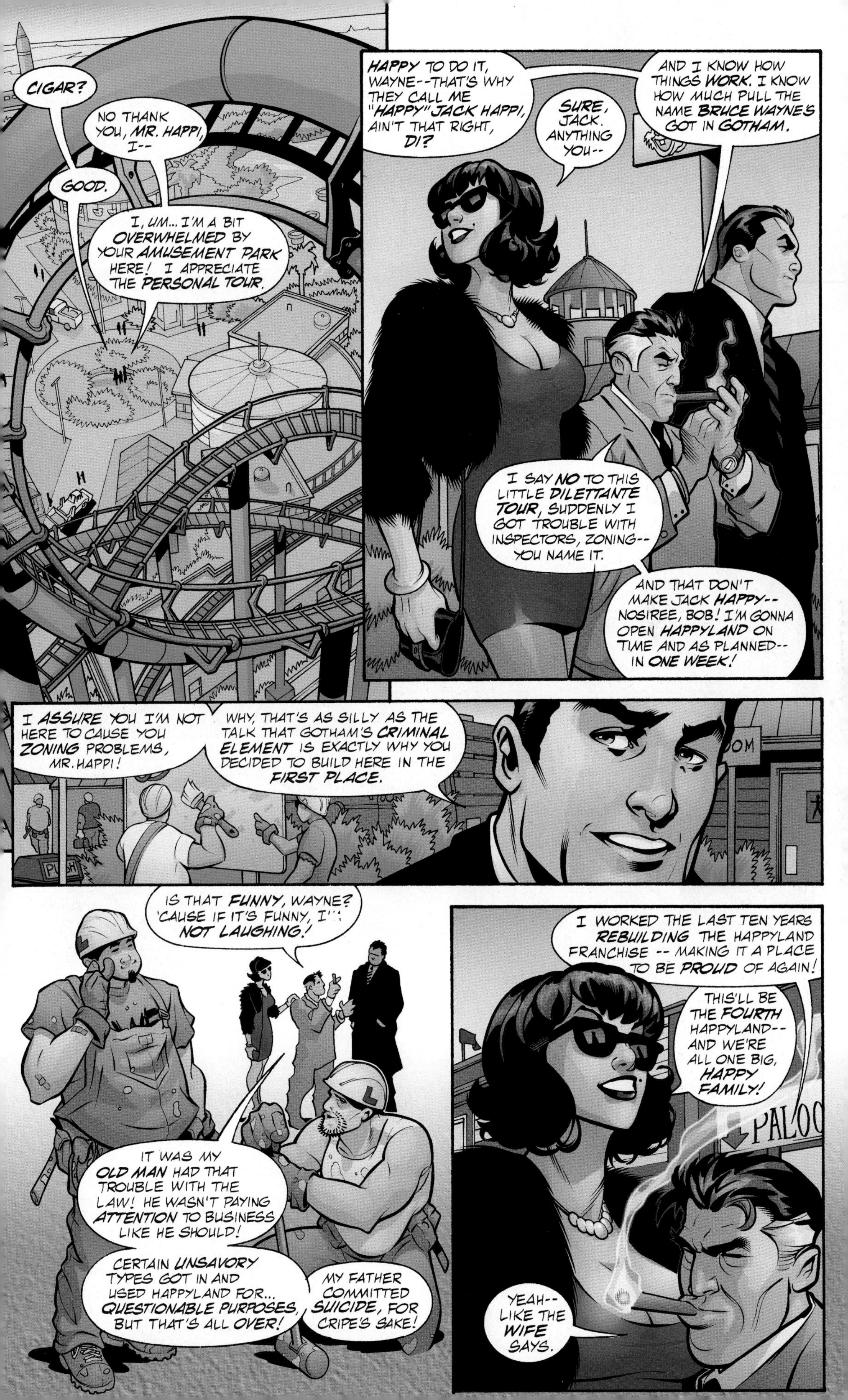
CIGAR?
NO THANK YOU, MR. HAPPI, I--
GOOD.
I, UM... I'M A BIT OVERWHELMED BY YOUR AMUSEMENT PARK HERE! I APPRECIATE THE PERSONAL TOUR.
HAPPY TO DO IT, WAYNE--THAT'S WHY THEY CALL ME "HAPPY" JACK HAPPI, AIN'T THAT RIGHT, DI?
SURE, JACK. ANYTHING YOU--
AND I KNOW HOW THINGS WORK. I KNOW HOW MUCH PULL THE NAME BRUCE WAYNE'S GOT IN GOTHAM.
I SAY NO TO THIS LITTLE DILETTANTE TOUR, SUDDENLY I GOT TROUBLE WITH INSPECTORS, ZONING--YOU NAME IT.
AND THAT DON'T MAKE JACK HAPPY--NOSIREE, BOB! I'M GONNA OPEN HAPPYLAND ON TIME AND AS PLANNED--IN ONE WEEK!
I ASSURE YOU I'M NOT HERE TO CAUSE YOU ZONING PROBLEMS, MR. HAPPI!
WHY, THAT'S AS SILLY AS THE TALK THAT GOTHAM'S CRIMINAL ELEMENT IS EXACTLY WHY YOU DECIDED TO BUILD HERE IN THE FIRST PLACE.
IS THAT FUNNY, WAYNE? 'CAUSE IF IT'S FUNNY, I'M NOT LAUGHING!
IT WAS MY OLD MAN HAD THAT TROUBLE WITH THE LAW! HE WASN'T PAYING ATTENTION TO BUSINESS LIKE HE SHOULD!
CERTAIN UNSAVORY TYPES GOT IN AND USED HAPPYLAND FOR... QUESTIONABLE PURPOSES, BUT THAT'S ALL OVER!
MY FATHER COMMITTED SUICIDE, FOR CRIPE'S SAKE!
I WORKED THE LAST TEN YEARS REBUILDING THE HAPPYLAND FRANCHISE -- MAKING IT A PLACE TO BE PROUD OF AGAIN!
THIS'LL BE THE FOURTH HAPPYLAND--AND WE'RE ALL ONE BIG, HAPPY FAMILY!
YEAH--LIKE THE WIFE SAYS.

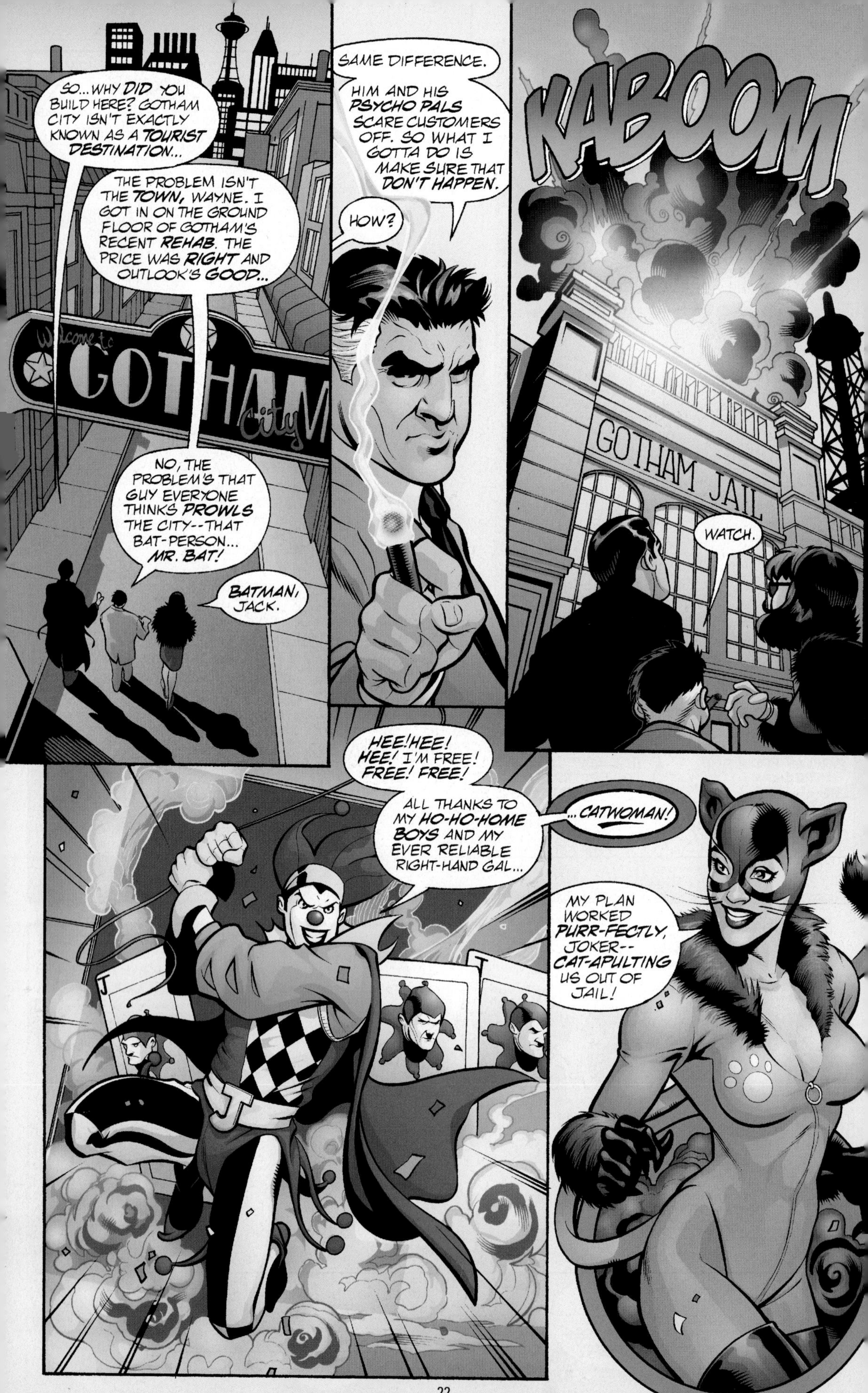
SO... WHY DID YOU BUILD HERE? GOTHAM CITY ISN'T EXACTLY KNOWN AS A TOURIST DESTINATION...
THE PROBLEM ISN'T THE TOWN, WAYNE. I GOT IN ON THE GROUND FLOOR OF GOTHAM'S RECENT REHAB. THE PRICE WAS RIGHT AND OUTLOOK'S GOOD...
GOTHAM
NO, THE PROBLEM'S THAT GUY EVERYONE THINKS PROWLS THE CITY--THAT BAT-PERSON... MR. BAT!
BATMAN, JACK.
SAME DIFFERENCE.
HIM AND HIS PSYCHO PALS SCARE CUSTOMERS OFF. SO WHAT I GOTTA DO IS MAKE SURE THAT DON'T HAPPEN.
HOW?
KABOOM
GOTHAM JAIL
WATCH.
HEE! HEE! HEE! I'M FREE! FREE! FREE!
ALL THANKS TO MY HO-HO-HOME BOYS AND MY EVER RELIABLE RIGHT-HAND GAL...
...CATWOMAN!
MY PLAN WORKED PURR-FECTLY, JOKER-- CAT-APULTING US OUT OF JAIL!

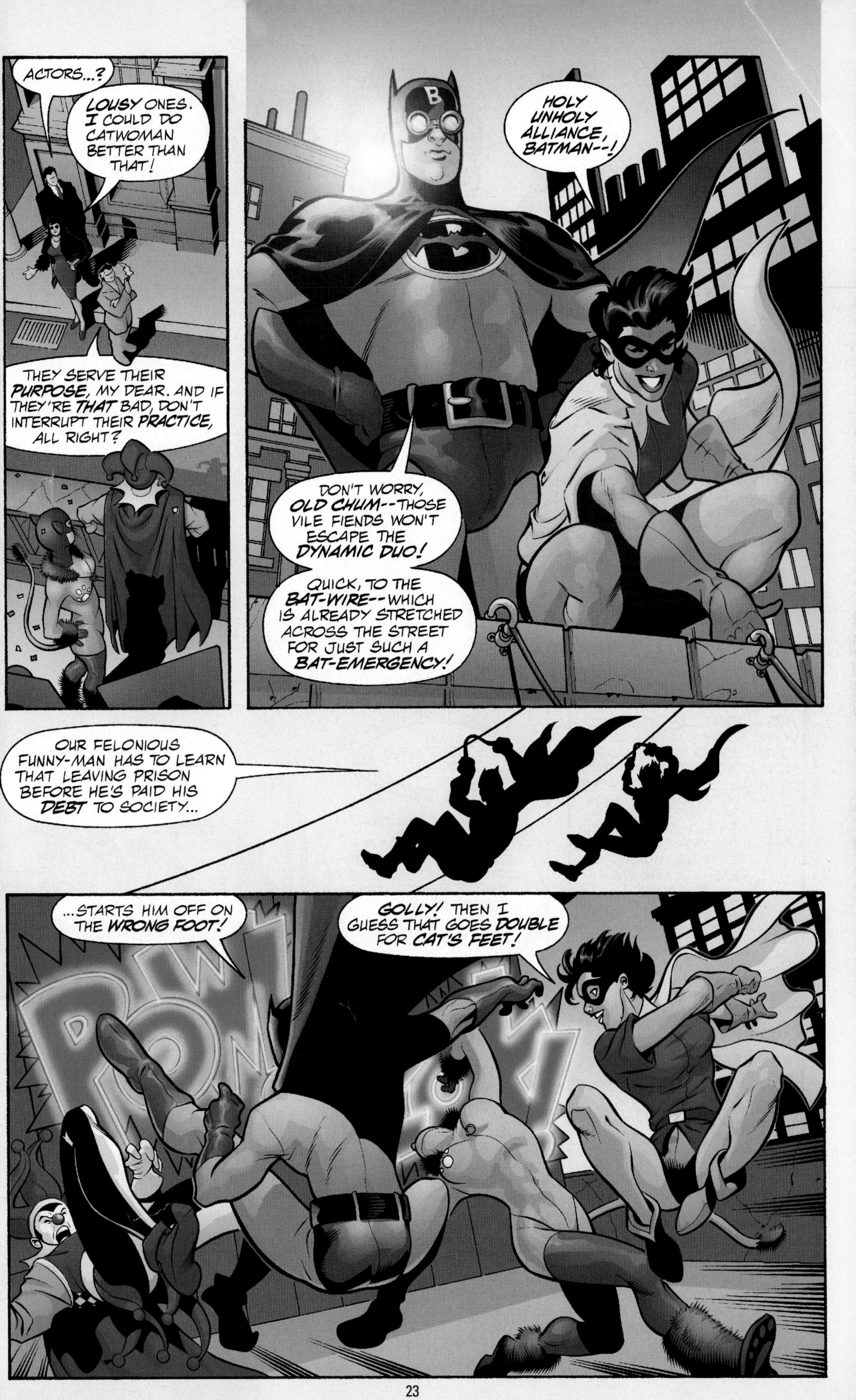
ACTORS...?
LOUSY ONES. I COULD DO CATWOMAN BETTER THAN THAT!
THEY SERVE THEIR PURPOSE, MY DEAR. AND IF THEY'RE THAT BAD, DON'T INTERRUPT THEIR PRACTICE, ALL RIGHT?
HOLY UNHOLY ALLIANCE, BATMAN--!
DON'T WORRY, OLD CHUM--THOSE VILE FIENDS WON'T ESCAPE THE DYNAMIC DUO!
QUICK, TO THE BAT-WIRE--WHICH IS ALREADY STRETCHED ACROSS THE STREET FOR JUST SUCH A BAT-EMERGENCY!
OUR FELONIOUS FUNNY-MAN HAS TO LEARN THAT LEAVING PRISON BEFORE HE'S PAID HIS DEBT TO SOCIETY...
...STARTS HIM OFF ON THE WRONG FOOT!
GOLLY! THEN I GUESS THAT GOES DOUBLE FOR CAT'S FEET!

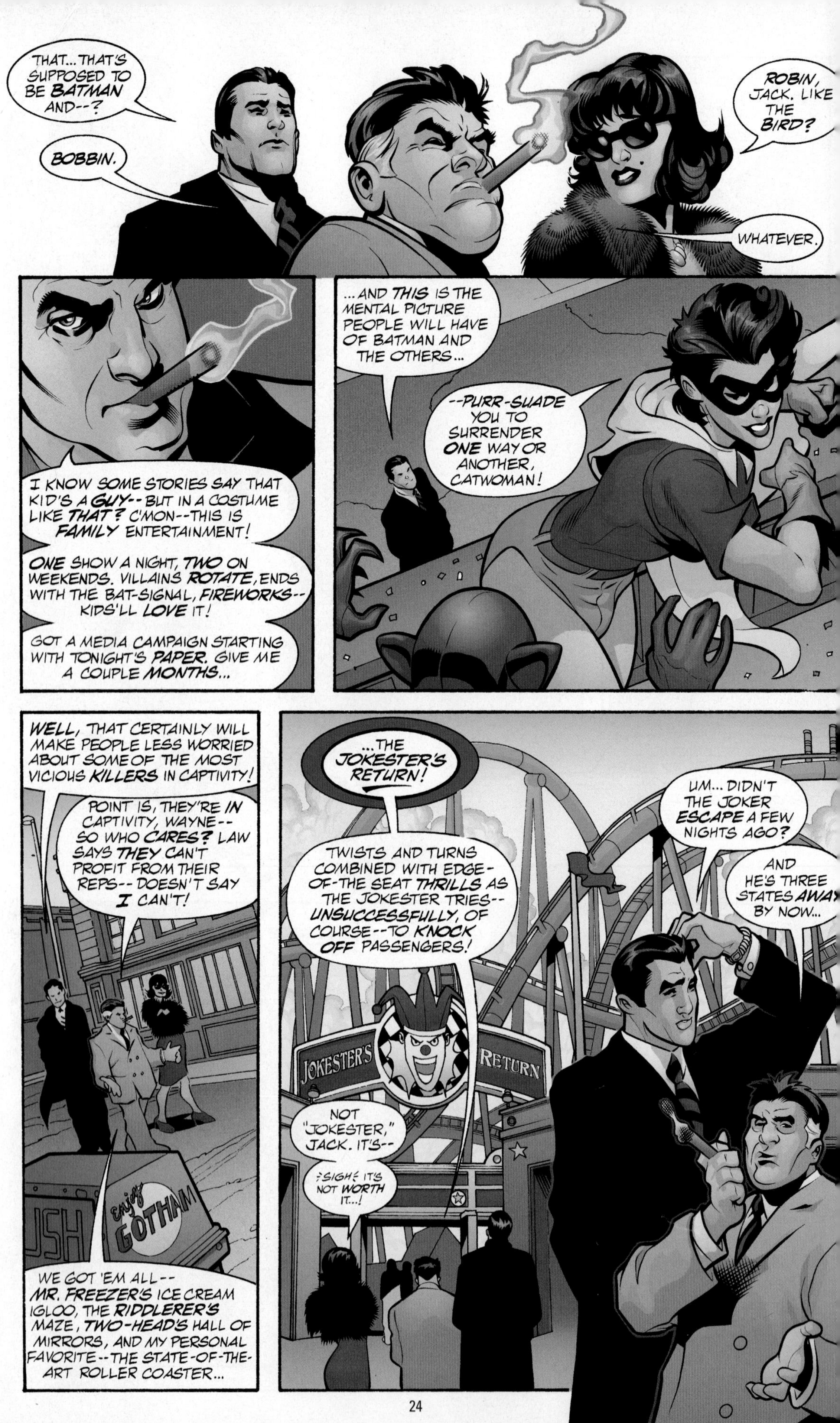
THAT... THAT'S SUPPOSED TO BE BATMAN AND--?
BOBBIN.
ROBIN, JACK. LIKE THE BIRD?
WHATEVER.
I KNOW SOME STORIES SAY THAT KID'S A GUY-- BUT IN A COSTUME LIKE THAT? C'MON--THIS IS FAMILY ENTERTAINMENT!
ONE SHOW A NIGHT, TWO ON WEEKENDS. VILLAINS ROTATE, ENDS WITH THE BAT-SIGNAL, FIREWORKS-- KIDS'LL LOVE IT!
GOT A MEDIA CAMPAIGN STARTING WITH TONIGHT'S PAPER. GIVE ME A COUPLE MONTHS...
...AND THIS IS THE MENTAL PICTURE PEOPLE WILL HAVE OF BATMAN AND THE OTHERS...
--PURR-SUADE YOU TO SURRENDER ONE WAY OR ANOTHER, CATWOMAN!
WELL, THAT CERTAINLY WILL MAKE PEOPLE LESS WORRIED ABOUT SOME OF THE MOST VICIOUS KILLERS IN CAPTIVITY!
POINT IS, THEY'RE IN CAPTIVITY, WAYNE-- SO WHO CARES? LAW SAYS THEY CAN'T PROFIT FROM THEIR REPS-- DOESN'T SAY I CAN'T!
Enjoy GOTHAM
WE GOT 'EM ALL-- MR. FREEZER'S ICE CREAM IGLOO, THE RIDDLERER'S MAZE, TWO-HEAD'S HALL OF MIRRORS, AND MY PERSONAL FAVORITE--THE STATE-OF-THE-ART ROLLER COASTER...
...THE JOKESTER'S RETURN!
TWISTS AND TURNS COMBINED WITH EDGE-OF-THE SEAT THRILLS AS THE JOKESTER TRIES-- UNSUCCESSFULLY, OF COURSE--TO KNOCK OFF PASSENGERS!
JOKESTER'S RETURN
NOT "JOKESTER," JACK. IT'S--
SIGH IT'S NOT WORTH IT...!
UM... DIDN'T THE JOKER ESCAPE A FEW NIGHTS AGO?
AND HE'S THREE STATES AWAY BY NOW...

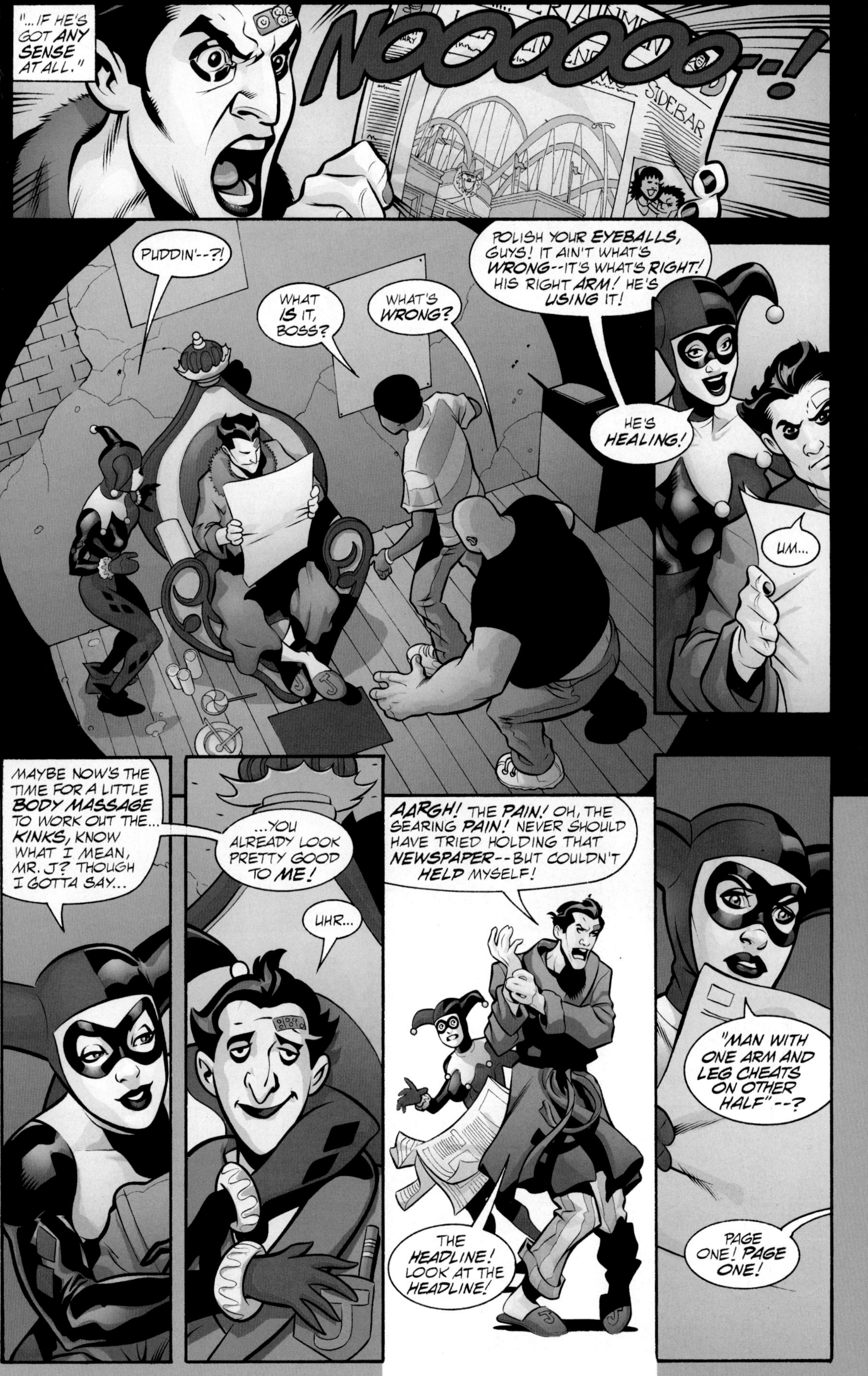
"...IF HE'S GOT ANY SENSE AT ALL."
NOOOOOO--!
SIDEBAR
PUDDIN'--?!
WHAT IS IT, BOSS?
WHAT'S WRONG?
POLISH YOUR EYEBALLS, GUYS! IT AIN'T WHAT'S WRONG--IT'S WHAT'S RIGHT! HIS RIGHT ARM! HE'S USING IT!
HE'S HEALING!
UM...
MAYBE NOW'S THE TIME FOR A LITTLE BODY MASSAGE TO WORK OUT THE... KINKS, KNOW WHAT I MEAN, MR. J? THOUGH I GOTTA SAY...
...YOU ALREADY LOOK PRETTY GOOD TO ME!
UHR...
AARGH! THE PAIN! OH, THE SEARING PAIN! NEVER SHOULD HAVE TRIED HOLDING THAT NEWSPAPER--BUT COULDN'T HELP MYSELF!
THE HEADLINE! LOOK AT THE HEADLINE!
"MAN WITH ONE ARM AND LEG CHEATS ON OTHER HALF"--?
PAGE ONE! PAGE ONE!

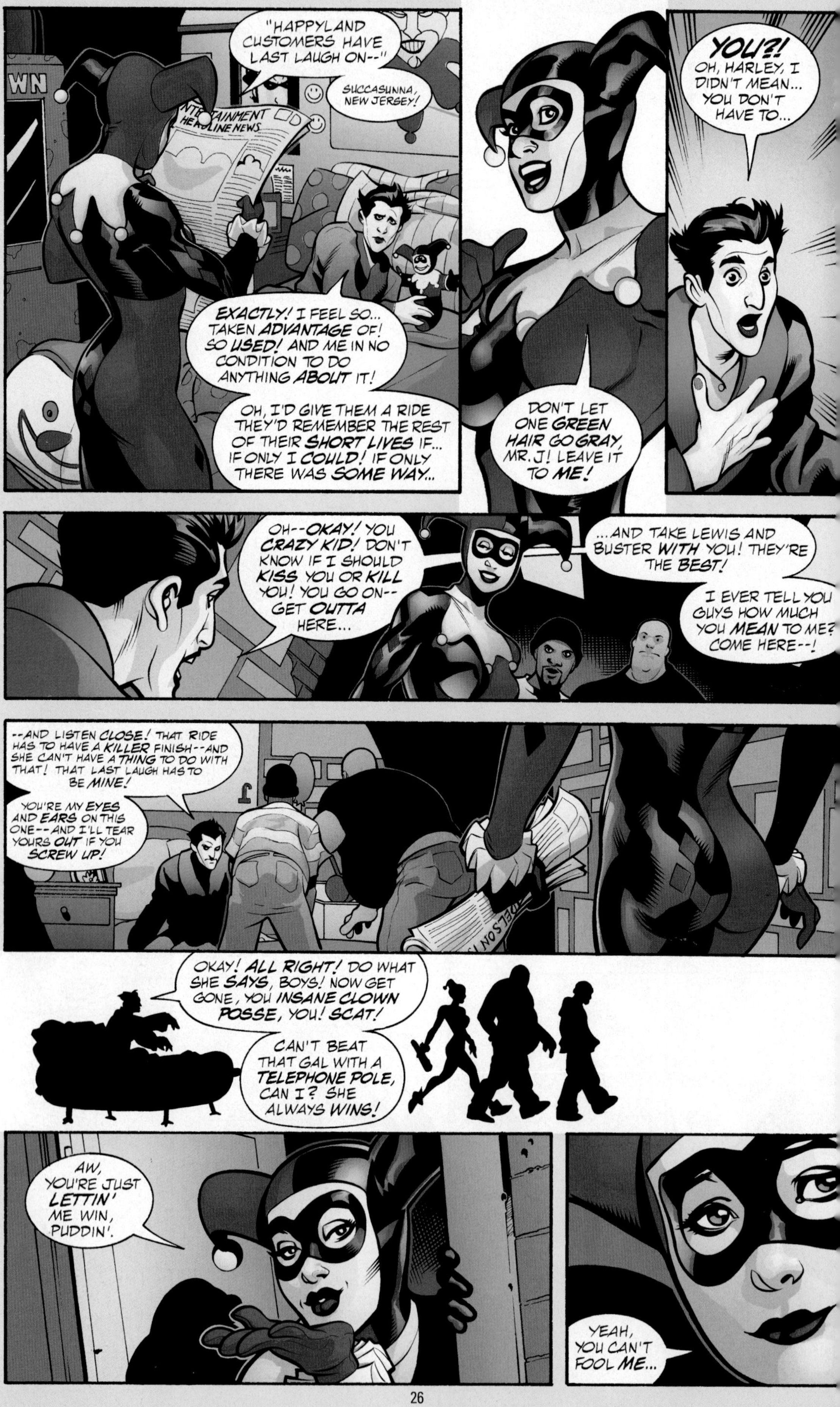

"HAPPYLAND CUSTOMERS HAVE LAST LAUGH ON--"
SUCCASUNNA, NEW JERSEY!
EXACTLY! I FEEL SO... TAKEN ADVANTAGE OF! SO USED! AND ME IN NO CONDITION TO DO ANYTHING ABOUT IT!
OH, I'D GIVE THEM A RIDE THEY'D REMEMBER THE REST OF THEIR SHORT LIVES IF... IF ONLY I COULD! IF ONLY THERE WAS SOME WAY...
DON'T LET ONE GREEN HAIR GO GRAY, MR. J! LEAVE IT TO ME!
YOU?! OH, HARLEY, I DIDN'T MEAN... YOU DON'T HAVE TO...
OH--OKAY! YOU CRAZY KID! DON'T KNOW IF I SHOULD KISS YOU OR KILL YOU! YOU GO ON-- GET OUTTA HERE...
...AND TAKE LEWIS AND BUSTER WITH YOU! THEY'RE THE BEST!
I EVER TELL YOU GUYS HOW MUCH YOU MEAN TO ME? COME HERE--!
--AND LISTEN CLOSE! THAT RIDE HAS TO HAVE A KILLER FINISH--AND SHE CAN'T HAVE A THING TO DO WITH THAT! THAT LAST LAUGH HAS TO BE MINE!
YOU'RE MY EYES AND EARS ON THIS ONE--AND I'LL TEAR YOURS OUT IF YOU SCREW UP!
OKAY! ALL RIGHT! DO WHAT SHE SAYS, BOYS! NOW GET GONE, YOU INSANE CLOWN POSSE, YOU! SCAT!
CAN'T BEAT THAT GAL WITH A TELEPHONE POLE, CAN I? SHE ALWAYS WINS!
AW, YOU'RE JUST LETTIN' ME WIN, PUDDIN'.
YEAH, YOU CAN'T FOOL ME...

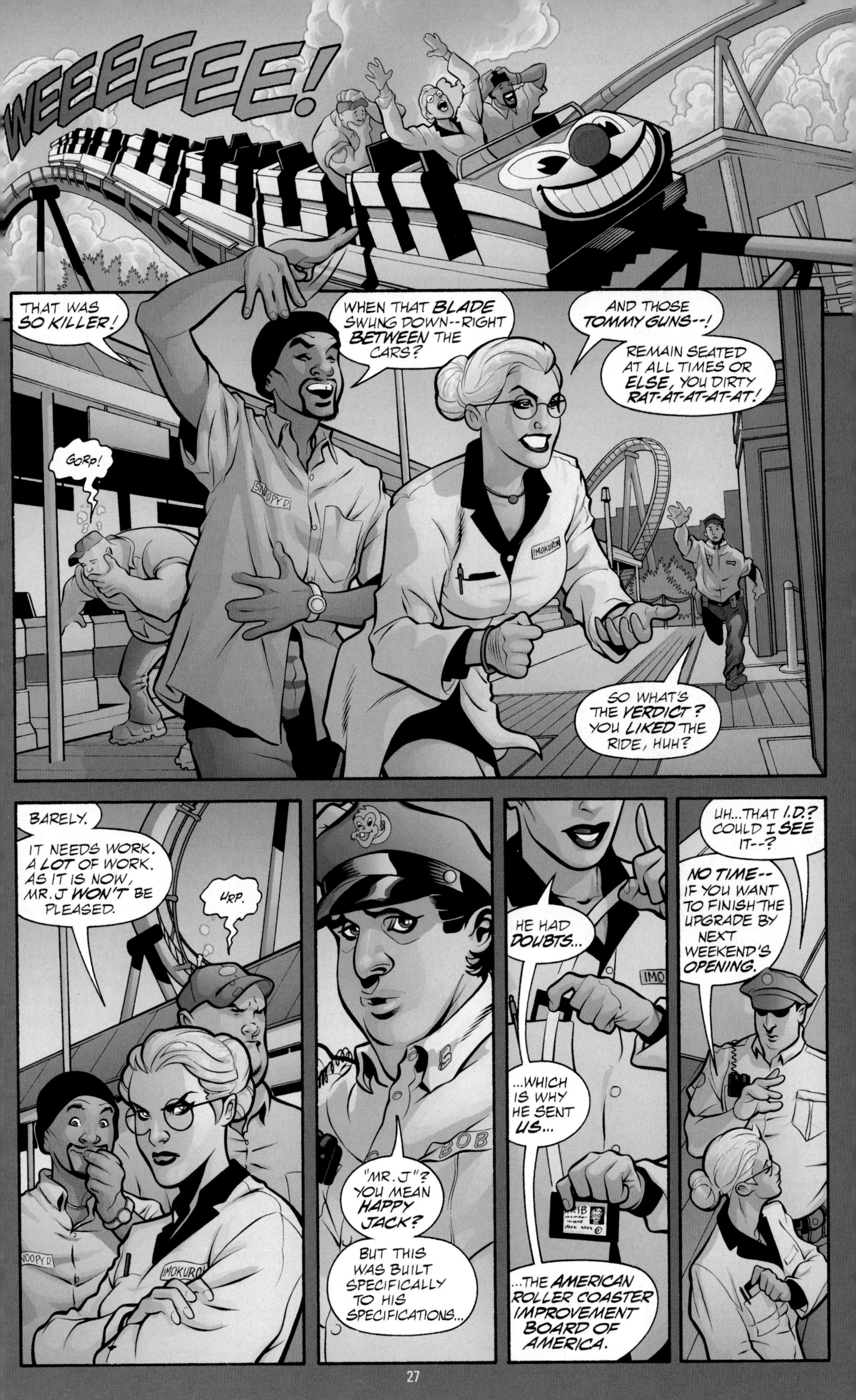
WEEEEEE!
THAT WAS SO KILLER!
WHEN THAT BLADE SWUNG DOWN--RIGHT BETWEEN THE CARS?
AND THOSE TOMMY GUNS--!
REMAIN SEATED AT ALL TIMES OR ELSE, YOU DIRTY RAT-AT-AT-AT-AT!
GORP!
SO WHAT'S THE VERDICT? YOU LIKED THE RIDE, HUH?
BARELY.
IT NEEDS WORK. A LOT OF WORK. AS IT IS NOW, MR. J WON'T BE PLEASED.
URP.
"MR. J"? YOU MEAN HAPPY JACK?
BUT THIS WAS BUILT SPECIFICALLY TO HIS SPECIFICATIONS...
HE HAD DOUBTS...
...WHICH IS WHY HE SENT US...
...THE AMERICAN ROLLER COASTER IMPROVEMENT BOARD OF AMERICA.
UH...THAT I.D.? COULD I SEE IT--?
NO TIME-- IF YOU WANT TO FINISH THE UPGRADE BY NEXT WEEKEND'S OPENING.

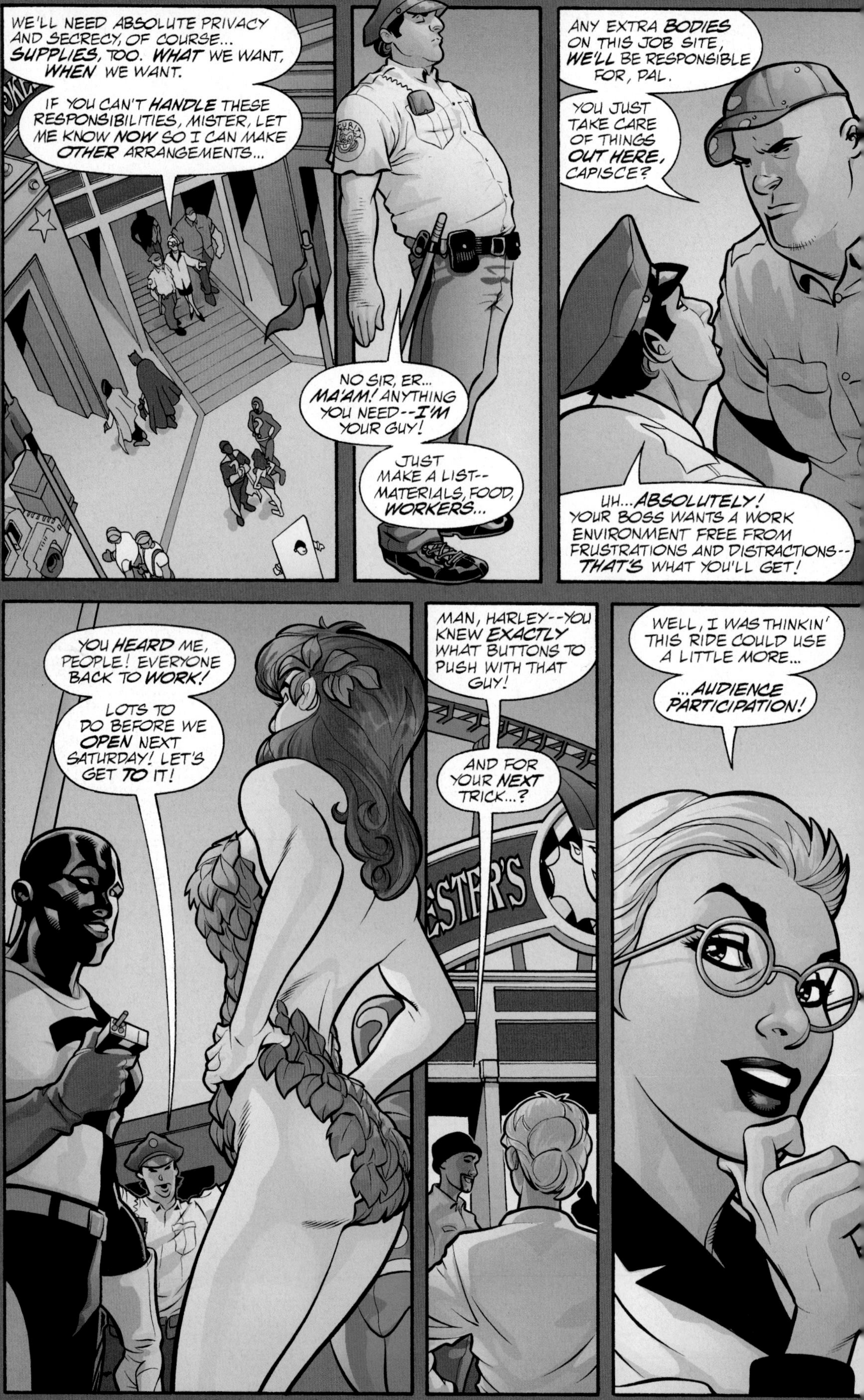

WE'LL NEED ABSOLUTE PRIVACY AND SECRECY, OF COURSE... SUPPLIES, TOO. WHAT WE WANT, WHEN WE WANT.
IF YOU CAN'T HANDLE THESE RESPONSIBILITIES, MISTER, LET ME KNOW NOW SO I CAN MAKE OTHER ARRANGEMENTS...
NO SIR, ER... MA'AM! ANYTHING YOU NEED--I'M YOUR GUY!
JUST MAKE A LIST--MATERIALS, FOOD, WORKERS...
ANY EXTRA BODIES ON THIS JOB SITE, WE'LL BE RESPONSIBLE FOR, PAL.
YOU JUST TAKE CARE OF THINGS OUT HERE, CAPISCE?
UH...ABSOLUTELY! YOUR BOSS WANTS A WORK ENVIRONMENT FREE FROM FRUSTRATIONS AND DISTRACTIONS--THAT'S WHAT YOU'LL GET!
YOU HEARD ME, PEOPLE! EVERYONE BACK TO WORK!
LOTS TO DO BEFORE WE OPEN NEXT SATURDAY! LET'S GET TO IT!
MAN, HARLEY--YOU KNEW EXACTLY WHAT BUTTONS TO PUSH WITH THAT GUY!
AND FOR YOUR NEXT TRICK...?
WELL, I WAS THINKIN' THIS RIDE COULD USE A LITTLE MORE...
...AUDIENCE PARTICIPATION!

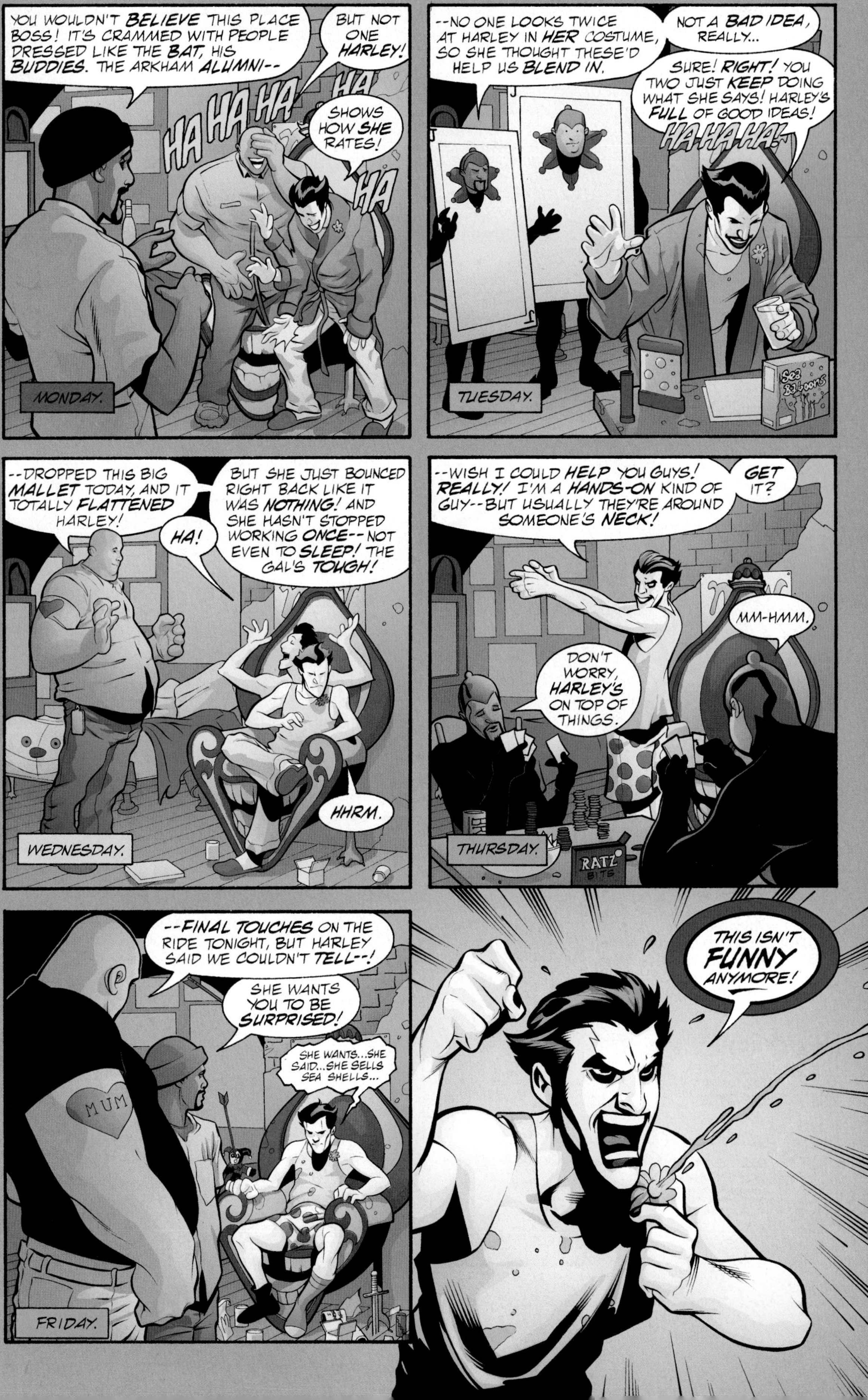
YOU WOULDN'T BELIEVE THIS PLACE BOSS! IT'S CRAMMED WITH PEOPLE DRESSED LIKE THE BAT, HIS BUDDIES. THE ARKHAM ALUMNI--
BUT NOT ONE HARLEY!
HA HA HA HA HA HA
SHOWS HOW SHE RATES!
MONDAY.
--NO ONE LOOKS TWICE AT HARLEY IN HER COSTUME, SO SHE THOUGHT THESE'D HELP US BLEND IN.
NOT A BAD IDEA, REALLY...
SURE! RIGHT! YOU TWO JUST KEEP DOING WHAT SHE SAYS! HARLEY'S FULL OF GOOD IDEAS!
HA HA HA!
TUESDAY.
--DROPPED THIS BIG MALLET TODAY, AND IT TOTALLY FLATTENED HARLEY!
HA!
BUT SHE JUST BOUNCED RIGHT BACK LIKE IT WAS NOTHING! AND SHE HASN'T STOPPED WORKING ONCE-- NOT EVEN TO SLEEP! THE GAL'S TOUGH!
HHRM.
WEDNESDAY.
--WISH I COULD HELP YOU GUYS! REALLY! I'M A HANDS-ON KIND OF GUY-- BUT USUALLY THEY'RE AROUND SOMEONE'S NECK!
GET IT?
MM-HMM.
DON'T WORRY, HARLEY'S ON TOP OF THINGS.
THURSDAY.
RATZ BITS
--FINAL TOUCHES ON THE RIDE TONIGHT, BUT HARLEY SAID WE COULDN'T TELL--!
SHE WANTS YOU TO BE SURPRISED!
SHE WANTS...SHE SAID...SHE SELLS SEA SHELLS...
MUM
FRIDAY.
THIS ISN'T FUNNY ANYMORE!

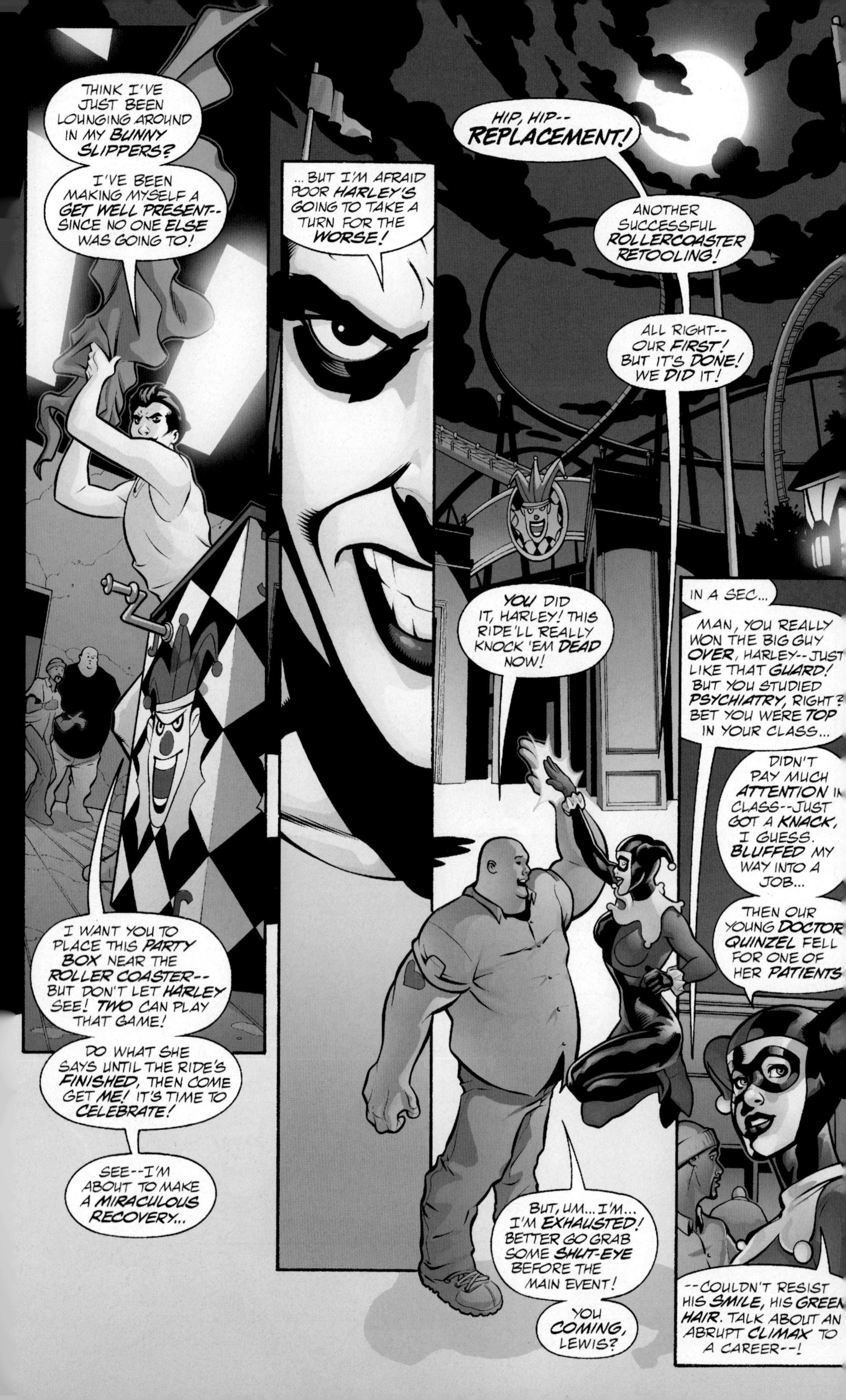
THINK I'VE JUST BEEN LOUNGING AROUND IN MY BUNNY SLIPPERS?
I'VE BEEN MAKING MYSELF A GET WELL PRESENT-- SINCE NO ONE ELSE WAS GOING TO!
I WANT YOU TO PLACE THIS PARTY BOX NEAR THE ROLLER COASTER-- BUT DON'T LET HARLEY SEE! TWO CAN PLAY THAT GAME!
DO WHAT SHE SAYS UNTIL THE RIDE'S FINISHED, THEN COME GET ME! IT'S TIME TO CELEBRATE!
SEE--I'M ABOUT TO MAKE A MIRACULOUS RECOVERY...
... BUT I'M AFRAID POOR HARLEY'S GOING TO TAKE A TURN FOR THE WORSE!
HIP, HIP-- REPLACEMENT!
ANOTHER SUCCESSFUL ROLLERCOASTER RETOOLING!
ALL RIGHT-- OUR FIRST! BUT IT'S DONE! WE DID IT!
YOU DID IT, HARLEY! THIS RIDE'LL REALLY KNOCK 'EM DEAD NOW!
BUT, UM... I'M... I'M EXHAUSTED! BETTER GO GRAB SOME SHUT-EYE BEFORE THE MAIN EVENT!
YOU COMING, LEWIS?
IN A SEC...
MAN, YOU REALLY WON THE BIG GUY OVER, HARLEY--JUST LIKE THAT GUARD! BUT YOU STUDIED PSYCHIATRY, RIGHT? BET YOU WERE TOP IN YOUR CLASS...
DIDN'T PAY MUCH ATTENTION IN CLASS--JUST GOT A KNACK, I GUESS. BLUFFED MY WAY INTO A JOB...
THEN OUR YOUNG DOCTOR QUINZEL FELL FOR ONE OF HER PATIENTS
--COULDN'T RESIST HIS SMILE, HIS GREEN HAIR. TALK ABOUT AN ABRUPT CLIMAX TO A CAREER--!

BUT ENOUGH ABOUT **ME!** HOW'D **YOU** HOOK UP WITH MR. J, LEWIS?

HEY, **YOU'RE** THE ONE WHO CAN READ PEOPLE LIKE A BOOK-- **YOU** TELL ME!

OOO-KAY...

YOU WANTED TO BE A **CLOWN,** BUT YOU HAD TO JOIN THE **MILITARY** TO PAY FOR CLOWN SCHOOL.

DURING A ROUTINE INVASION, YOU WERE EXPOSED TO AN EXPERIMENTAL **NERVE GAS** THAT LEFT YOU ALLERGIC TO **GREASE PAINT.**

EMBITTERED, YOU REJECTED ALL AUTHORITY AND TURNED TO A LIFE OF **CRIME.**

AND I LIKE TO THINK YOU **KILLED** A MAN-- IT'S THE **ROMANTIC** IN ME!

AFRAID MY STORY AIN'T ALL **THAT,** HARLEY. I MADE SOME **BIG MISTAKES** WHEN I WAS YOUNG...THINGS I CAN'T **FIX,** CAN'T **UNDO...**

BUT I GOT A **GIRL,** AND WE **LOVE** EACH OTHER, AND WE GOT A **BABY.** I SEND WHAT **MONEY** I CAN...

...BUT YOU DON'T WORK FOR THE **JOKER** FOR THE **MONEY.**

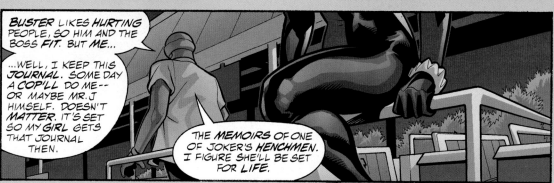

BUSTER LIKES **HURTING** PEOPLE, SO HIM AND THE BOSS **FIT.** BUT ME...

...WELL, I KEEP THIS **JOURNAL.** SOME DAY A COP'LL DO ME-- OR MAYBE MR. J HIMSELF. DOESN'T **MATTER.** IT'S SET SO MY **GIRL** GETS THAT JOURNAL THEN.

THE **MEMOIRS** OF ONE OF JOKER'S **HENCHMEN.** I FIGURE SHE'LL BE SET FOR **LIFE.**

WHAT ABOUT **YOU,** HARLEY? WHY DO **YOU** STICK?

WOULD YOU BELIEVE...

...HE REMINDS ME OF AN **OLD BOYFRIEND?**

REMEMBER MERRY MO INSIDE THE V

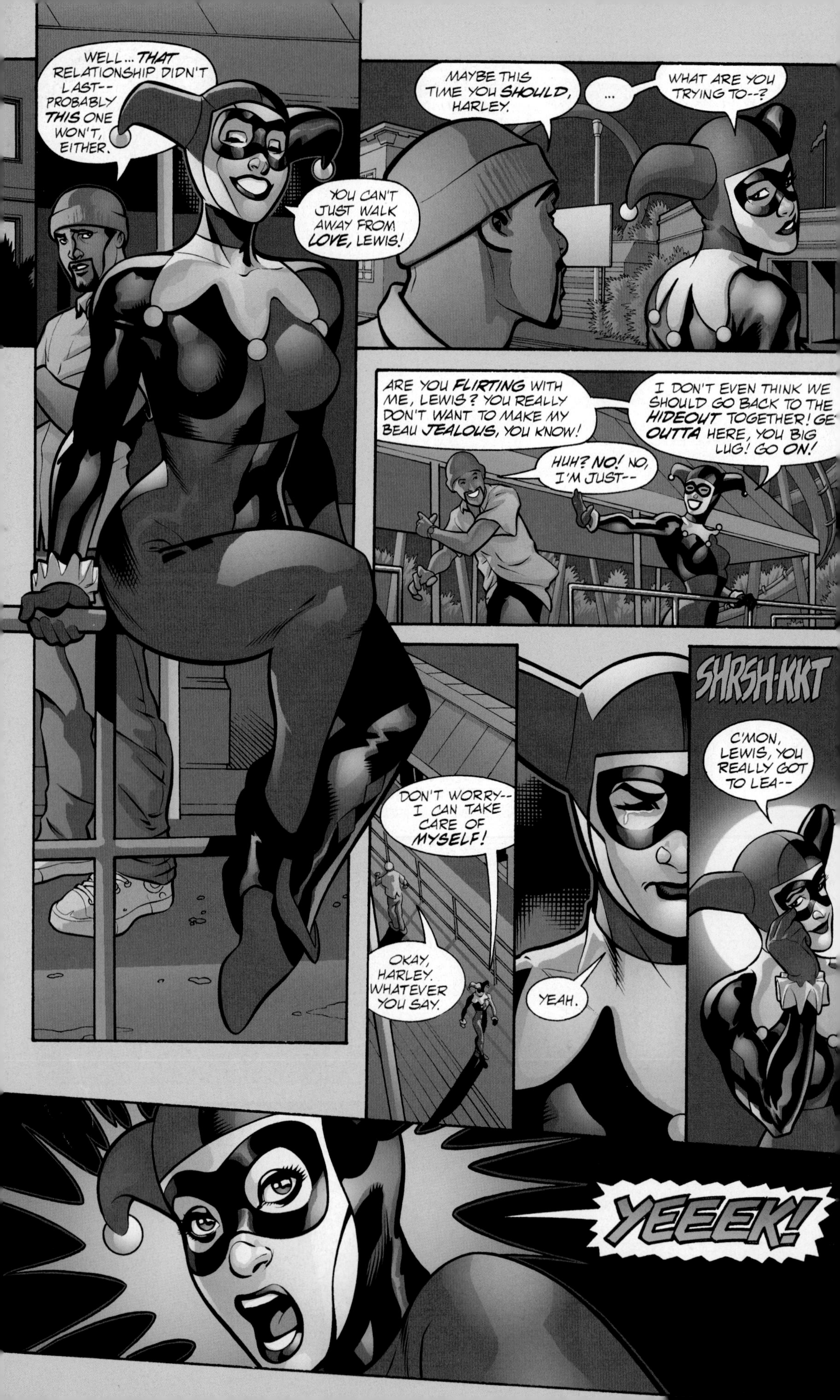

WELL... THAT RELATIONSHIP DIDN'T LAST-- PROBABLY THIS ONE WON'T, EITHER.
YOU CAN'T JUST WALK AWAY FROM LOVE, LEWIS!
MAYBE THIS TIME YOU SHOULD, HARLEY.
...
WHAT ARE YOU TRYING TO--?
ARE YOU FLIRTING WITH ME, LEWIS? YOU REALLY DON'T WANT TO MAKE MY BEAU JEALOUS, YOU KNOW!
HUH? NO! NO, I'M JUST--
I DON'T EVEN THINK WE SHOULD GO BACK TO THE HIDEOUT TOGETHER! GET OUTTA HERE, YOU BIG LUG! GO ON!
DON'T WORRY-- I CAN TAKE CARE OF MYSELF!
OKAY, HARLEY. WHATEVER YOU SAY.
YEAH.
SHRSH-KKT
C'MON, LEWIS, YOU REALLY GOT TO LEA--
YEEEK!

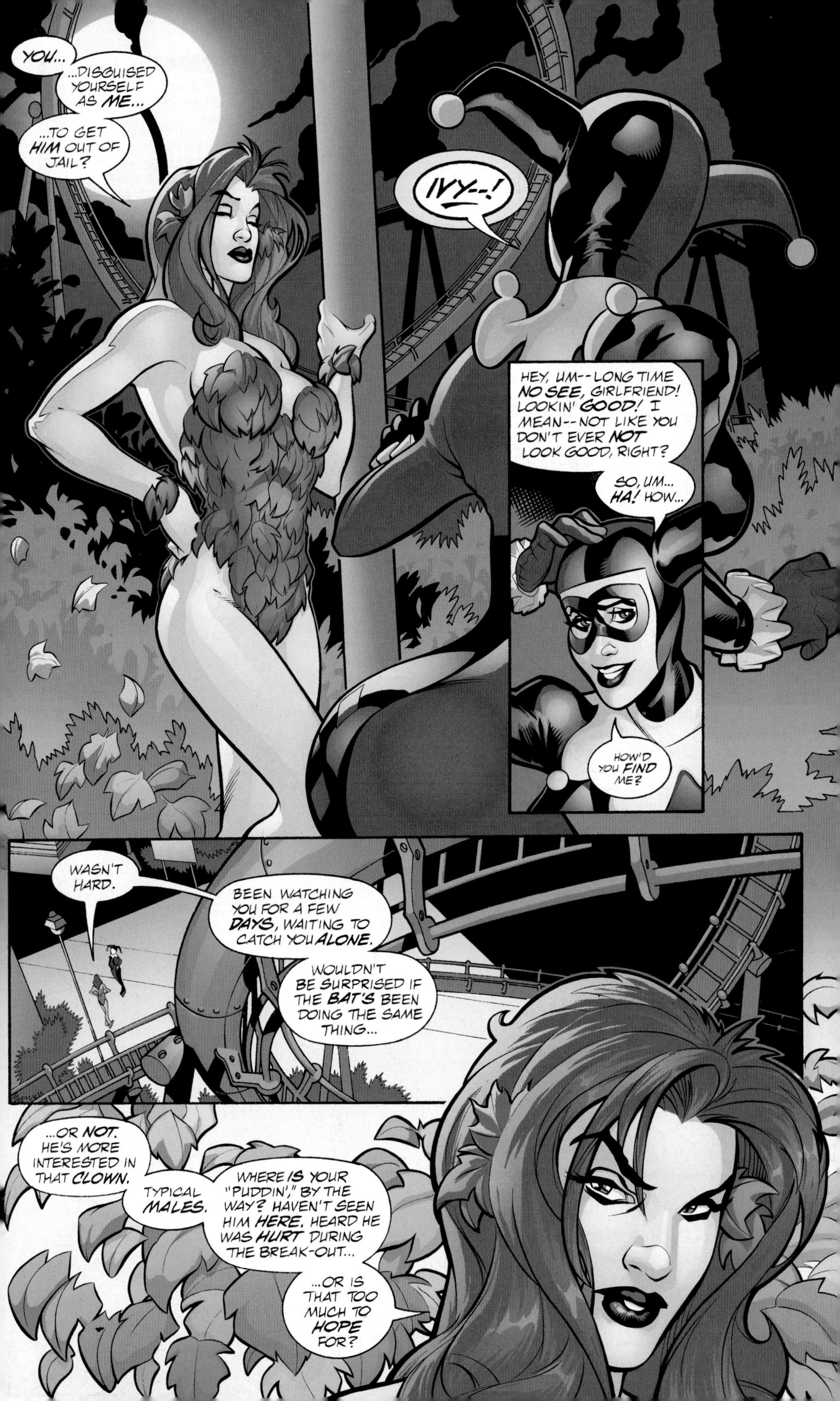
YOU...
...DISGUISED YOURSELF AS ME...
...TO GET HIM OUT OF JAIL?
IVY--!
HEY, UM--LONG TIME NO SEE, GIRLFRIEND! LOOKIN' GOOD! I MEAN--NOT LIKE YOU DON'T EVER NOT LOOK GOOD, RIGHT?
SO, UM... HA! HOW...
HOW'D YOU FIND ME?
WASN'T HARD.
BEEN WATCHING YOU FOR A FEW DAYS, WAITING TO CATCH YOU ALONE.
WOULDN'T BE SURPRISED IF THE BAT'S BEEN DOING THE SAME THING...
...OR NOT. HE'S MORE INTERESTED IN THAT CLOWN.
TYPICAL MALES.
WHERE IS YOUR "PUDDIN'," BY THE WAY? HAVEN'T SEEN HIM HERE. HEARD HE WAS HURT DURING THE BREAK-OUT...
...OR IS THAT TOO MUCH TO HOPE FOR?

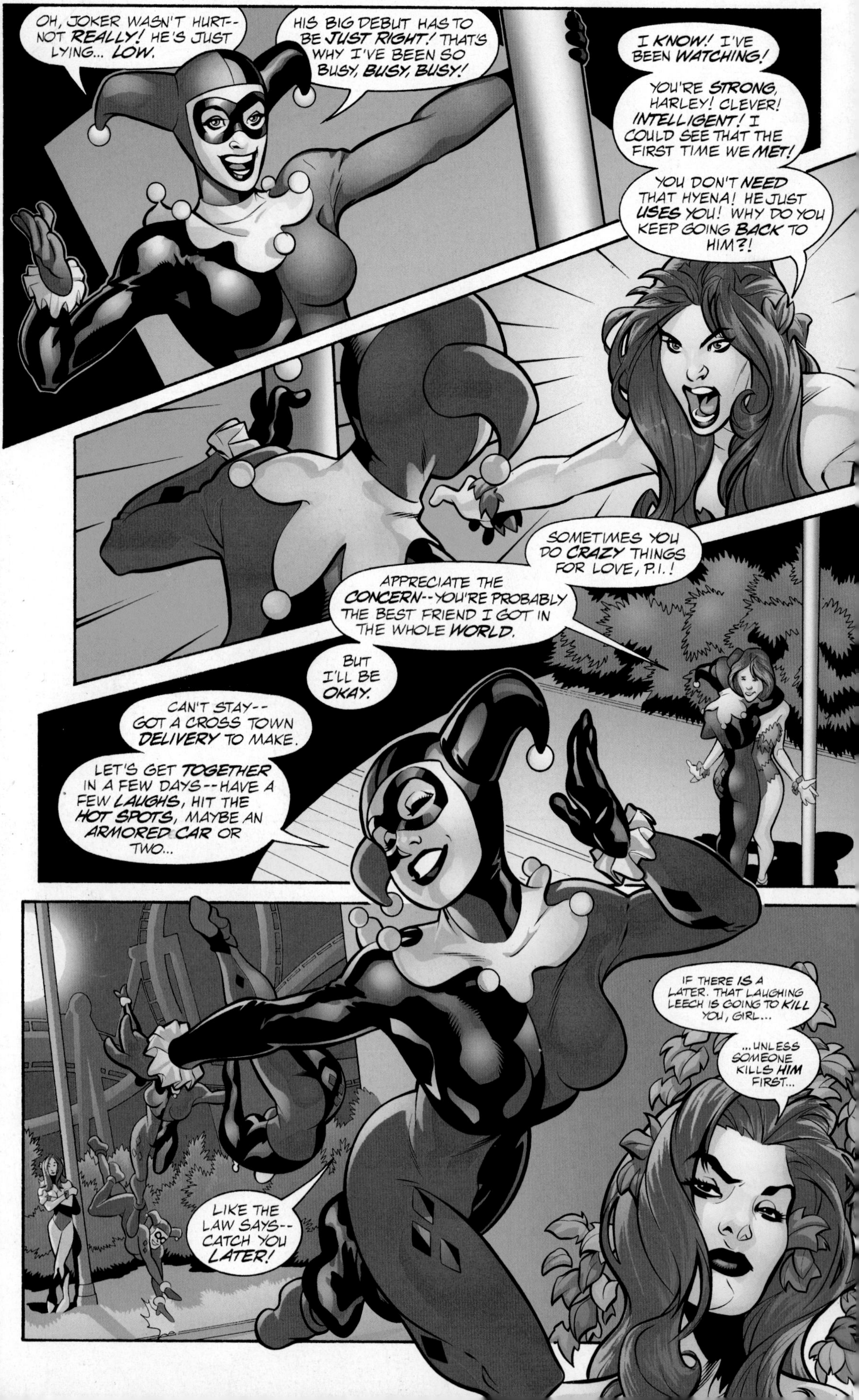

OH, JOKER WASN'T HURT--NOT REALLY! HE'S JUST LYING... LOW.
HIS BIG DEBUT HAS TO BE JUST RIGHT! THAT'S WHY I'VE BEEN SO BUSY, BUSY, BUSY!
I KNOW! I'VE BEEN WATCHING!
YOU'RE STRONG, HARLEY! CLEVER! INTELLIGENT! I COULD SEE THAT THE FIRST TIME WE MET!
YOU DON'T NEED THAT HYENA! HE JUST USES YOU! WHY DO YOU KEEP GOING BACK TO HIM?!
SOMETIMES YOU DO CRAZY THINGS FOR LOVE, P.I.!
APPRECIATE THE CONCERN--YOU'RE PROBABLY THE BEST FRIEND I GOT IN THE WHOLE WORLD.
BUT I'LL BE OKAY.
CAN'T STAY--GOT A CROSS TOWN DELIVERY TO MAKE.
LET'S GET TOGETHER IN A FEW DAYS--HAVE A FEW LAUGHS, HIT THE HOT SPOTS, MAYBE AN ARMORED CAR OR TWO...
LIKE THE LAW SAYS--CATCH YOU LATER!
IF THERE IS A LATER. THAT LAUGHING LEECH IS GOING TO KILL YOU, GIRL...
...UNLESS SOMEONE KILLS HIM FIRST...

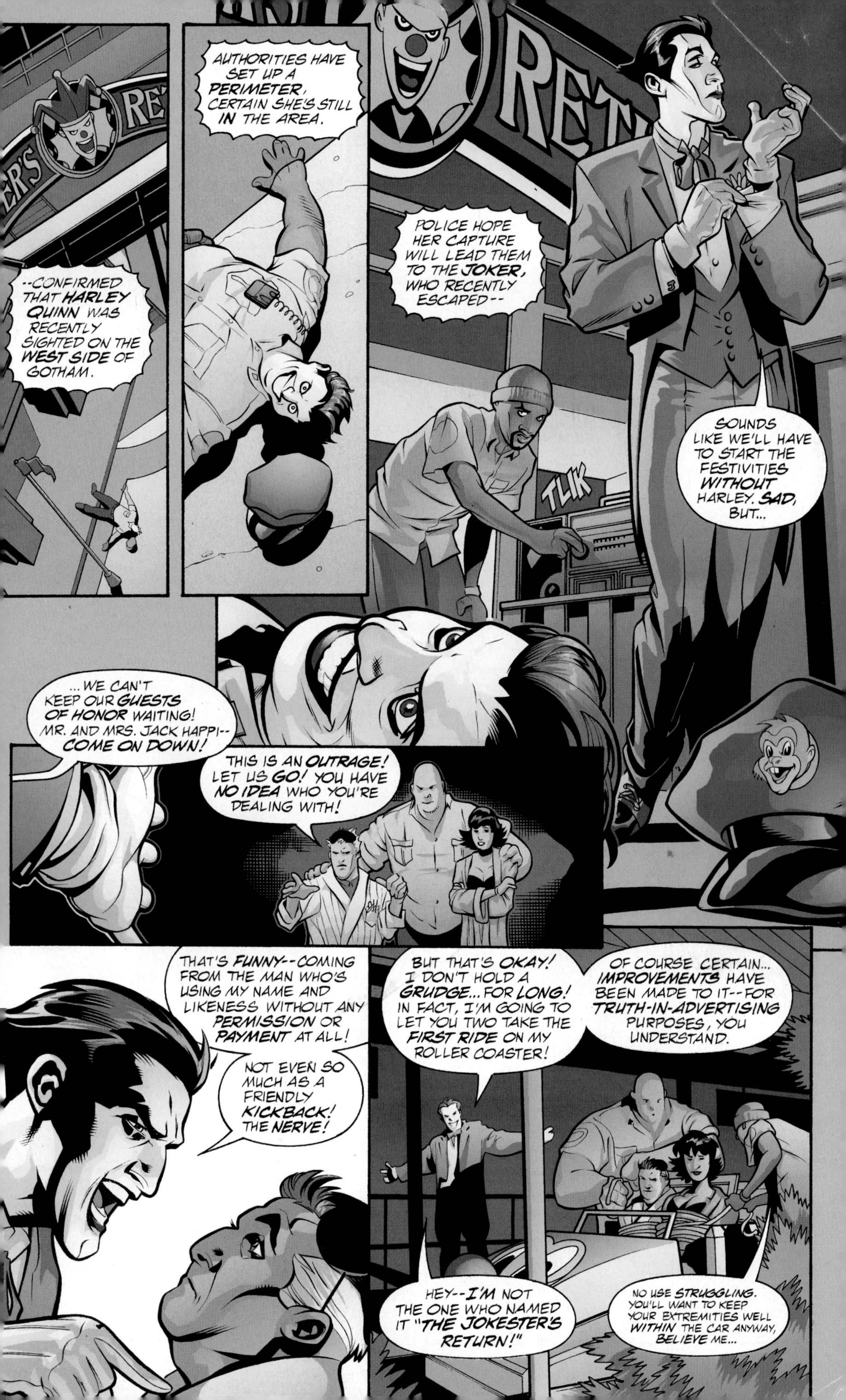
--CONFIRMED THAT HARLEY QUINN WAS RECENTLY SIGHTED ON THE WEST SIDE OF GOTHAM.
AUTHORITIES HAVE SET UP A PERIMETER, CERTAIN SHE'S STILL IN THE AREA.
POLICE HOPE HER CAPTURE WILL LEAD THEM TO THE JOKER, WHO RECENTLY ESCAPED--
TLIK
SOUNDS LIKE WE'LL HAVE TO START THE FESTIVITIES WITHOUT HARLEY. SAD, BUT...
...WE CAN'T KEEP OUR GUESTS OF HONOR WAITING! MR. AND MRS. JACK HAPPI-- COME ON DOWN!
THIS IS AN OUTRAGE! LET US GO! YOU HAVE NO IDEA WHO YOU'RE DEALING WITH!
THAT'S FUNNY--COMING FROM THE MAN WHO'S USING MY NAME AND LIKENESS WITHOUT ANY PERMISSION OR PAYMENT AT ALL!
NOT EVEN SO MUCH AS A FRIENDLY KICKBACK! THE NERVE!
BUT THAT'S OKAY! I DON'T HOLD A GRUDGE...FOR LONG! IN FACT, I'M GOING TO LET YOU TWO TAKE THE FIRST RIDE ON MY ROLLER COASTER!
OF COURSE CERTAIN... IMPROVEMENTS HAVE BEEN MADE TO IT--FOR TRUTH-IN-ADVERTISING PURPOSES, YOU UNDERSTAND.
HEY--I'M NOT THE ONE WHO NAMED IT "THE JOKESTER'S RETURN!"
NO USE STRUGGLING. YOU'LL WANT TO KEEP YOUR EXTREMITIES WELL WITHIN THE CAR ANYWAY, BELIEVE ME...

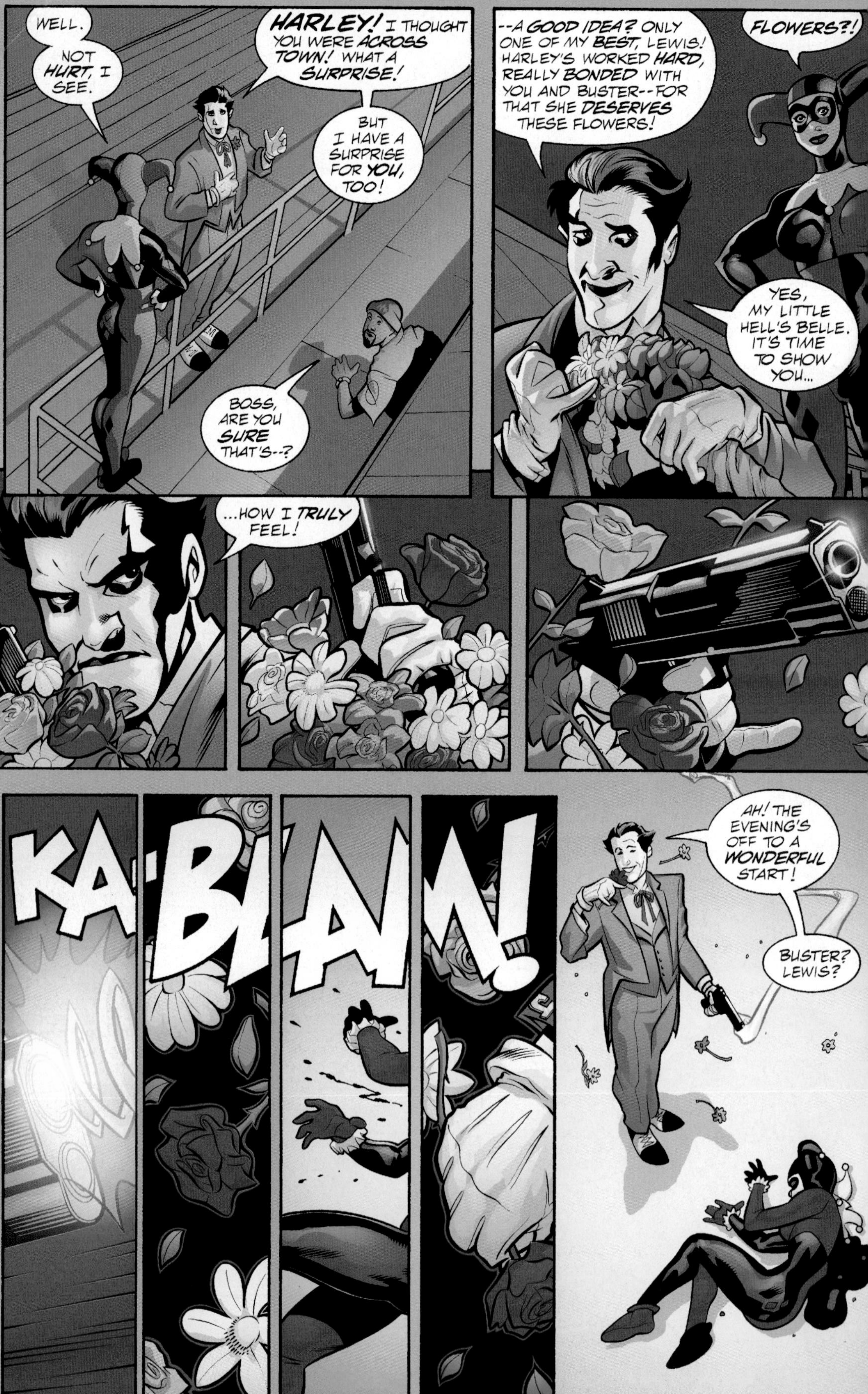
WELL.
NOT HURT, I SEE.
HARLEY! I THOUGHT YOU WERE ACROSS TOWN! WHAT A SURPRISE!
BUT I HAVE A SURPRISE FOR YOU, TOO!
BOSS, ARE YOU SURE THAT'S--?
--A GOOD IDEA? ONLY ONE OF MY BEST, LEWIS! HARLEY'S WORKED HARD, REALLY BONDED WITH YOU AND BUSTER--FOR THAT SHE DESERVES THESE FLOWERS!
FLOWERS?!
YES, MY LITTLE HELL'S BELLE. IT'S TIME TO SHOW YOU...
...HOW I TRULY FEEL!
KA-BLAM!
AH! THE EVENING'S OFF TO A WONDERFUL START!
BUSTER? LEWIS?

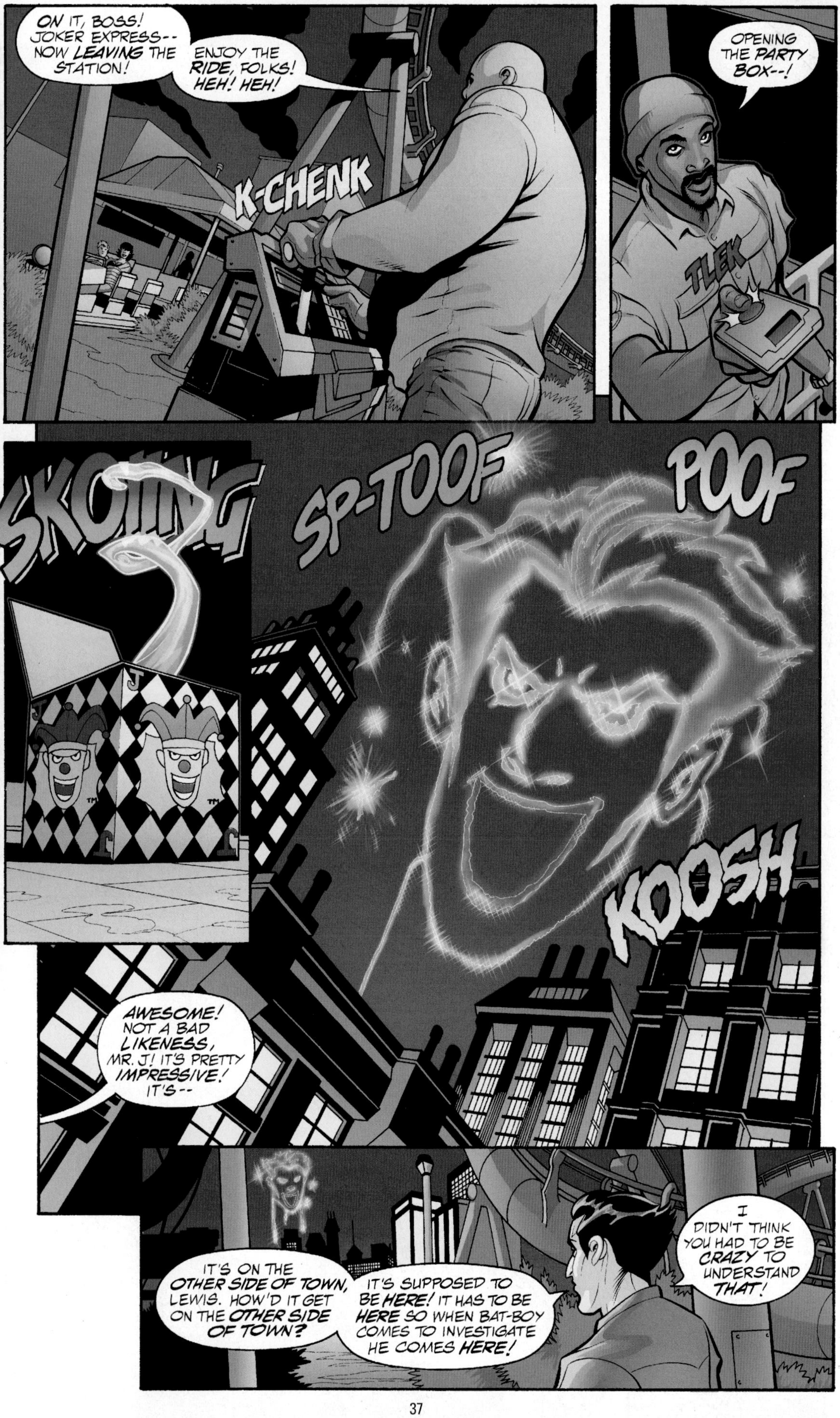
ON IT, BOSS! JOKER EXPRESS-- NOW LEAVING THE STATION!
ENJOY THE RIDE, FOLKS! HEH! HEH!
K-CHENK
OPENING THE PARTY BOX--!
TLEK
SKOTING
SP-TOOF
POOF
KOOSH
AWESOME! NOT A BAD LIKENESS, MR. J! IT'S PRETTY IMPRESSIVE! IT'S--
IT'S ON THE OTHER SIDE OF TOWN, LEWIS. HOW'D IT GET ON THE OTHER SIDE OF TOWN?
IT'S SUPPOSED TO BE HERE! IT HAS TO BE HERE SO WHEN BAT-BOY COMES TO INVESTIGATE HE COMES HERE!
I DIDN'T THINK YOU HAD TO BE CRAZY TO UNDERSTAND THAT!

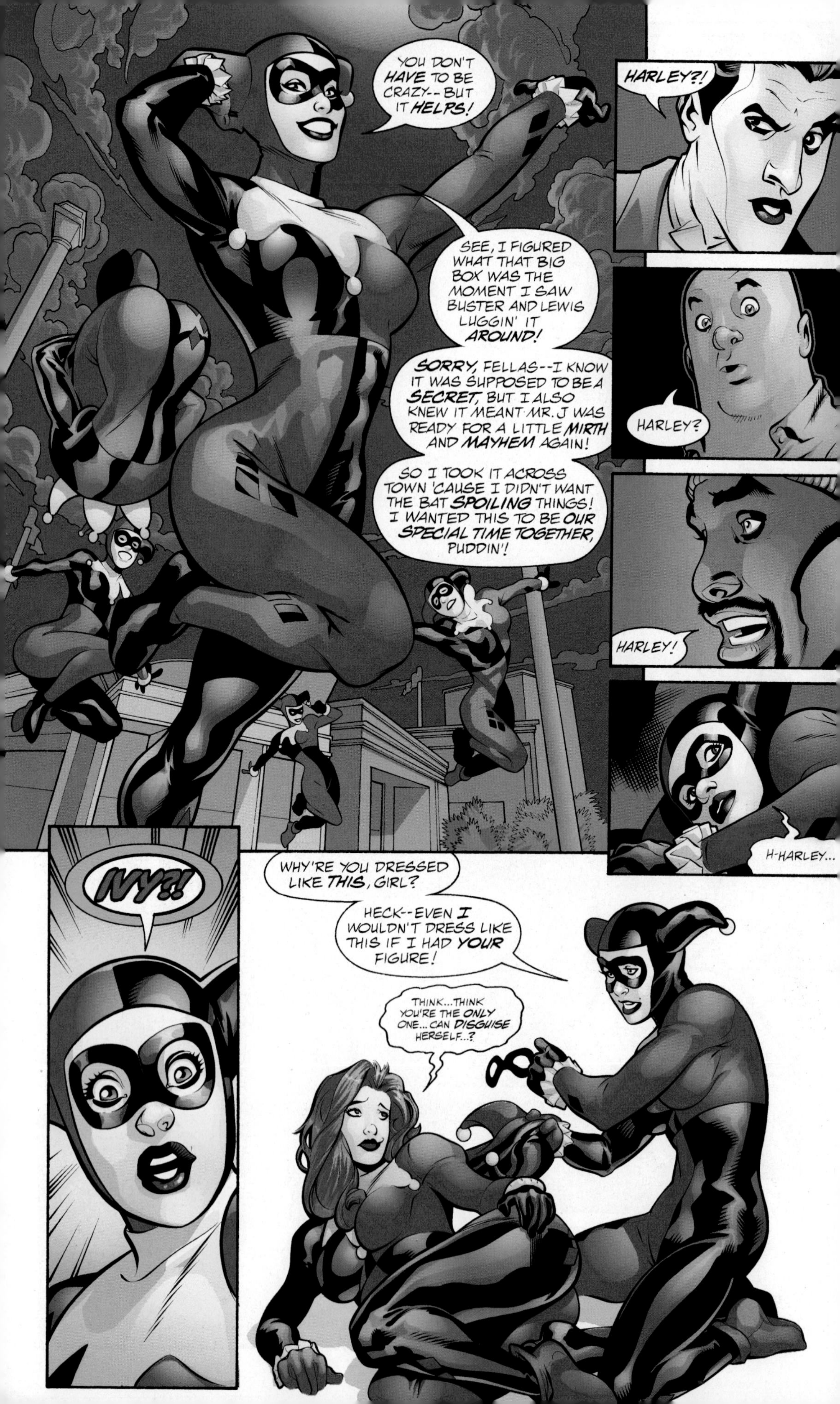
YOU DON'T HAVE TO BE CRAZY-- BUT IT HELPS!
SEE, I FIGURED WHAT THAT BIG BOX WAS THE MOMENT I SAW BUSTER AND LEWIS LUGGIN' IT AROUND!
SORRY, FELLAS--I KNOW IT WAS SUPPOSED TO BE A SECRET, BUT I ALSO KNEW IT MEANT MR. J WAS READY FOR A LITTLE MIRTH AND MAYHEM AGAIN!
SO I TOOK IT ACROSS TOWN 'CAUSE I DIDN'T WANT THE BAT SPOILING THINGS! I WANTED THIS TO BE OUR SPECIAL TIME TOGETHER, PUDDIN'!
HARLEY?!
HARLEY?
HARLEY!
H-HARLEY...
IVY?!
WHY'RE YOU DRESSED LIKE THIS, GIRL?
HECK--EVEN I WOULDN'T DRESS LIKE THIS IF I HAD YOUR FIGURE!
THINK...THINK YOU'RE THE ONLY ONE...CAN DISGUISE HERSELF...?

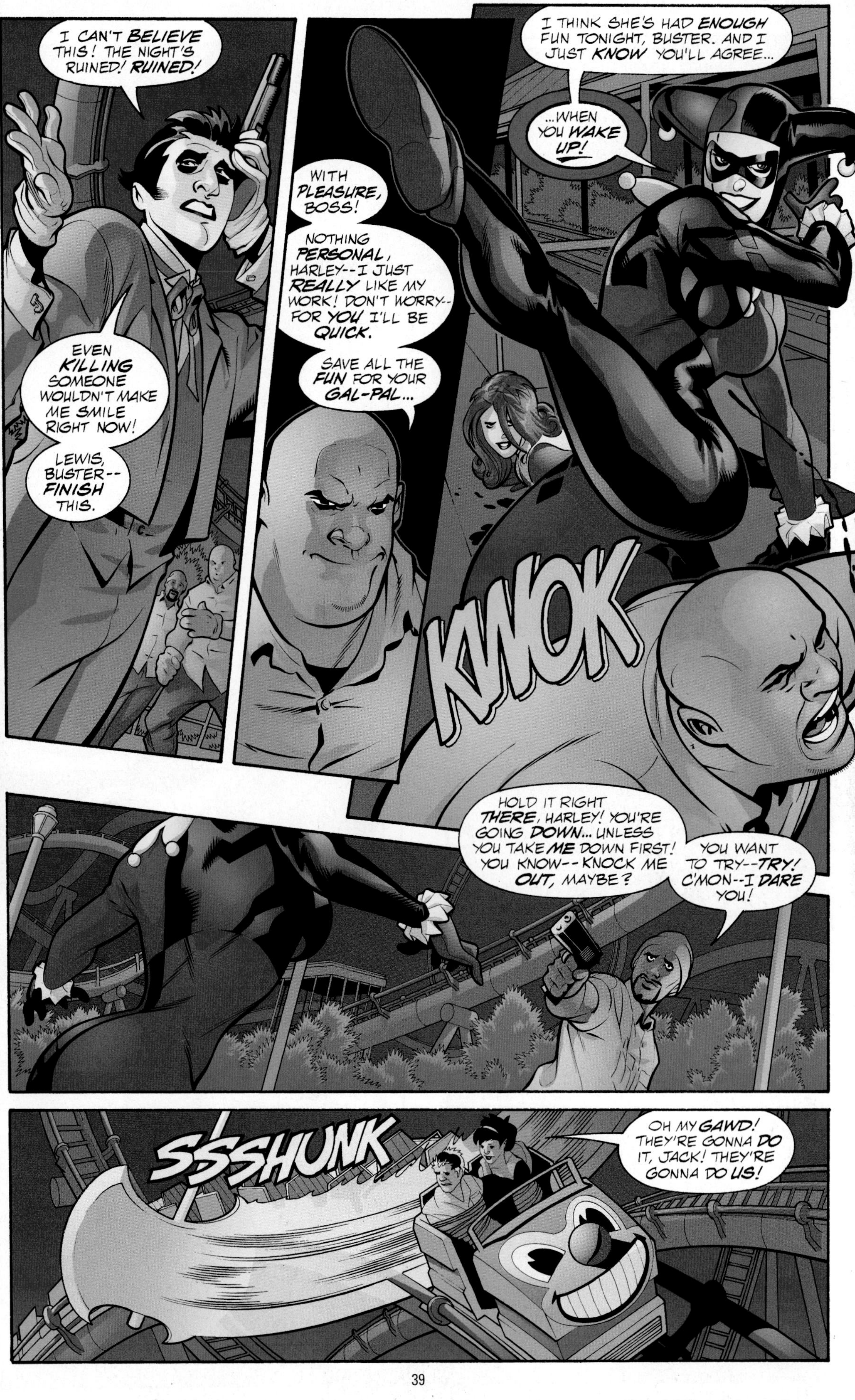
I CAN'T BELIEVE THIS! THE NIGHT'S RUINED! RUINED!
EVEN KILLING SOMEONE WOULDN'T MAKE ME SMILE RIGHT NOW!
LEWIS, BUSTER-- FINISH THIS.
WITH PLEASURE, BOSS!
NOTHING PERSONAL, HARLEY--I JUST REALLY LIKE MY WORK! DON'T WORRY-- FOR YOU I'LL BE QUICK.
SAVE ALL THE FUN FOR YOUR GAL-PAL...
I THINK SHE'S HAD ENOUGH FUN TONIGHT, BUSTER. AND I JUST KNOW YOU'LL AGREE...
...WHEN YOU WAKE UP!
KNOK
HOLD IT RIGHT THERE, HARLEY! YOU'RE GOING DOWN... UNLESS YOU TAKE ME DOWN FIRST! YOU KNOW--KNOCK ME OUT, MAYBE?
YOU WANT TO TRY--TRY! C'MON--I DARE YOU!
SSSHUNK
OH MY GAWD! THEY'RE GONNA DO IT, JACK! THEY'RE GONNA DO US!

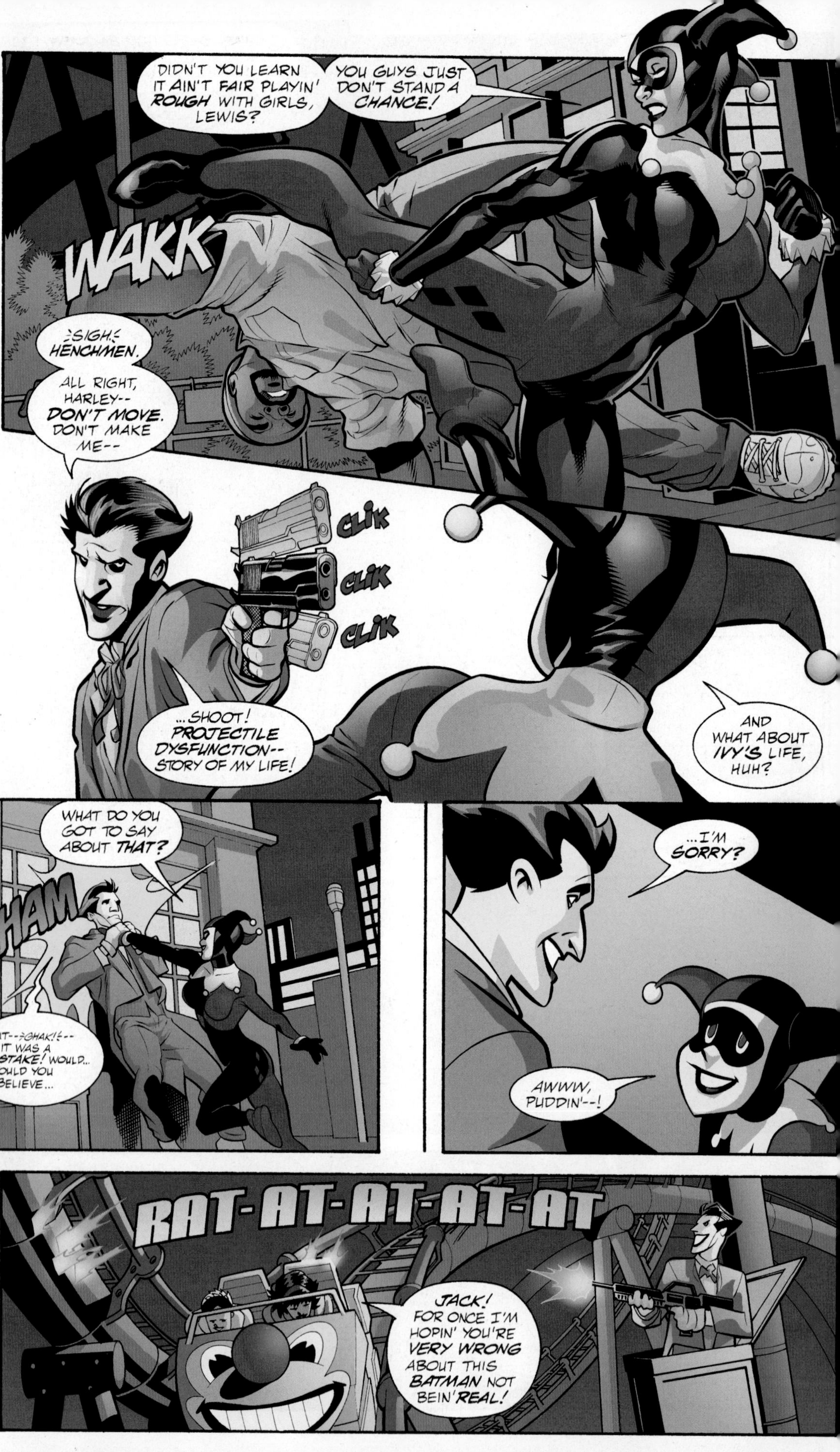
DIDN'T YOU LEARN IT AIN'T FAIR PLAYIN' ROUGH WITH GIRLS, LEWIS?
YOU GUYS JUST DON'T STAND A CHANCE!
WAKK
:SIGH: HENCHMEN.
ALL RIGHT, HARLEY-- DON'T MOVE. DON'T MAKE ME--
CLIK
CLIK
CLIK
...SHOOT! PROJECTILE DYSFUNCTION-- STORY OF MY LIFE!
AND WHAT ABOUT IVY'S LIFE, HUH?
WHAT DO YOU GOT TO SAY ABOUT THAT?
WHAM
IT--:GHAK!:-- IT WAS A MISTAKE! WOULD... WOULD YOU BELIEVE...
...I'M SORRY?
AWWW, PUDDIN'--!
RAT-AT-AT-AT-AT
JACK! FOR ONCE I'M HOPIN' YOU'RE VERY WRONG ABOUT THIS BATMAN NOT BEIN' REAL!

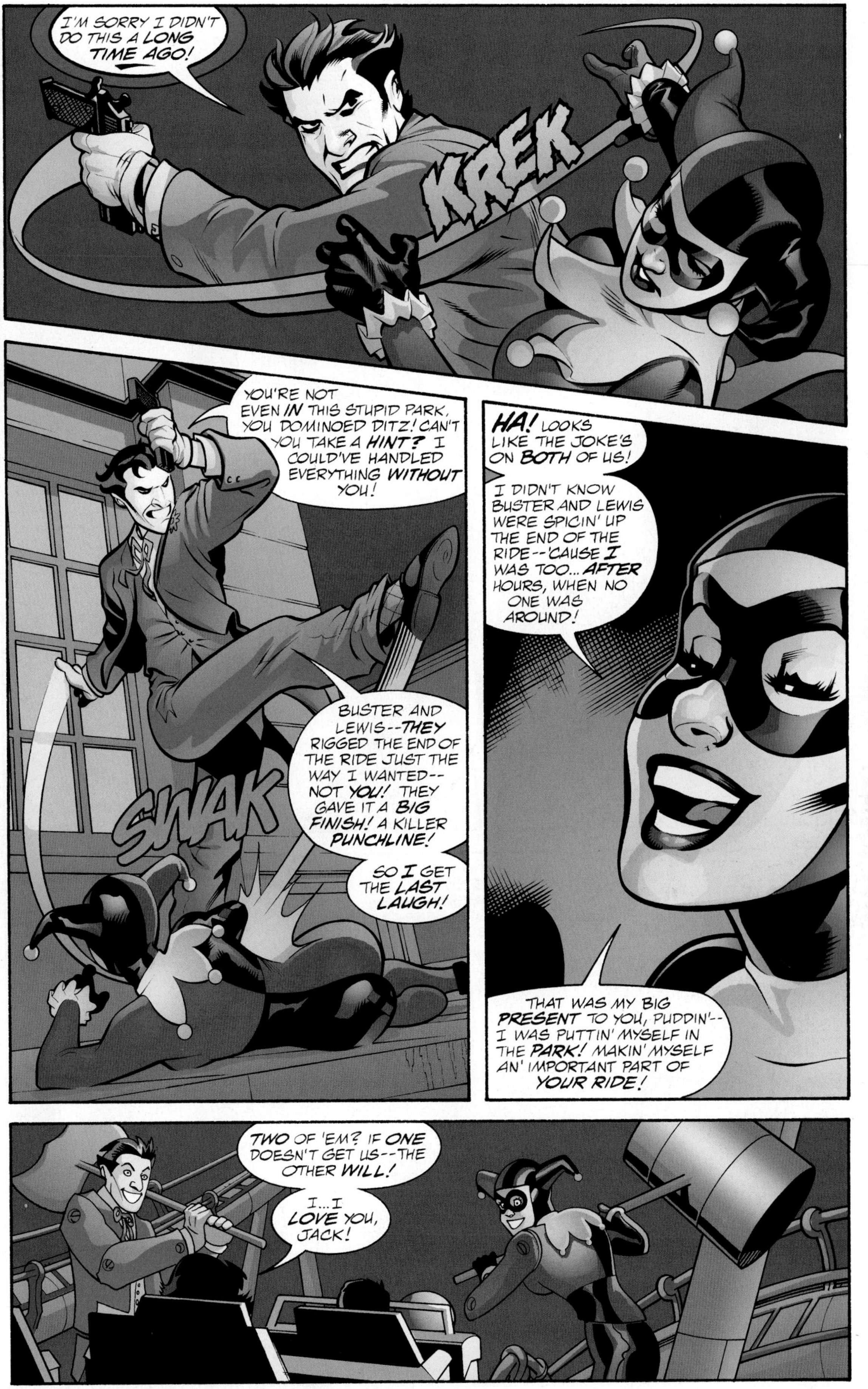
I'M SORRY I DIDN'T DO THIS A LONG TIME AGO!
KREK
YOU'RE NOT EVEN IN THIS STUPID PARK, YOU DOMINOED DITZ! CAN'T YOU TAKE A HINT? I COULD'VE HANDLED EVERYTHING WITHOUT YOU!
SWAK
BUSTER AND LEWIS--THEY RIGGED THE END OF THE RIDE JUST THE WAY I WANTED--NOT YOU! THEY GAVE IT A BIG FINISH! A KILLER PUNCHLINE!
SO I GET THE LAST LAUGH!
HA! LOOKS LIKE THE JOKE'S ON BOTH OF US!
I DIDN'T KNOW BUSTER AND LEWIS WERE SPICIN' UP THE END OF THE RIDE--'CAUSE I WAS TOO... AFTER HOURS, WHEN NO ONE WAS AROUND!
THAT WAS MY BIG PRESENT TO YOU, PUDDIN'--I WAS PUTTIN' MYSELF IN THE PARK! MAKIN' MYSELF AN' IMPORTANT PART OF YOUR RIDE!
TWO OF 'EM? IF ONE DOESN'T GET US--THE OTHER WILL!
I...I LOVE YOU, JACK!

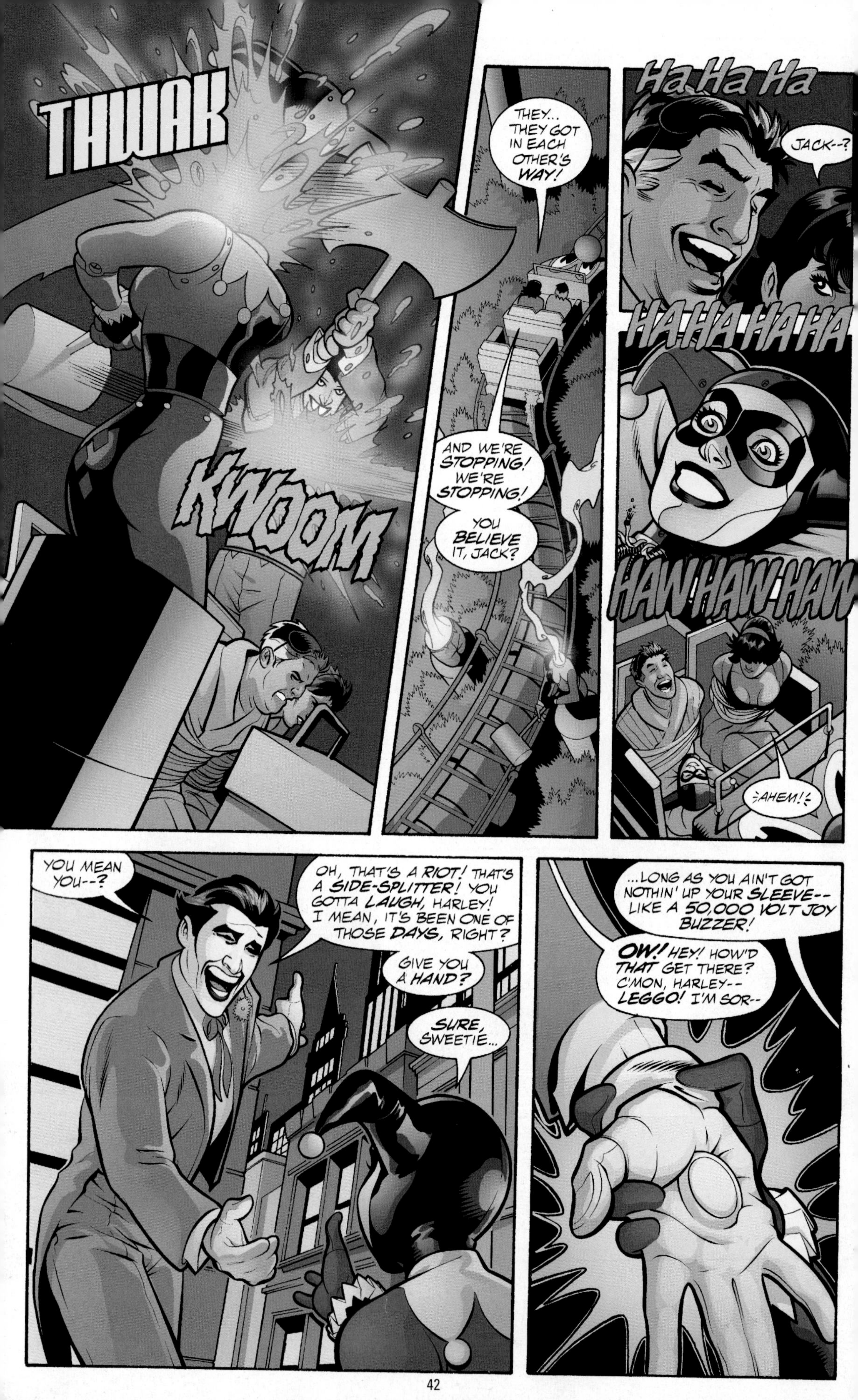
THWAK
KWOOM
THEY... THEY GOT IN EACH OTHER'S WAY!
AND WE'RE STOPPING! WE'RE STOPPING!
YOU BELIEVE IT, JACK?
Ha Ha Ha Ha
JACK--?
HA HA HA HA HA
HAW HAW HAW
AHEM!
YOU MEAN YOU--?
OH, THAT'S A RIOT! THAT'S A SIDE-SPLITTER! YOU GOTTA LAUGH, HARLEY! I MEAN, IT'S BEEN ONE OF THOSE DAYS, RIGHT?
GIVE YOU A HAND?
SURE, SWEETIE...
...LONG AS YOU AIN'T GOT NOTHIN' UP YOUR SLEEVE-- LIKE A 50,000 VOLT JOY BUZZER!
OW! HEY! HOW'D THAT GET THERE? C'MON, HARLEY-- LEGGO! I'M SOR--

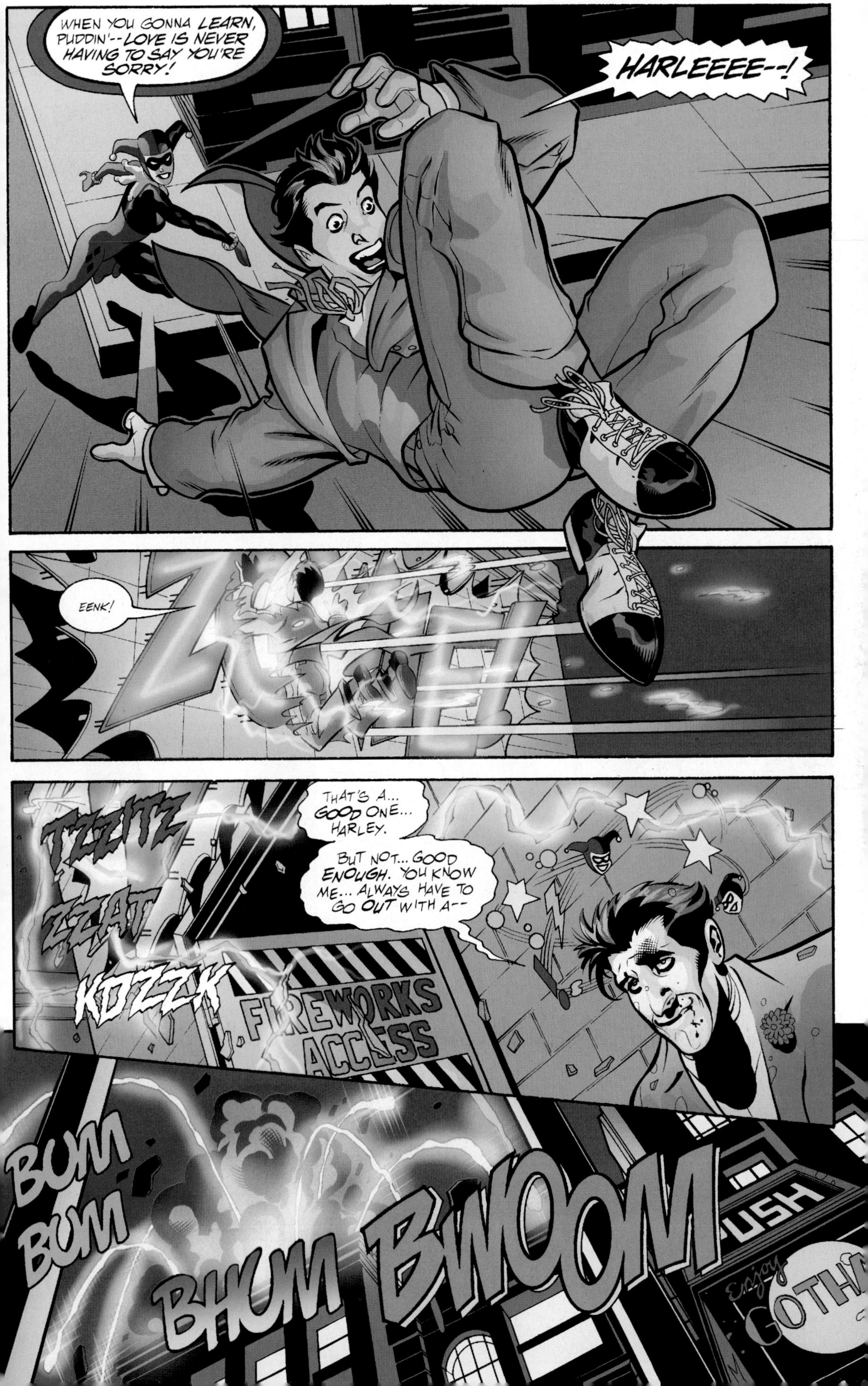

WHEN YOU GONNA LEARN, PUDDIN'--LOVE IS NEVER HAVING TO SAY YOU'RE SORRY!
HARLEEEE--!
EEENK!
TZZITZ
ZZAT
KDZZZK
THAT'S A... GOOD ONE... HARLEY.
BUT NOT... GOOD ENOUGH. YOU KNOW ME... ALWAYS HAVE TO GO OUT WITH A--
FIREWORKS ACCESS
BUM
BUM
BHUM
BWOOM
PUSH
Enjoy
GOTH

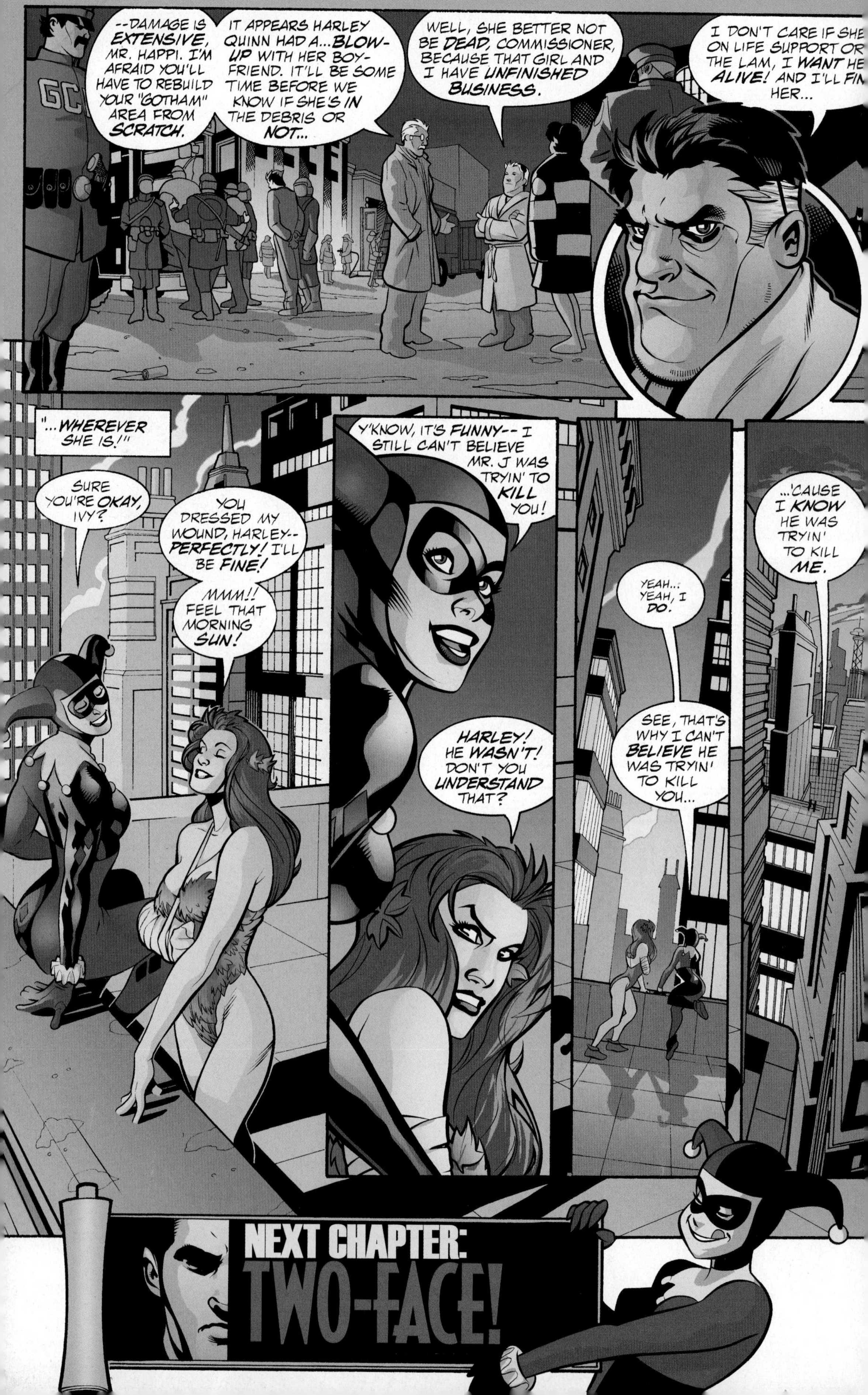
--DAMAGE IS EXTENSIVE, MR. HAPPI. I'M AFRAID YOU'LL HAVE TO REBUILD YOUR "GOTHAM" AREA FROM SCRATCH.
IT APPEARS HARLEY QUINN HAD A...BLOW-UP WITH HER BOY-FRIEND. IT'LL BE SOME TIME BEFORE WE KNOW IF SHE'S IN THE DEBRIS OR NOT...
WELL, SHE BETTER NOT BE DEAD, COMMISSIONER, BECAUSE THAT GIRL AND I HAVE UNFINISHED BUSINESS.
I DON'T CARE IF SHE ON LIFE SUPPORT OR THE LAM, I WANT HE ALIVE! AND I'LL FIN HER...
"...WHEREVER SHE IS!"
SURE YOU'RE OKAY, IVY?
YOU DRESSED MY WOUND, HARLEY--PERFECTLY! I'LL BE FINE!
MMM!! FEEL THAT MORNING SUN!
Y'KNOW, IT'S FUNNY-- I STILL CAN'T BELIEVE MR. J WAS TRYIN' TO KILL YOU!
HARLEY! HE WASN'T! DON'T YOU UNDERSTAND THAT?
YEAH... YEAH, I DO.
SEE, THAT'S WHY I CAN'T BELIEVE HE WAS TRYIN' TO KILL YOU...
...'CAUSE I KNOW HE WAS TRYIN' TO KILL ME.
NEXT CHAPTER:
TWO-FACE!

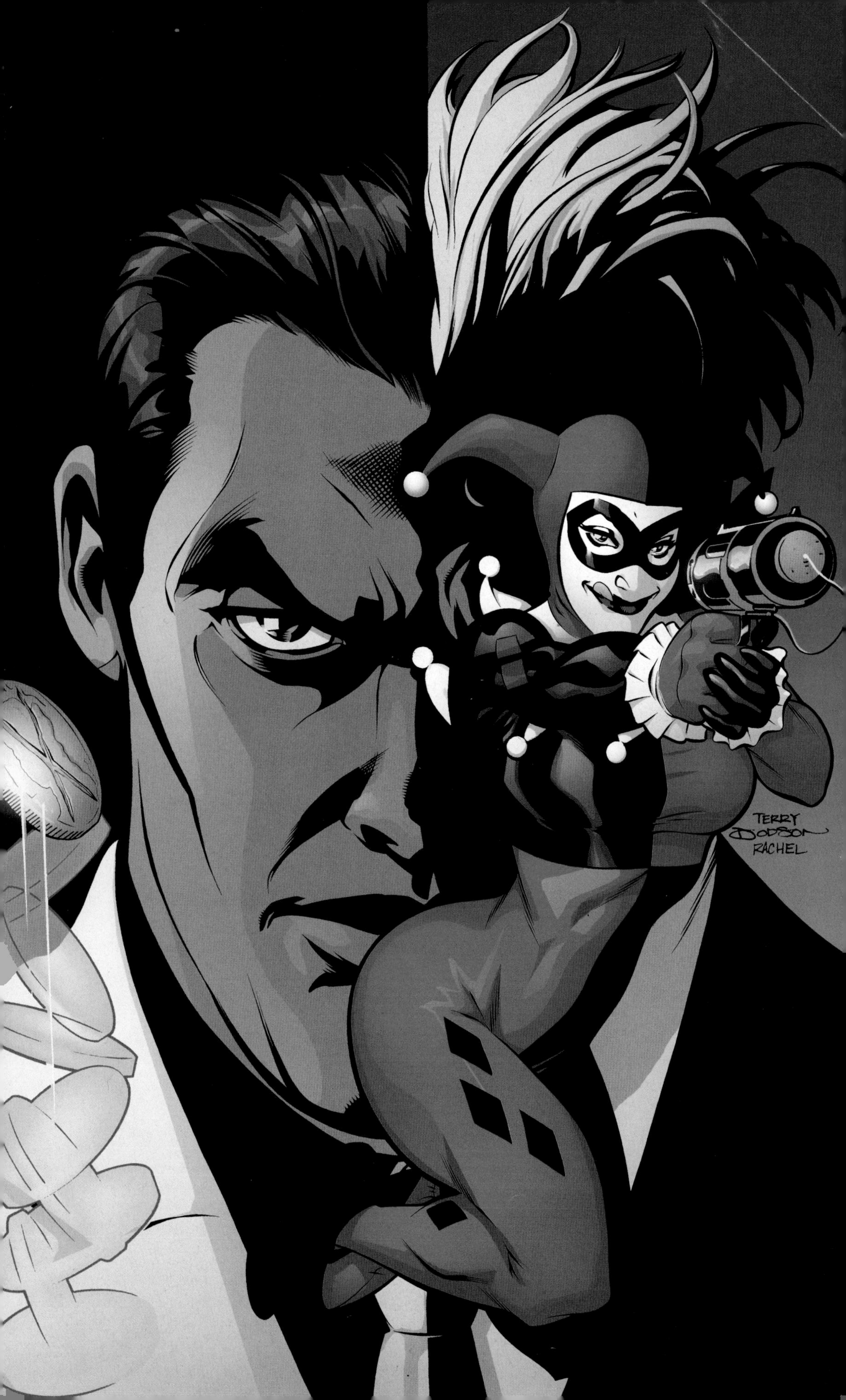
TERRY
DODSON
RACHEL

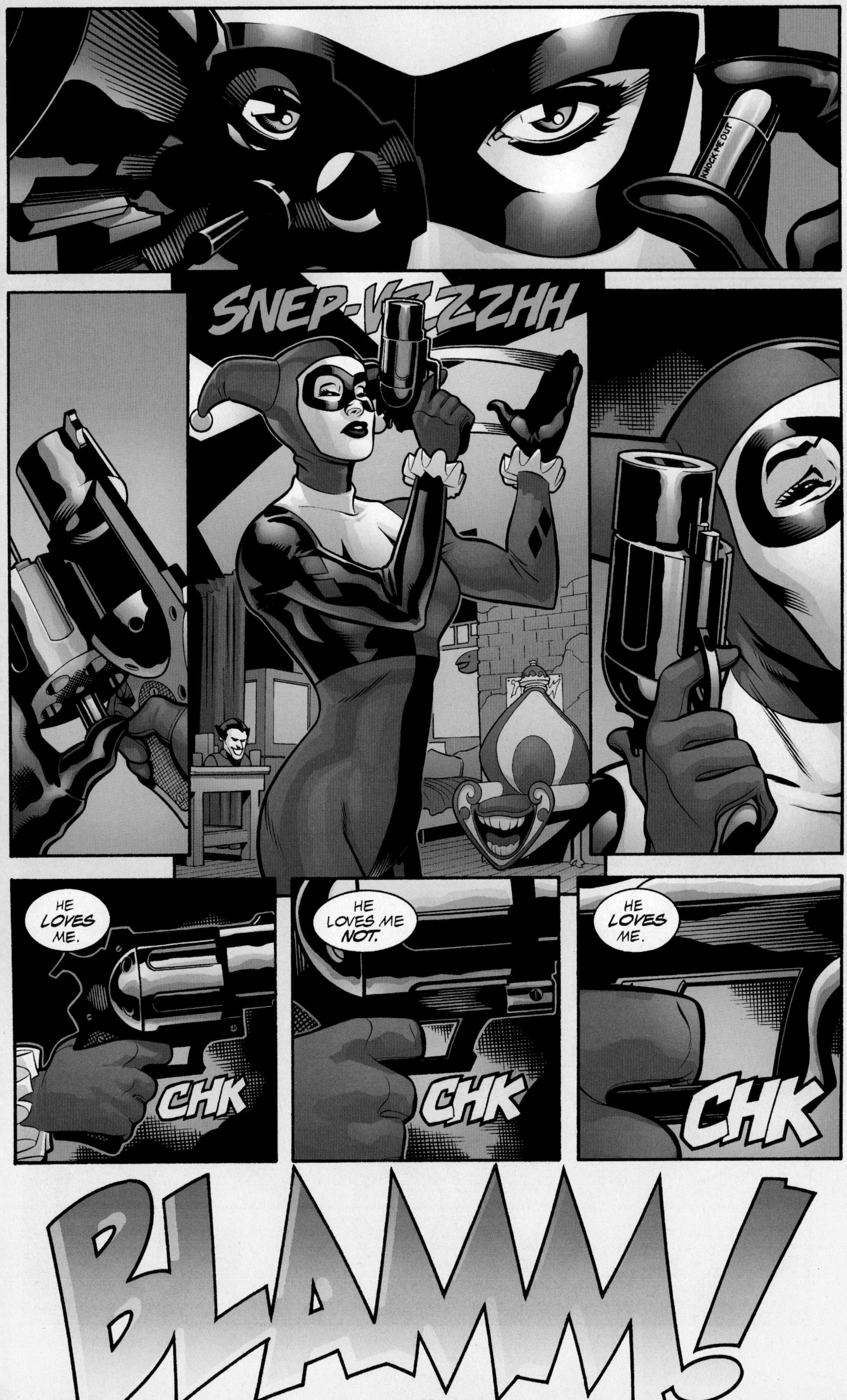

KNOCK ME OUT
SNEP-VZZZHH
HE LOVES ME.
CHK
HE LOVES ME NOT.
CHK
HE LOVES ME.
CHK
BLAMM!

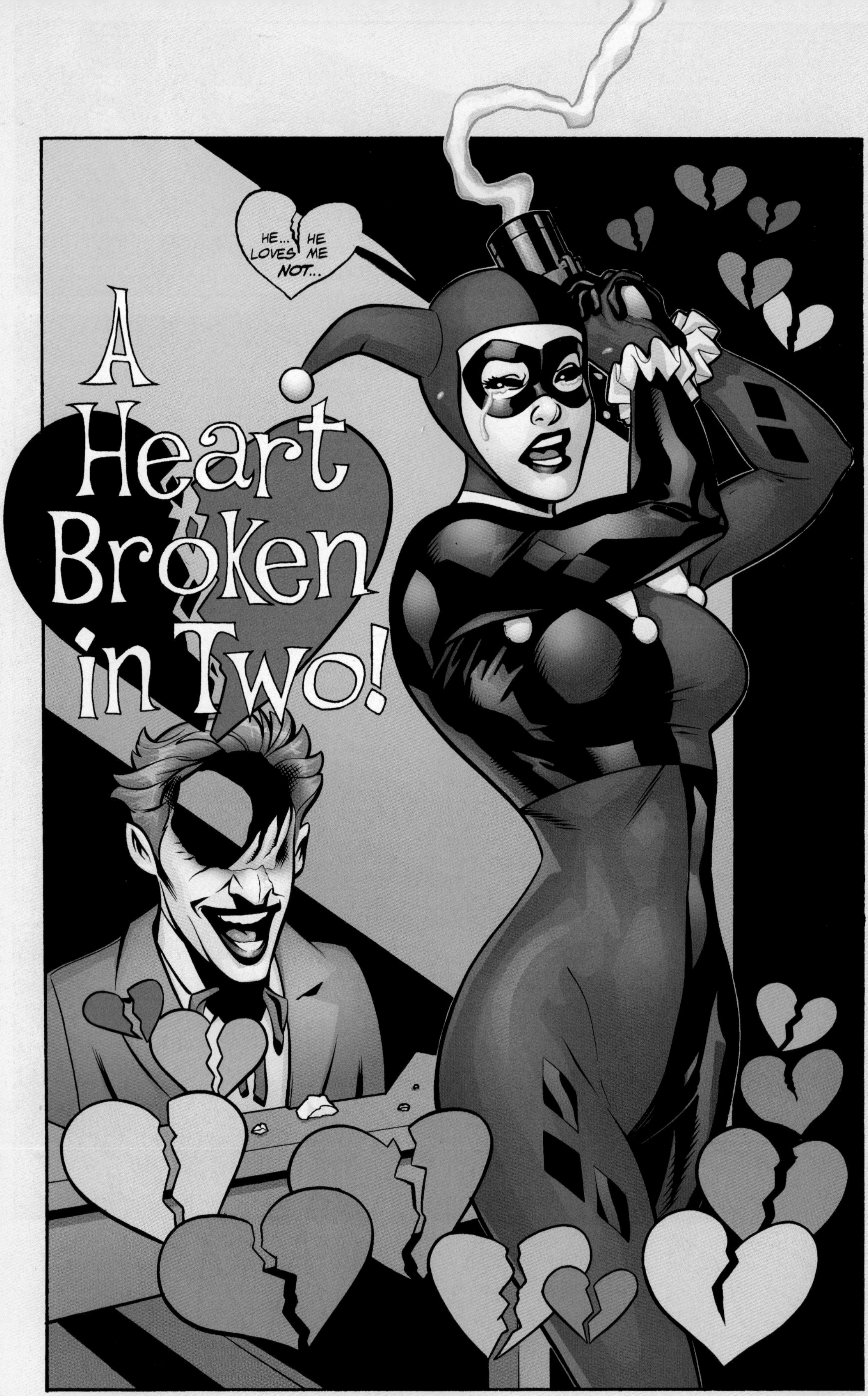
HE... HE LOVES ME NOT...
A Heart Broken in Two!

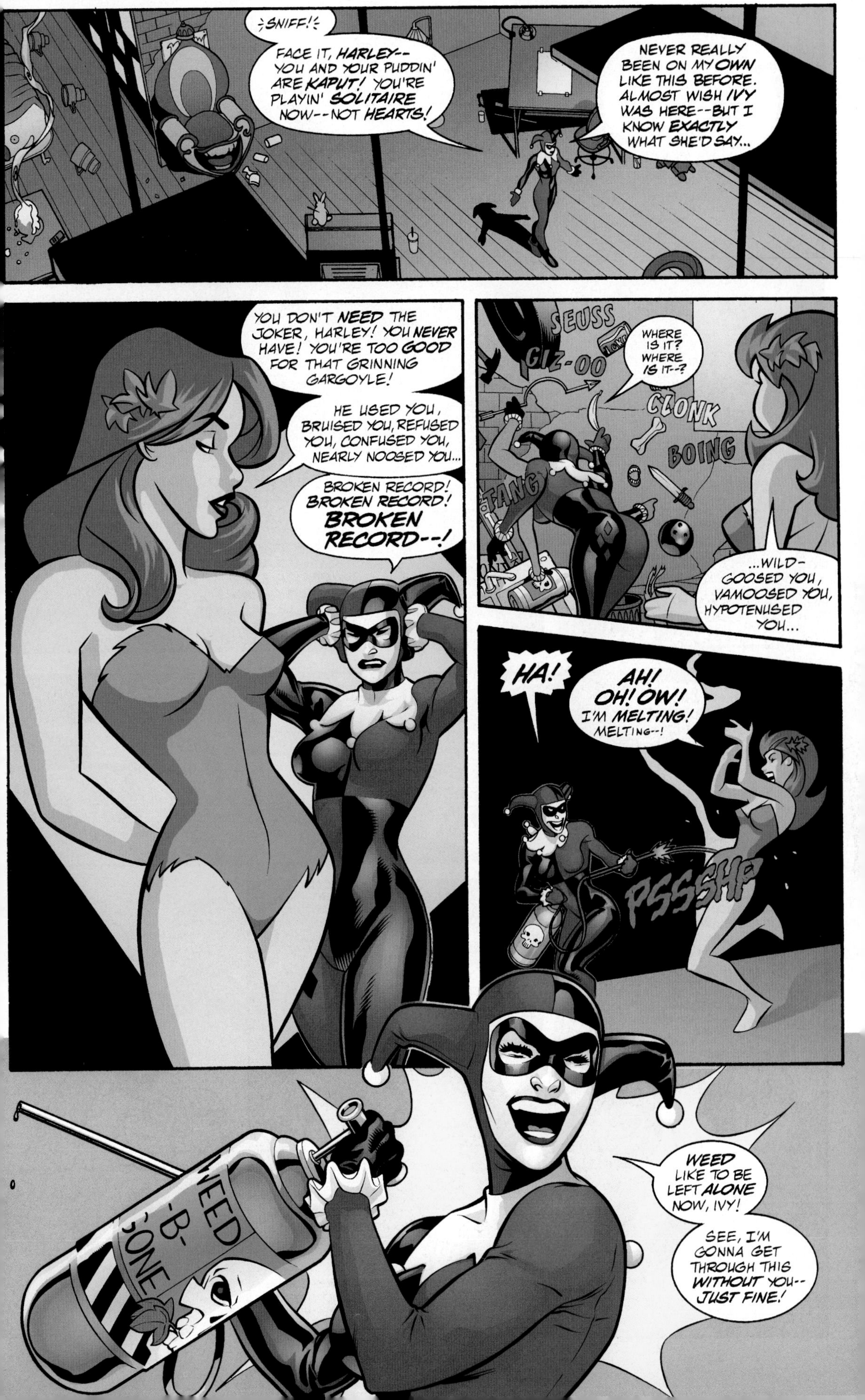

SNIFF!
FACE IT, HARLEY-- YOU AND YOUR PUDDIN' ARE KAPUT! YOU'RE PLAYIN' SOLITAIRE NOW--NOT HEARTS!
NEVER REALLY BEEN ON MY OWN LIKE THIS BEFORE. ALMOST WISH IVY WAS HERE--BUT I KNOW EXACTLY WHAT SHE'D SAY...
YOU DON'T NEED THE JOKER, HARLEY! YOU NEVER HAVE! YOU'RE TOO GOOD FOR THAT GRINNING GARGOYLE!
HE USED YOU, BRUISED YOU, REFUSED YOU, CONFUSED YOU, NEARLY NOOSED YOU...
BROKEN RECORD! BROKEN RECORD! BROKEN RECORD--!
SEUSS
GIZ-OO
WHERE IS IT? WHERE IS IT--?
CLONK
BOING
TANG
...WILD-GOOSED YOU, VAMOOSED YOU, HYPOTENUSED YOU...
HA!
AH! OH! OW! I'M MELTING! MELTING--!
PSSSHP
WEED-B-GONE
WEED LIKE TO BE LEFT ALONE NOW, IVY!
SEE, I'M GONNA GET THROUGH THIS WITHOUT YOU-- JUST FINE!

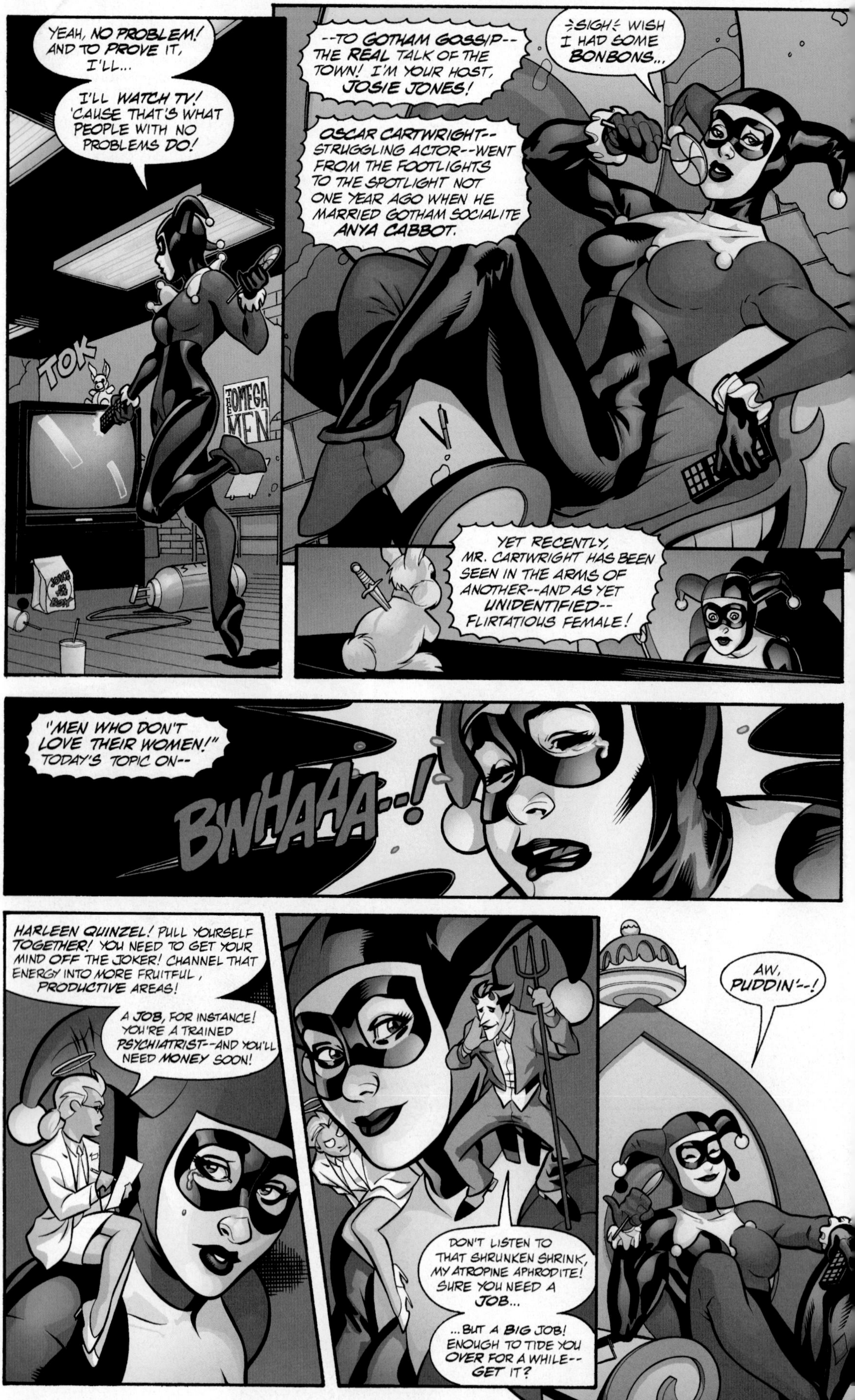
YEAH, NO PROBLEM! AND TO PROVE IT, I'LL...
I'LL WATCH TV! 'CAUSE THAT'S WHAT PEOPLE WITH NO PROBLEMS DO!
TOK
THE OMEGA MEN
--TO GOTHAM GOSSIP-- THE REAL TALK OF THE TOWN! I'M YOUR HOST, JOSIE JONES!
OSCAR CARTWRIGHT-- STRUGGLING ACTOR--WENT FROM THE FOOTLIGHTS TO THE SPOTLIGHT NOT ONE YEAR AGO WHEN HE MARRIED GOTHAM SOCIALITE ANYA CABBOT.
SIGH WISH I HAD SOME BONBONS...
YET RECENTLY, MR. CARTWRIGHT HAS BEEN SEEN IN THE ARMS OF ANOTHER--AND AS YET UNIDENTIFIED-- FLIRTATIOUS FEMALE!
"MEN WHO DON'T LOVE THEIR WOMEN!" TODAY'S TOPIC ON--
BWHAAA--!
HARLEEN QUINZEL! PULL YOURSELF TOGETHER! YOU NEED TO GET YOUR MIND OFF THE JOKER! CHANNEL THAT ENERGY INTO MORE FRUITFUL, PRODUCTIVE AREAS!
A JOB, FOR INSTANCE! YOU'RE A TRAINED PSYCHIATRIST--AND YOU'LL NEED MONEY SOON!
DON'T LISTEN TO THAT SHRUNKEN SHRINK, MY ATROPINE APHRODITE! SURE YOU NEED A JOB...
...BUT A BIG JOB! ENOUGH TO TIDE YOU OVER FOR A WHILE-- GET IT?
AW, PUDDIN'--!

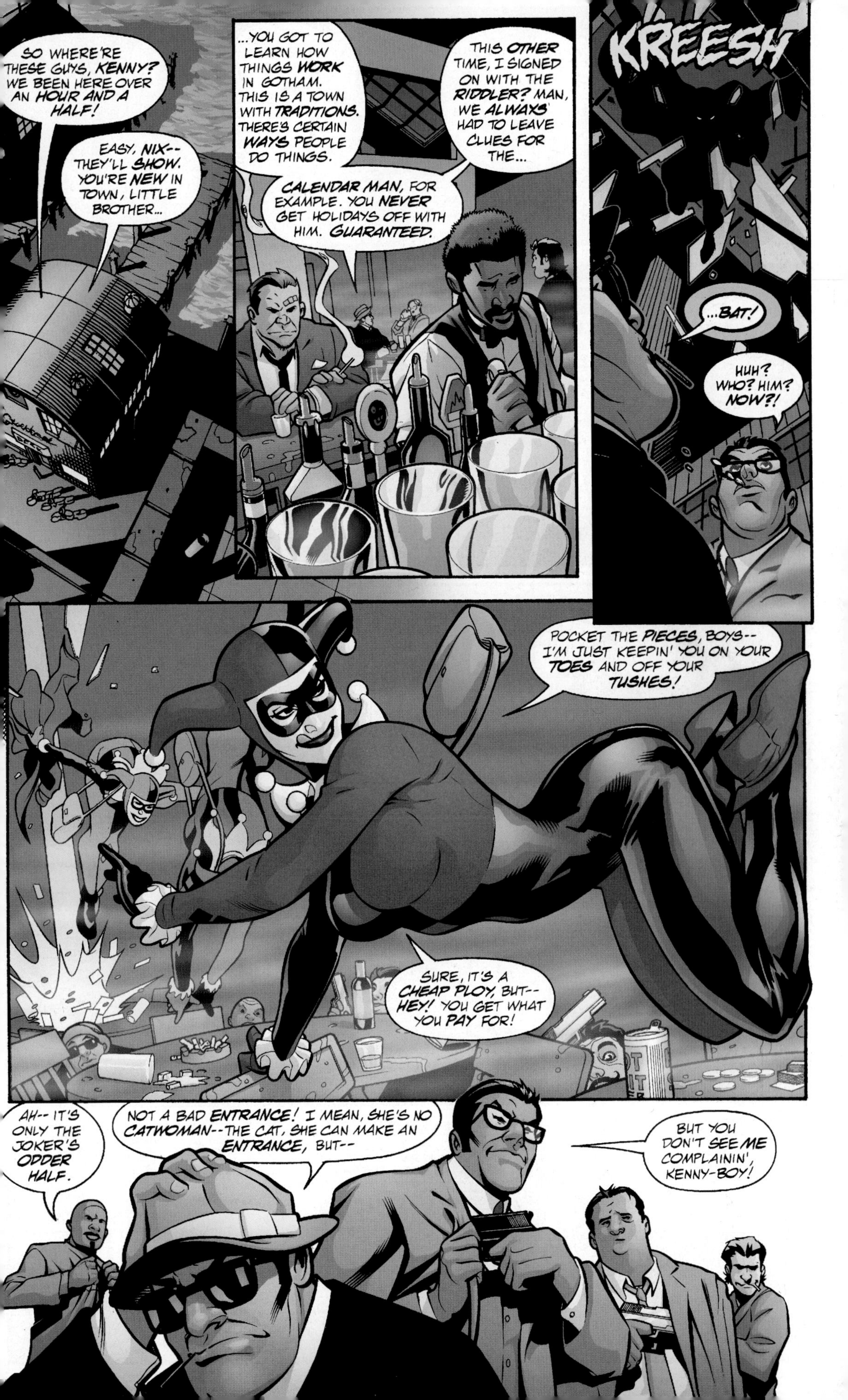
SO WHERE'RE THESE GUYS, KENNY? WE BEEN HERE OVER AN HOUR AND A HALF!
EASY, NIX-- THEY'LL SHOW. YOU'RE NEW IN TOWN, LITTLE BROTHER...
...YOU GOT TO LEARN HOW THINGS WORK IN GOTHAM. THIS IS A TOWN WITH TRADITIONS. THERE'S CERTAIN WAYS PEOPLE DO THINGS.
CALENDAR MAN, FOR EXAMPLE. YOU NEVER GET HOLIDAYS OFF WITH HIM. GUARANTEED.
THIS OTHER TIME, I SIGNED ON WITH THE RIDDLER? MAN, WE ALWAYS HAD TO LEAVE CLUES FOR THE...
KREESH
...BAT!
HUH? WHO? HIM? NOW?!
POCKET THE PIECES, BOYS-- I'M JUST KEEPIN' YOU ON YOUR TOES AND OFF YOUR TUSHES!
SURE, IT'S A CHEAP PLOY, BUT-- HEY! YOU GET WHAT YOU PAY FOR!
AH-- IT'S ONLY THE JOKER'S ODDER HALF.
NOT A BAD ENTRANCE! I MEAN, SHE'S NO CATWOMAN-- THE CAT, SHE CAN MAKE AN ENTRANCE, BUT--
BUT YOU DON'T SEE ME COMPLAININ', KENNY-BOY!

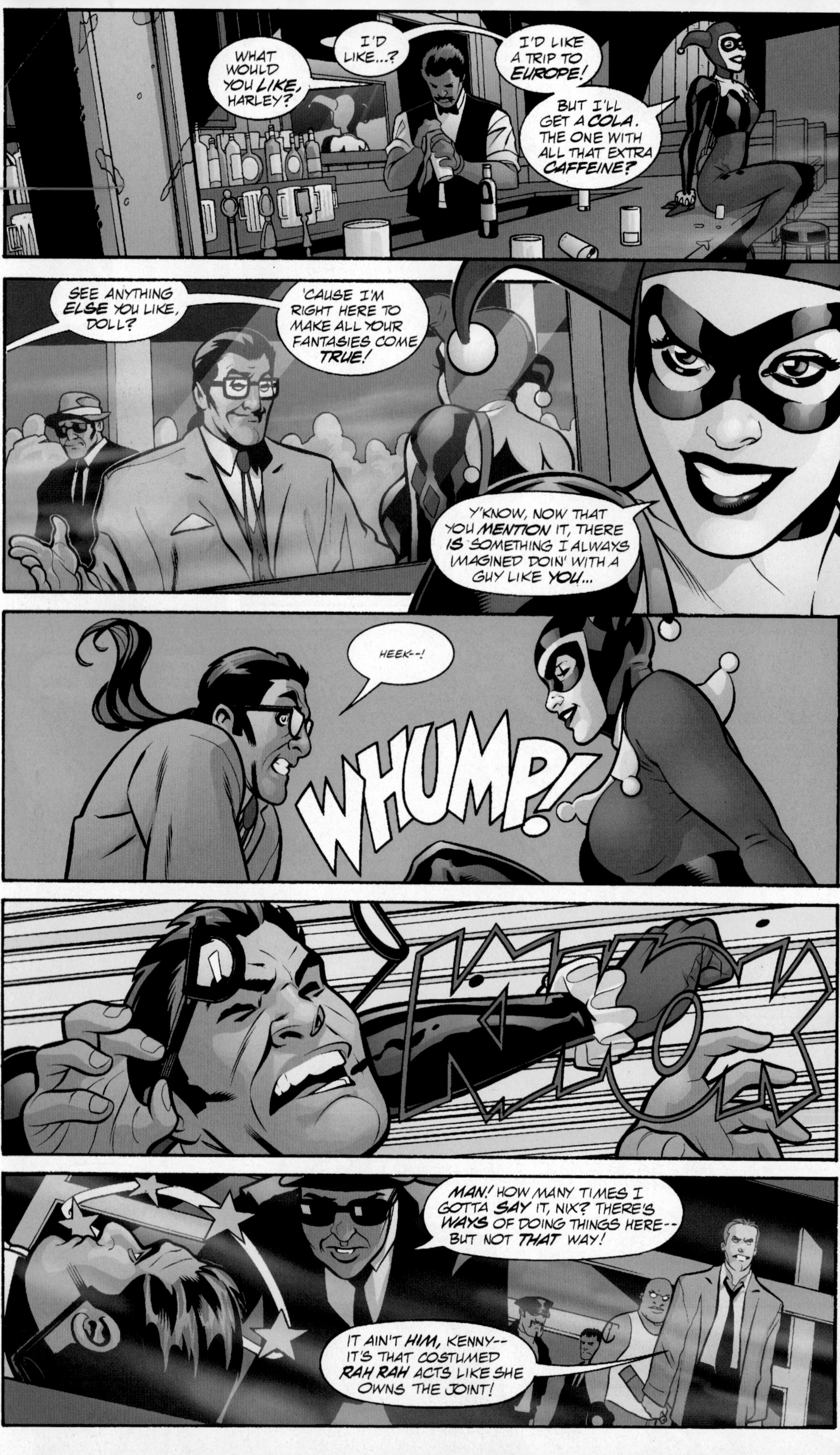
WHAT WOULD YOU LIKE, HARLEY?
I'D LIKE...?
I'D LIKE A TRIP TO EUROPE!
BUT I'LL GET A COLA. THE ONE WITH ALL THAT EXTRA CAFFEINE?
SEE ANYTHING ELSE YOU LIKE, DOLL?
'CAUSE I'M RIGHT HERE TO MAKE ALL YOUR FANTASIES COME TRUE!
Y'KNOW, NOW THAT YOU MENTION IT, THERE IS SOMETHING I ALWAYS IMAGINED DOIN' WITH A GUY LIKE YOU...
HEEK--!
WHUMP!
MAN! HOW MANY TIMES I GOTTA SAY IT, NIX? THERE'S WAYS OF DOING THINGS HERE-- BUT NOT THAT WAY!
IT AIN'T HIM, KENNY-- IT'S THAT COSTUMED RAH RAH ACTS LIKE SHE OWNS THE JOINT!

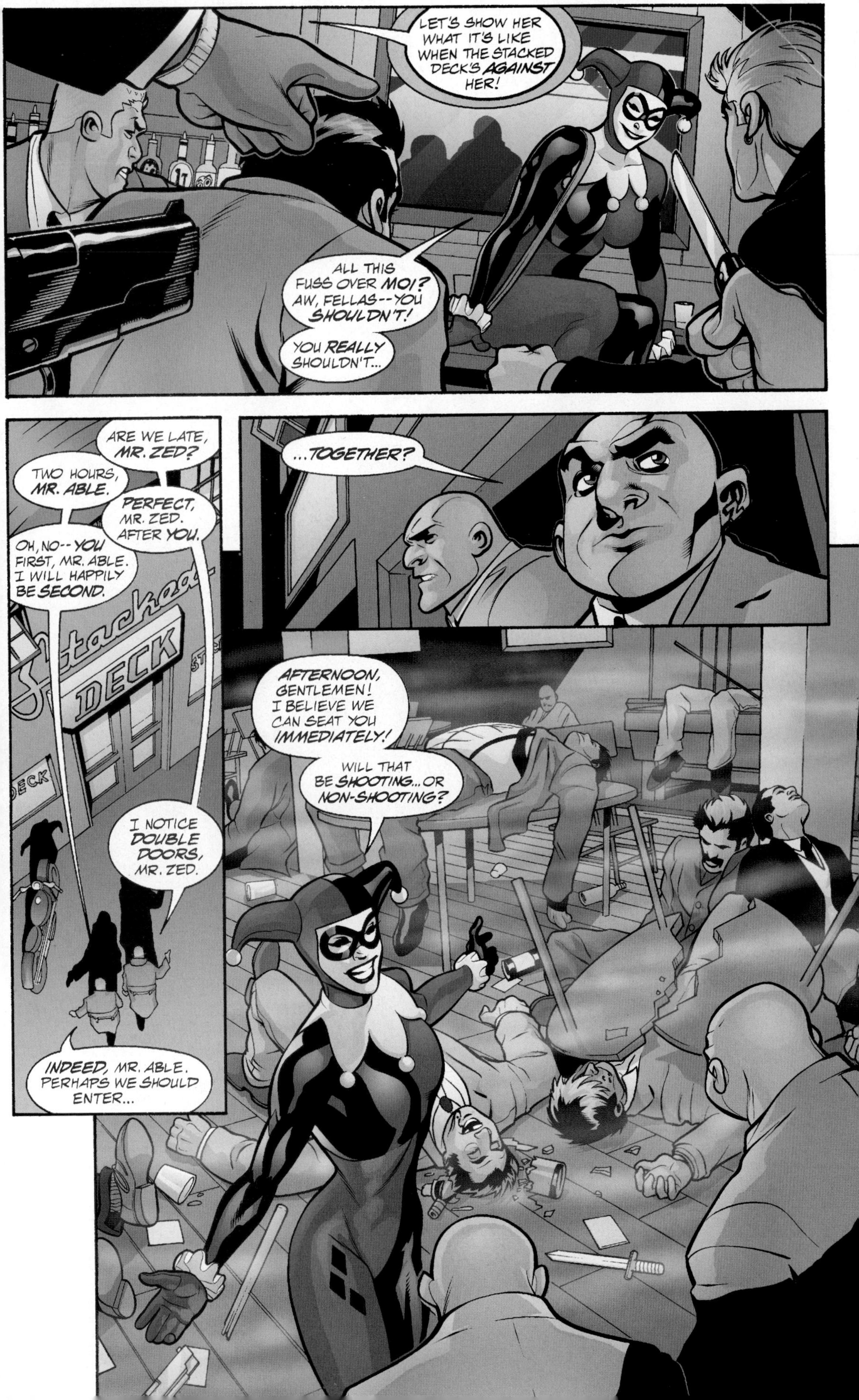
LET'S SHOW HER WHAT IT'S LIKE WHEN THE STACKED DECK'S AGAINST HER!
ALL THIS FUSS OVER MOI? AW, FELLAS--YOU SHOULDN'T!
YOU REALLY SHOULDN'T...
ARE WE LATE, MR. ZED?
TWO HOURS, MR. ABLE.
PERFECT, MR. ZED. AFTER YOU.
OH, NO--YOU FIRST, MR. ABLE. I WILL HAPPILY BE SECOND.
Stacked DECK
I NOTICE DOUBLE DOORS, MR. ZED.
INDEED, MR. ABLE. PERHAPS WE SHOULD ENTER...
...TOGETHER?
AFTERNOON, GENTLEMEN! I BELIEVE WE CAN SEAT YOU IMMEDIATELY!
WILL THAT BE SHOOTING...OR NON-SHOOTING?

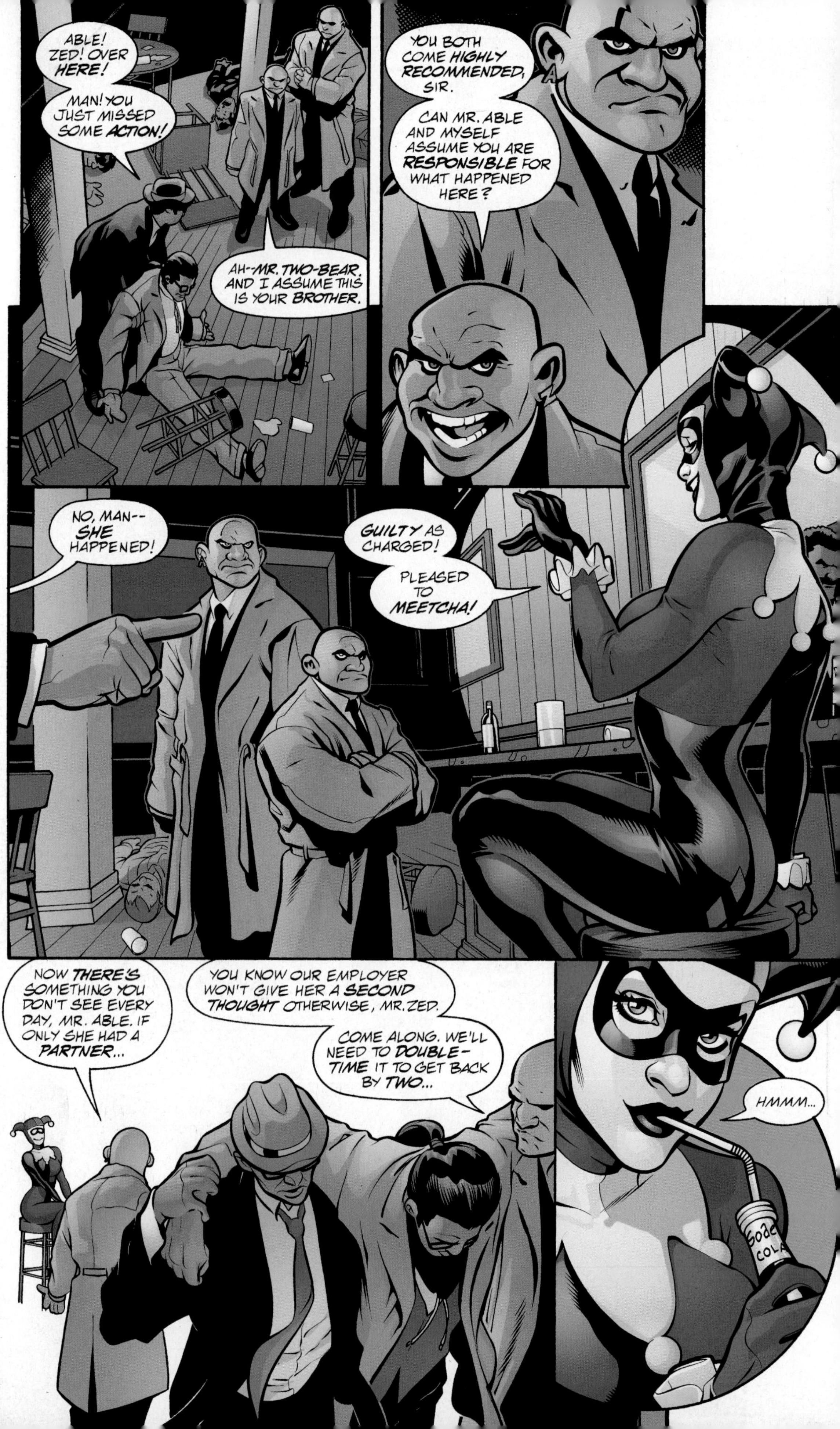
ABLE! ZED! OVER HERE!
MAN! YOU JUST MISSED SOME ACTION!
AH--MR. TWO-BEAR. AND I ASSUME THIS IS YOUR BROTHER.
YOU BOTH COME HIGHLY RECOMMENDED, SIR.
CAN MR. ABLE AND MYSELF ASSUME YOU ARE RESPONSIBLE FOR WHAT HAPPENED HERE?
NO, MAN-- SHE HAPPENED!
GUILTY AS CHARGED!
PLEASED TO MEETCHA!
NOW THERE'S SOMETHING YOU DON'T SEE EVERY DAY, MR. ABLE. IF ONLY SHE HAD A PARTNER...
YOU KNOW OUR EMPLOYER WON'T GIVE HER A SECOND THOUGHT OTHERWISE, MR. ZED.
COME ALONG. WE'LL NEED TO DOUBLE-TIME IT TO GET BACK BY TWO...
HMMM...
SODA COLA

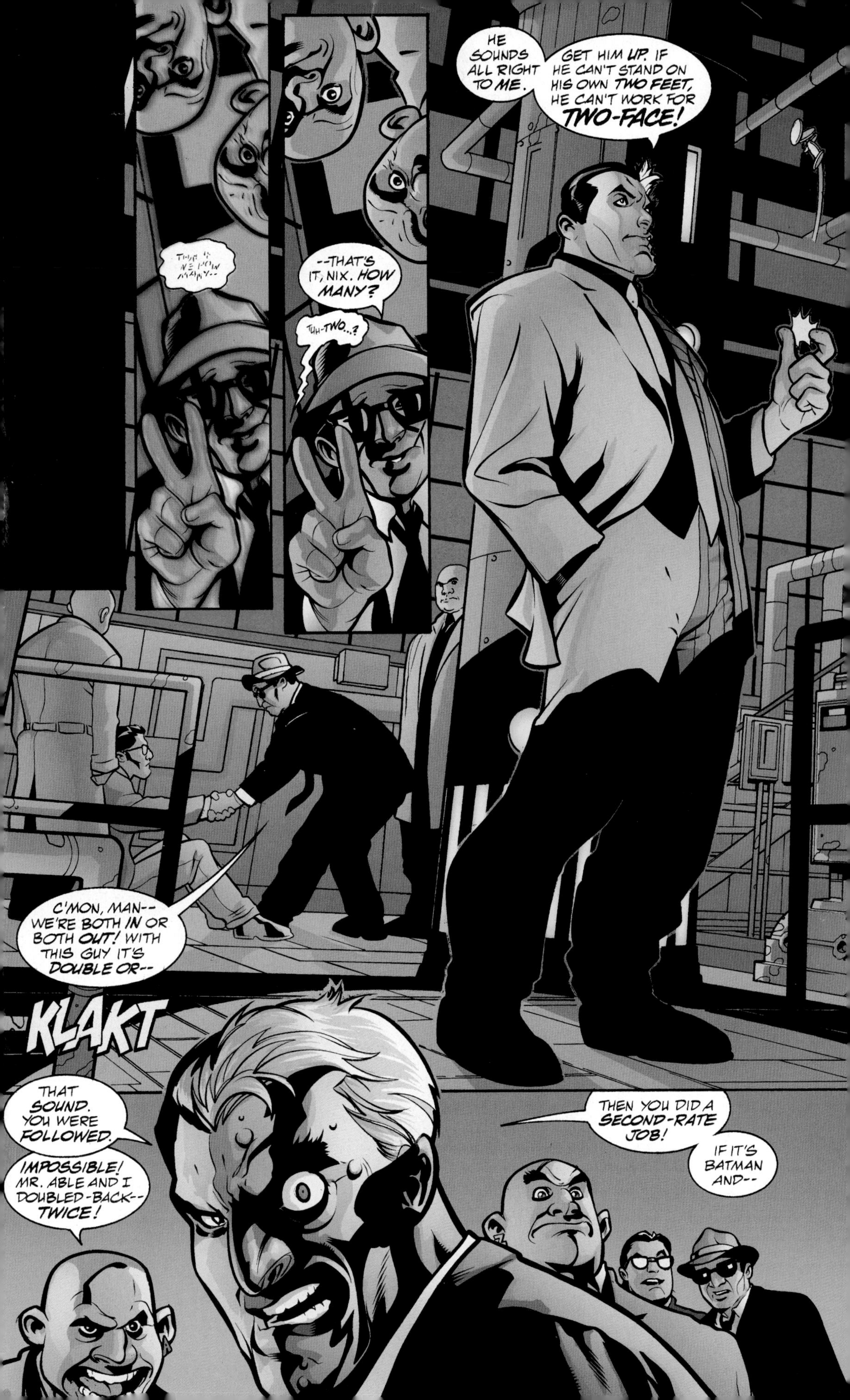
--THAT'S IT, NIX. HOW MANY?
TUH-TWO...?
HE SOUNDS ALL RIGHT TO ME.
GET HIM UP. IF HE CAN'T STAND ON HIS OWN TWO FEET, HE CAN'T WORK FOR TWO-FACE!
C'MON, MAN-- WE'RE BOTH IN OR BOTH OUT! WITH THIS GUY IT'S DOUBLE OR--
KLAKT
THAT SOUND. YOU WERE FOLLOWED.
IMPOSSIBLE! MR. ABLE AND I DOUBLED-BACK-- TWICE!
THEN YOU DID A SECOND-RATE JOB!
IF IT'S BATMAN AND--

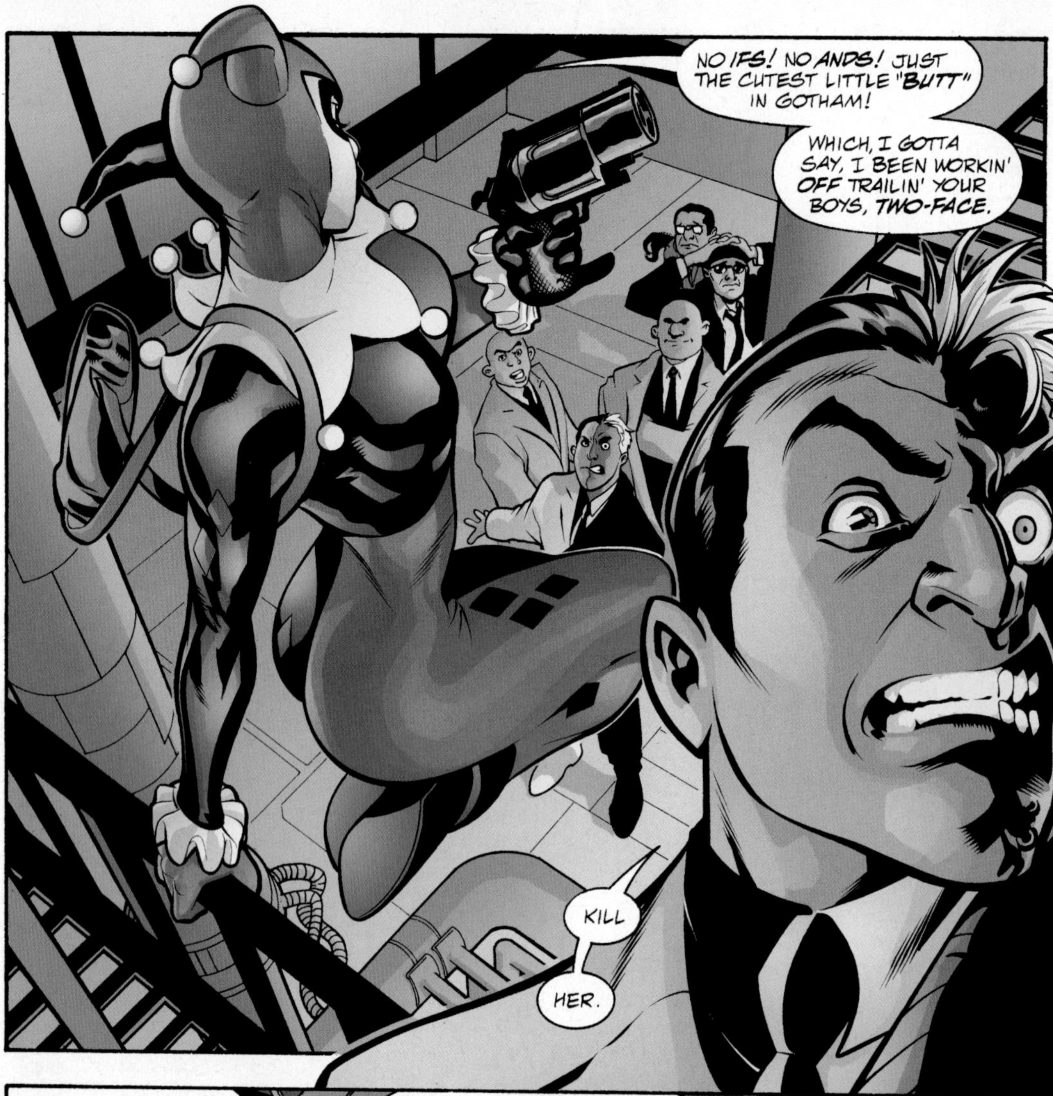
NO IFS! NO ANDS! JUST THE CUTEST LITTLE "BUTT" IN GOTHAM!
WHICH, I GOTTA SAY, I BEEN WORKIN' OFF TRAILIN' YOUR BOYS, TWO-FACE.
KILL
HER.

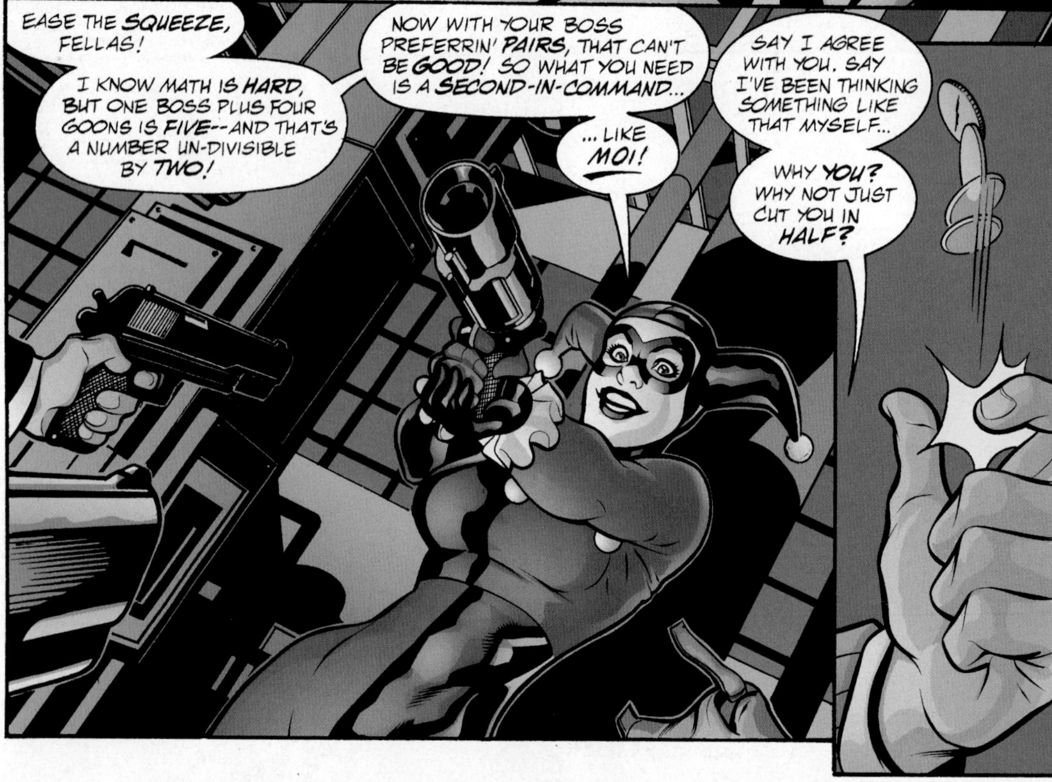
EASE THE SQUEEZE, FELLAS!
I KNOW MATH IS HARD, BUT ONE BOSS PLUS FOUR GOONS IS FIVE--AND THAT'S A NUMBER UN-DIVISIBLE BY TWO!
NOW WITH YOUR BOSS PREFERRIN' PAIRS, THAT CAN'T BE GOOD! SO WHAT YOU NEED IS A SECOND-IN-COMMAND...
...LIKE MOI!
SAY I AGREE WITH YOU. SAY I'VE BEEN THINKING SOMETHING LIKE THAT MYSELF...
WHY YOU? WHY NOT JUST CUT YOU IN HALF?

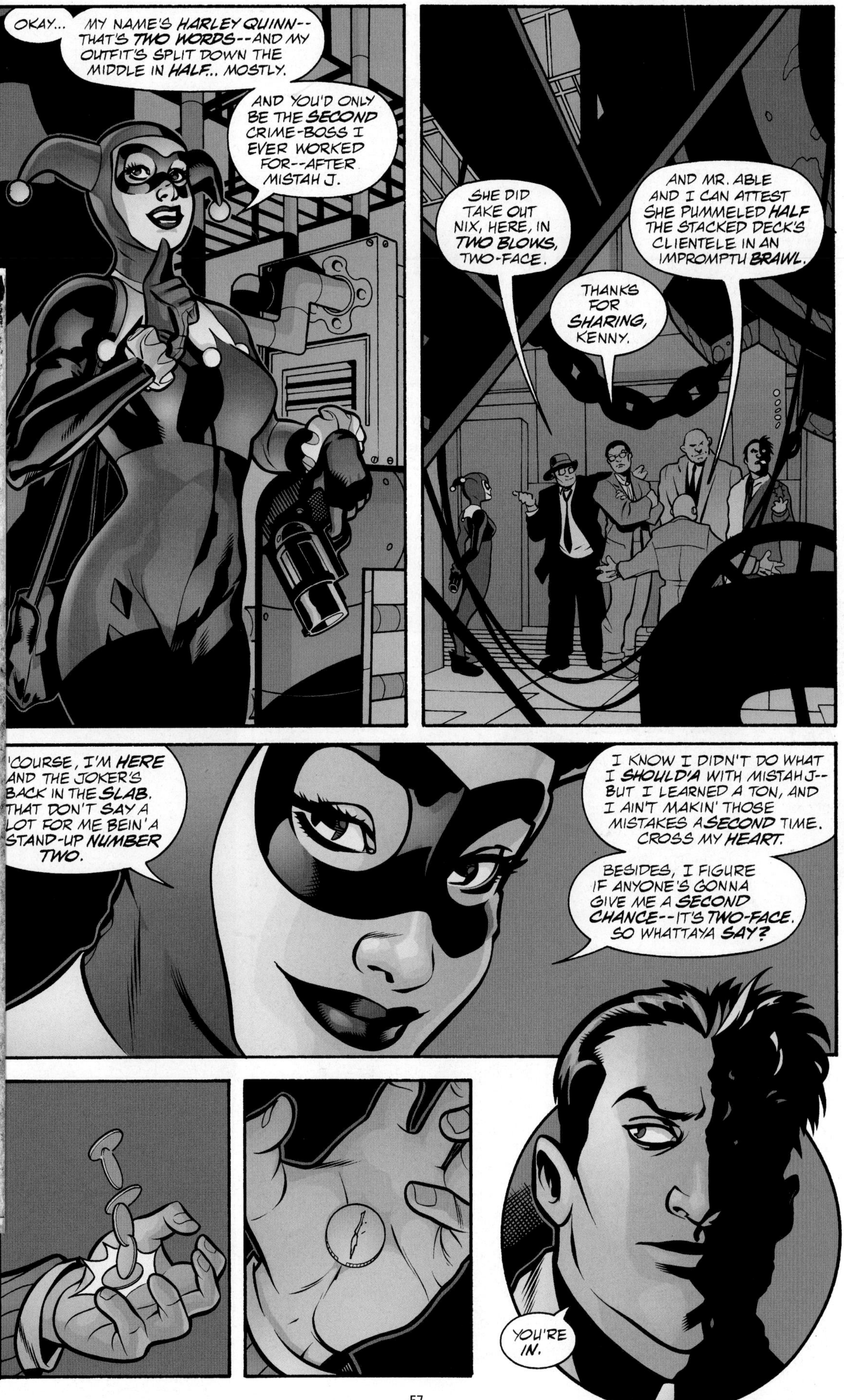

OKAY...
MY NAME'S HARLEY QUINN--THAT'S TWO WORDS--AND MY OUTFIT'S SPLIT DOWN THE MIDDLE IN HALF... MOSTLY.
AND YOU'D ONLY BE THE SECOND CRIME-BOSS I EVER WORKED FOR--AFTER MISTAH J.
SHE DID TAKE OUT NIX, HERE, IN TWO BLOWS, TWO-FACE.
AND MR. ABLE AND I CAN ATTEST SHE PUMMELED HALF THE STACKED DECK'S CLIENTELE IN AN IMPROMPTU BRAWL.
THANKS FOR SHARING, KENNY.
'COURSE, I'M HERE AND THE JOKER'S BACK IN THE SLAB. THAT DON'T SAY A LOT FOR ME BEIN' A STAND-UP NUMBER TWO.
I KNOW I DIDN'T DO WHAT I SHOULD'A WITH MISTAH J--BUT I LEARNED A TON, AND I AIN'T MAKIN' THOSE MISTAKES A SECOND TIME. CROSS MY HEART.
BESIDES, I FIGURE IF ANYONE'S GONNA GIVE ME A SECOND CHANCE--IT'S TWO-FACE. SO WHATTAYA SAY?
YOU'RE IN.

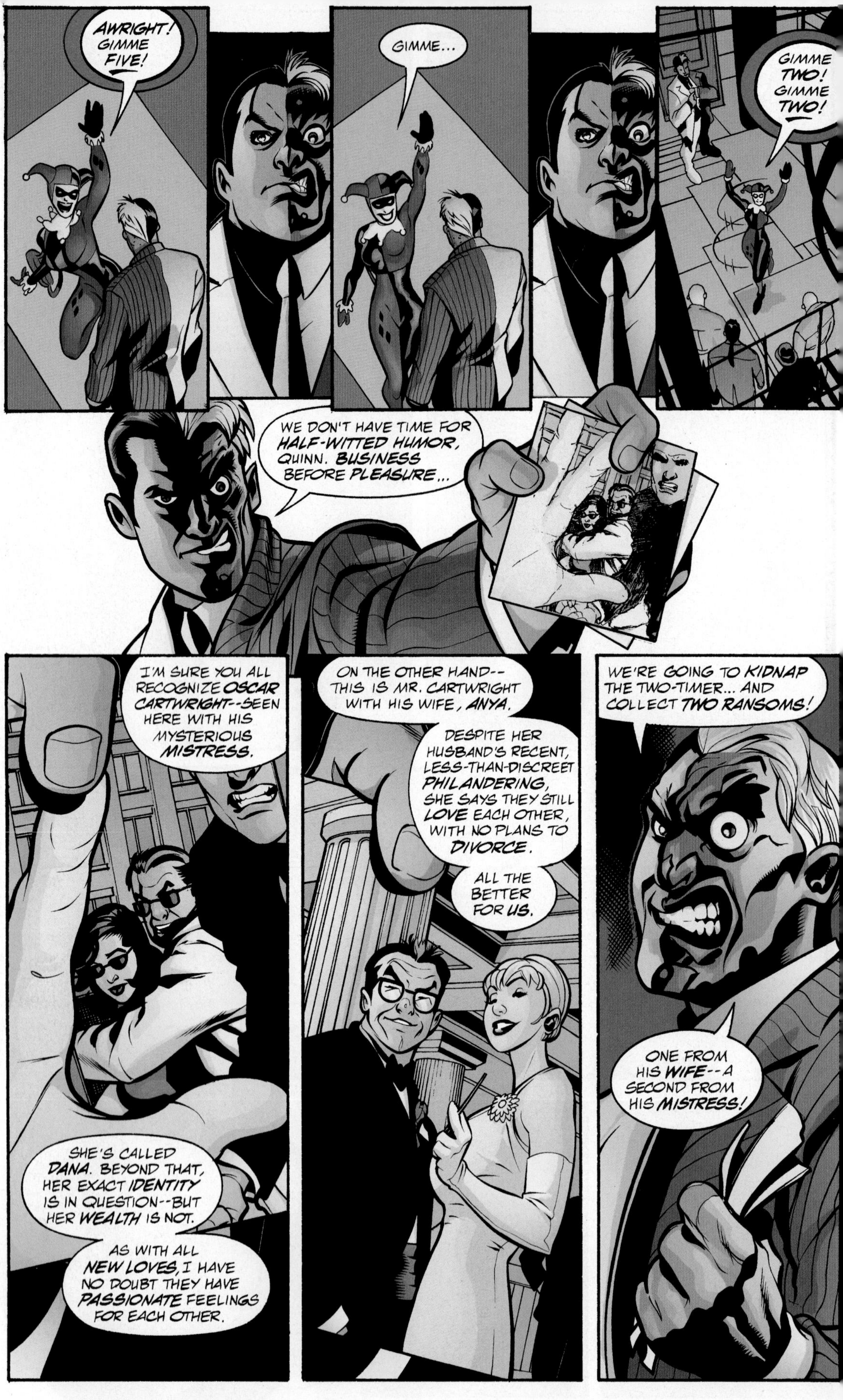
AWRIGHT! GIMME FIVE!
GIMME...
GIMME TWO! GIMME TWO!
WE DON'T HAVE TIME FOR HALF-WITTED HUMOR, QUINN. BUSINESS BEFORE PLEASURE...
I'M SURE YOU ALL RECOGNIZE OSCAR CARTWRIGHT--SEEN HERE WITH HIS MYSTERIOUS MISTRESS.
SHE'S CALLED DANA. BEYOND THAT, HER EXACT IDENTITY IS IN QUESTION--BUT HER WEALTH IS NOT.
AS WITH ALL NEW LOVES, I HAVE NO DOUBT THEY HAVE PASSIONATE FEELINGS FOR EACH OTHER.
ON THE OTHER HAND-- THIS IS MR. CARTWRIGHT WITH HIS WIFE, ANYA.
DESPITE HER HUSBAND'S RECENT, LESS-THAN-DISCREET PHILANDERING, SHE SAYS THEY STILL LOVE EACH OTHER, WITH NO PLANS TO DIVORCE.
ALL THE BETTER FOR US.
WE'RE GOING TO KIDNAP THE TWO-TIMER... AND COLLECT TWO RANSOMS!
ONE FROM HIS WIFE--A SECOND FROM HIS MISTRESS!

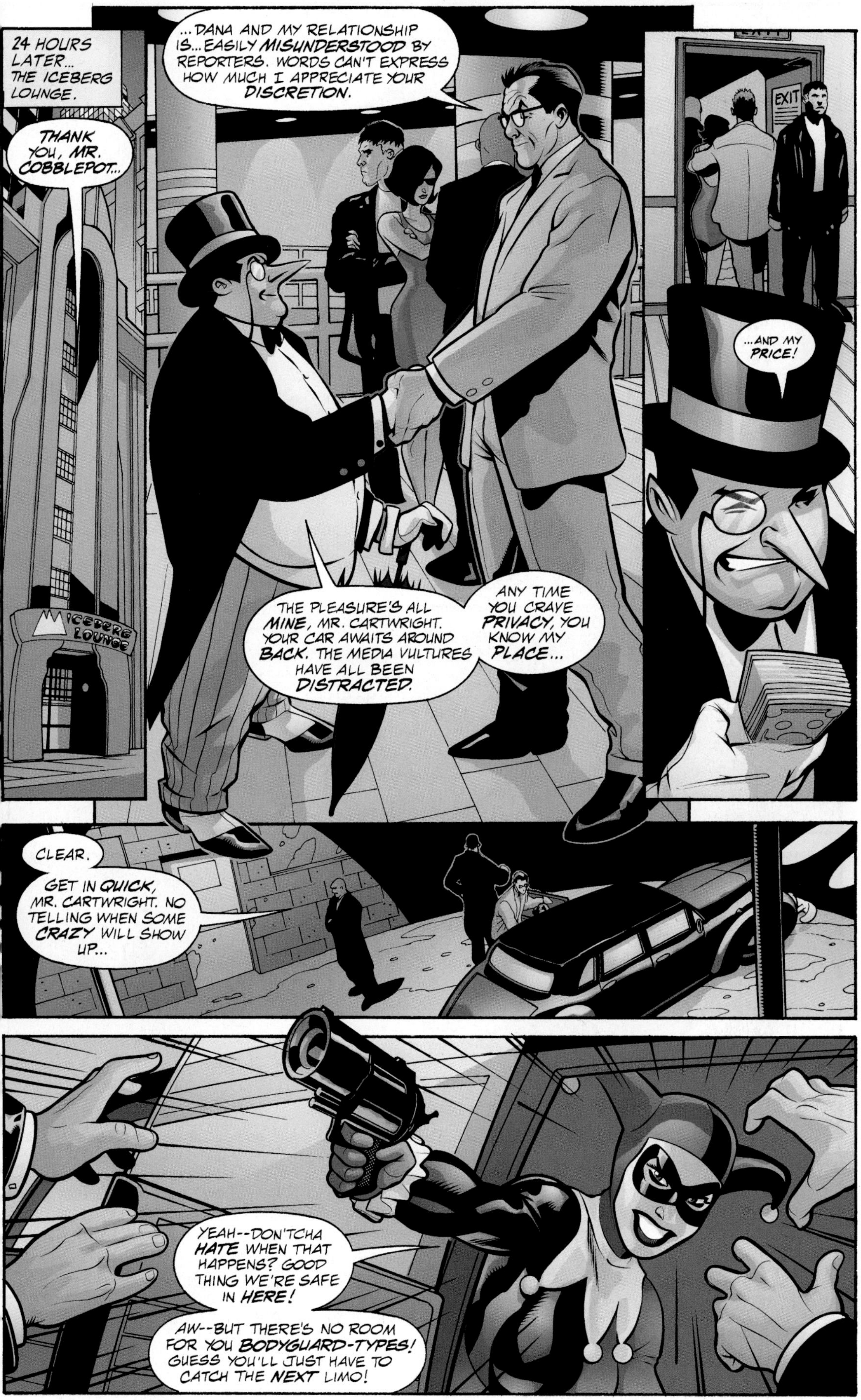
24 HOURS LATER... THE ICEBERG LOUNGE.
THANK YOU, MR. COBBLEPOT...
...DANA AND MY RELATIONSHIP IS...EASILY MISUNDERSTOOD BY REPORTERS. WORDS CAN'T EXPRESS HOW MUCH I APPRECIATE YOUR DISCRETION.
ICEBERG LOUNGE
THE PLEASURE'S ALL MINE, MR. CARTWRIGHT. YOUR CAR AWAITS AROUND BACK. THE MEDIA VULTURES HAVE ALL BEEN DISTRACTED.
ANY TIME YOU CRAVE PRIVACY, YOU KNOW MY PLACE...
EXIT
...AND MY PRICE!
CLEAR.
GET IN QUICK, MR. CARTWRIGHT. NO TELLING WHEN SOME CRAZY WILL SHOW UP...
YEAH--DON'TCHA HATE WHEN THAT HAPPENS? GOOD THING WE'RE SAFE IN HERE!
AW--BUT THERE'S NO ROOM FOR YOU BODYGUARD-TYPES! GUESS YOU'LL JUST HAVE TO CATCH THE NEXT LIMO!

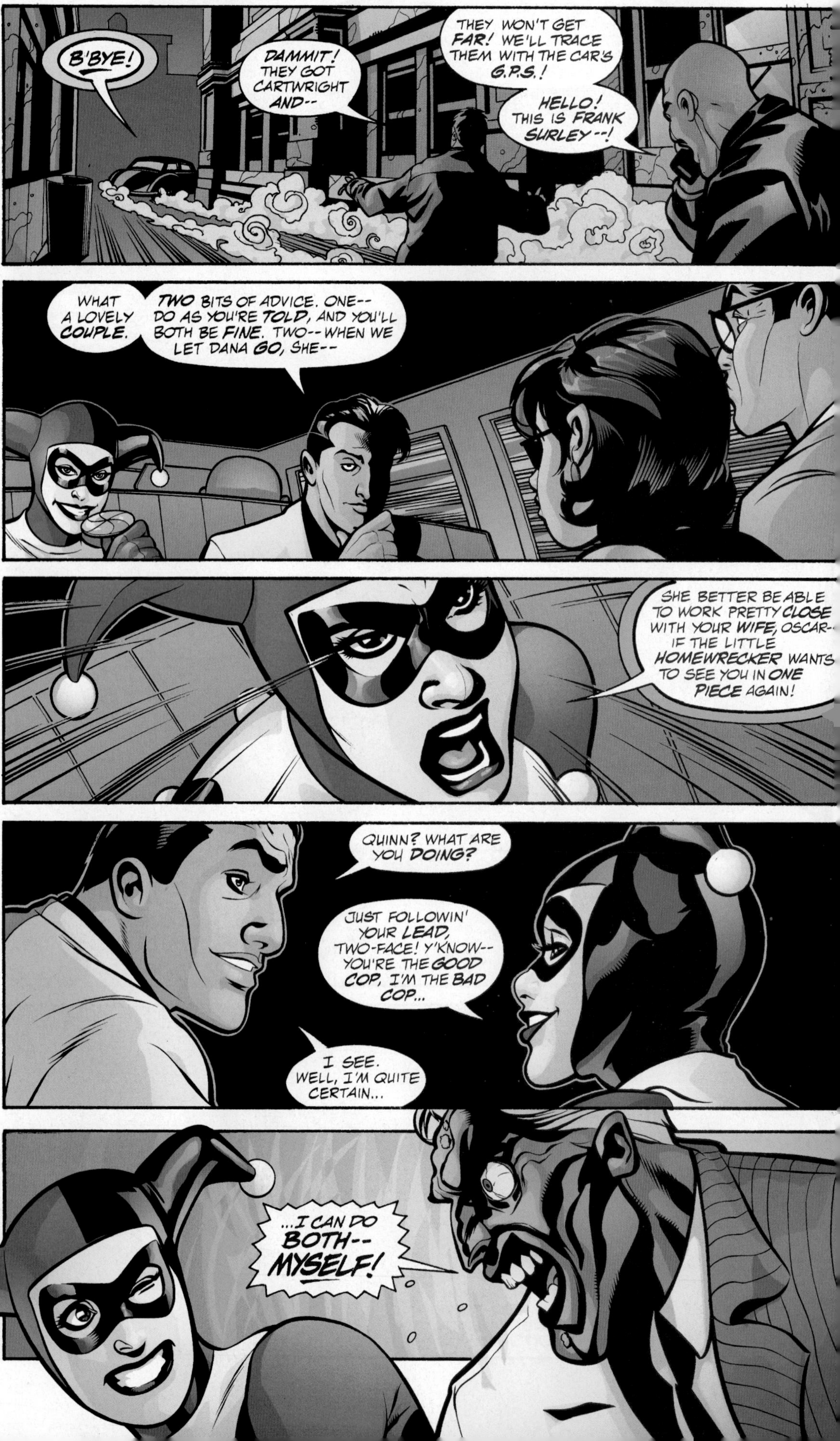
B'BYE!
DAMMIT! THEY GOT CARTWRIGHT AND--
THEY WON'T GET FAR! WE'LL TRACE THEM WITH THE CAR'S G.P.S.!
HELLO! THIS IS FRANK SURLEY--!
WHAT A LOVELY COUPLE.
TWO BITS OF ADVICE. ONE-- DO AS YOU'RE TOLD, AND YOU'LL BOTH BE FINE. TWO--WHEN WE LET DANA GO, SHE--
SHE BETTER BE ABLE TO WORK PRETTY CLOSE WITH YOUR WIFE, OSCAR-- IF THE LITTLE HOMEWRECKER WANTS TO SEE YOU IN ONE PIECE AGAIN!
QUINN? WHAT ARE YOU DOING?
JUST FOLLOWIN' YOUR LEAD, TWO-FACE! Y'KNOW-- YOU'RE THE GOOD COP, I'M THE BAD COP...
I SEE. WELL, I'M QUITE CERTAIN...
...I CAN DO BOTH-- MYSELF!

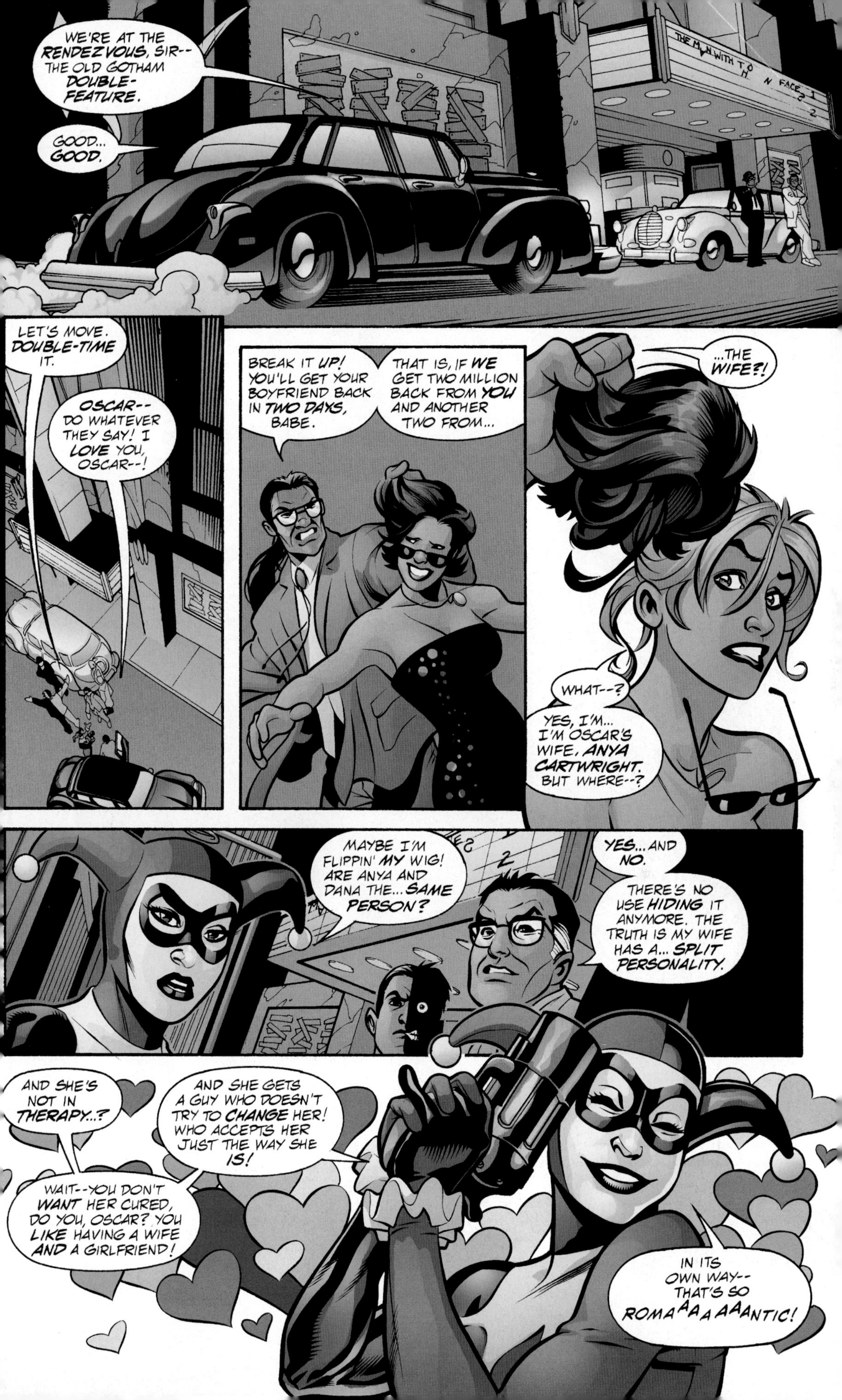

WE'RE AT THE RENDEZVOUS, SIR-- THE OLD GOTHAM DOUBLE-FEATURE.
GOOD... GOOD.
LET'S MOVE. DOUBLE-TIME IT.
OSCAR-- DO WHATEVER THEY SAY! I LOVE YOU, OSCAR--!
BREAK IT UP! YOU'LL GET YOUR BOYFRIEND BACK IN TWO DAYS, BABE.
THAT IS, IF WE GET TWO MILLION BACK FROM YOU AND ANOTHER TWO FROM...
...THE WIFE?!
WHAT--?
YES, I'M... I'M OSCAR'S WIFE, ANYA CARTWRIGHT. BUT WHERE--?
MAYBE I'M FLIPPIN' MY WIG! ARE ANYA AND DANA THE... SAME PERSON?
YES... AND NO.
THERE'S NO USE HIDING IT ANYMORE. THE TRUTH IS MY WIFE HAS A... SPLIT PERSONALITY.
AND SHE'S NOT IN THERAPY...?
AND SHE GETS A GUY WHO DOESN'T TRY TO CHANGE HER! WHO ACCEPTS HER JUST THE WAY SHE IS!
WAIT--YOU DON'T WANT HER CURED, DO YOU, OSCAR? YOU LIKE HAVING A WIFE AND A GIRLFRIEND!
IN ITS OWN WAY-- THAT'S SO ROMAAAAAAANTIC!

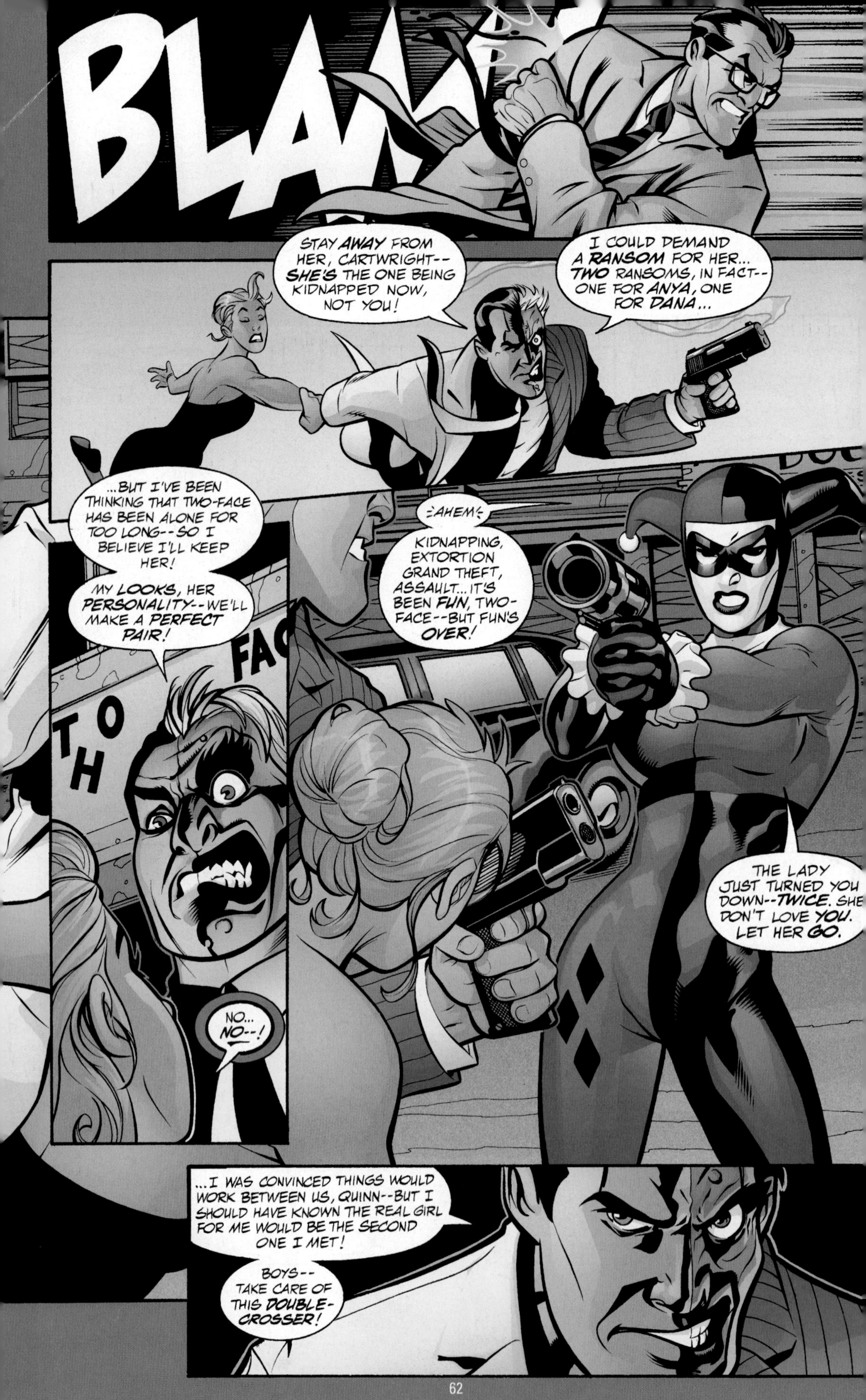
BLAM
STAY AWAY FROM HER, CARTWRIGHT-- SHE'S THE ONE BEING KIDNAPPED NOW, NOT YOU!
I COULD DEMAND A RANSOM FOR HER... TWO RANSOMS, IN FACT-- ONE FOR ANYA, ONE FOR DANA...
...BUT I'VE BEEN THINKING THAT TWO-FACE HAS BEEN ALONE FOR TOO LONG--SO I BELIEVE I'LL KEEP HER!
MY LOOKS, HER PERSONALITY--WE'LL MAKE A PERFECT PAIR!
AHEM
KIDNAPPING, EXTORTION GRAND THEFT, ASSAULT... IT'S BEEN FUN, TWO-FACE--BUT FUN'S OVER!
THE LADY JUST TURNED YOU DOWN--TWICE. SHE DON'T LOVE YOU. LET HER GO.
NO... NO--!
...I WAS CONVINCED THINGS WOULD WORK BETWEEN US, QUINN--BUT I SHOULD HAVE KNOWN THE REAL GIRL FOR ME WOULD BE THE SECOND ONE I MET!
BOYS-- TAKE CARE OF THIS DOUBLE-CROSSER!

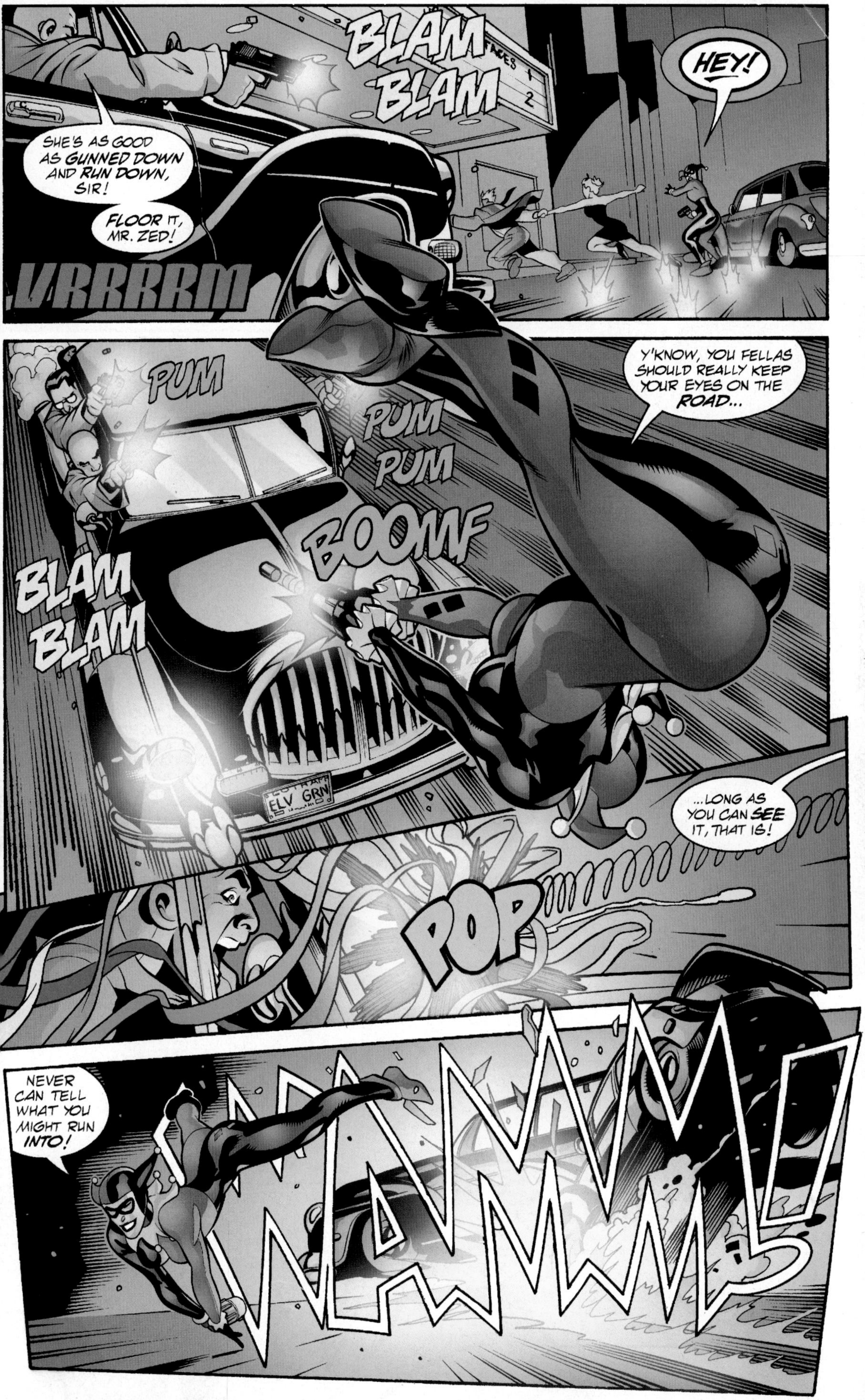
BLAM
BLAM
HEY!
SHE'S AS GOOD AS GUNNED DOWN AND RUN DOWN, SIR!
FLOOR IT, MR. ZED!
VRRRRM
PUM
PUM PUM
Y'KNOW, YOU FELLAS SHOULD REALLY KEEP YOUR EYES ON THE ROAD...
BOOMF
BLAM BLAM
GOTHAM ELV GRN
...LONG AS YOU CAN SEE IT, THAT IS!
POP
NEVER CAN TELL WHAT YOU MIGHT RUN INTO!

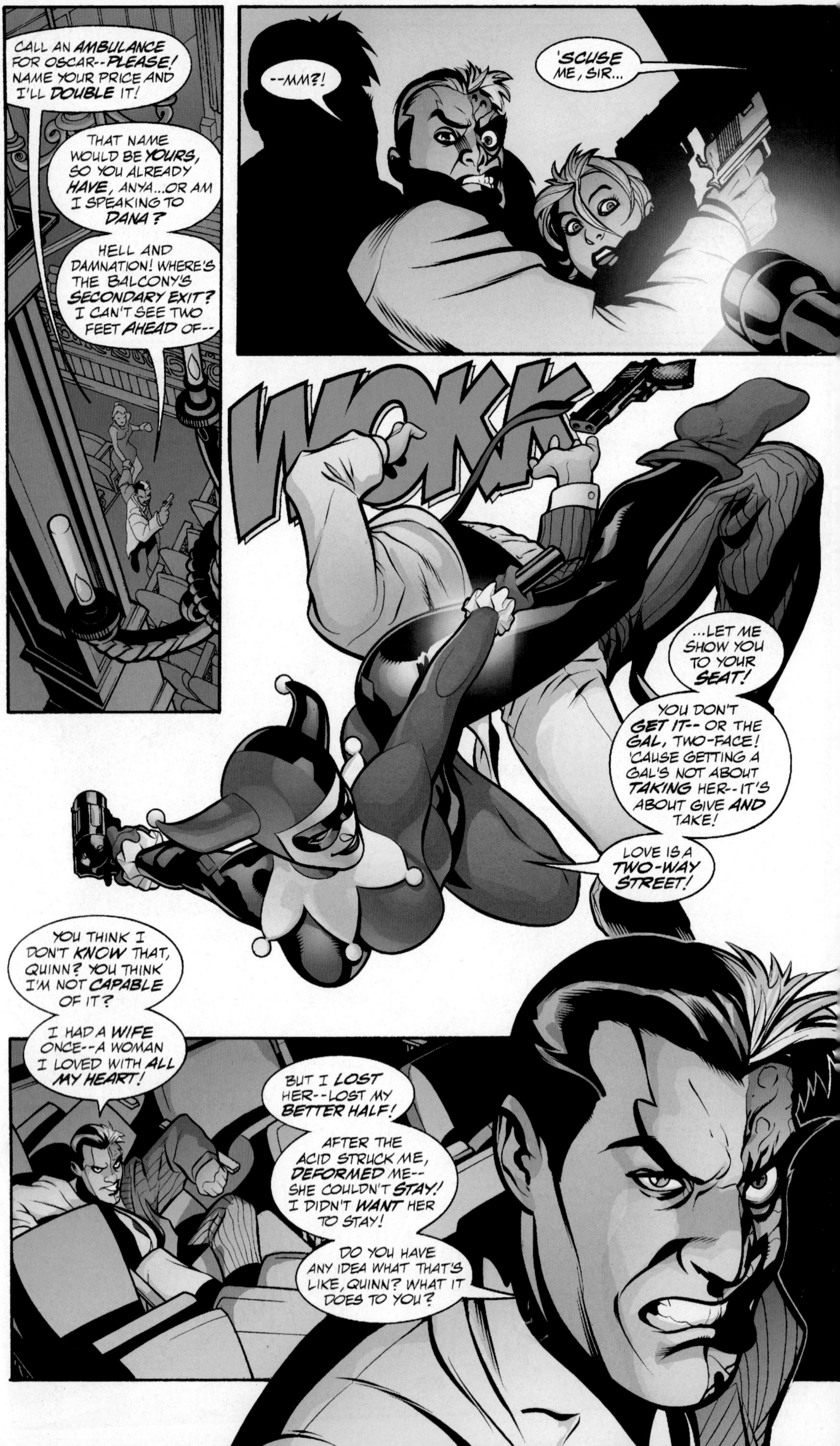
CALL AN AMBULANCE FOR OSCAR--PLEASE! NAME YOUR PRICE AND I'LL DOUBLE IT!
THAT NAME WOULD BE YOURS, SO YOU ALREADY HAVE, ANYA...OR AM I SPEAKING TO DANA?
HELL AND DAMNATION! WHERE'S THE BALCONY'S SECONDARY EXIT? I CAN'T SEE TWO FEET AHEAD OF--
--MM?!
'SCUSE ME, SIR...
WOKK
...LET ME SHOW YOU TO YOUR SEAT!
YOU DON'T GET IT-- OR THE GAL, TWO-FACE! 'CAUSE GETTING A GAL'S NOT ABOUT TAKING HER--IT'S ABOUT GIVE AND TAKE!
LOVE IS A TWO-WAY STREET!
YOU THINK I DON'T KNOW THAT, QUINN? YOU THINK I'M NOT CAPABLE OF IT?
I HAD A WIFE ONCE--A WOMAN I LOVED WITH ALL MY HEART!
BUT I LOST HER--LOST MY BETTER HALF!
AFTER THE ACID STRUCK ME, DEFORMED ME-- SHE COULDN'T STAY! I DIDN'T WANT HER TO STAY!
DO YOU HAVE ANY IDEA WHAT THAT'S LIKE, QUINN? WHAT IT DOES TO YOU?

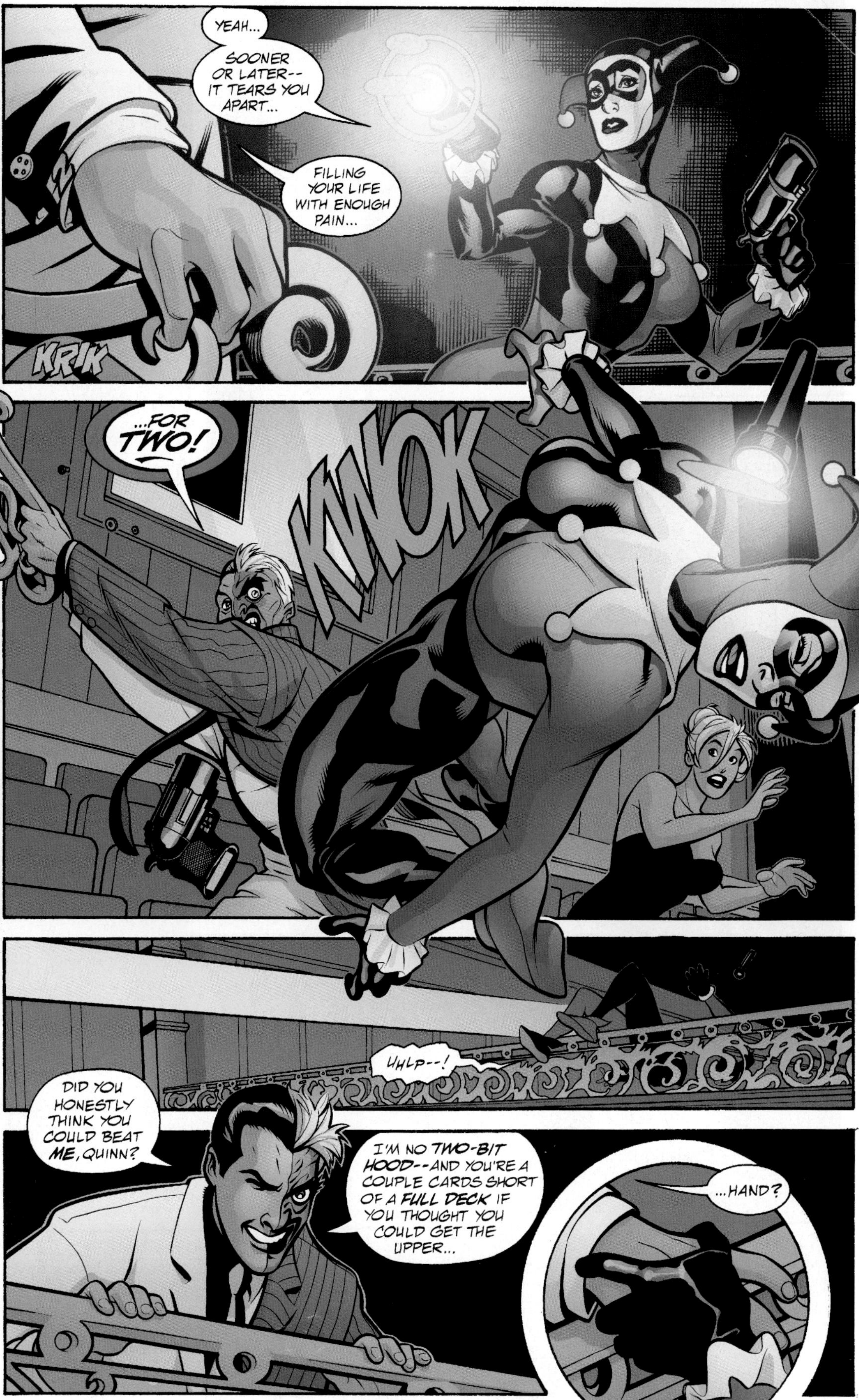
YEAH...
SOONER OR LATER-- IT TEARS YOU APART...
FILLING YOUR LIFE WITH ENOUGH PAIN...
KRIK
...FOR TWO!
KWOK
UHLP--!
!
DID YOU HONESTLY THINK YOU COULD BEAT ME, QUINN?
I'M NO TWO-BIT HOOD--AND YOU'RE A COUPLE CARDS SHORT OF A FULL DECK IF YOU THOUGHT YOU COULD GET THE UPPER...
...HAND?

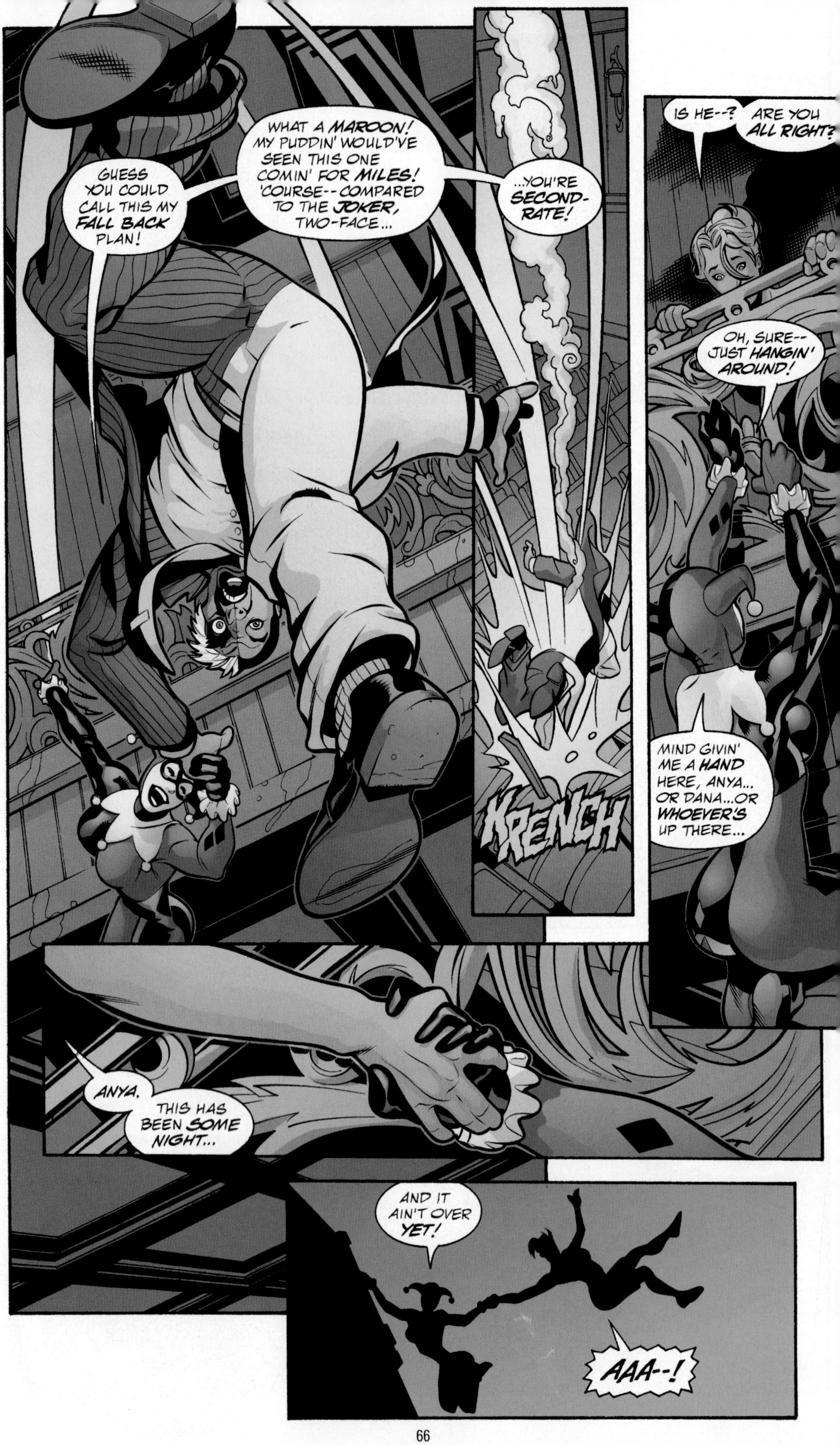

GUESS YOU COULD CALL THIS MY FALL BACK PLAN!
WHAT A MAROON! MY PUDDIN' WOULD'VE SEEN THIS ONE COMIN' FOR MILES! 'COURSE-- COMPARED TO THE JOKER, TWO-FACE...
...YOU'RE SECOND-RATE!
KRENCH
IS HE--?
ARE YOU ALL RIGHT?
OH, SURE-- JUST HANGIN' AROUND!
MIND GIVIN' ME A HAND HERE, ANYA... OR DANA...OR WHOEVER'S UP THERE...
ANYA.
THIS HAS BEEN SOME NIGHT...
AND IT AIN'T OVER YET!
AAA--!

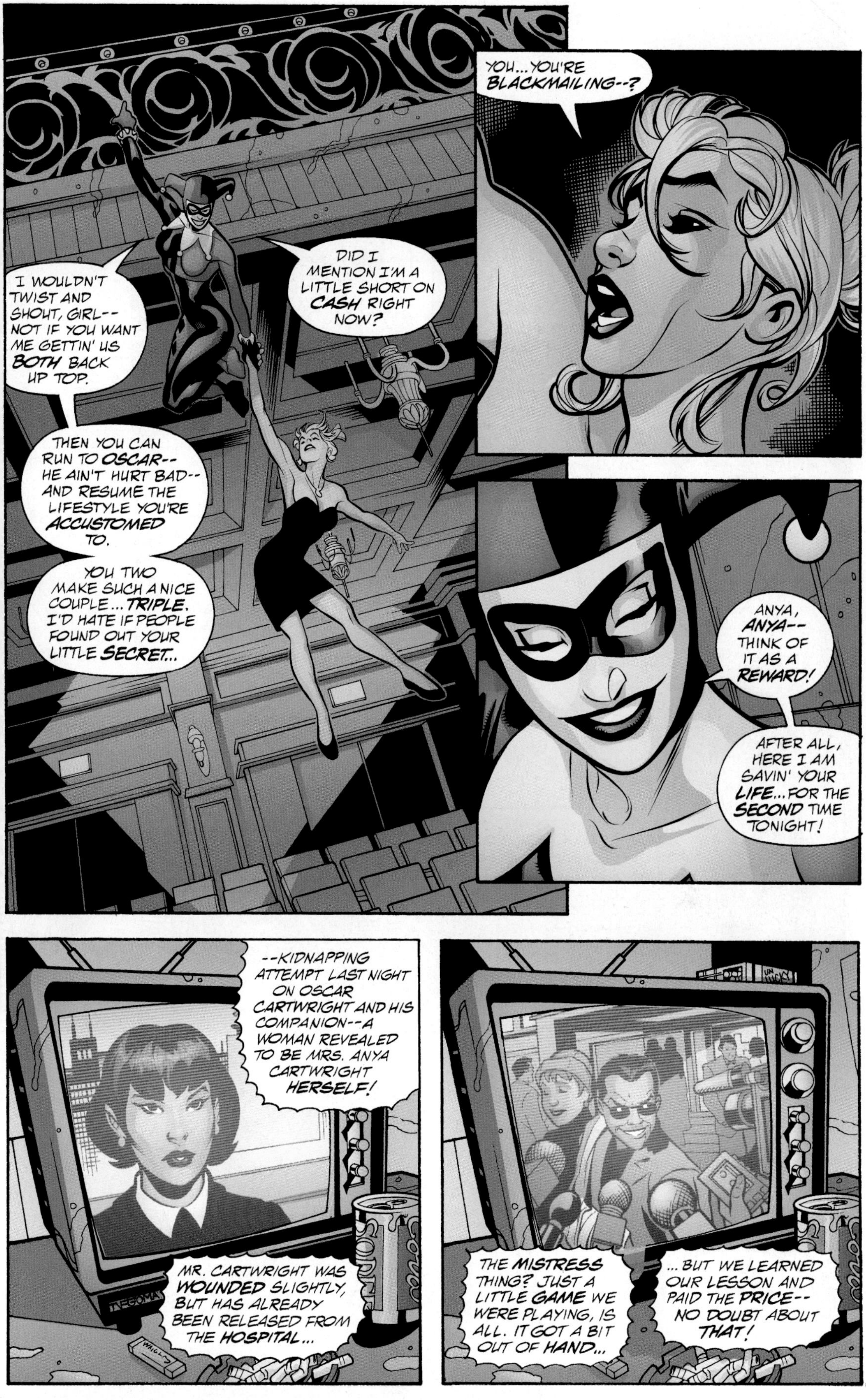
I WOULDN'T TWIST AND SHOUT, GIRL-- NOT IF YOU WANT ME GETTIN' US BOTH BACK UP TOP.
DID I MENTION I'M A LITTLE SHORT ON CASH RIGHT NOW?
THEN YOU CAN RUN TO OSCAR-- HE AIN'T HURT BAD-- AND RESUME THE LIFESTYLE YOU'RE ACCUSTOMED TO.
YOU TWO MAKE SUCH A NICE COUPLE... TRIPLE. I'D HATE IF PEOPLE FOUND OUT YOUR LITTLE SECRET...
YOU... YOU'RE BLACKMAILING--?
ANYA, ANYA-- THINK OF IT AS A REWARD!
AFTER ALL, HERE I AM SAVIN' YOUR LIFE... FOR THE SECOND TIME TONIGHT!
--KIDNAPPING ATTEMPT LAST NIGHT ON OSCAR CARTWRIGHT AND HIS COMPANION--A WOMAN REVEALED TO BE MRS. ANYA CARTWRIGHT HERSELF!
MR. CARTWRIGHT WAS WOUNDED SLIGHTLY, BUT HAS ALREADY BEEN RELEASED FROM THE HOSPITAL...
THE MISTRESS THING? JUST A LITTLE GAME WE WERE PLAYING, IS ALL. IT GOT A BIT OUT OF HAND...
...BUT WE LEARNED OUR LESSON AND PAID THE PRICE-- NO DOUBT ABOUT THAT!

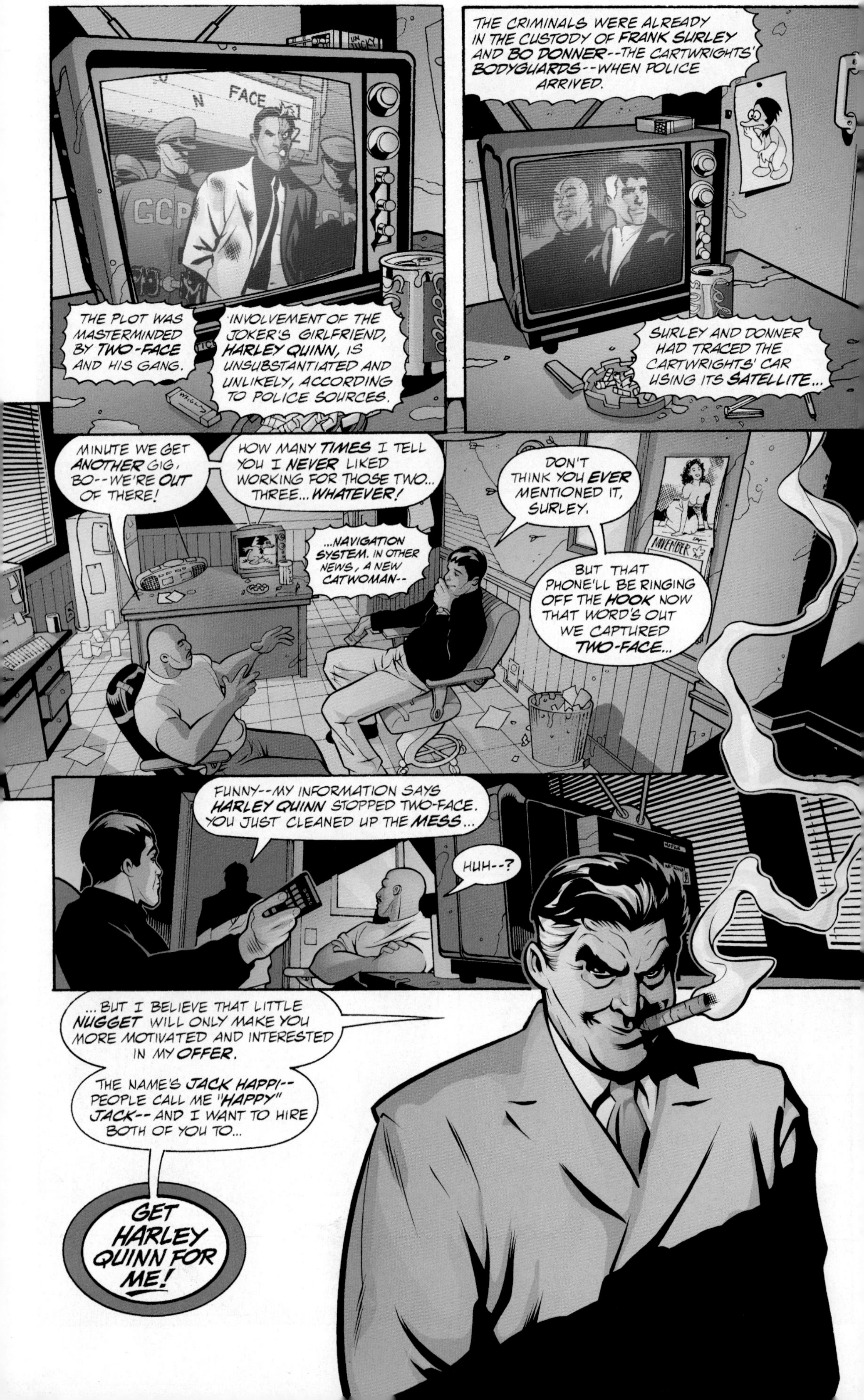
FACE
GCPD
THE CRIMINALS WERE ALREADY IN THE CUSTODY OF FRANK SURLEY AND BO DONNER--THE CARTWRIGHTS' BODYGUARDS--WHEN POLICE ARRIVED.
THE PLOT WAS MASTERMINDED BY TWO-FACE AND HIS GANG.
INVOLVEMENT OF THE JOKER'S GIRLFRIEND, HARLEY QUINN, IS UNSUBSTANTIATED AND UNLIKELY, ACCORDING TO POLICE SOURCES.
SURLEY AND DONNER HAD TRACED THE CARTWRIGHTS' CAR USING ITS SATELLITE...
MINUTE WE GET ANOTHER GIG, BO--WE'RE OUT OF THERE!
HOW MANY TIMES I TELL YOU I NEVER LIKED WORKING FOR THOSE TWO... THREE... WHATEVER!
...NAVIGATION SYSTEM. IN OTHER NEWS, A NEW CATWOMAN--
DON'T THINK YOU EVER MENTIONED IT, SURLEY.
NOVEMBER
BUT THAT PHONE'LL BE RINGING OFF THE HOOK NOW THAT WORD'S OUT WE CAPTURED TWO-FACE...
FUNNY--MY INFORMATION SAYS HARLEY QUINN STOPPED TWO-FACE. YOU JUST CLEANED UP THE MESS...
HUH--?
...BUT I BELIEVE THAT LITTLE NUGGET WILL ONLY MAKE YOU MORE MOTIVATED AND INTERESTED IN MY OFFER.
THE NAME'S JACK HAPPI--PEOPLE CALL ME "HAPPY" JACK--AND I WANT TO HIRE BOTH OF YOU TO...
GET HARLEY QUINN FOR ME!

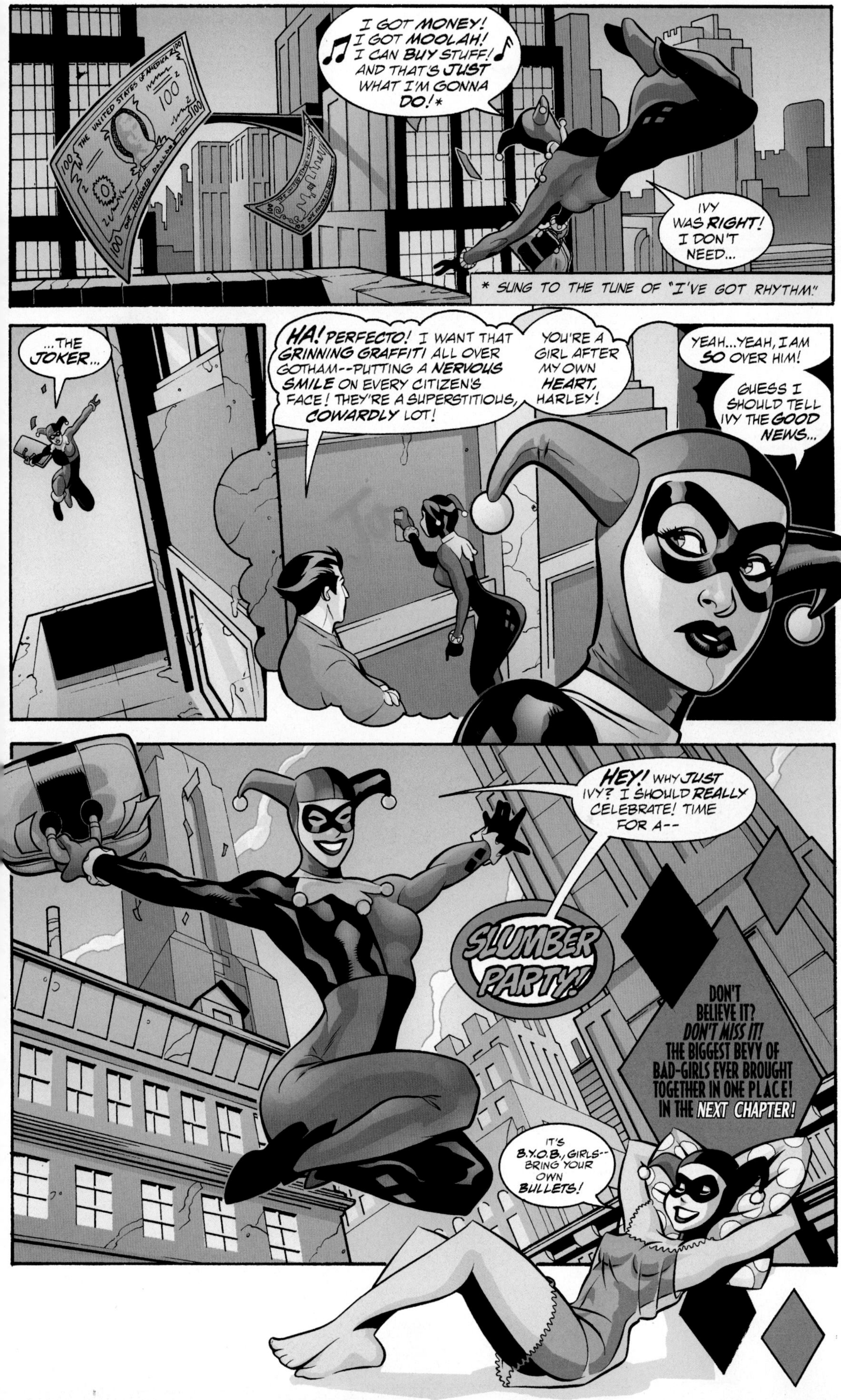
I GOT MONEY! I GOT MOOLAH! I CAN BUY STUFF! AND THAT'S JUST WHAT I'M GONNA DO!*
IVY WAS RIGHT! I DON'T NEED...
* SUNG TO THE TUNE OF "I'VE GOT RHYTHM."
...THE JOKER...
HA! PERFECTO! I WANT THAT GRINNING GRAFFITI ALL OVER GOTHAM--PUTTING A NERVOUS SMILE ON EVERY CITIZEN'S FACE! THEY'RE A SUPERSTITIOUS, COWARDLY LOT!
YOU'RE A GIRL AFTER MY OWN HEART, HARLEY!
YEAH...YEAH, I AM SO OVER HIM!
GUESS I SHOULD TELL IVY THE GOOD NEWS...
HEY! WHY JUST IVY? I SHOULD REALLY CELEBRATE! TIME FOR A--
SLUMBER PARTY!
DON'T BELIEVE IT? DON'T MISS IT! THE BIGGEST BEVY OF BAD-GIRLS EVER BROUGHT TOGETHER IN ONE PLACE! IN THE NEXT CHAPTER!
IT'S B.Y.O.B., GIRLS--BRING YOUR OWN BULLETS!

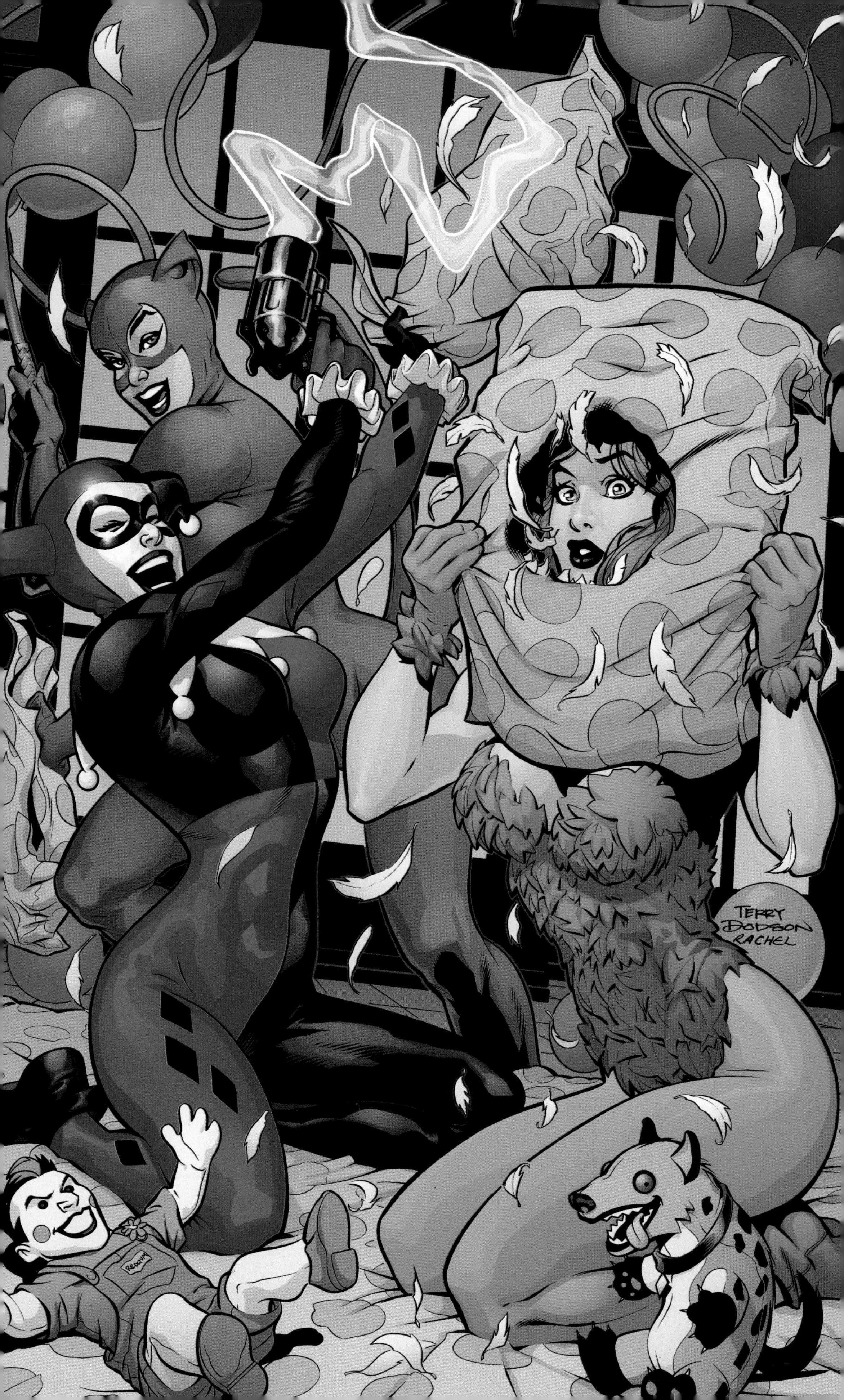
TERRY
DODSON
RACHEL
REDRUM

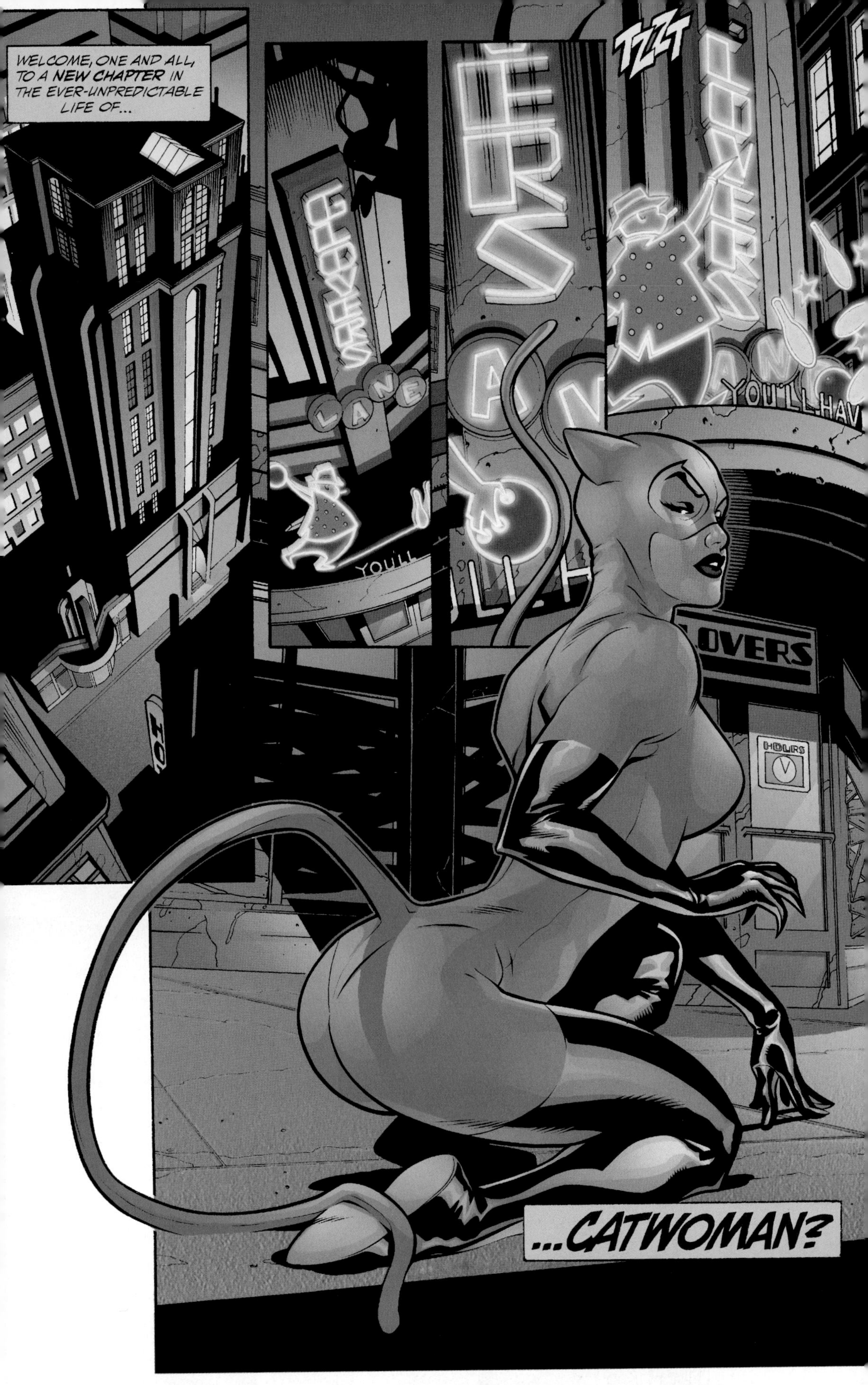
WELCOME, ONE AND ALL, TO A **NEW CHAPTER** IN THE EVER-UNPREDICTABLE LIFE OF...
TZZZT
LANE
LOVERS
HOURS
...CATWOMAN?

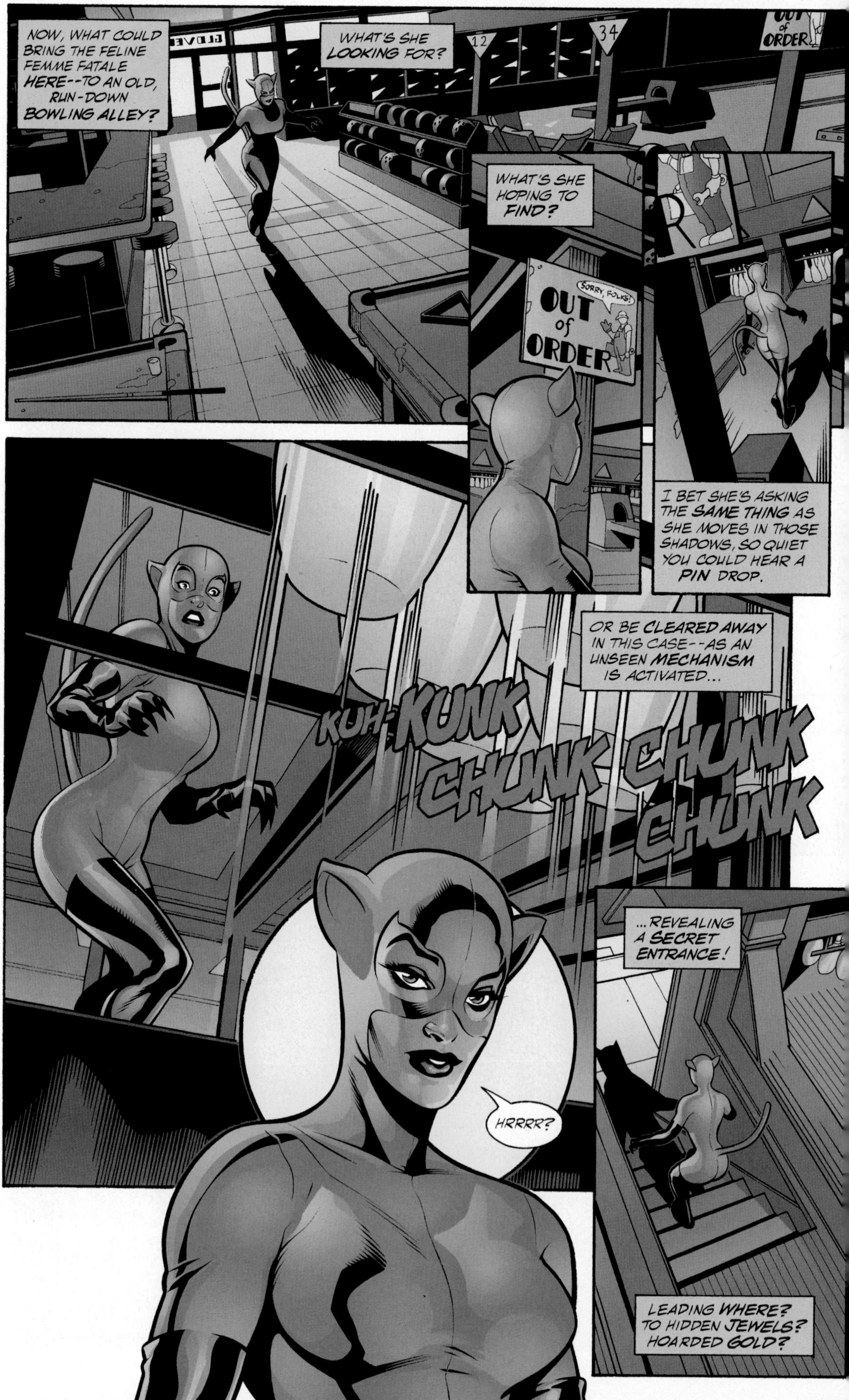
NOW, WHAT COULD BRING THE FELINE FEMME FATALE HERE--TO AN OLD, RUN-DOWN BOWLING ALLEY?
WHAT'S SHE LOOKING FOR?
12
34
OUT of ORDER
WHAT'S SHE HOPING TO FIND?
SORRY, FOLKS!
OUT of ORDER
I BET SHE'S ASKING THE SAME THING AS SHE MOVES IN THOSE SHADOWS, SO QUIET YOU COULD HEAR A PIN DROP.
OR BE CLEARED AWAY IN THIS CASE--AS AN UNSEEN MECHANISM IS ACTIVATED...
KUH-KUNK
CHUNK CHUNK CHUNK
HRRRR?
...REVEALING A SECRET ENTRANCE!
LEADING WHERE? TO HIDDEN JEWELS? HOARDED GOLD?

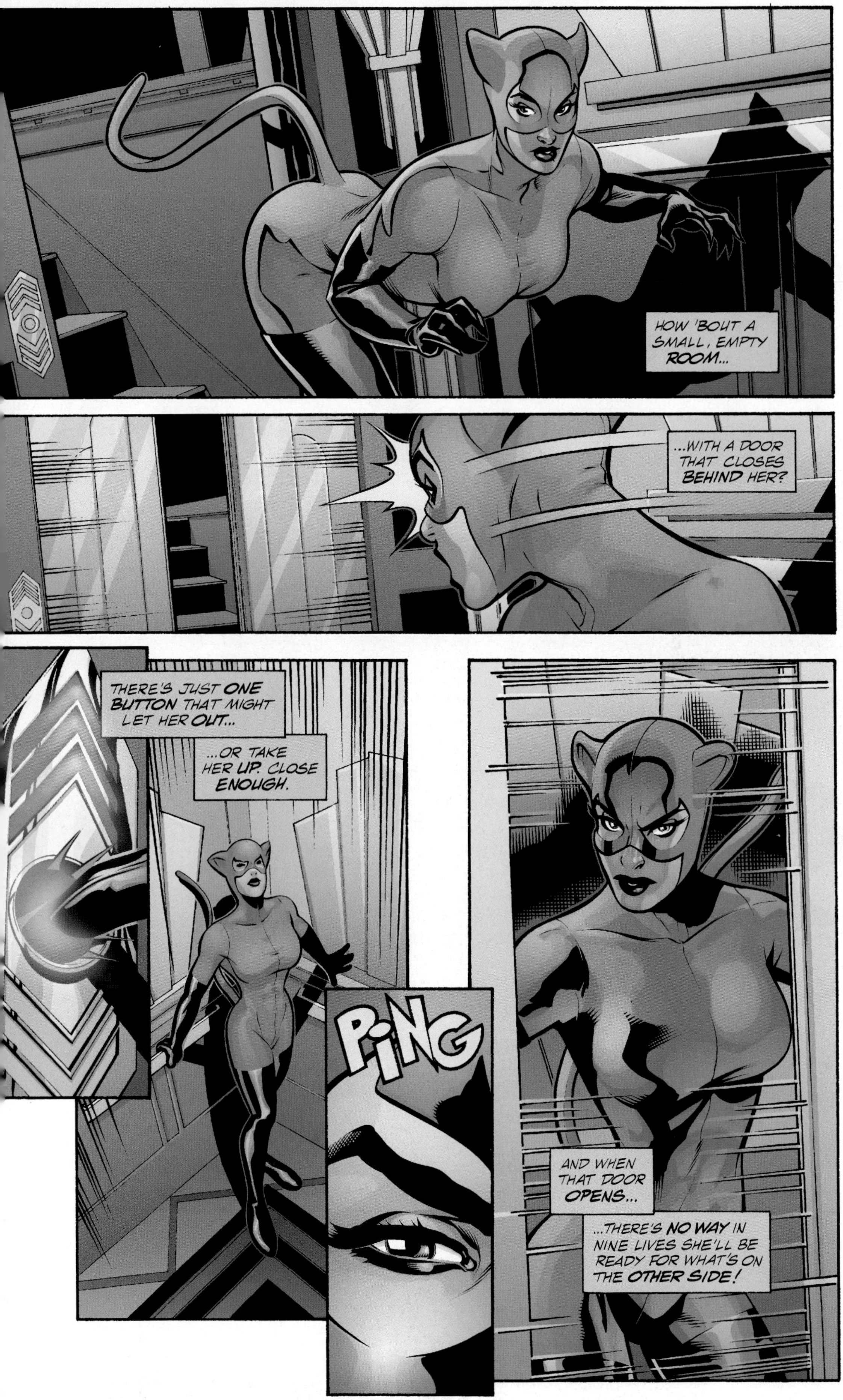
HOW 'BOUT A SMALL, EMPTY ROOM...
...WITH A DOOR THAT CLOSES BEHIND HER?
THERE'S JUST ONE BUTTON THAT MIGHT LET HER OUT...
...OR TAKE HER UP. CLOSE ENOUGH.
PING
AND WHEN THAT DOOR OPENS...
...THERE'S NO WAY IN NINE LIVES SHE'LL BE READY FOR WHAT'S ON THE OTHER SIDE!

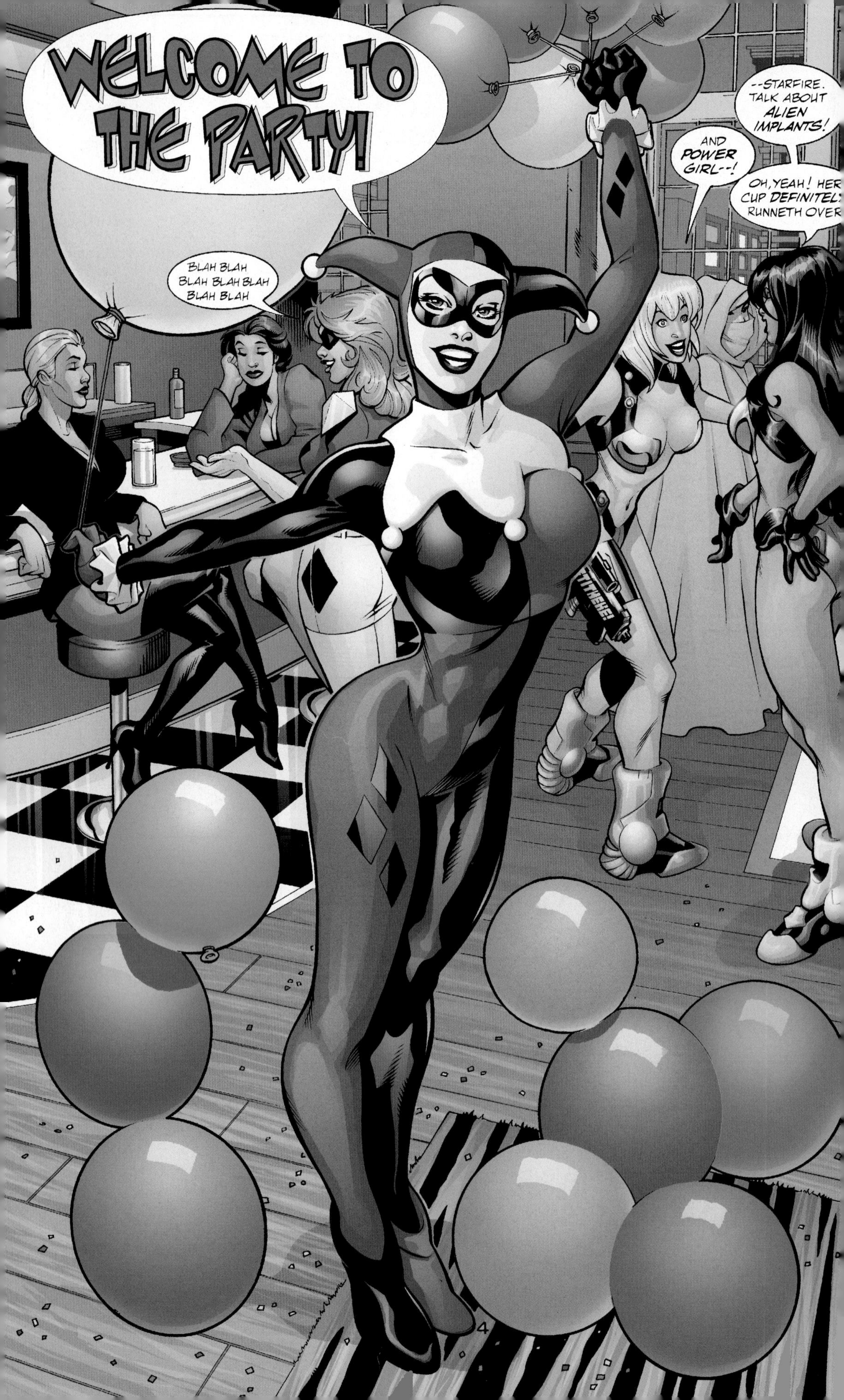
WELCOME TO THE PARTY!
BLAH BLAH
BLAH BLAH BLAH
BLAH BLAH
AND POWER GIRL--!
--STARFIRE. TALK ABOUT ALIEN IMPLANTS!
OH, YEAH! HER CUP DEFINITEL RUNNETH OVER

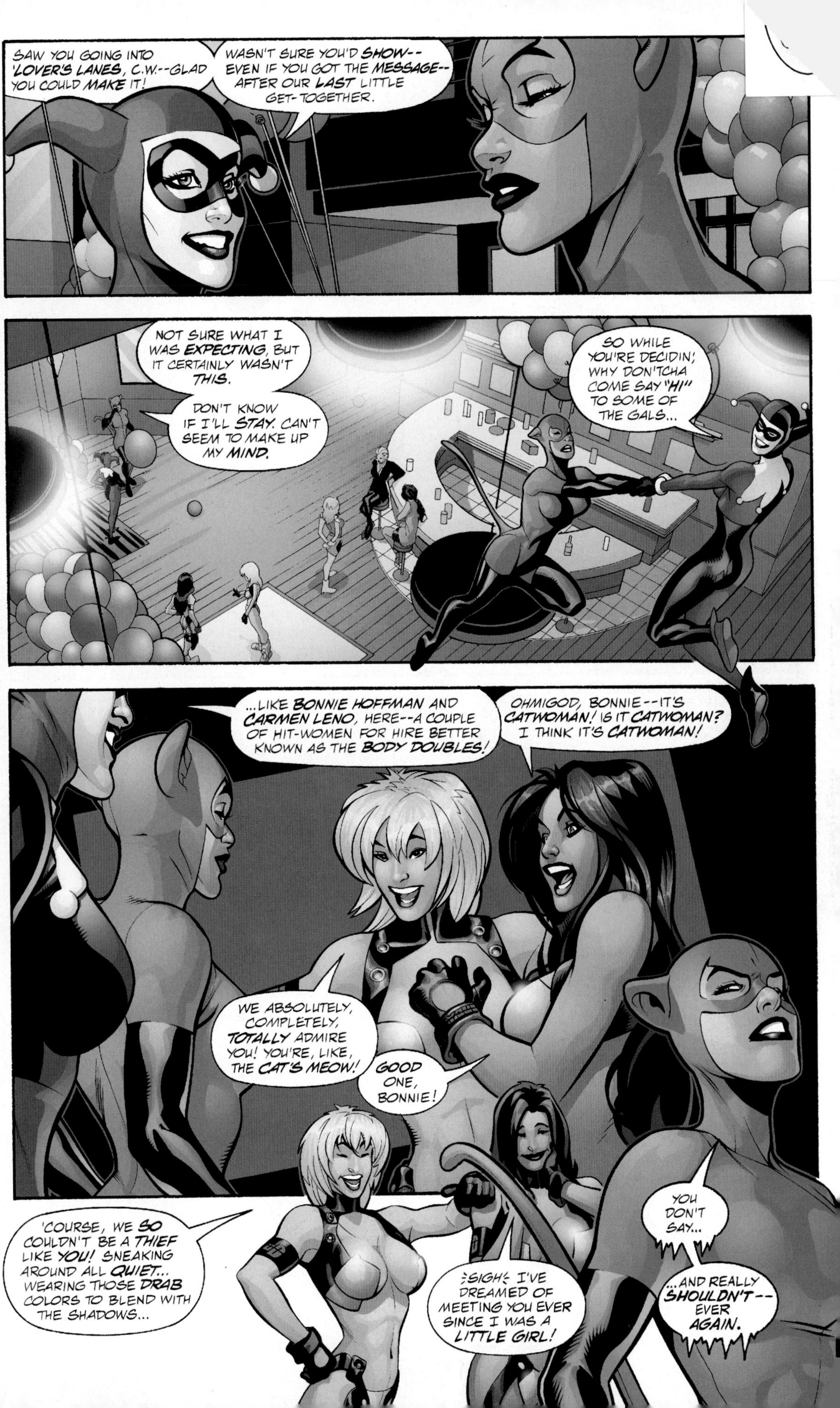
SAW YOU GOING INTO 'LOVER'S LANES, C.W.--GLAD YOU COULD MAKE IT!
WASN'T SURE YOU'D SHOW-- EVEN IF YOU GOT THE MESSAGE-- AFTER OUR LAST LITTLE GET-TOGETHER.
NOT SURE WHAT I WAS EXPECTING, BUT IT CERTAINLY WASN'T THIS.
DON'T KNOW IF I'LL STAY. CAN'T SEEM TO MAKE UP MY MIND.
SO WHILE YOU'RE DECIDIN', WHY DON'TCHA COME SAY "HI" TO SOME OF THE GALS...
...LIKE BONNIE HOFFMAN AND CARMEN LENO, HERE--A COUPLE OF HIT-WOMEN FOR HIRE BETTER KNOWN AS THE BODY DOUBLES!
OHMIGOD, BONNIE--IT'S CATWOMAN! IS IT CATWOMAN? I THINK IT'S CATWOMAN!
WE ABSOLUTELY, COMPLETELY, TOTALLY ADMIRE YOU! YOU'RE, LIKE, THE CAT'S MEOW!
GOOD ONE, BONNIE!
'COURSE, WE SO COULDN'T BE A THIEF LIKE YOU! SNEAKING AROUND ALL QUIET... WEARING THOSE DRAB COLORS TO BLEND WITH THE SHADOWS...
SIGH I'VE DREAMED OF MEETING YOU EVER SINCE I WAS A LITTLE GIRL!
YOU DON'T SAY...
...AND REALLY SHOULDN'T-- EVER AGAIN.

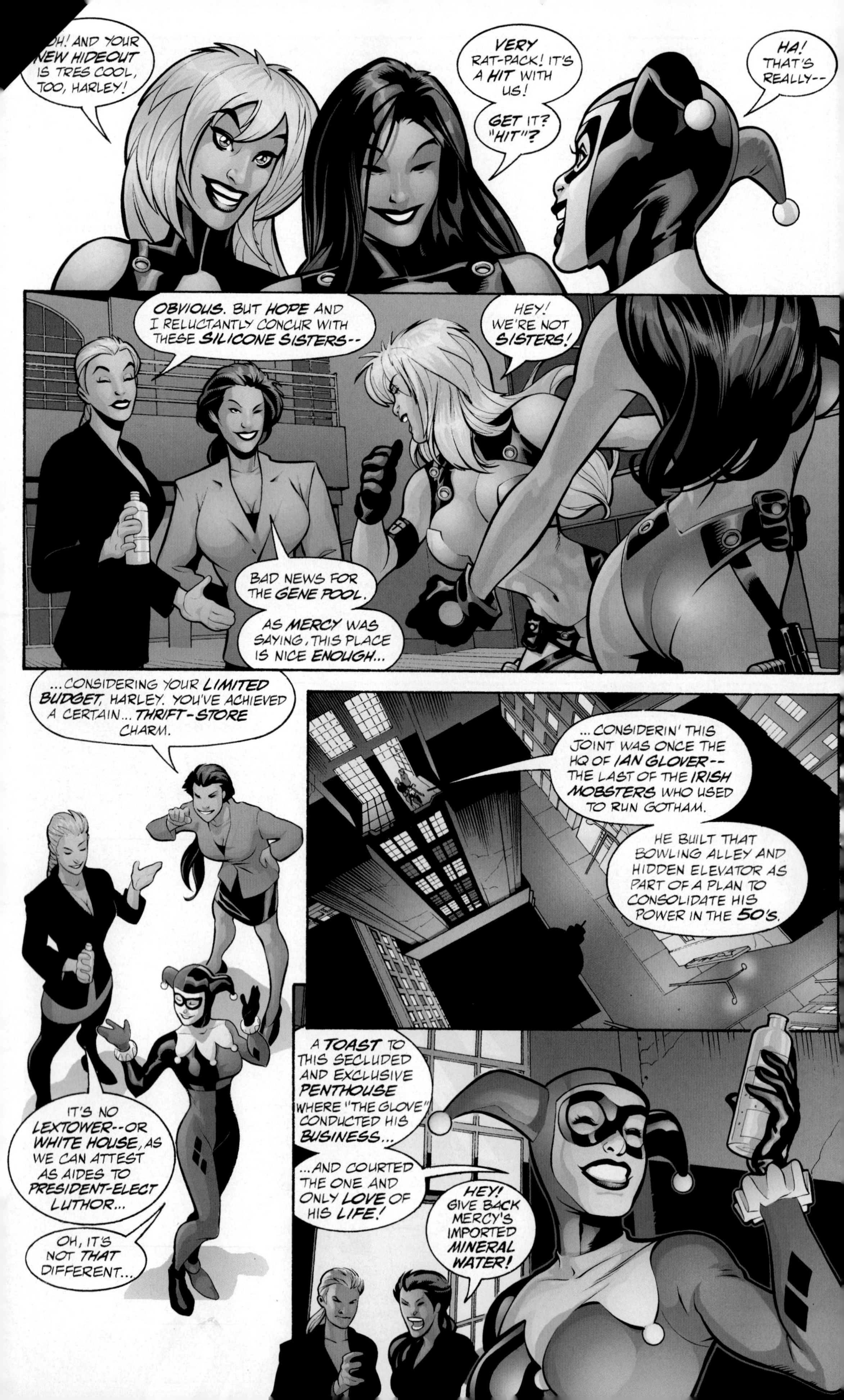
OH! AND YOUR NEW HIDEOUT IS TRES COOL, TOO, HARLEY!
VERY RAT-PACK! IT'S A HIT WITH US!
GET IT? "HIT"?
HA! THAT'S REALLY--
OBVIOUS. BUT HOPE AND I RELUCTANTLY CONCUR WITH THESE SILICONE SISTERS--
HEY! WE'RE NOT SISTERS!
BAD NEWS FOR THE GENE POOL.
AS MERCY WAS SAYING, THIS PLACE IS NICE ENOUGH...
...CONSIDERING YOUR LIMITED BUDGET, HARLEY. YOU'VE ACHIEVED A CERTAIN... THRIFT-STORE CHARM.
IT'S NO LEXTOWER--OR WHITE HOUSE, AS WE CAN ATTEST AS AIDES TO PRESIDENT-ELECT LUTHOR...
OH, IT'S NOT THAT DIFFERENT...
...CONSIDERIN' THIS JOINT WAS ONCE THE HQ OF IAN GLOVER-- THE LAST OF THE IRISH MOBSTERS WHO USED TO RUN GOTHAM.
HE BUILT THAT BOWLING ALLEY AND HIDDEN ELEVATOR AS PART OF A PLAN TO CONSOLIDATE HIS POWER IN THE 50'S.
A TOAST TO THIS SECLUDED AND EXCLUSIVE PENTHOUSE WHERE "THE GLOVE" CONDUCTED HIS BUSINESS...
...AND COURTED THE ONE AND ONLY LOVE OF HIS LIFE!
HEY! GIVE BACK MERCY'S IMPORTED MINERAL WATER!

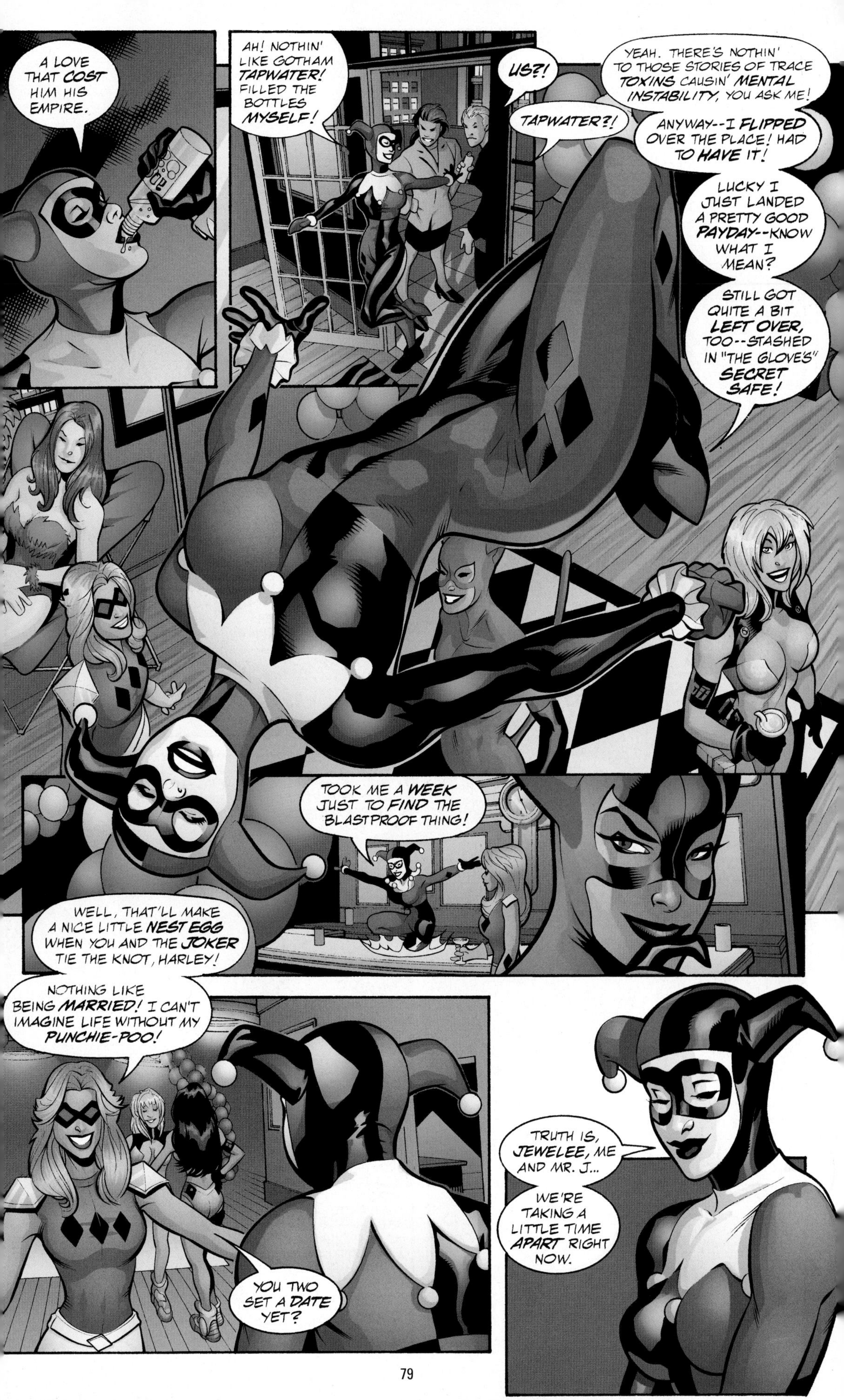
A LOVE THAT COST HIM HIS EMPIRE.
AH! NOTHIN' LIKE GOTHAM TAPWATER! FILLED THE BOTTLES MYSELF!
US?!
TAPWATER?!
YEAH. THERE'S NOTHIN' TO THOSE STORIES OF TRACE TOXINS CAUSIN' MENTAL INSTABILITY, YOU ASK ME!
ANYWAY--I FLIPPED OVER THE PLACE! HAD TO HAVE IT!
LUCKY I JUST LANDED A PRETTY GOOD PAYDAY--KNOW WHAT I MEAN?
STILL GOT QUITE A BIT LEFT OVER, TOO--STASHED IN "THE GLOVE'S" SECRET SAFE!
TOOK ME A WEEK JUST TO FIND THE BLASTPROOF THING!
WELL, THAT'LL MAKE A NICE LITTLE NEST EGG WHEN YOU AND THE JOKER TIE THE KNOT, HARLEY!
NOTHING LIKE BEING MARRIED! I CAN'T IMAGINE LIFE WITHOUT MY PUNCHIE-POO!
YOU TWO SET A DATE YET?
TRUTH IS, JEWELEE, ME AND MR. J...
WE'RE TAKING A LITTLE TIME APART RIGHT NOW.

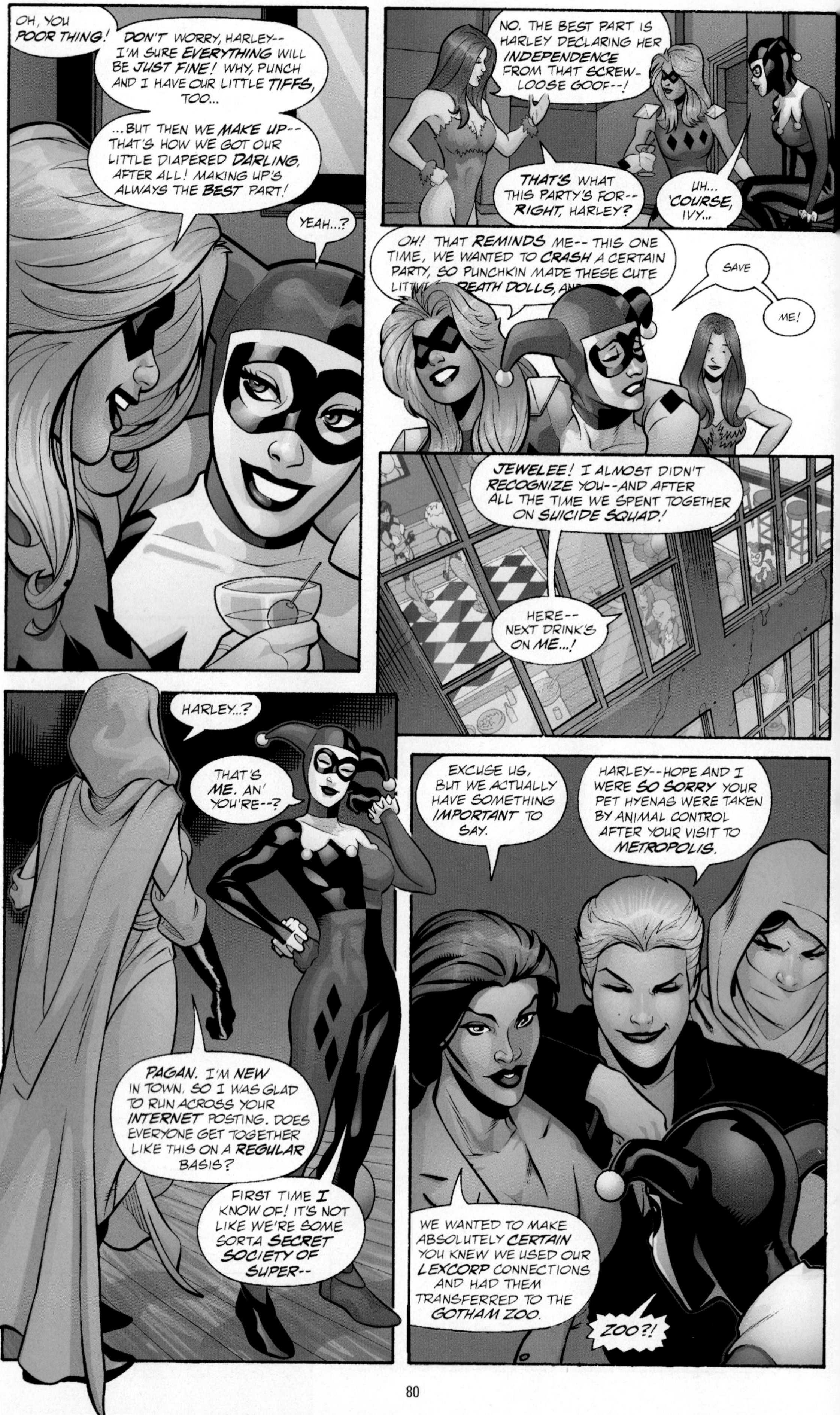

OH, YOU POOR THING!
DON'T WORRY, HARLEY-- I'M SURE EVERYTHING WILL BE JUST FINE! WHY, PUNCH AND I HAVE OUR LITTLE TIFFS, TOO...
...BUT THEN WE MAKE UP-- THAT'S HOW WE GOT OUR LITTLE DIAPERED DARLING, AFTER ALL! MAKING UP'S ALWAYS THE BEST PART!
YEAH...?
NO. THE BEST PART IS HARLEY DECLARING HER INDEPENDENCE FROM THAT SCREW-LOOSE GOOF--!
THAT'S WHAT THIS PARTY'S FOR-- RIGHT, HARLEY?
UH... 'COURSE, IVY...
OH! THAT REMINDS ME-- THIS ONE TIME, WE WANTED TO CRASH A CERTAIN PARTY, SO PUNCHKIN MADE THESE CUTE
SAVE
ME!
JEWELEE! I ALMOST DIDN'T RECOGNIZE YOU--AND AFTER ALL THE TIME WE SPENT TOGETHER ON SUICIDE SQUAD!
HERE-- NEXT DRINK'S ON ME...!
HARLEY...?
THAT'S ME. AN' YOU'RE--?
PAGAN. I'M NEW IN TOWN, SO I WAS GLAD TO RUN ACROSS YOUR INTERNET POSTING. DOES EVERYONE GET TOGETHER LIKE THIS ON A REGULAR BASIS?
FIRST TIME I KNOW OF! IT'S NOT LIKE WE'RE SOME SORTA SECRET SOCIETY OF SUPER--
EXCUSE US, BUT WE ACTUALLY HAVE SOMETHING IMPORTANT TO SAY.
HARLEY--HOPE AND I WERE SO SORRY YOUR PET HYENAS WERE TAKEN BY ANIMAL CONTROL AFTER YOUR VISIT TO METROPOLIS.
WE WANTED TO MAKE ABSOLUTELY CERTAIN YOU KNEW WE USED OUR LEXCORP CONNECTIONS AND HAD THEM TRANSFERRED TO THE GOTHAM ZOO.
ZOO?!

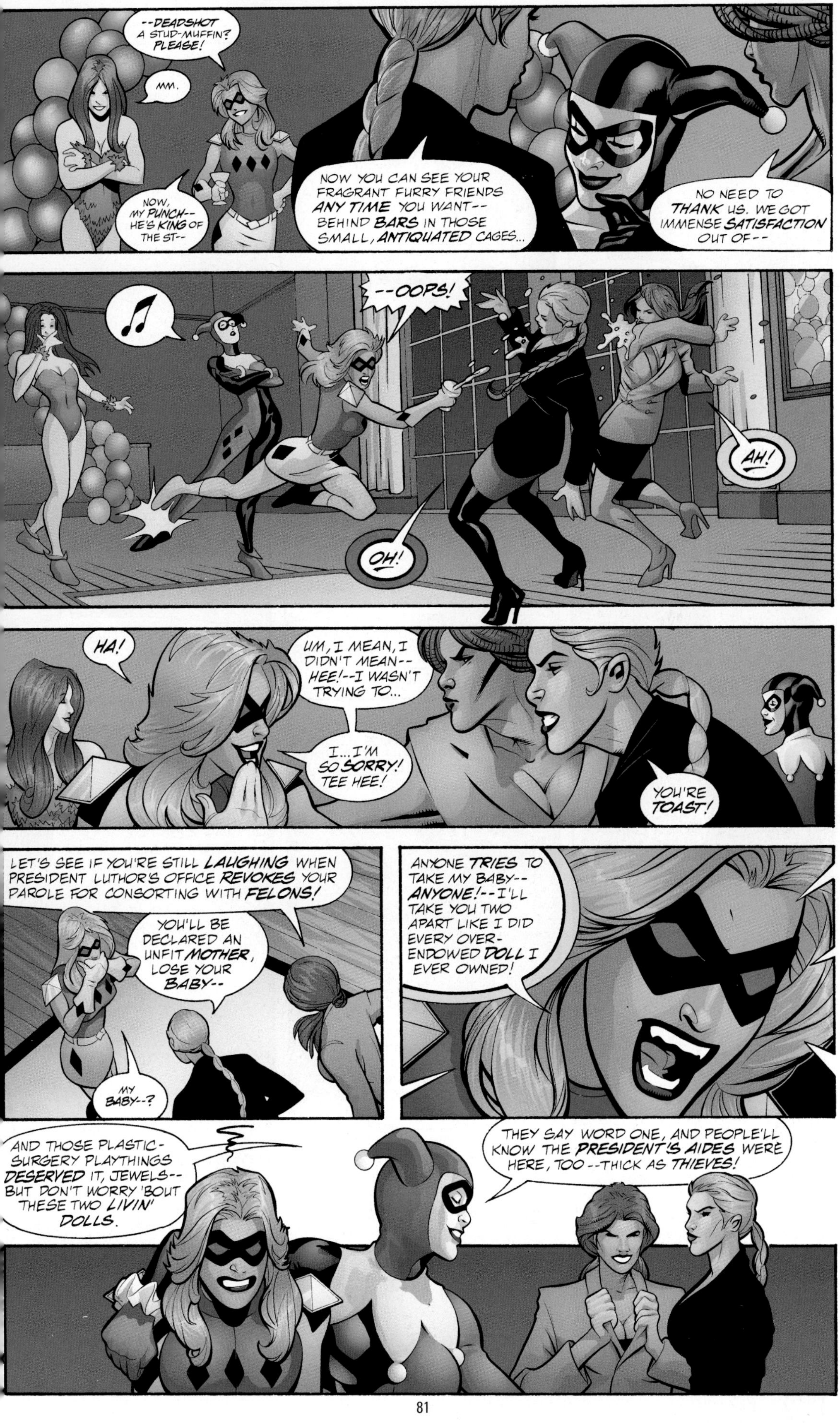
--DEADSHOT A STUD-MUFFIN? PLEASE!
MM.
NOW, MY PUNCH-- HE'S KING OF THE ST--
NOW YOU CAN SEE YOUR FRAGRANT FURRY FRIENDS ANY TIME YOU WANT-- BEHIND BARS IN THOSE SMALL, ANTIQUATED CAGES...
NO NEED TO THANK US. WE GOT IMMENSE SATISFACTION OUT OF--
--OOPS!
OH!
AH!
HA!
UM, I MEAN, I DIDN'T MEAN-- HEE!--I WASN'T TRYING TO...
I...I'M SO SORRY! TEE HEE!
YOU'RE TOAST!
LET'S SEE IF YOU'RE STILL LAUGHING WHEN PRESIDENT LUTHOR'S OFFICE REVOKES YOUR PAROLE FOR CONSORTING WITH FELONS!
YOU'LL BE DECLARED AN UNFIT MOTHER, LOSE YOUR BABY--
MY BABY--?
ANYONE TRIES TO TAKE MY BABY-- ANYONE!--I'LL TAKE YOU TWO APART LIKE I DID EVERY OVER-ENDOWED DOLL I EVER OWNED!
AND THOSE PLASTIC-SURGERY PLAYTHINGS DESERVED IT, JEWELS-- BUT DON'T WORRY 'BOUT THESE TWO LIVIN' DOLLS.
THEY SAY WORD ONE, AND PEOPLE'LL KNOW THE PRESIDENT'S AIDES WERE HERE, TOO--THICK AS THIEVES!

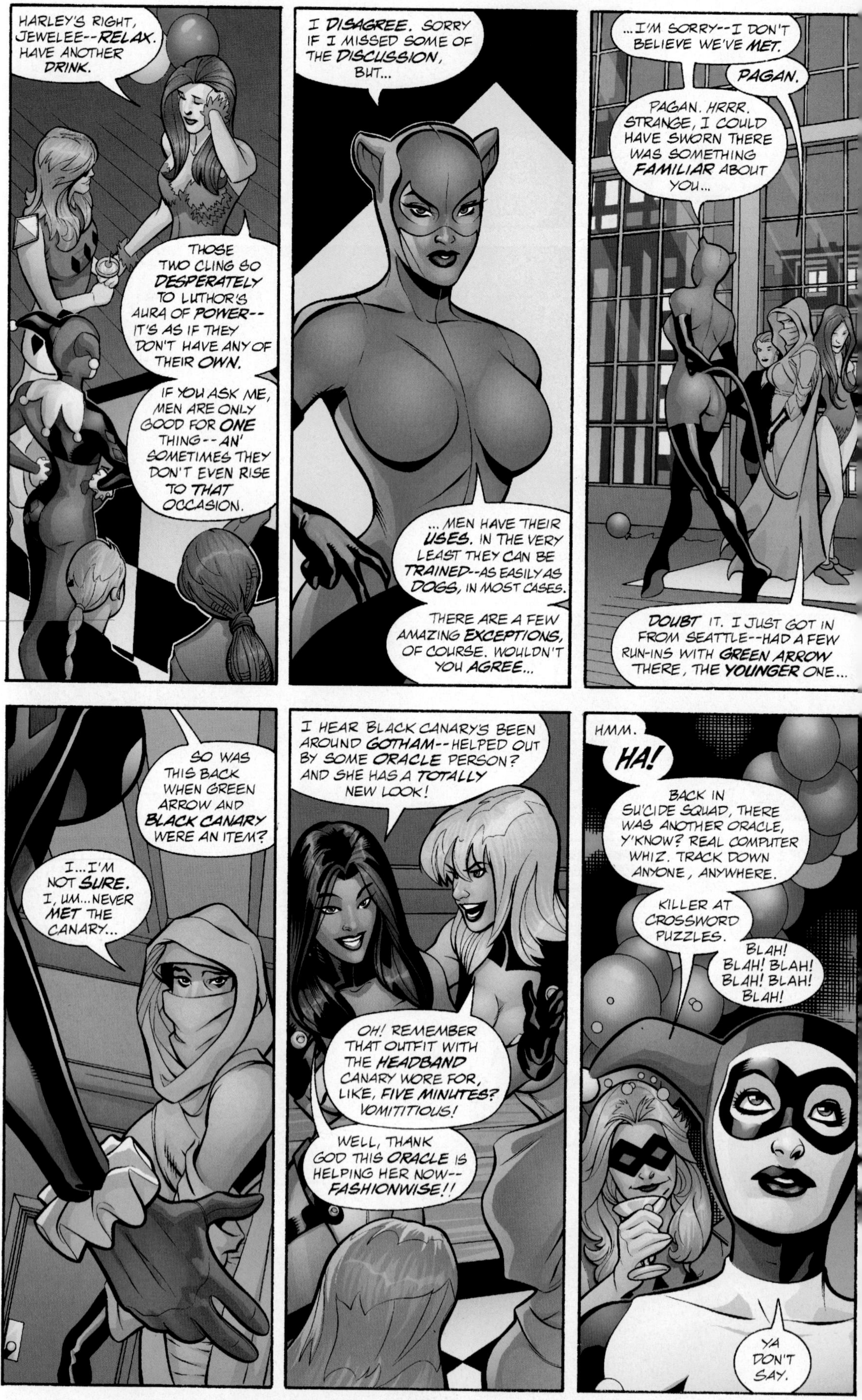
HARLEY'S RIGHT, JEWELEE--RELAX. HAVE ANOTHER DRINK.
THOSE TWO CLING SO DESPERATELY TO LUTHOR'S AURA OF POWER--IT'S AS IF THEY DON'T HAVE ANY OF THEIR OWN.
IF YOU ASK ME, MEN ARE ONLY GOOD FOR ONE THING--AN' SOMETIMES THEY DON'T EVEN RISE TO THAT OCCASION.
I DISAGREE. SORRY IF I MISSED SOME OF THE DISCUSSION, BUT...
...MEN HAVE THEIR USES. IN THE VERY LEAST THEY CAN BE TRAINED--AS EASILY AS DOGS, IN MOST CASES.
THERE ARE A FEW AMAZING EXCEPTIONS, OF COURSE. WOULDN'T YOU AGREE...
...I'M SORRY--I DON'T BELIEVE WE'VE MET.
PAGAN.
PAGAN. HRRR. STRANGE, I COULD HAVE SWORN THERE WAS SOMETHING FAMILIAR ABOUT YOU...
DOUBT IT. I JUST GOT IN FROM SEATTLE--HAD A FEW RUN-INS WITH GREEN ARROW THERE, THE YOUNGER ONE...
SO WAS THIS BACK WHEN GREEN ARROW AND BLACK CANARY WERE AN ITEM?
I...I'M NOT SURE. I, UM...NEVER MET THE CANARY...
I HEAR BLACK CANARY'S BEEN AROUND GOTHAM--HELPED OUT BY SOME ORACLE PERSON? AND SHE HAS A TOTALLY NEW LOOK!
OH! REMEMBER THAT OUTFIT WITH THE HEADBAND CANARY WORE FOR, LIKE, FIVE MINUTES? VOMITITIOUS!
WELL, THANK GOD THIS ORACLE IS HELPING HER NOW--FASHIONWISE!!
HMM.
HA!
BACK IN SU'CIDE SQUAD, THERE WAS ANOTHER ORACLE, Y'KNOW? REAL COMPUTER WHIZ. TRACK DOWN ANYONE, ANYWHERE.
KILLER AT CROSSWORD PUZZLES.
BLAH! BLAH! BLAH! BLAH! BLAH! BLAH!
YA DON'T SAY.

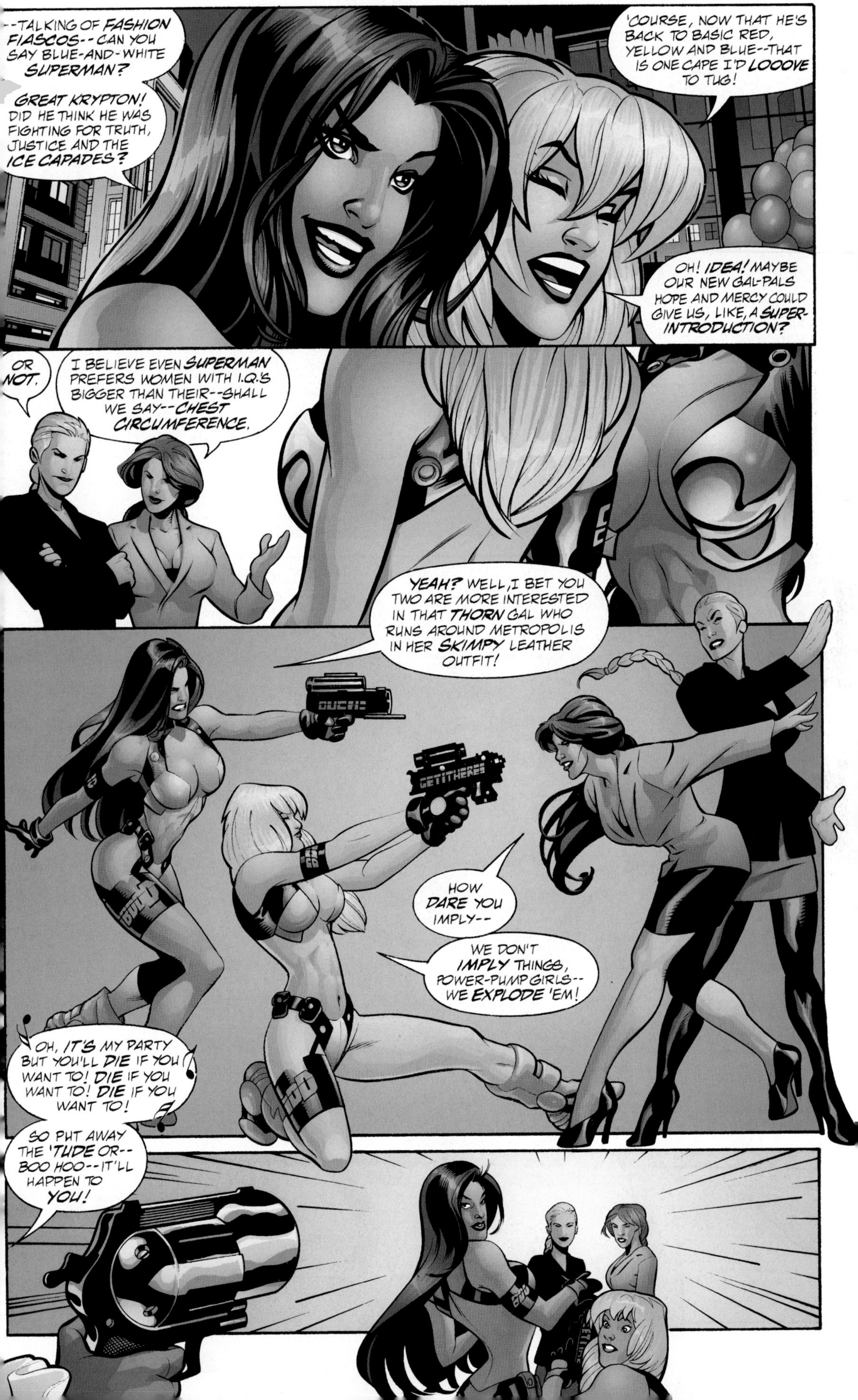
--TALKING OF FASHION FIASCOS--CAN YOU SAY BLUE-AND-WHITE SUPERMAN?
GREAT KRYPTON! DID HE THINK HE WAS FIGHTING FOR TRUTH, JUSTICE AND THE ICE CAPADES?
'COURSE, NOW THAT HE'S BACK TO BASIC RED, YELLOW AND BLUE--THAT IS ONE CAPE I'D LOOOVE TO TUG!
OH! IDEA! MAYBE OUR NEW GAL-PALS HOPE AND MERCY COULD GIVE US, LIKE, A SUPER-INTRODUCTION?
OR NOT.
I BELIEVE EVEN SUPERMAN PREFERS WOMEN WITH I.Q.'S BIGGER THAN THEIR--SHALL WE SAY--CHEST CIRCUMFERENCE.
YEAH? WELL, I BET YOU TWO ARE MORE INTERESTED IN THAT THORN GAL WHO RUNS AROUND METROPOLIS IN HER SKIMPY LEATHER OUTFIT!
OUCH!
GETITHERE!
HOW DARE YOU IMPLY--
WE DON'T IMPLY THINGS, POWER-PUMP GIRLS--WE EXPLODE 'EM!
OH, IT'S MY PARTY BUT YOU'LL DIE IF YOU WANT TO! DIE IF YOU WANT TO! DIE IF YOU WANT TO!
SO PUT AWAY THE 'TUDE OR--BOO HOO--IT'LL HAPPEN TO YOU!

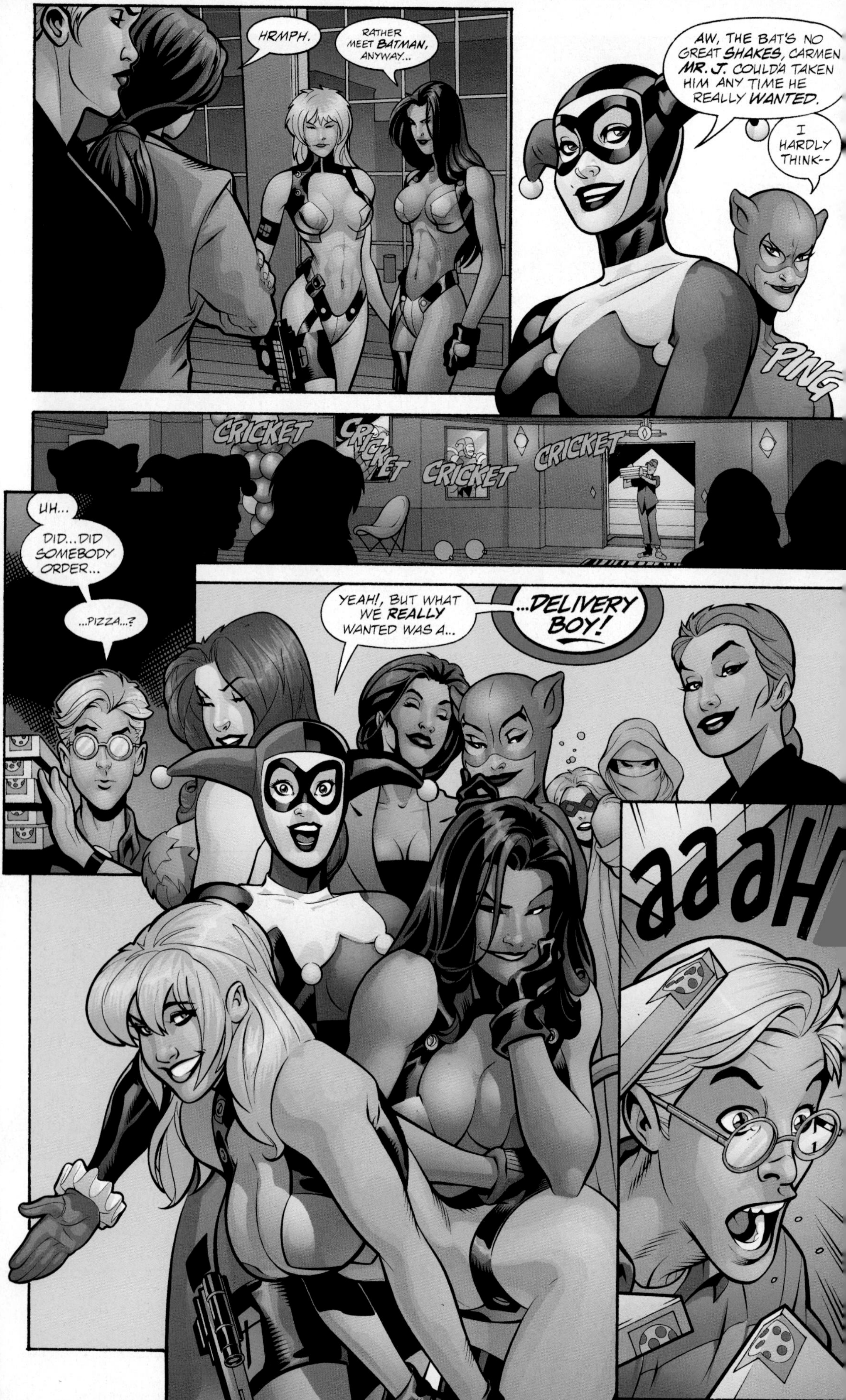

HRMPH.
RATHER MEET BATMAN, ANYWAY...
AW, THE BAT'S NO GREAT SHAKES, CARMEN. MR. J. COULD'A TAKEN HIM ANY TIME HE REALLY WANTED.
I HARDLY THINK--
PING
CRICKET
CRICKET
CRICKET
CRICKET
UH...
DID...DID SOMEBODY ORDER...
...PIZZA...?
YEAH!, BUT WHAT WE REALLY WANTED WAS A...
...DELIVERY BOY!
AAAH

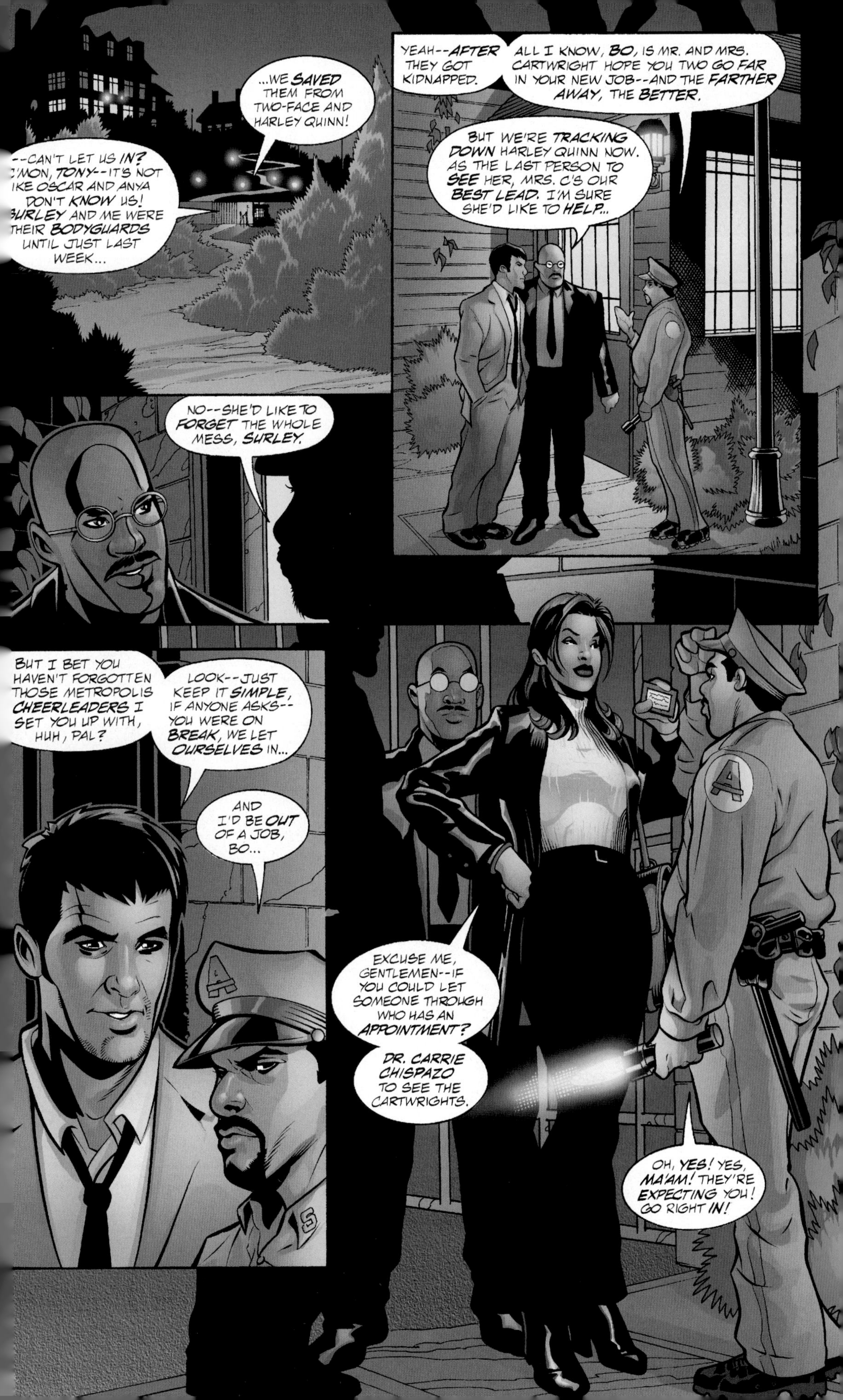
--CAN'T LET US IN? C'MON, TONY--IT'S NOT LIKE OSCAR AND ANYA DON'T KNOW US! SURLEY AND ME WERE THEIR BODYGUARDS UNTIL JUST LAST WEEK...
...WE SAVED THEM FROM TWO-FACE AND HARLEY QUINN!
YEAH--AFTER THEY GOT KIDNAPPED.
ALL I KNOW, BO, IS MR. AND MRS. CARTWRIGHT HOPE YOU TWO GO FAR IN YOUR NEW JOB--AND THE FARTHER AWAY, THE BETTER.
BUT WE'RE TRACKING DOWN HARLEY QUINN NOW. AS THE LAST PERSON TO SEE HER, MRS. C'S OUR BEST LEAD. I'M SURE SHE'D LIKE TO HELP...
NO--SHE'D LIKE TO FORGET THE WHOLE MESS, SURLEY.
BUT I BET YOU HAVEN'T FORGOTTEN THOSE METROPOLIS CHEERLEADERS I SET YOU UP WITH, HUH, PAL?
LOOK--JUST KEEP IT SIMPLE, IF ANYONE ASKS--YOU WERE ON BREAK, WE LET OURSELVES IN...
AND I'D BE OUT OF A JOB, BO...
EXCUSE ME, GENTLEMEN--IF YOU COULD LET SOMEONE THROUGH WHO HAS AN APPOINTMENT?
DR. CARRIE CHISPAZO TO SEE THE CARTWRIGHTS.
OH, YES! YES, MA'AM! THEY'RE EXPECTING YOU! GO RIGHT IN!

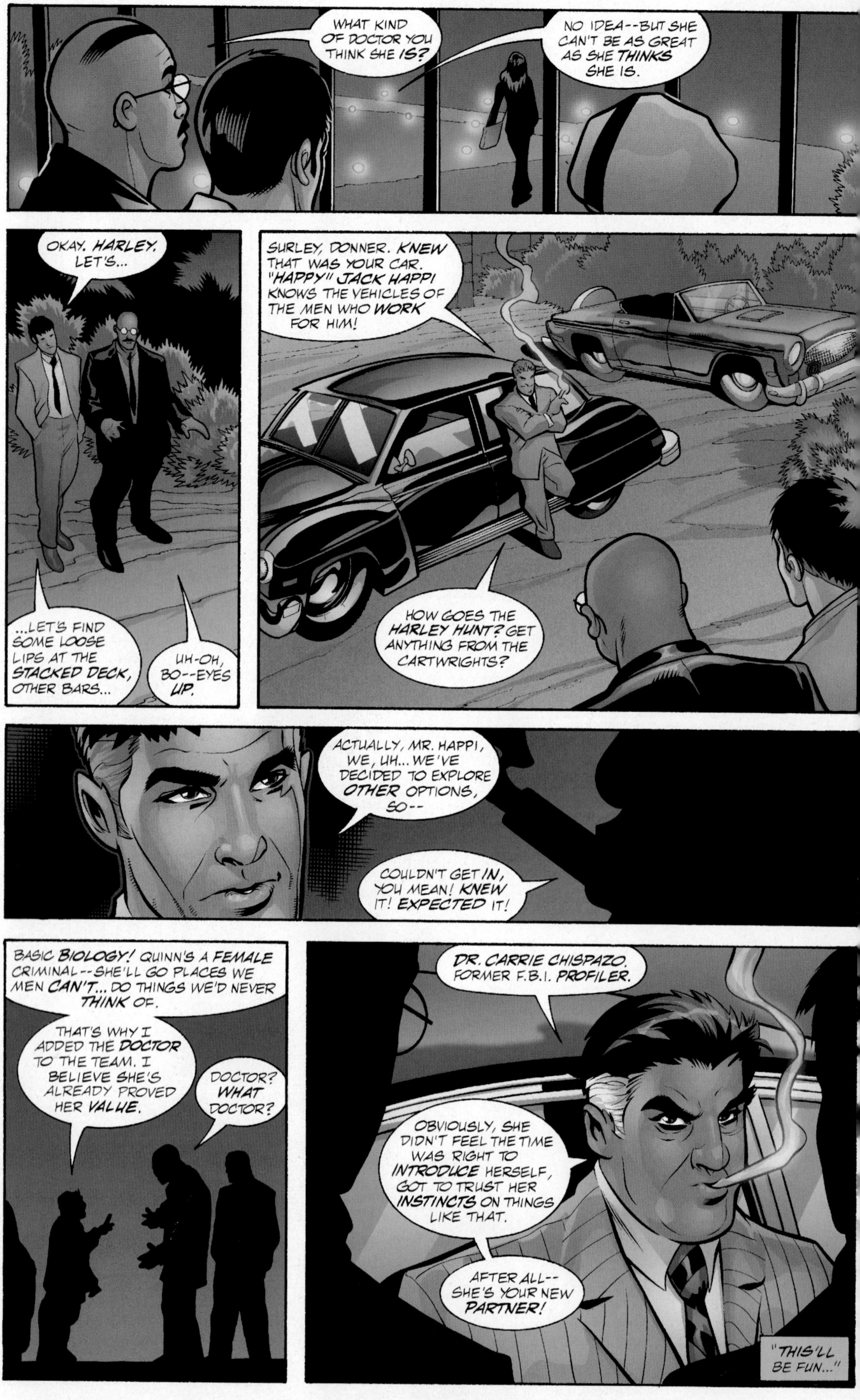
WHAT KIND OF DOCTOR YOU THINK SHE IS?
NO IDEA--BUT SHE CAN'T BE AS GREAT AS SHE THINKS SHE IS.
OKAY. HARLEY. LET'S...
...LET'S FIND SOME LOOSE LIPS AT THE STACKED DECK, OTHER BARS...
UH-OH, BO--EYES UP.
SURLEY, DONNER. KNEW THAT WAS YOUR CAR. "HAPPY" JACK HAPPI KNOWS THE VEHICLES OF THE MEN WHO WORK FOR HIM!
HOW GOES THE HARLEY HUNT? GET ANYTHING FROM THE CARTWRIGHTS?
ACTUALLY, MR. HAPPI, WE, UH... WE'VE DECIDED TO EXPLORE OTHER OPTIONS, SO--
COULDN'T GET IN, YOU MEAN! KNEW IT! EXPECTED IT!
BASIC BIOLOGY! QUINN'S A FEMALE CRIMINAL--SHE'LL GO PLACES WE MEN CAN'T... DO THINGS WE'D NEVER THINK OF.
THAT'S WHY I ADDED THE DOCTOR TO THE TEAM. I BELIEVE SHE'S ALREADY PROVED HER VALUE.
DOCTOR? WHAT DOCTOR?
DR. CARRIE CHISPAZO. FORMER F.B.I. PROFILER.
OBVIOUSLY, SHE DIDN'T FEEL THE TIME WAS RIGHT TO INTRODUCE HERSELF, GOT TO TRUST HER INSTINCTS ON THINGS LIKE THAT.
AFTER ALL--SHE'S YOUR NEW PARTNER!
"THIS'LL BE FUN..."

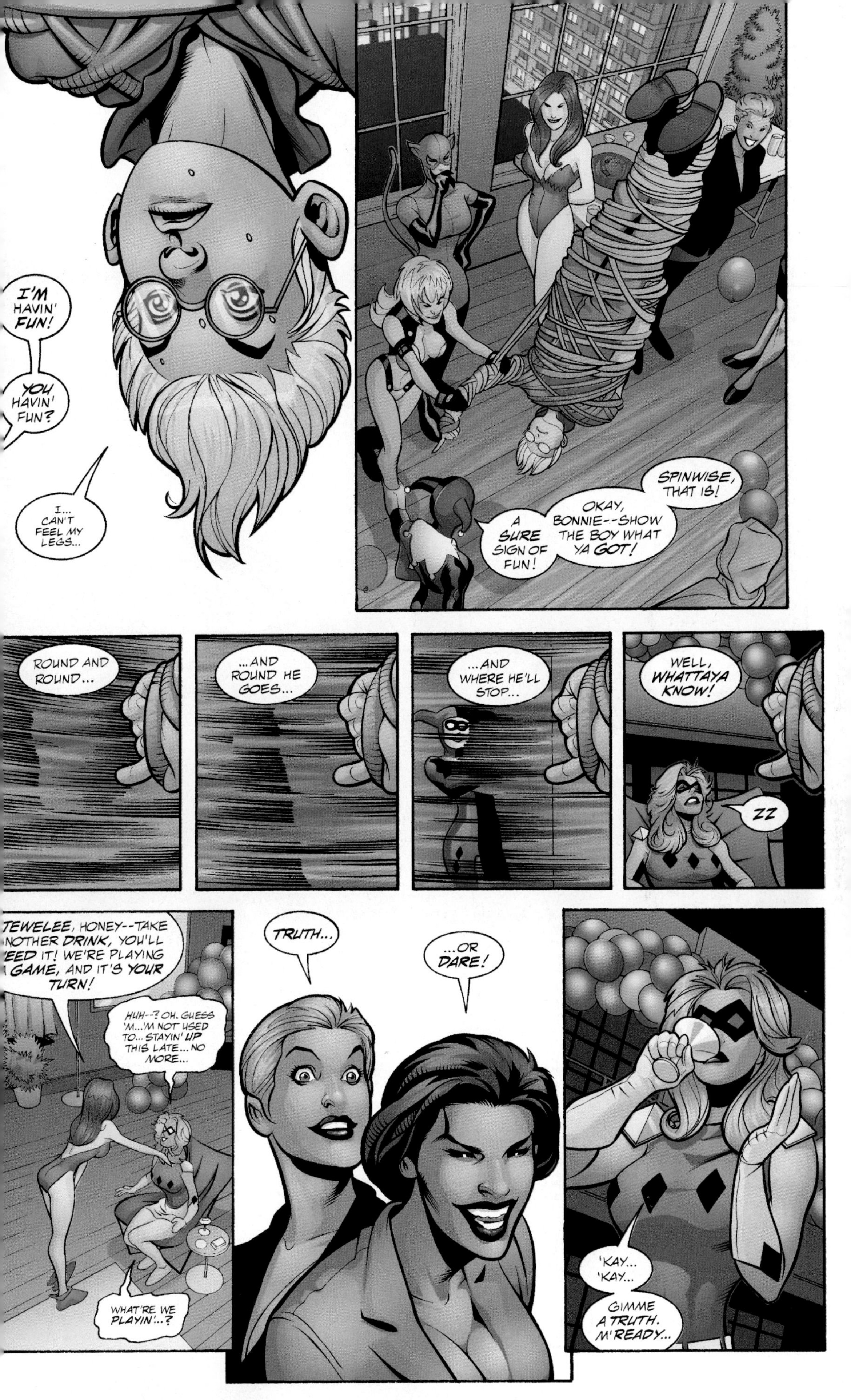
I'M HAVIN' FUN!
YOU HAVIN' FUN?
I... CAN'T FEEL MY LEGS...
SPINWISE, THAT IS!
OKAY, BONNIE--SHOW THE BOY WHAT YA GOT!
A SURE SIGN OF FUN!
ROUND AND ROUND...
...AND ROUND HE GOES...
...AND WHERE HE'LL STOP...
WELL, WHATTAYA KNOW!
ZZ
TEWELEE, HONEY--TAKE NOTHER DRINK, YOU'LL EED IT! WE'RE PLAYING A GAME, AND IT'S YOUR TURN!
HUH--? OH. GUESS 'M...'M NOT USED TO... STAYIN' UP THIS LATE... NO MORE...
WHAT'RE WE PLAYIN'...?
TRUTH...
...OR DARE!
'KAY... 'KAY... GIMME A TRUTH. M'READY...

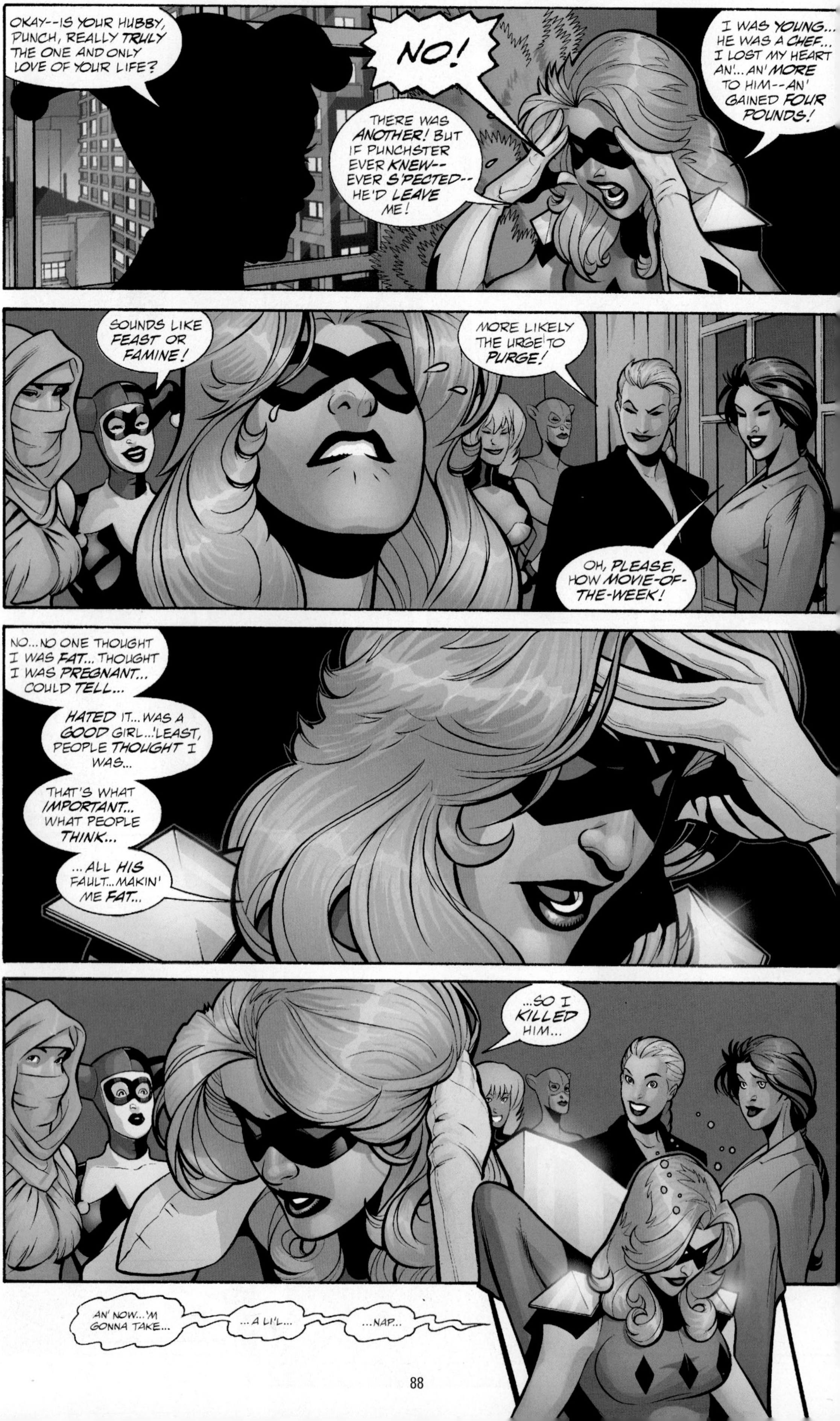
OKAY--IS YOUR HUBBY, PUNCH, REALLY TRULY THE ONE AND ONLY LOVE OF YOUR LIFE?
NO!
THERE WAS ANOTHER! BUT IF PUNCHSTER EVER KNEW-- EVER S'PECTED-- HE'D LEAVE ME!
I WAS YOUNG... HE WAS A CHEF... I LOST MY HEART AN'... AN' MORE TO HIM--AN' GAINED FOUR POUNDS!
SOUNDS LIKE FEAST OR FAMINE!
MORE LIKELY THE URGE TO PURGE!
OH, PLEASE, HOW MOVIE-OF-THE-WEEK!
NO... NO ONE THOUGHT I WAS FAT... THOUGHT I WAS PREGNANT... COULD TELL...
HATED IT... WAS A GOOD GIRL...'LEAST, PEOPLE THOUGHT I WAS...
THAT'S WHAT IMPORTANT... WHAT PEOPLE THINK...
...ALL HIS FAULT... MAKIN' ME FAT...
...SO I KILLED HIM...
AN' NOW... 'M GONNA TAKE...
...A LI'L...
...NAP...

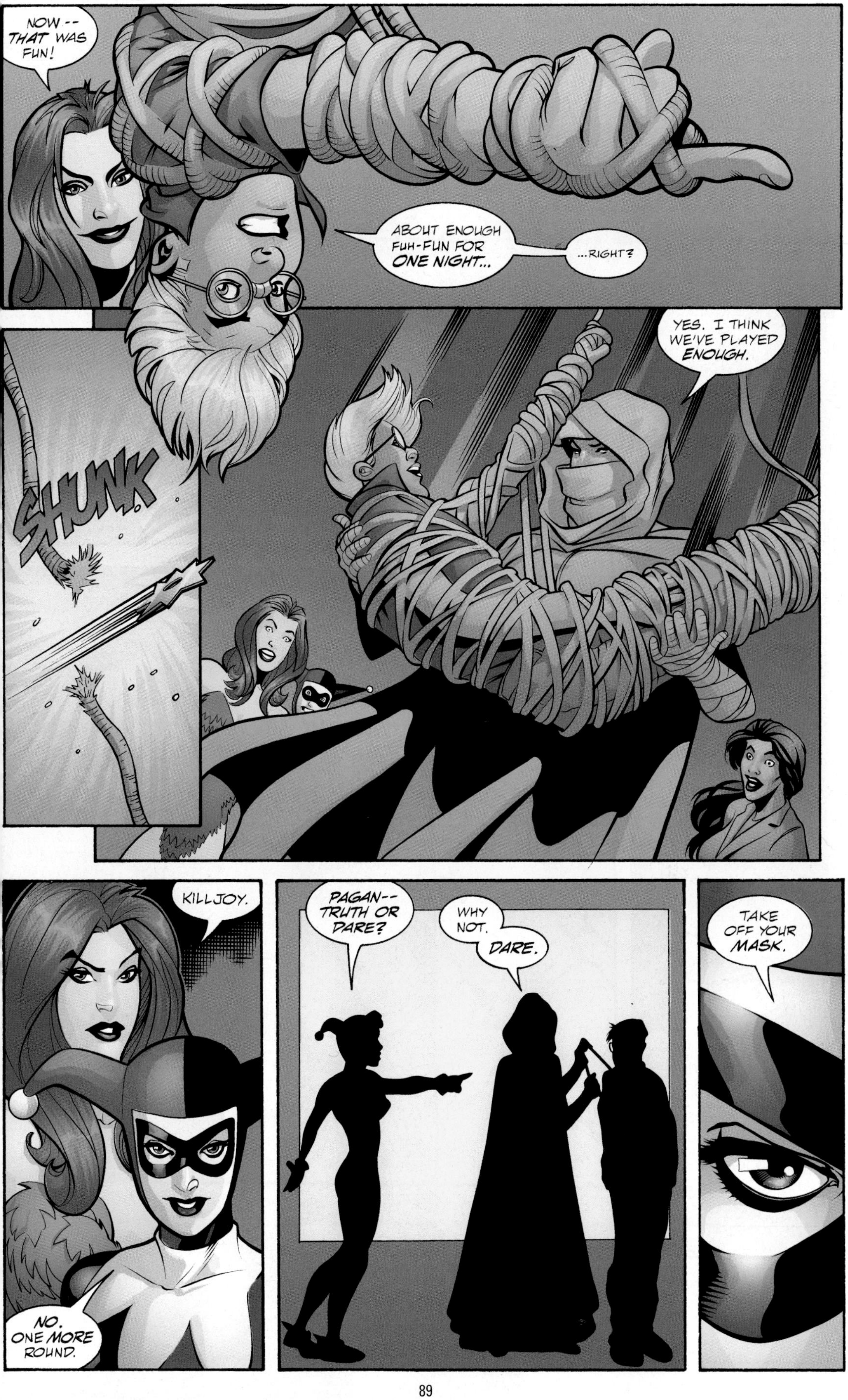
NOW -- THAT WAS FUN!
ABOUT ENOUGH FUH-FUN FOR ONE NIGHT...
...RIGHT?
YES. I THINK WE'VE PLAYED ENOUGH.
SHUNK
KILLJOY.
NO. ONE MORE ROUND.
PAGAN-- TRUTH OR DARE?
WHY NOT. DARE.
TAKE OFF YOUR MASK.

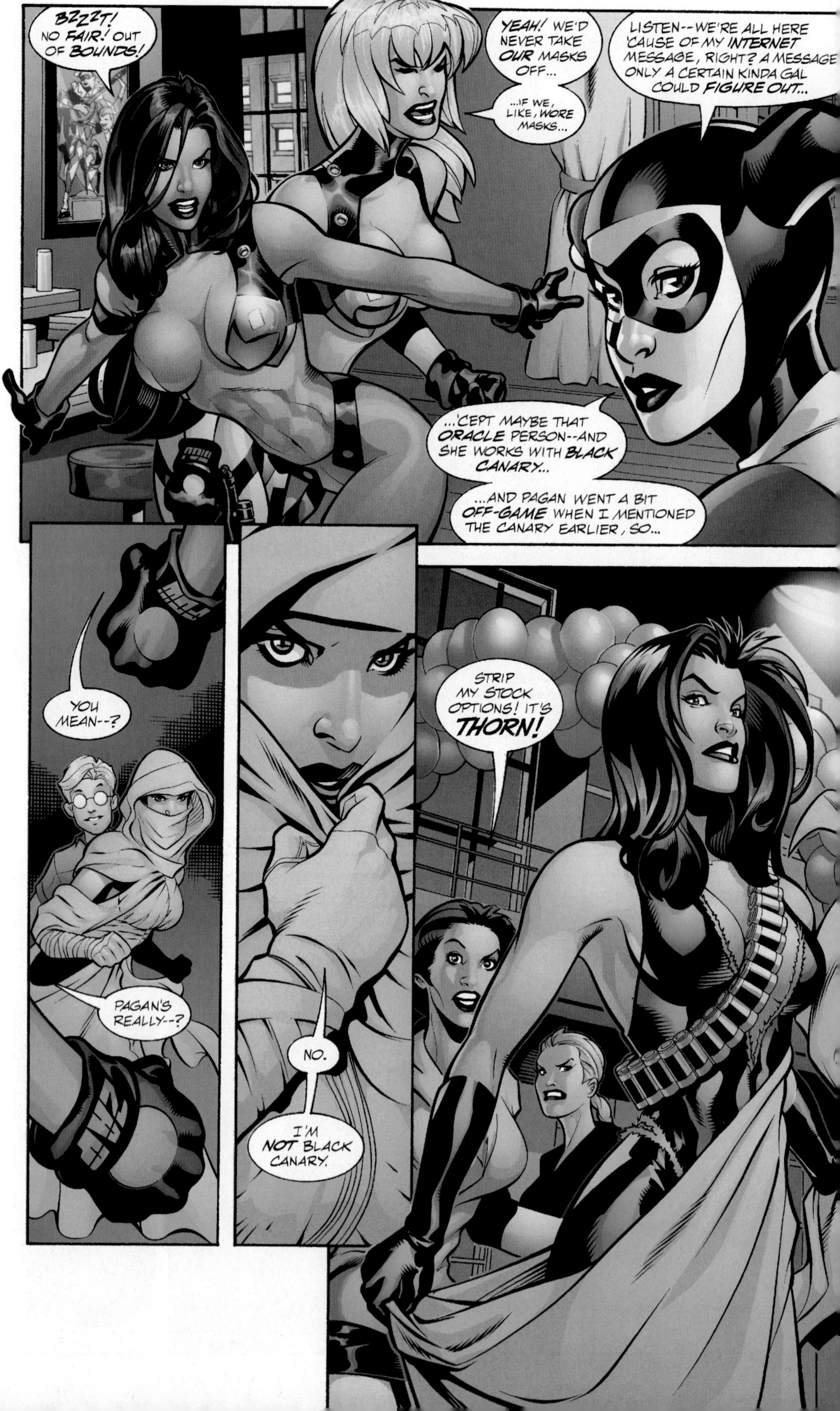

BZZZT! NO FAIR! OUT OF BOUNDS!
YEAH! WE'D NEVER TAKE OUR MASKS OFF...
...IF WE, LIKE, WORE MASKS...
LISTEN--WE'RE ALL HERE 'CAUSE OF MY INTERNET MESSAGE, RIGHT? A MESSAGE ONLY A CERTAIN KINDA GAL COULD FIGURE OUT...
...'CEPT MAYBE THAT ORACLE PERSON--AND SHE WORKS WITH BLACK CANARY...
...AND PAGAN WENT A BIT OFF-GAME WHEN I MENTIONED THE CANARY EARLIER, SO...
YOU MEAN--?
PAGAN'S REALLY--?
NO.
I'M NOT BLACK CANARY.
STRIP MY STOCK OPTIONS! IT'S THORN!

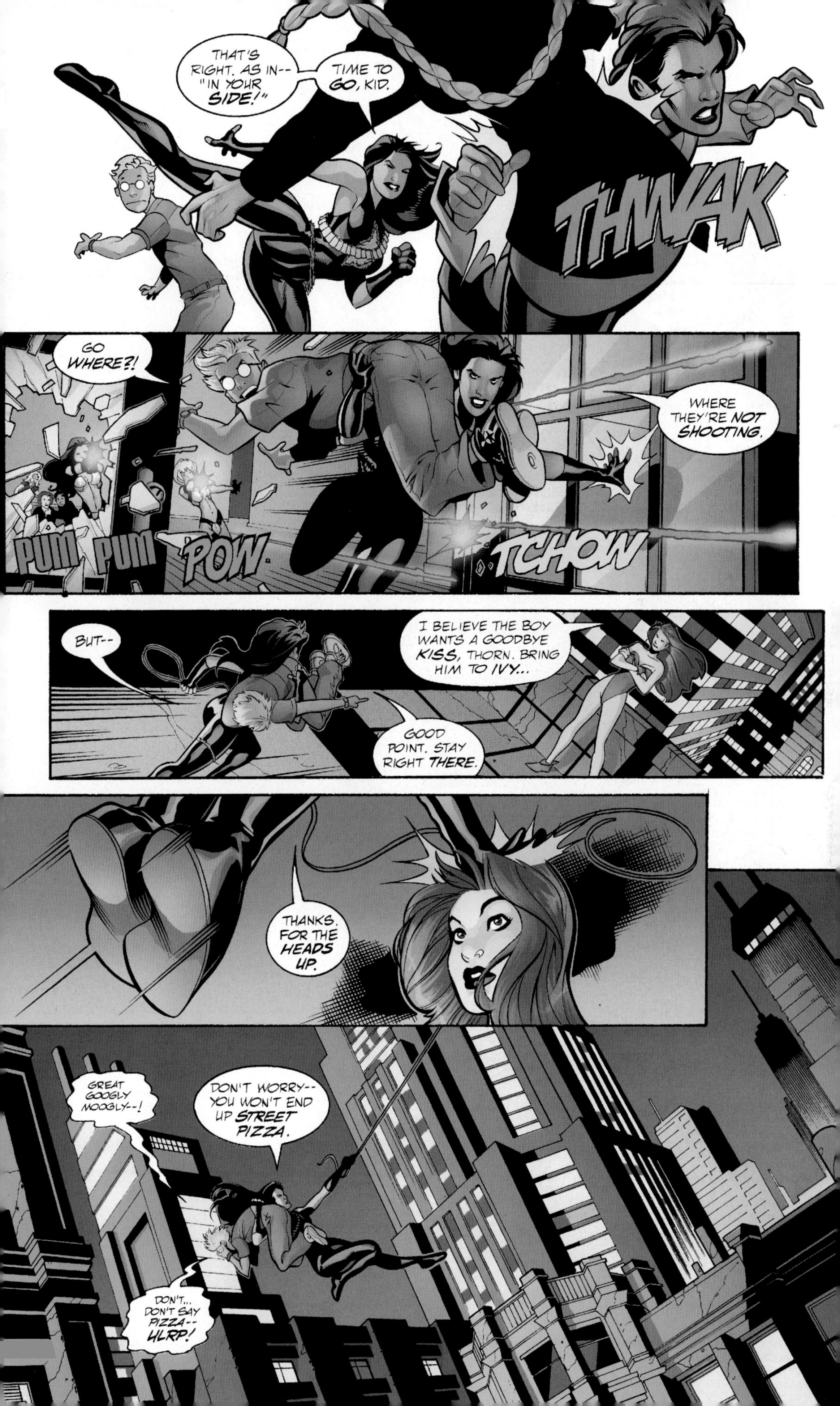

THAT'S RIGHT. AS IN-- "IN YOUR SIDE!"
TIME TO GO, KID.
THWAK
GO WHERE?!
WHERE THEY'RE NOT SHOOTING.
PUM PUM POW
TCHOW
BUT--
I BELIEVE THE BOY WANTS A GOODBYE KISS, THORN. BRING HIM TO IVY...
GOOD POINT. STAY RIGHT THERE.
THANKS. FOR THE HEADS UP.
GREAT GOOGLY MOOGLY--!
DON'T WORRY-- YOU WON'T END UP STREET PIZZA.
DON'T... DON'T SAY PIZZA-- ULRP!

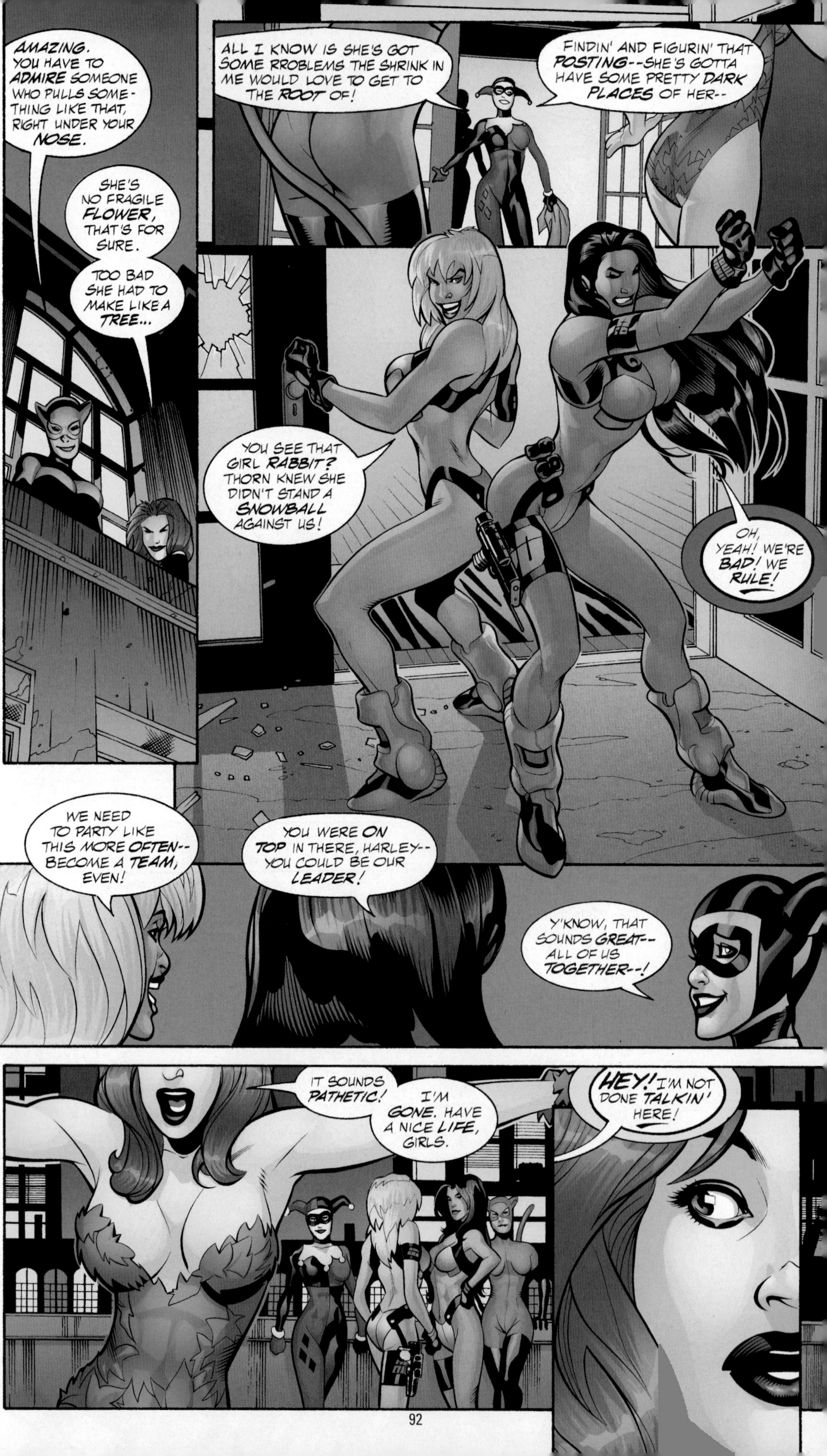

AMAZING. YOU HAVE TO ADMIRE SOMEONE WHO PULLS SOME-THING LIKE THAT, RIGHT UNDER YOUR NOSE.
ALL I KNOW IS SHE'S GOT SOME RROBLEMS THE SHRINK IN ME WOULD LOVE TO GET TO THE ROOT OF!
FINDIN' AND FIGURIN' THAT POSTING--SHE'S GOTTA HAVE SOME PRETTY DARK PLACES OF HER--
SHE'S NO FRAGILE FLOWER, THAT'S FOR SURE.
TOO BAD SHE HAD TO MAKE LIKE A TREE...
YOU SEE THAT GIRL RABBIT? THORN KNEW SHE DIDN'T STAND A SNOWBALL AGAINST US!
OH, YEAH! WE'RE BAD! WE RULE!
WE NEED TO PARTY LIKE THIS MORE OFTEN--BECOME A TEAM, EVEN!
YOU WERE ON TOP IN THERE, HARLEY--YOU COULD BE OUR LEADER!
Y'KNOW, THAT SOUNDS GREAT--ALL OF US TOGETHER--!
IT SOUNDS PATHETIC!
I'M GONE. HAVE A NICE LIFE, GIRLS.
HEY! I'M NOT DONE TALKIN' HERE!

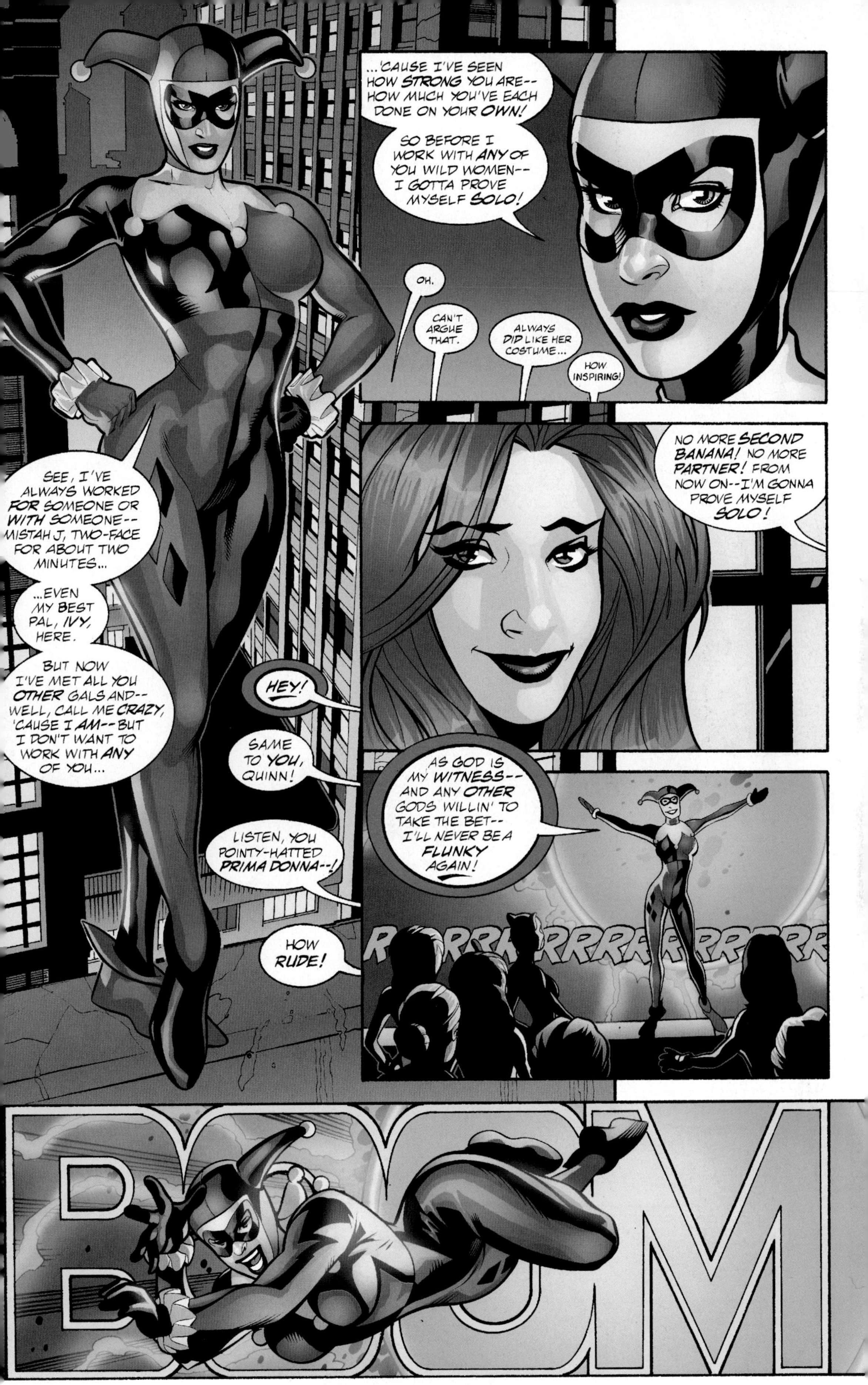
...'CAUSE I'VE SEEN HOW STRONG YOU ARE-- HOW MUCH YOU'VE EACH DONE ON YOUR OWN!
SO BEFORE I WORK WITH ANY OF YOU WILD WOMEN-- I GOTTA PROVE MYSELF SOLO!
OH.
CAN'T ARGUE THAT.
ALWAYS DID LIKE HER COSTUME...
HOW INSPIRING!
SEE, I'VE ALWAYS WORKED FOR SOMEONE OR WITH SOMEONE-- MISTAH J, TWO-FACE FOR ABOUT TWO MINUTES...
...EVEN MY BEST PAL, IVY, HERE.
BUT NOW I'VE MET ALL YOU OTHER GALS AND-- WELL, CALL ME CRAZY, 'CAUSE I AM--BUT I DON'T WANT TO WORK WITH ANY OF YOU...
HEY!
SAME TO YOU, QUINN!
LISTEN, YOU POINTY-HATTED PRIMA DONNA--!
HOW RUDE!
NO MORE SECOND BANANA! NO MORE PARTNER! FROM NOW ON--I'M GONNA PROVE MYSELF SOLO!
AS GOD IS MY WITNESS-- AND ANY OTHER GODS WILLIN' TO TAKE THE BET-- I'LL NEVER BE A FLUNKY AGAIN!
RRRRRRRRRRRRRRRR
BOOM

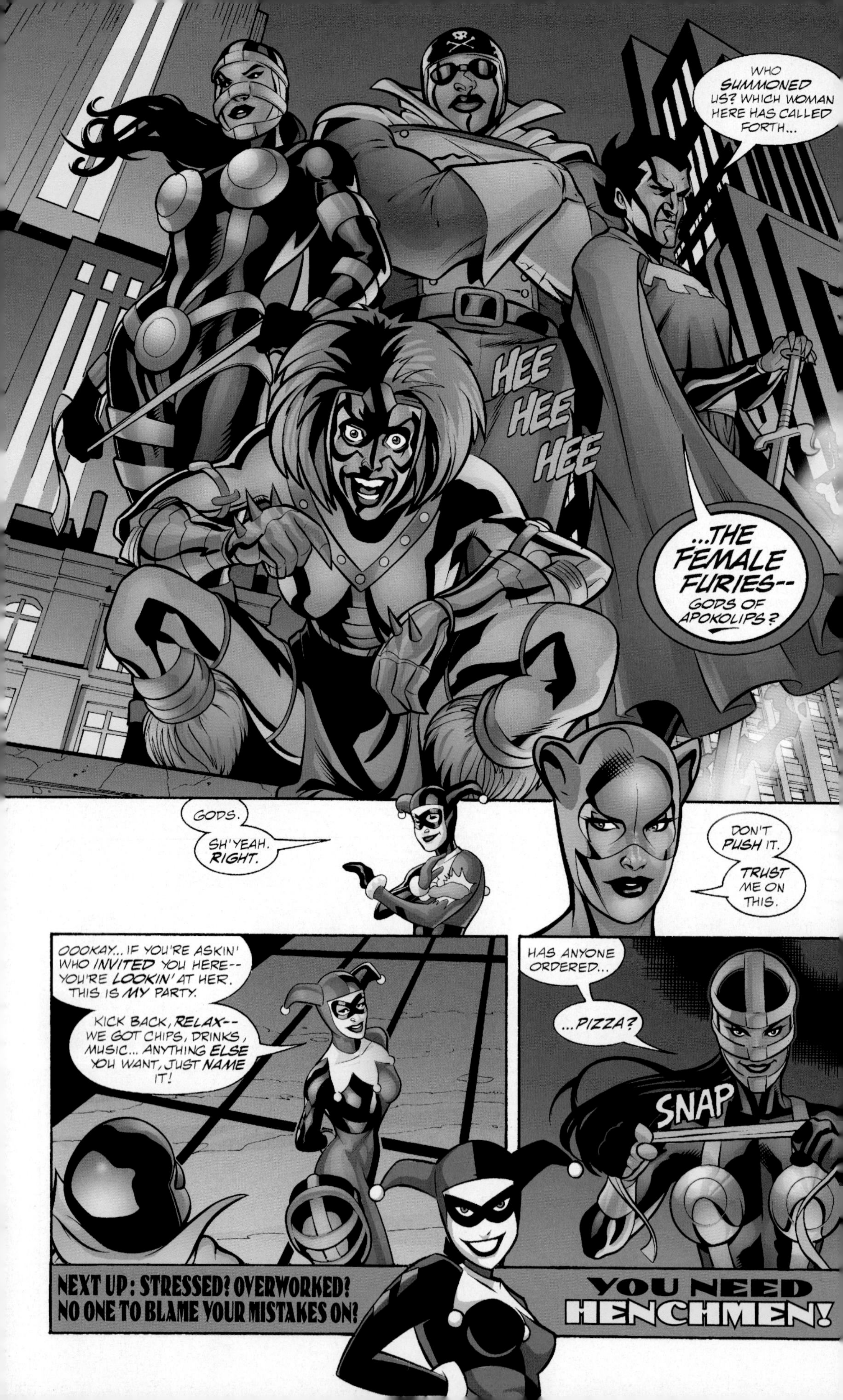
WHO SUMMONED US? WHICH WOMAN HERE HAS CALLED FORTH...
HEE HEE HEE
...THE FEMALE FURIES-- GODS OF APOKOLIPS?
GODS.
SH'YEAH. RIGHT.
DON'T PUSH IT.
TRUST ME ON THIS.
OOOKAY... IF YOU'RE ASKIN' WHO INVITED YOU HERE-- YOU'RE LOOKIN' AT HER. THIS IS MY PARTY.
KICK BACK, RELAX-- WE GOT CHIPS, DRINKS, MUSIC... ANYTHING ELSE YOU WANT, JUST NAME IT!
HAS ANYONE ORDERED...
...PIZZA?
SNAP
NEXT UP : STRESSED? OVERWORKED? NO ONE TO BLAME YOUR MISTAKES ON?
YOU NEED HENCHMEN!

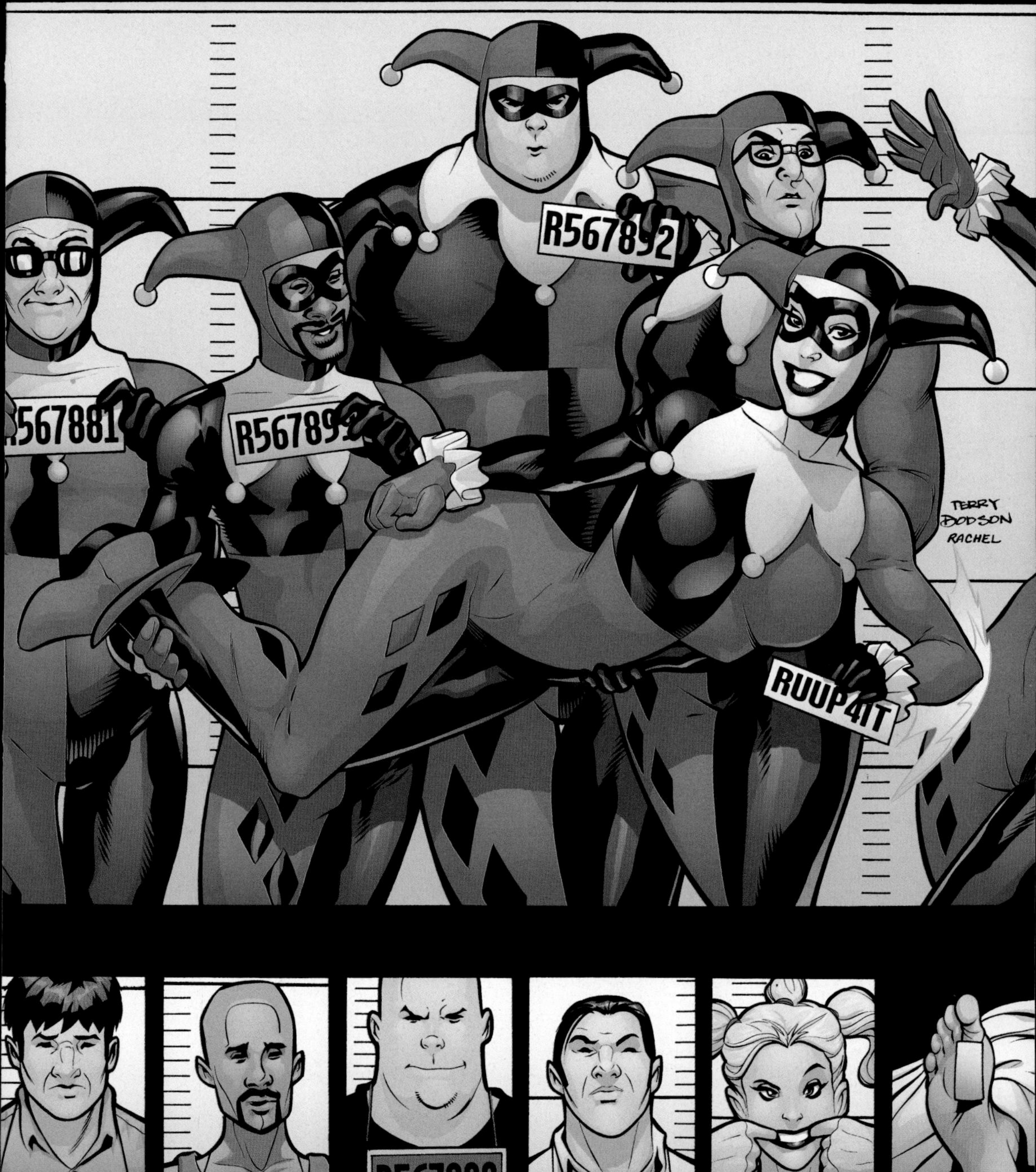
R567881
R56789
R567892
RUUP4IT
TERRY
DODSON
RACHEL

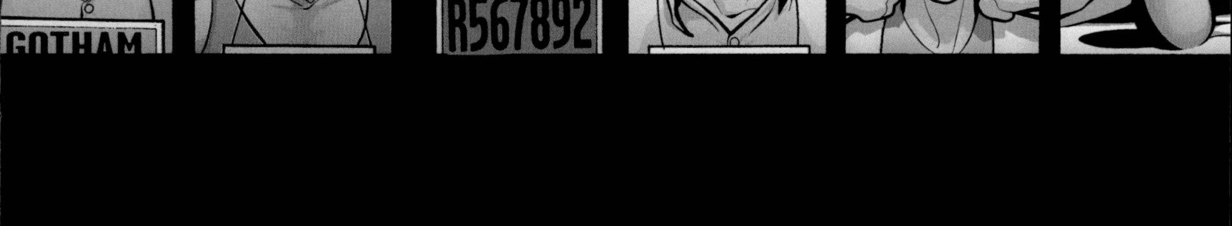
GOTHAM
R567892

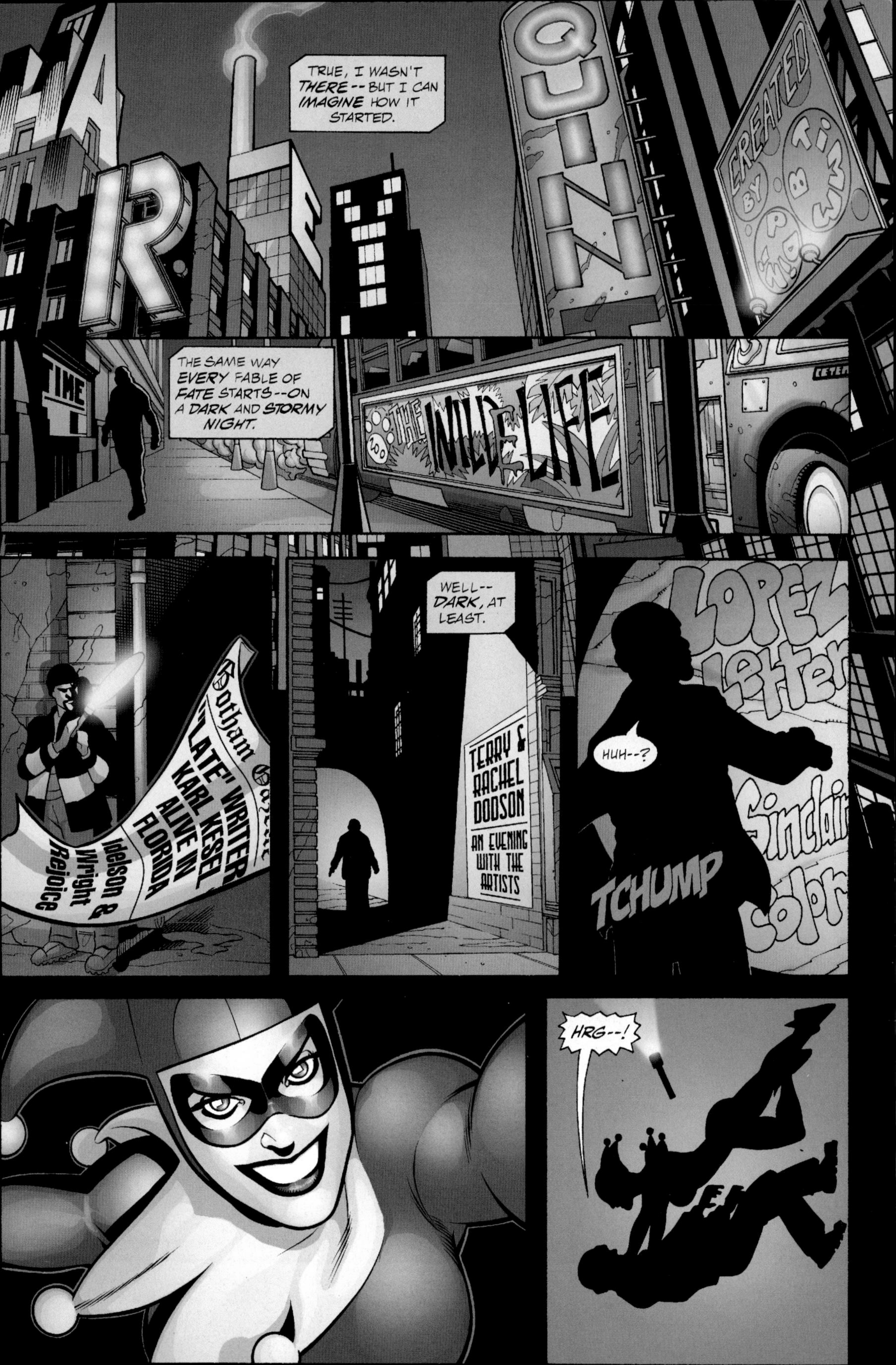
TRUE, I WASN'T THERE--BUT I CAN IMAGINE HOW IT STARTED.
QUINN
CREATED BY
THE SAME WAY EVERY FABLE OF FATE STARTS--ON A DARK AND STORMY NIGHT.
TIME
THE WILDE LIFE
"LATE" WRITER KARL KESEL ALIVE IN FLORIDA
Idelson & Wright Rejoice
WELL--DARK, AT LEAST.
TERRY & RACHEL DODSON
AN EVENING WITH THE ARTISTS
LOPEZ
Sinclair
HUH--?
TCHUMP
HRG--!

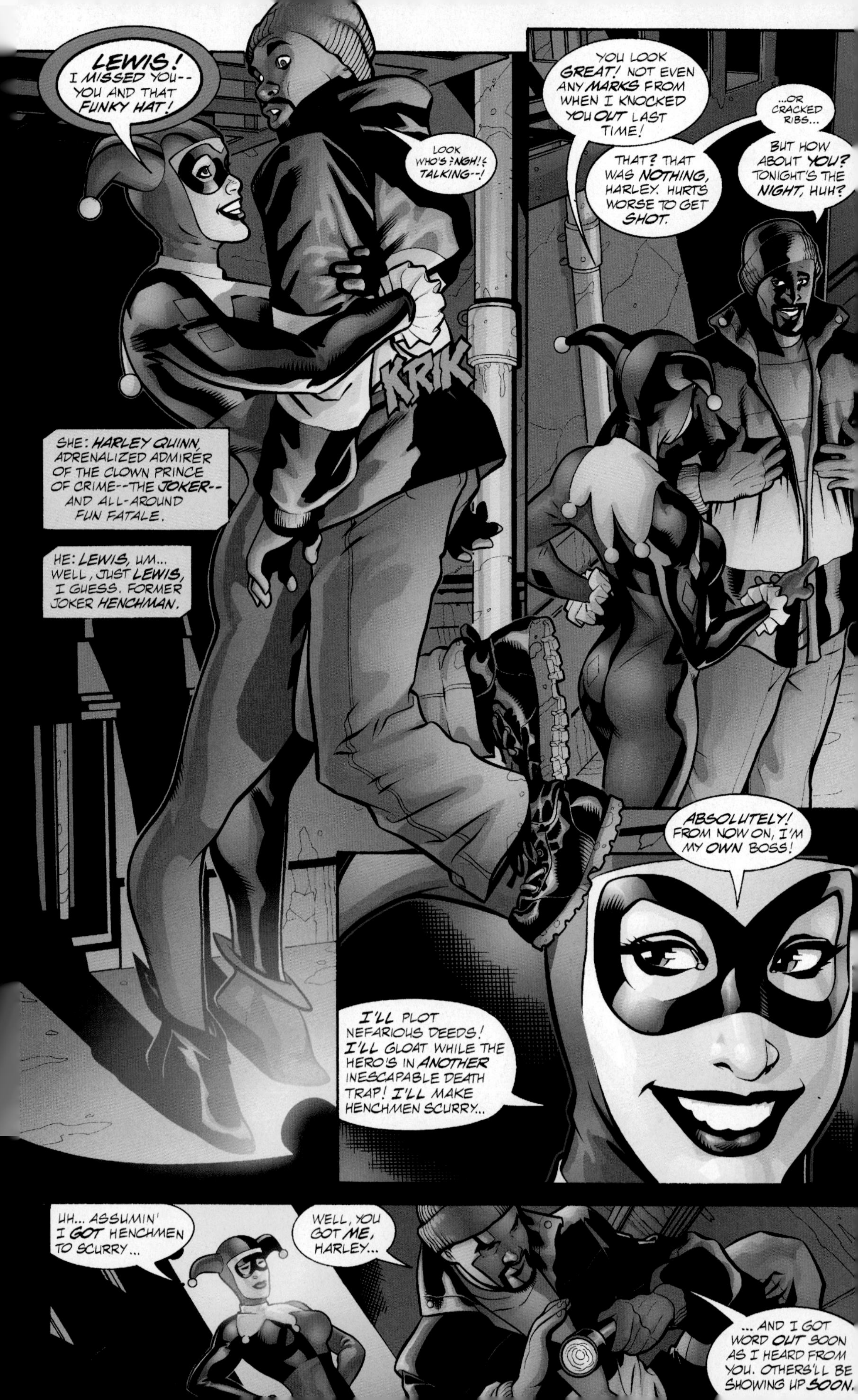

LEWIS! I MISSED YOU-- YOU AND THAT FUNKY HAT!
LOOK WHO'S ?NGH!¿ TALKING--!
KRIK
SHE: HARLEY QUINN, ADRENALIZED ADMIRER OF THE CLOWN PRINCE OF CRIME--THE JOKER-- AND ALL-AROUND FUN FATALE.
HE: LEWIS, UM... WELL, JUST LEWIS, I GUESS. FORMER JOKER HENCHMAN.
YOU LOOK GREAT! NOT EVEN ANY MARKS FROM WHEN I KNOCKED YOU OUT LAST TIME!
THAT? THAT WAS NOTHING, HARLEY. HURTS WORSE TO GET SHOT.
...OR CRACKED RIBS...
BUT HOW ABOUT YOU? TONIGHT'S THE NIGHT, HUH?
ABSOLUTELY! FROM NOW ON, I'M MY OWN BOSS!
I'LL PLOT NEFARIOUS DEEDS! I'LL GLOAT WHILE THE HERO'S IN ANOTHER INESCAPABLE DEATH TRAP! I'LL MAKE HENCHMEN SCURRY...
UH... ASSUMIN' I GOT HENCHMEN TO SCURRY...
WELL, YOU GOT ME, HARLEY...
... AND I GOT WORD OUT SOON AS I HEARD FROM YOU. OTHERS'LL BE SHOWING UP SOON.

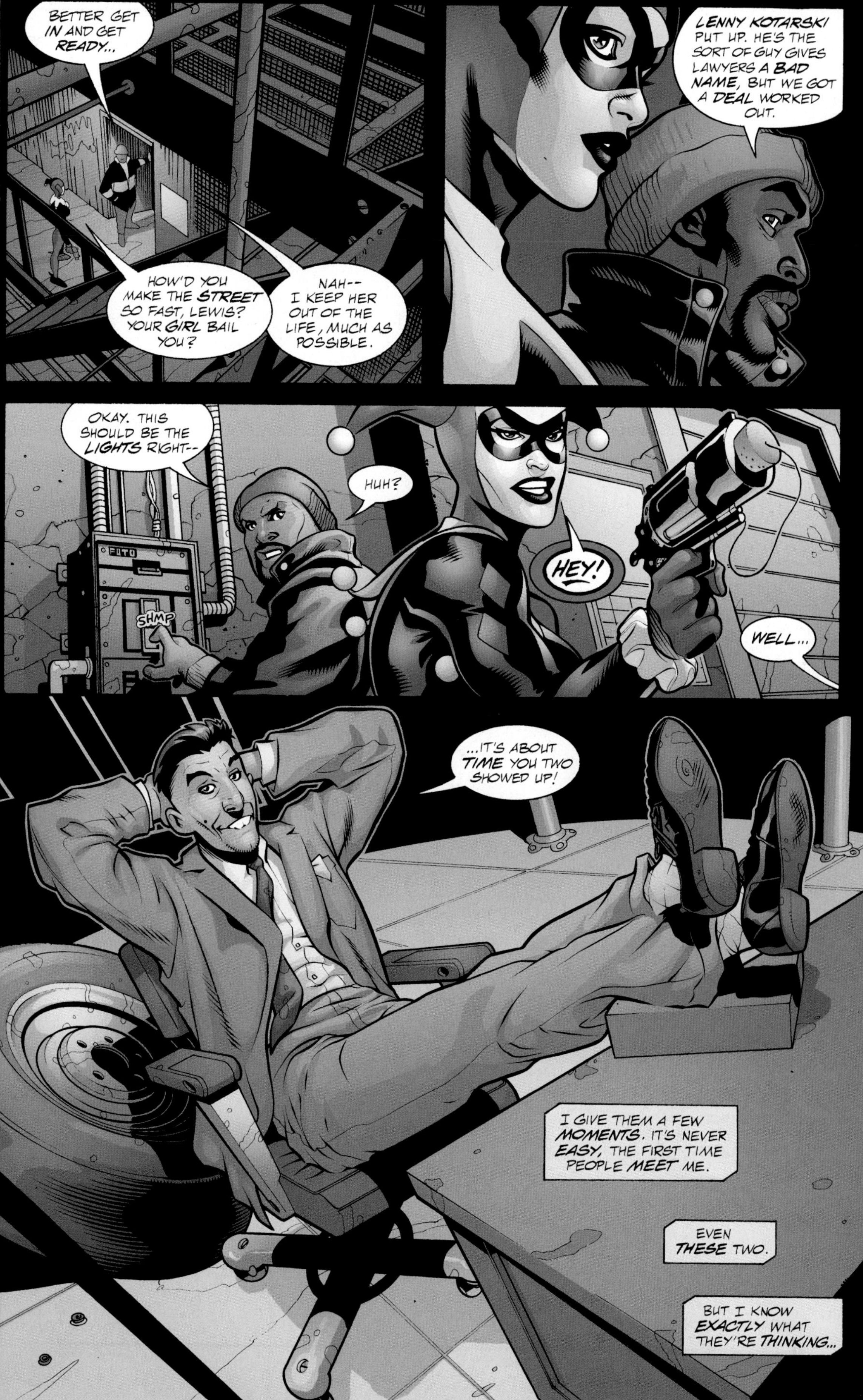
BETTER GET IN AND GET READY...
HOW'D YOU MAKE THE STREET SO FAST, LEWIS? YOUR GIRL BAIL YOU?
NAH-- I KEEP HER OUT OF THE LIFE, MUCH AS POSSIBLE.
LENNY KOTARSKI PUT UP. HE'S THE SORT OF GUY GIVES LAWYERS A BAD NAME, BUT WE GOT A DEAL WORKED OUT.
OKAY. THIS SHOULD BE THE LIGHTS RIGHT--
SHMP
HUH?
HEY!
WELL...
...IT'S ABOUT TIME YOU TWO SHOWED UP!
I GIVE THEM A FEW MOMENTS. IT'S NEVER EASY, THE FIRST TIME PEOPLE MEET ME.
EVEN THESE TWO.
BUT I KNOW EXACTLY WHAT THEY'RE THINKING...

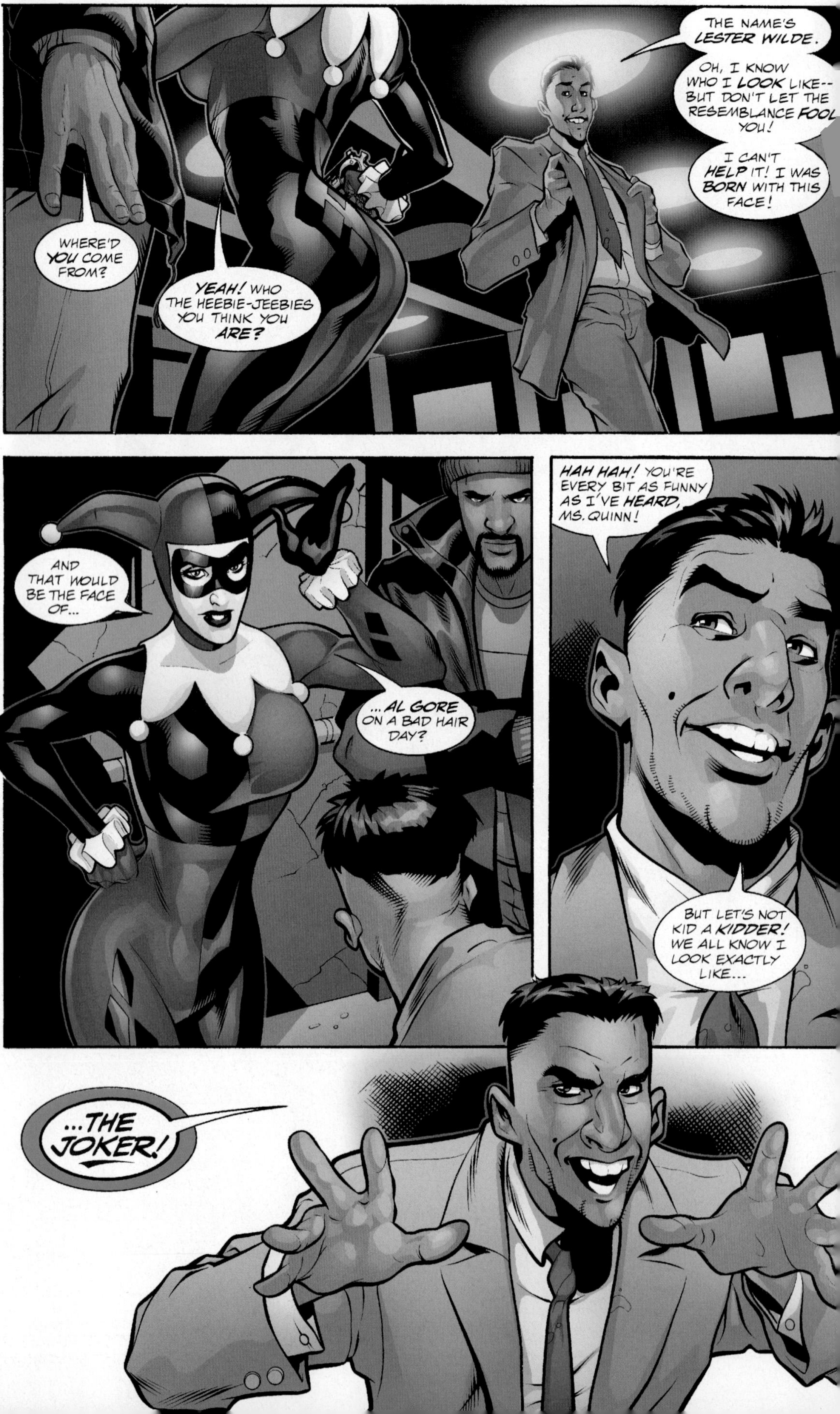
THE NAME'S LESTER WILDE.
OH, I KNOW WHO I LOOK LIKE--BUT DON'T LET THE RESEMBLANCE FOOL YOU!
I CAN'T HELP IT! I WAS BORN WITH THIS FACE!
WHERE'D YOU COME FROM?
YEAH! WHO THE HEEBIE-JEEBIES YOU THINK YOU ARE?
AND THAT WOULD BE THE FACE OF...
...AL GORE ON A BAD HAIR DAY?
HAH HAH! YOU'RE EVERY BIT AS FUNNY AS I'VE HEARD, MS. QUINN!
BUT LET'S NOT KID A KIDDER! WE ALL KNOW I LOOK EXACTLY LIKE...
...THE JOKER!

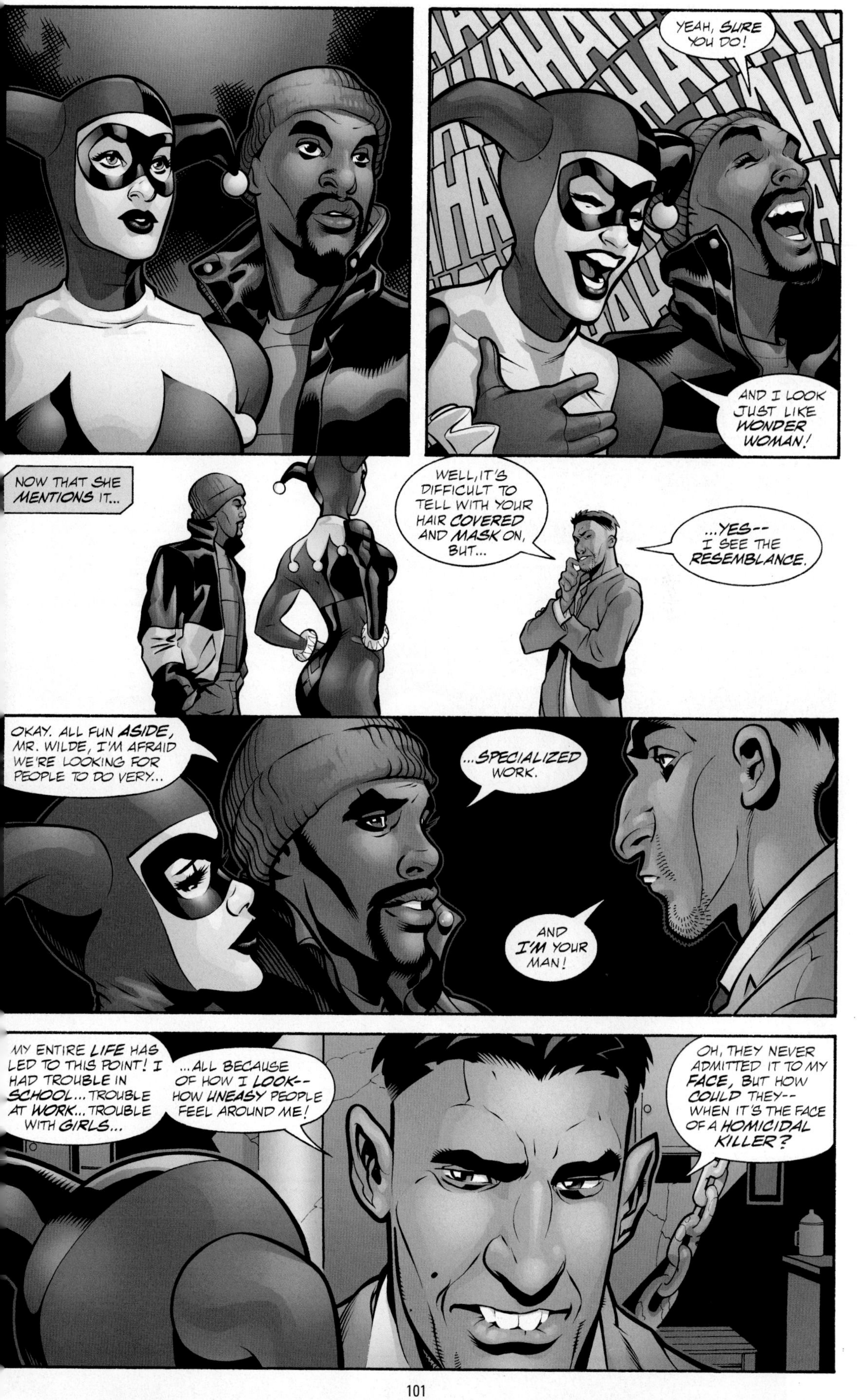
HAHAHA
YEAH, SURE YOU DO!
AND I LOOK JUST LIKE WONDER WOMAN!
NOW THAT SHE MENTIONS IT...
WELL, IT'S DIFFICULT TO TELL WITH YOUR HAIR COVERED AND MASK ON, BUT...
...YES-- I SEE THE RESEMBLANCE.
OKAY. ALL FUN ASIDE, MR. WILDE, I'M AFRAID WE'RE LOOKING FOR PEOPLE TO DO VERY...
...SPECIALIZED WORK.
AND I'M YOUR MAN!
MY ENTIRE LIFE HAS LED TO THIS POINT! I HAD TROUBLE IN SCHOOL... TROUBLE AT WORK... TROUBLE WITH GIRLS...
...ALL BECAUSE OF HOW I LOOK-- HOW UNEASY PEOPLE FEEL AROUND ME!
OH, THEY NEVER ADMITTED IT TO MY FACE, BUT HOW COULD THEY-- WHEN IT'S THE FACE OF A HOMICIDAL KILLER?

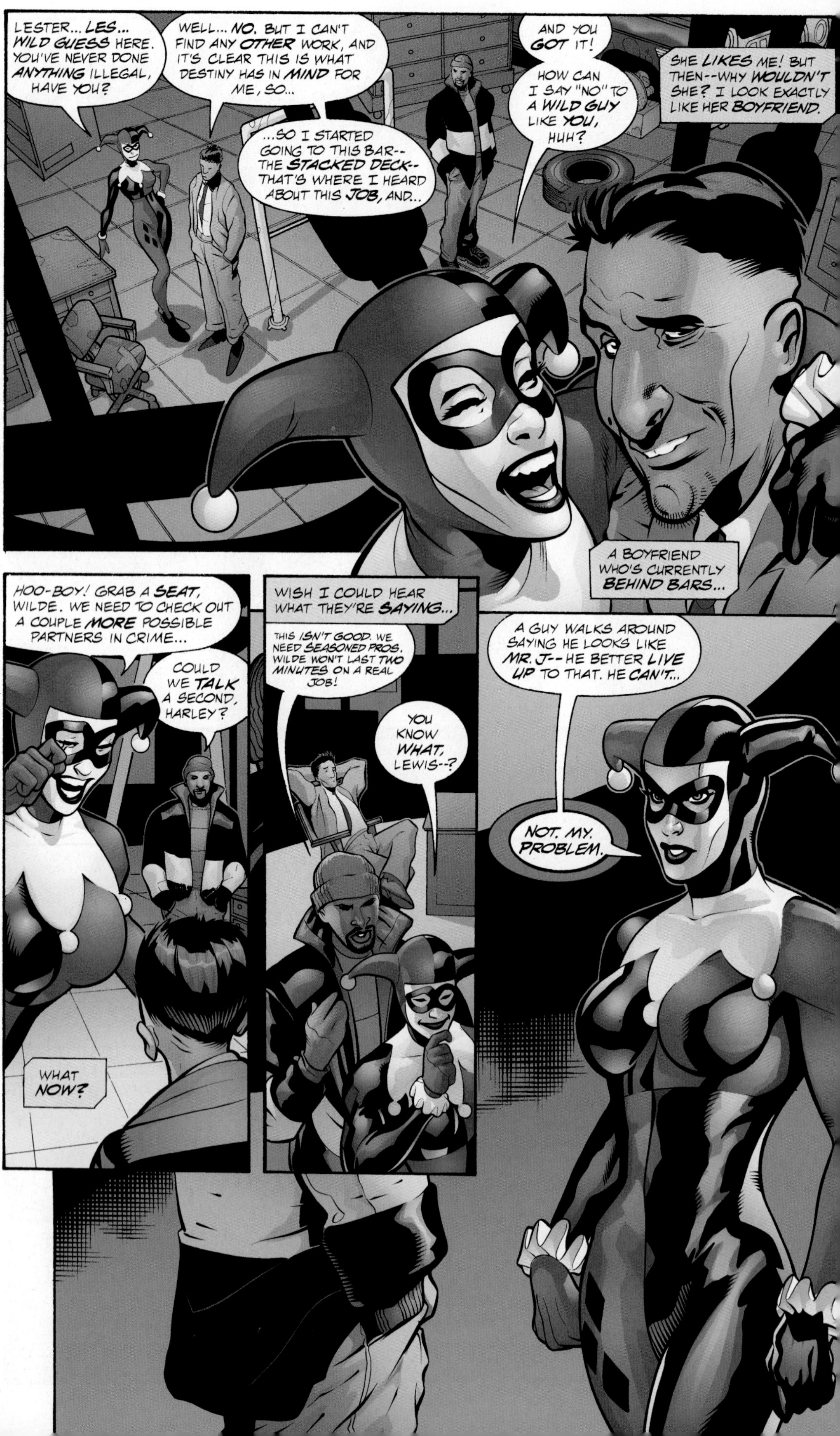
LESTER... LES... WILD GUESS HERE. YOU'VE NEVER DONE ANYTHING ILLEGAL, HAVE YOU?
WELL... NO. BUT I CAN'T FIND ANY OTHER WORK, AND IT'S CLEAR THIS IS WHAT DESTINY HAS IN MIND FOR ME, SO...
...SO I STARTED GOING TO THIS BAR-- THE STACKED DECK-- THAT'S WHERE I HEARD ABOUT THIS JOB, AND...
AND YOU GOT IT!
HOW CAN I SAY "NO" TO A WILD GUY LIKE YOU, HUH?
SHE LIKES ME! BUT THEN--WHY WOULDN'T SHE? I LOOK EXACTLY LIKE HER BOYFRIEND.
A BOYFRIEND WHO'S CURRENTLY BEHIND BARS...
HOO-BOY! GRAB A SEAT, WILDE. WE NEED TO CHECK OUT A COUPLE MORE POSSIBLE PARTNERS IN CRIME...
COULD WE TALK A SECOND, HARLEY?
WHAT NOW?
WISH I COULD HEAR WHAT THEY'RE SAYING...
THIS ISN'T GOOD. WE NEED SEASONED PROS. WILDE WON'T LAST TWO MINUTES ON A REAL JOB!
YOU KNOW WHAT, LEWIS--?
A GUY WALKS AROUND SAYING HE LOOKS LIKE MR. J-- HE BETTER LIVE UP TO THAT. HE CAN'T...
NOT. MY. PROBLEM.

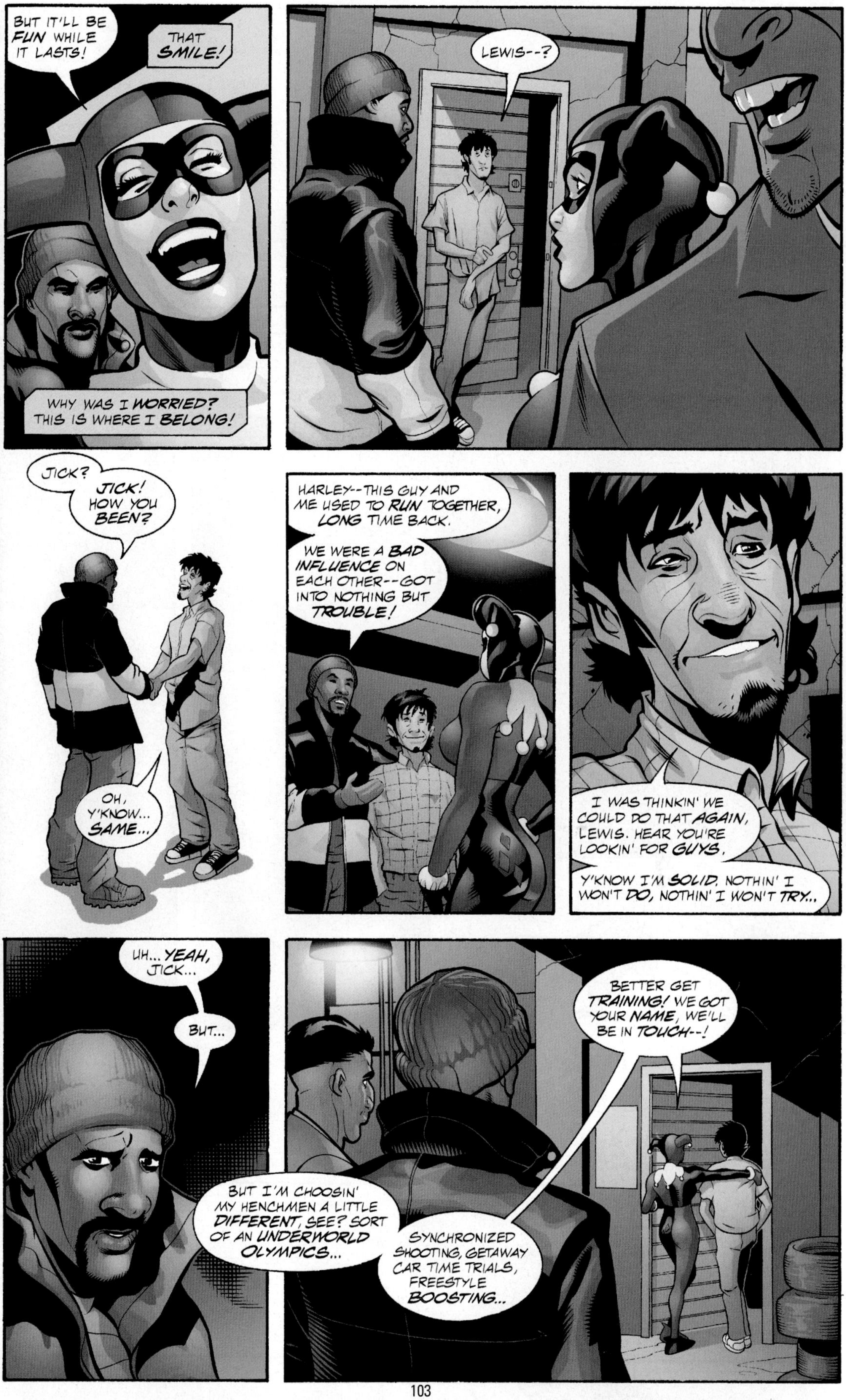

BUT IT'LL BE FUN WHILE IT LASTS!
THAT SMILE!
WHY WAS I WORRIED? THIS IS WHERE I BELONG!
LEWIS--?
JICK? JICK! HOW YOU BEEN?
OH, Y'KNOW... SAME...
HARLEY--THIS GUY AND ME USED TO RUN TOGETHER, LONG TIME BACK.
WE WERE A BAD INFLUENCE ON EACH OTHER--GOT INTO NOTHING BUT TROUBLE!
I WAS THINKIN' WE COULD DO THAT AGAIN, LEWIS. HEAR YOU'RE LOOKIN' FOR GUYS.
Y'KNOW I'M SOLID. NOTHIN' I WON'T DO, NOTHIN' I WON'T TRY...
UH... YEAH, JICK...
BUT...
BUT I'M CHOOSIN' MY HENCHMEN A LITTLE DIFFERENT, SEE? SORT OF AN UNDERWORLD OLYMPICS...
SYNCHRONIZED SHOOTING, GETAWAY CAR TIME TRIALS, FREESTYLE BOOSTING...
BETTER GET TRAINING! WE GOT YOUR NAME, WE'LL BE IN TOUCH--!

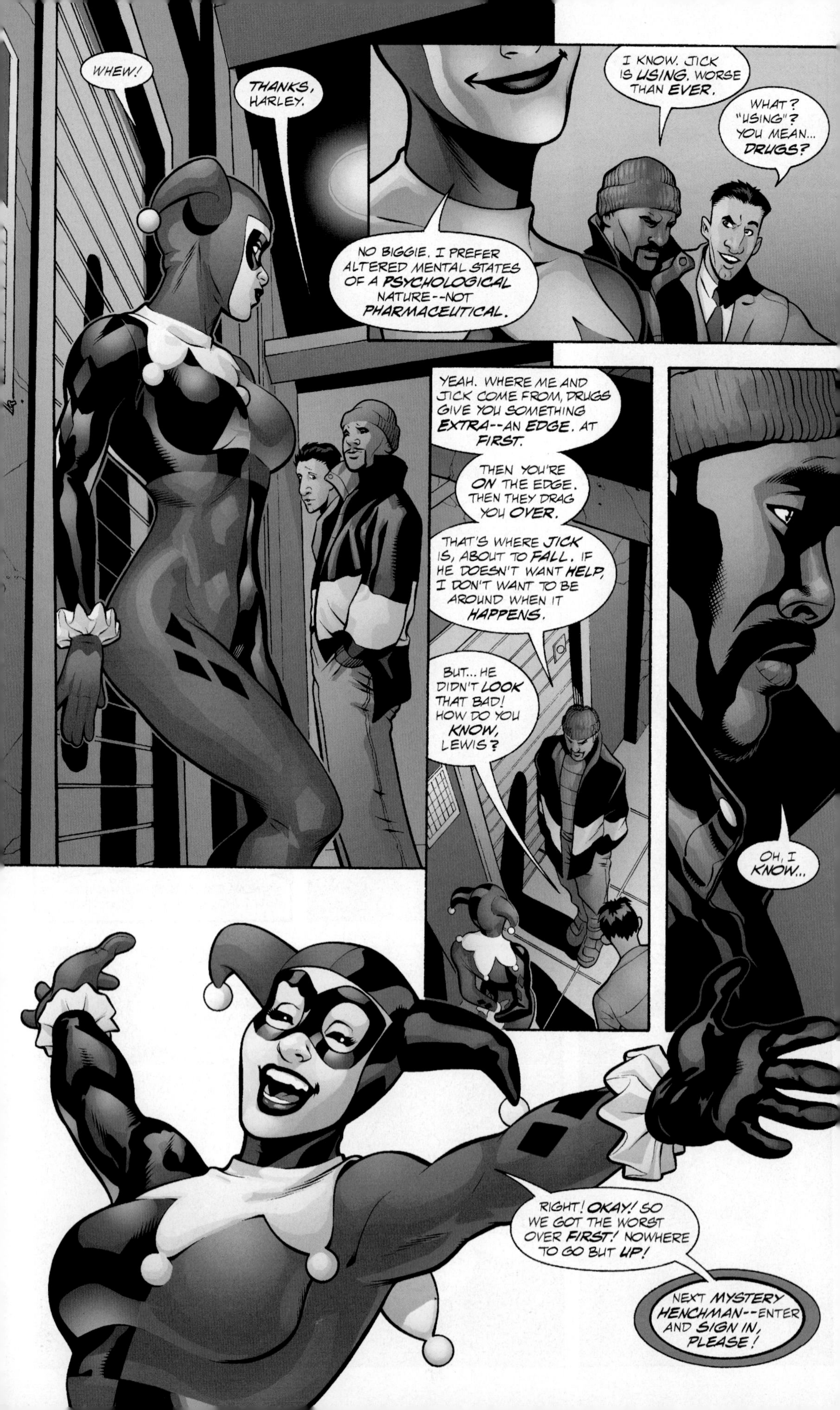
WHEW!
THANKS, HARLEY.
I KNOW. JICK IS USING. WORSE THAN EVER.
WHAT? "USING"? YOU MEAN... DRUGS?
NO BIGGIE. I PREFER ALTERED MENTAL STATES OF A PSYCHOLOGICAL NATURE--NOT PHARMACEUTICAL.
YEAH. WHERE ME AND JICK COME FROM, DRUGS GIVE YOU SOMETHING EXTRA--AN EDGE. AT FIRST.
THEN YOU'RE ON THE EDGE. THEN THEY DRAG YOU OVER.
THAT'S WHERE JICK IS, ABOUT TO FALL. IF HE DOESN'T WANT HELP, I DON'T WANT TO BE AROUND WHEN IT HAPPENS.
BUT... HE DIDN'T LOOK THAT BAD! HOW DO YOU KNOW, LEWIS?
OH, I KNOW...
RIGHT! OKAY! SO WE GOT THE WORST OVER FIRST! NOWHERE TO GO BUT UP!
NEXT MYSTERY HENCHMAN--ENTER AND SIGN IN, PLEASE!

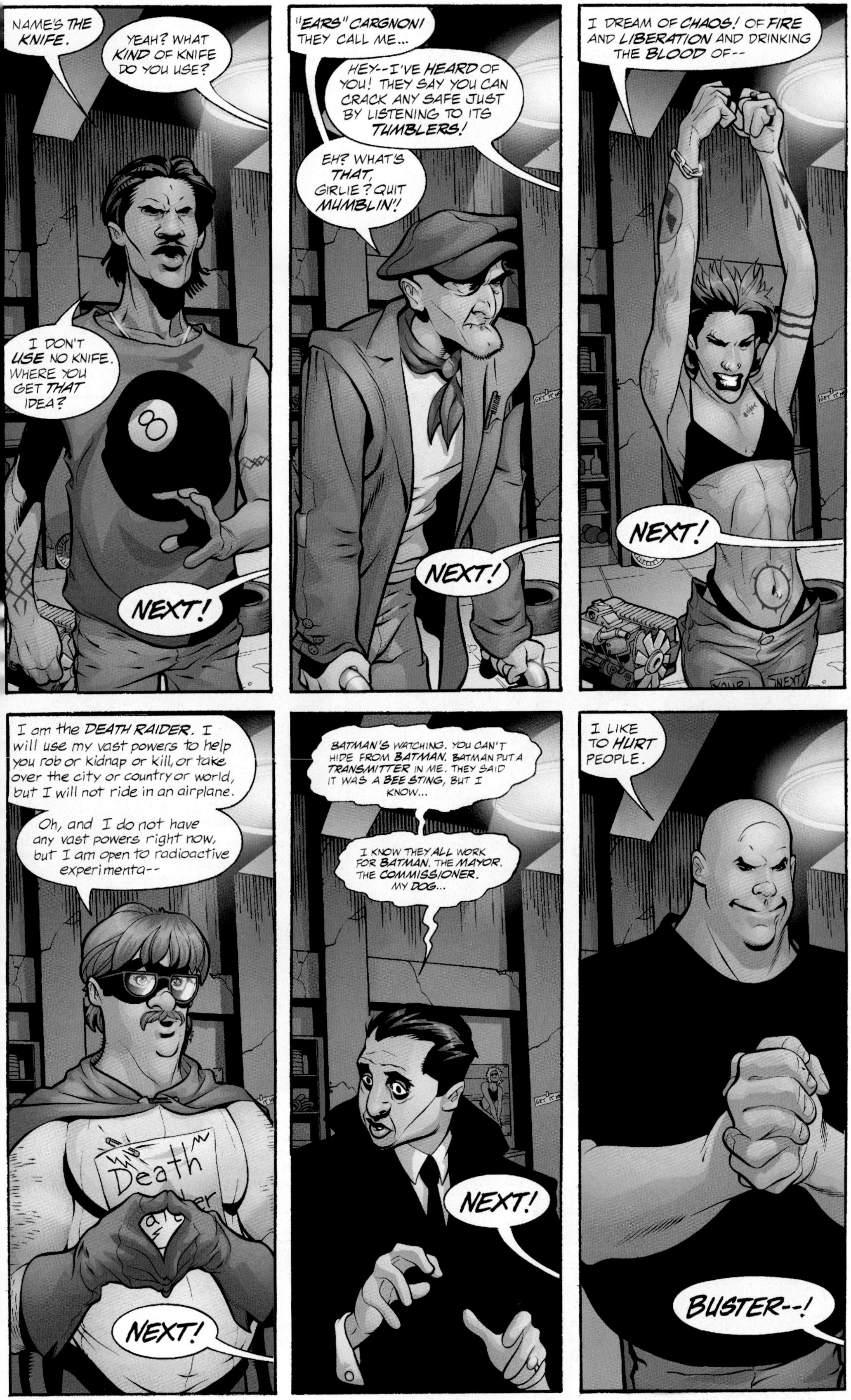
NAME'S THE KNIFE.
YEAH? WHAT KIND OF KNIFE DO YOU USE?
I DON'T USE NO KNIFE. WHERE YOU GET THAT IDEA?
NEXT!
"EARS" CARGNONI THEY CALL ME...
HEY--I'VE HEARD OF YOU! THEY SAY YOU CAN CRACK ANY SAFE JUST BY LISTENING TO ITS TUMBLERS!
EH? WHAT'S THAT, GIRLIE? QUIT MUMBLIN'!
NEXT!
I DREAM OF CHAOS! OF FIRE AND LIBERATION AND DRINKING THE BLOOD OF--
NEXT!
I am the DEATH RAIDER. I will use my vast powers to help you rob or kidnap or kill, or take over the city or country or world, but I will not ride in an airplane.
Oh, and I do not have any vast powers right now, but I am open to radioactive experimenta--
Death
NEXT!
BATMAN'S WATCHING. YOU CAN'T HIDE FROM BATMAN. BATMAN PUT A TRANSMITTER IN ME. THEY SAID IT WAS A BEE STING, BUT I KNOW...
I KNOW THEY ALL WORK FOR BATMAN. THE MAYOR. THE COMMISSIONER. MY DOG...
NEXT!
I LIKE TO HURT PEOPLE.
BUSTER--!

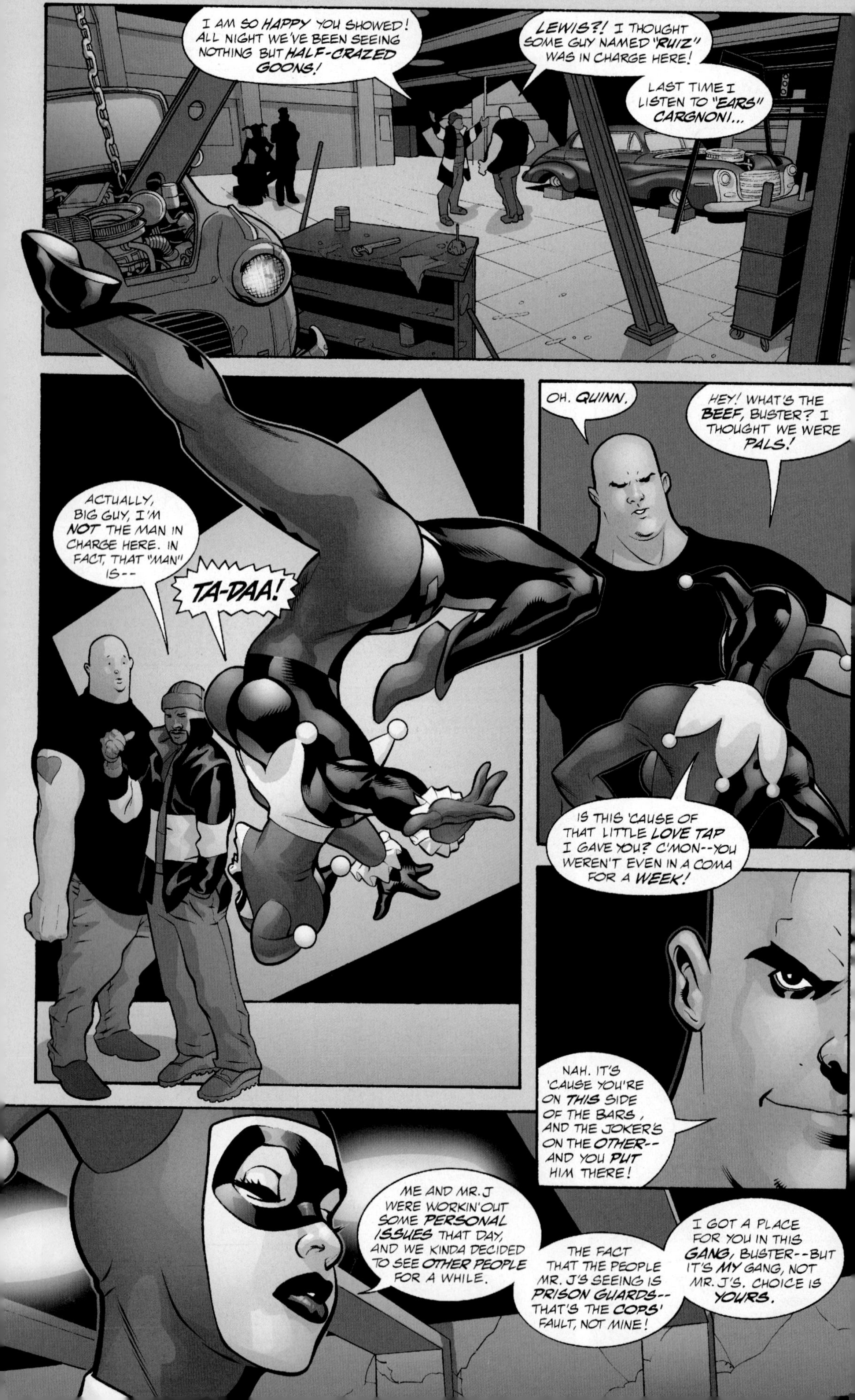
I AM SO HAPPY YOU SHOWED! ALL NIGHT WE'VE BEEN SEEING NOTHING BUT HALF-CRAZED GOONS!
LEWIS?! I THOUGHT SOME GUY NAMED "RUIZ" WAS IN CHARGE HERE!
LAST TIME I LISTEN TO "EARS" CARGNONI...
ACTUALLY, BIG GUY, I'M NOT THE MAN IN CHARGE HERE. IN FACT, THAT "MAN" IS--
TA-DAA!
OH. QUINN.
HEY! WHAT'S THE BEEF, BUSTER? I THOUGHT WE WERE PALS!
IS THIS 'CAUSE OF THAT LITTLE LOVE TAP I GAVE YOU? C'MON--YOU WEREN'T EVEN IN A COMA FOR A WEEK!
NAH. IT'S 'CAUSE YOU'RE ON THIS SIDE OF THE BARS, AND THE JOKER'S ON THE OTHER--AND YOU PUT HIM THERE!
ME AND MR. J WERE WORKIN' OUT SOME PERSONAL ISSUES THAT DAY, AND WE KINDA DECIDED TO SEE OTHER PEOPLE FOR A WHILE.
THE FACT THAT THE PEOPLE MR. J'S SEEING IS PRISON GUARDS--THAT'S THE COPS' FAULT, NOT MINE!
I GOT A PLACE FOR YOU IN THIS GANG, BUSTER--BUT IT'S MY GANG, NOT MR. J'S. CHOICE IS YOURS.

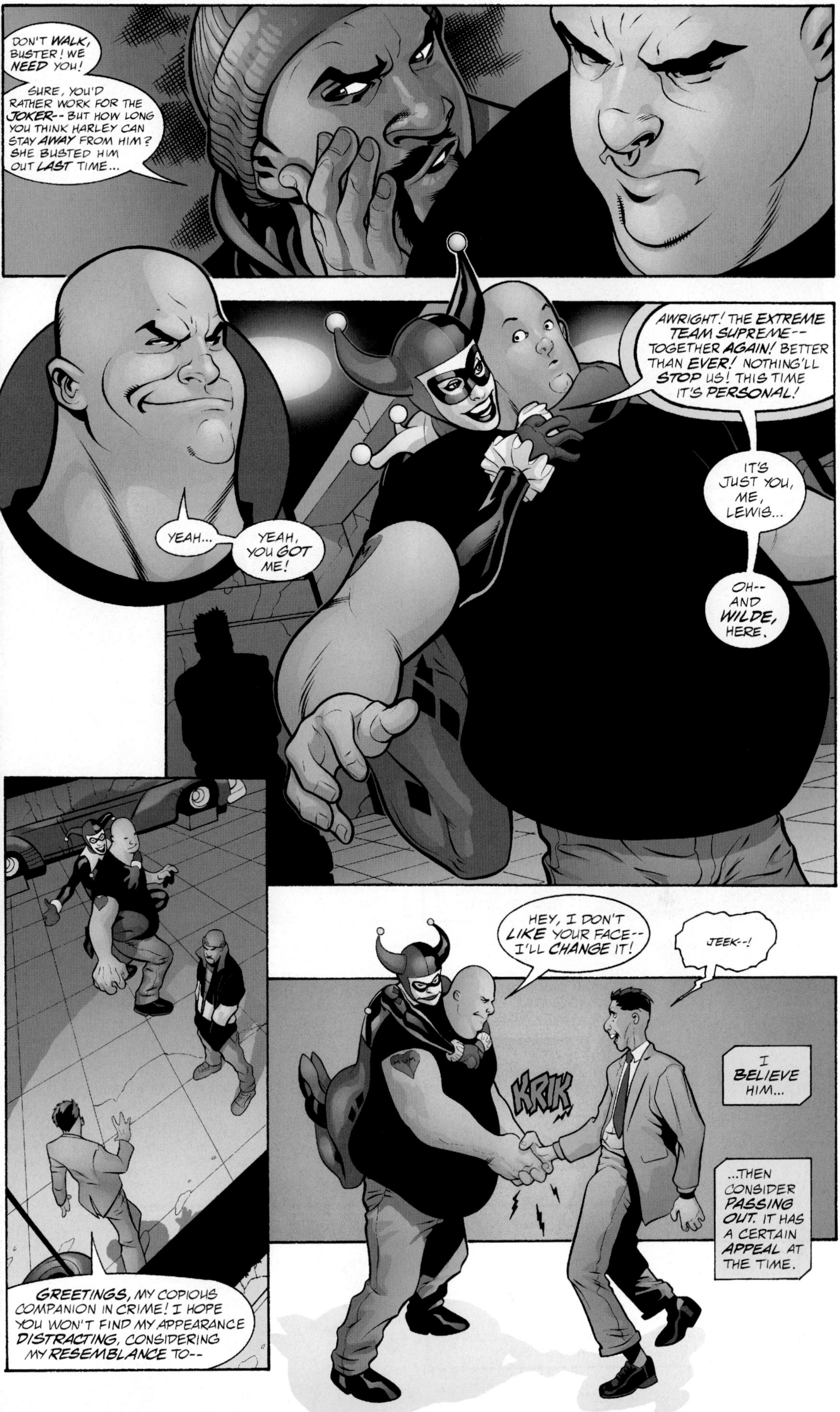
DON'T WALK, BUSTER! WE NEED YOU!
SURE, YOU'D RATHER WORK FOR THE JOKER-- BUT HOW LONG YOU THINK HARLEY CAN STAY AWAY FROM HIM? SHE BUSTED HIM OUT LAST TIME...
AWRIGHT! THE EXTREME TEAM SUPREME-- TOGETHER AGAIN! BETTER THAN EVER! NOTHING'LL STOP US! THIS TIME IT'S PERSONAL!
YEAH...
YEAH, YOU GOT ME!
IT'S JUST YOU, ME, LEWIS...
OH-- AND WILDE, HERE.
GREETINGS, MY COPIOUS COMPANION IN CRIME! I HOPE YOU WON'T FIND MY APPEARANCE DISTRACTING, CONSIDERING MY RESEMBLANCE TO--
HEY, I DON'T LIKE YOUR FACE-- I'LL CHANGE IT!
JEEK--!
KRIK
I BELIEVE HIM...
...THEN CONSIDER PASSING OUT. IT HAS A CERTAIN APPEAL AT THE TIME.

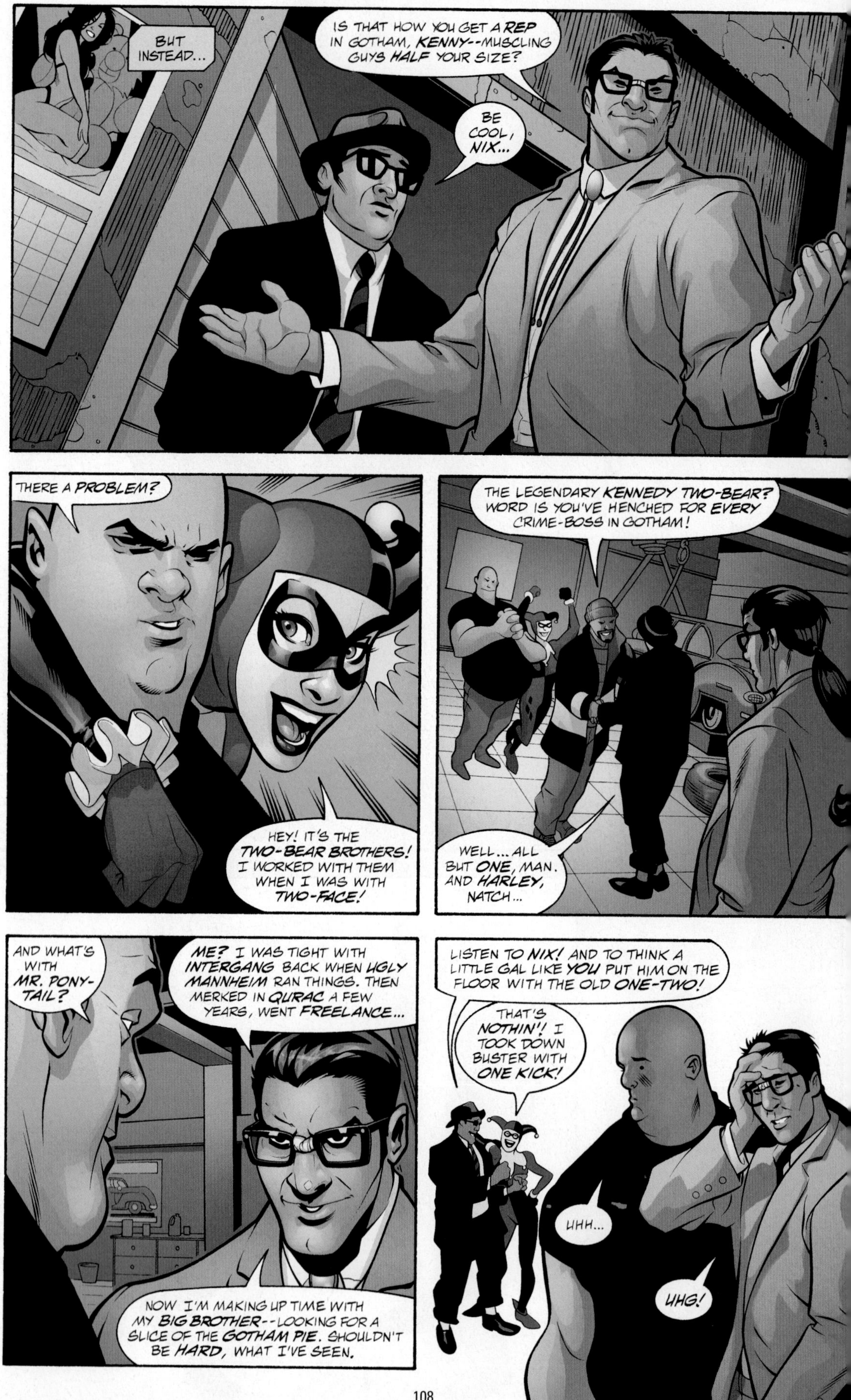
BUT INSTEAD...
IS THAT HOW YOU GET A REP IN GOTHAM, KENNY--MUSCLING GUYS HALF YOUR SIZE?
BE COOL, NIX...
THERE A PROBLEM?
HEY! IT'S THE TWO-BEAR BROTHERS! I WORKED WITH THEM WHEN I WAS WITH TWO-FACE!
THE LEGENDARY KENNEDY TWO-BEAR? WORD IS YOU'VE HENCHED FOR EVERY CRIME-BOSS IN GOTHAM!
WELL... ALL BUT ONE, MAN. AND HARLEY, NATCH...
AND WHAT'S WITH MR. PONY-TAIL?
ME? I WAS TIGHT WITH INTERGANG BACK WHEN UGLY MANNHEIM RAN THINGS. THEN MERKED IN QURAC A FEW YEARS, WENT FREELANCE...
NOW I'M MAKING UP TIME WITH MY BIG BROTHER--LOOKING FOR A SLICE OF THE GOTHAM PIE. SHOULDN'T BE HARD, WHAT I'VE SEEN.
LISTEN TO NIX! AND TO THINK A LITTLE GAL LIKE YOU PUT HIM ON THE FLOOR WITH THE OLD ONE-TWO!
THAT'S NOTHIN'! I TOOK DOWN BUSTER WITH ONE KICK!
UHH...
UHG!

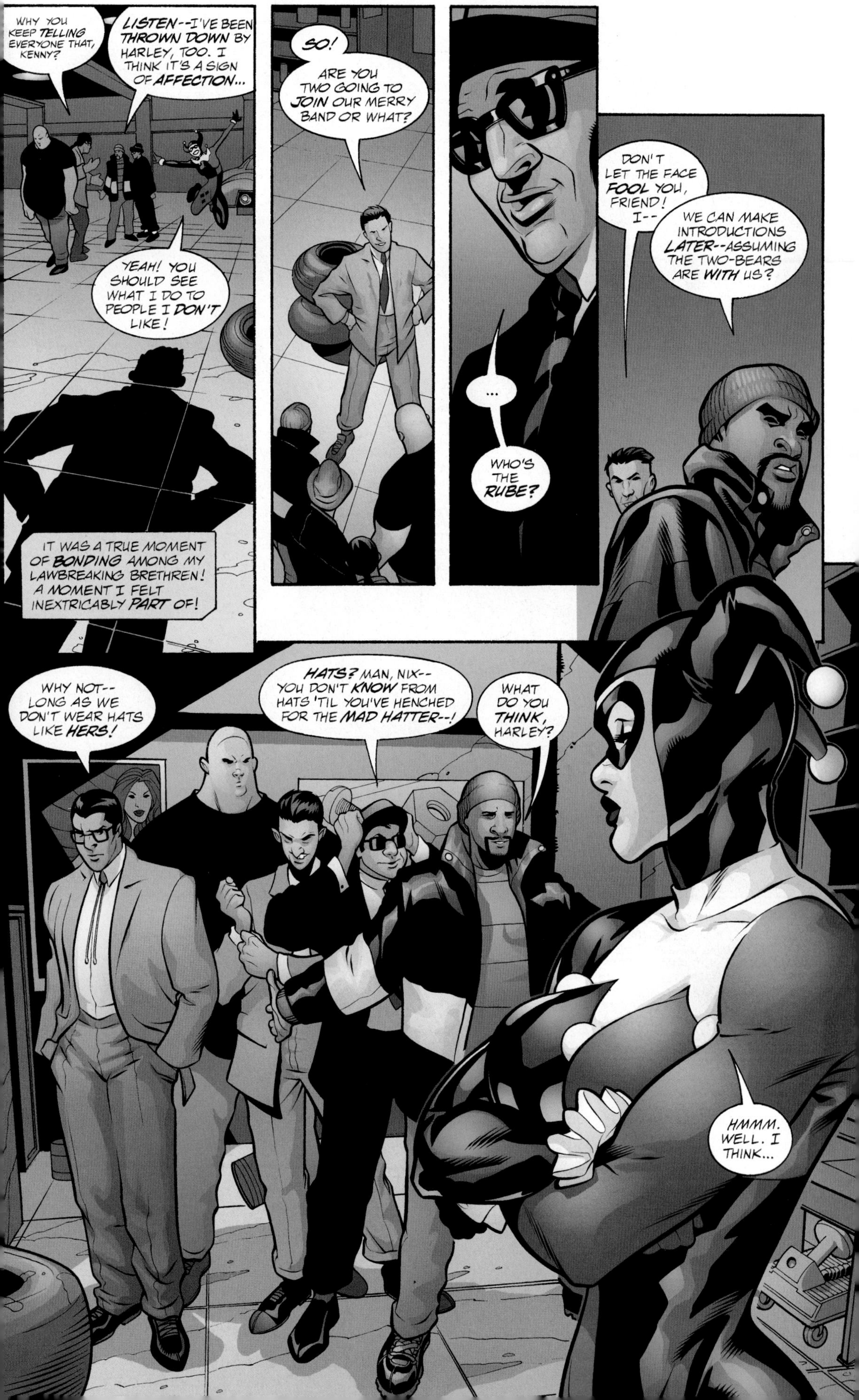
WHY YOU KEEP TELLING EVERYONE THAT, KENNY?
LISTEN--I'VE BEEN THROWN DOWN BY HARLEY, TOO. I THINK IT'S A SIGN OF AFFECTION...
YEAH! YOU SHOULD SEE WHAT I DO TO PEOPLE I DON'T LIKE!
IT WAS A TRUE MOMENT OF BONDING AMONG MY LAWBREAKING BRETHREN! A MOMENT I FELT INEXTRICABLY PART OF!
SO!
ARE YOU TWO GOING TO JOIN OUR MERRY BAND OR WHAT?
...
WHO'S THE RUBE?
DON'T LET THE FACE FOOL YOU, FRIEND! I--
WE CAN MAKE INTRODUCTIONS LATER--ASSUMING THE TWO-BEARS ARE WITH US?
WHY NOT--LONG AS WE DON'T WEAR HATS LIKE HERS!
HATS? MAN, NIX--YOU DON'T KNOW FROM HATS 'TIL YOU'VE HENCHED FOR THE MAD HATTER--!
WHAT DO YOU THINK, HARLEY?
HMMM. WELL. I THINK...

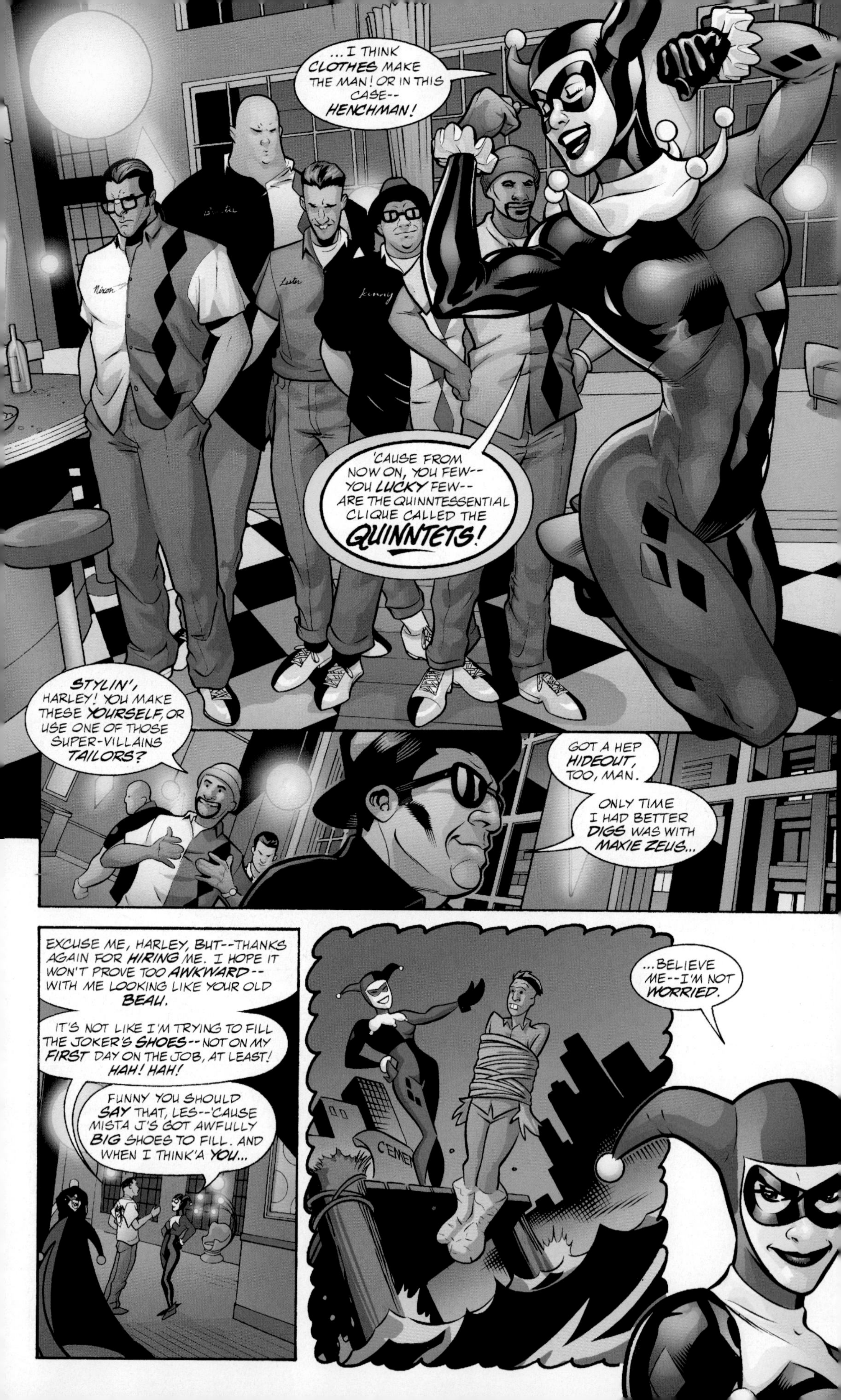
...I THINK CLOTHES MAKE THE MAN! OR IN THIS CASE-- HENCHMAN!
'CAUSE FROM NOW ON, YOU FEW-- YOU LUCKY FEW-- ARE THE QUINNTESSENTIAL CLIQUE CALLED THE QUINNTETS!
STYLIN', HARLEY! YOU MAKE THESE YOURSELF, OR USE ONE OF THOSE SUPER-VILLAINS TAILORS?
GOT A HEP HIDEOUT, TOO, MAN.
ONLY TIME I HAD BETTER DIGS WAS WITH MAXIE ZEUS...
EXCUSE ME, HARLEY, BUT--THANKS AGAIN FOR HIRING ME. I HOPE IT WON'T PROVE TOO AWKWARD-- WITH ME LOOKING LIKE YOUR OLD BEAU.
IT'S NOT LIKE I'M TRYING TO FILL THE JOKER'S SHOES--NOT ON MY FIRST DAY ON THE JOB, AT LEAST! HAH! HAH!
FUNNY YOU SHOULD SAY THAT, LES--'CAUSE MISTA J'S GOT AWFULLY BIG SHOES TO FILL. AND WHEN I THINK'A YOU...
...BELIEVE ME--I'M NOT WORRIED.

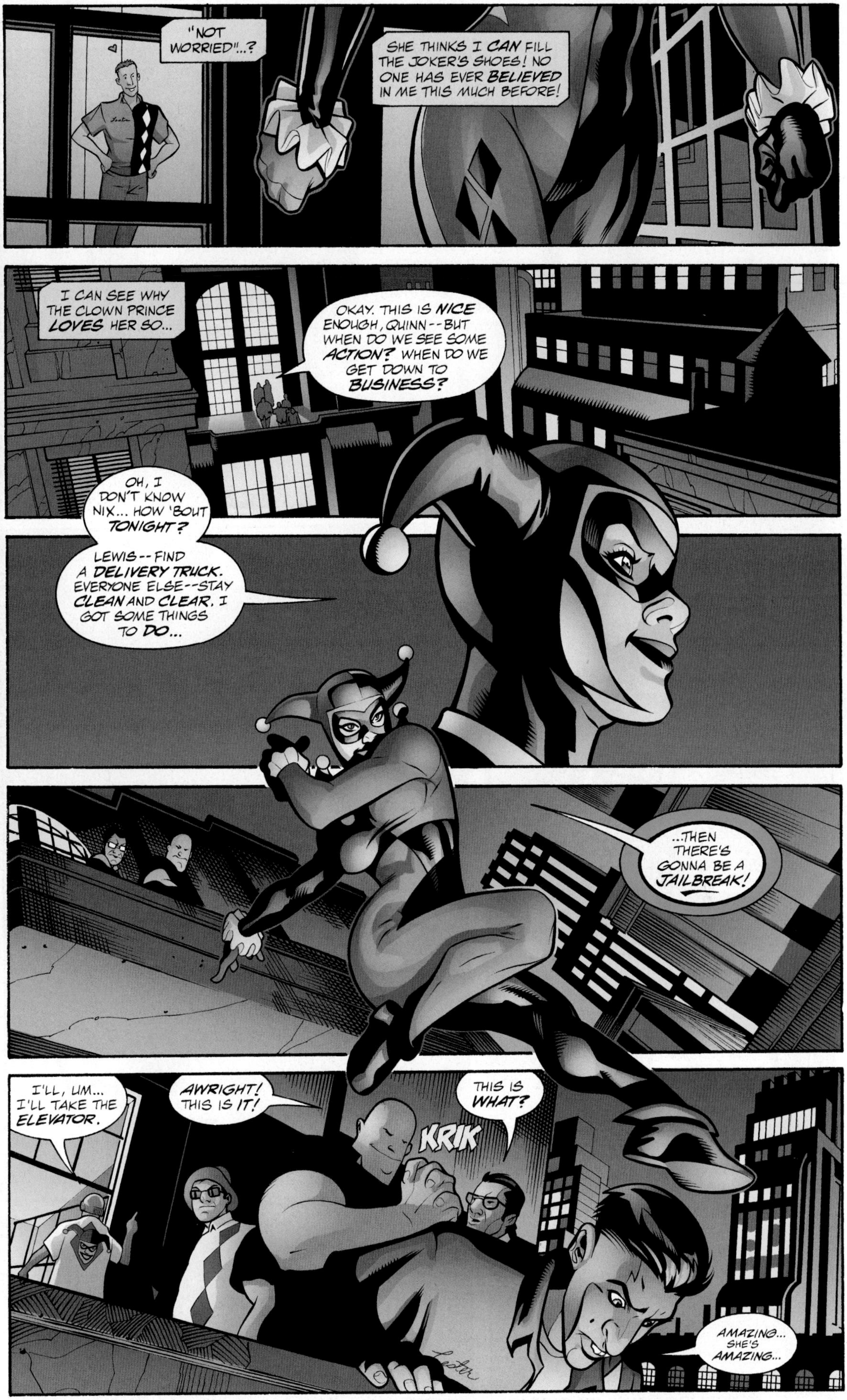
"NOT WORRIED"...?
SHE THINKS I CAN FILL THE JOKER'S SHOES! NO ONE HAS EVER BELIEVED IN ME THIS MUCH BEFORE!
I CAN SEE WHY THE CLOWN PRINCE LOVES HER SO...
OKAY. THIS IS NICE ENOUGH, QUINN--BUT WHEN DO WE SEE SOME ACTION? WHEN DO WE GET DOWN TO BUSINESS?
OH, I DON'T KNOW NIX... HOW 'BOUT TONIGHT?
LEWIS--FIND A DELIVERY TRUCK. EVERYONE ELSE--STAY CLEAN AND CLEAR. I GOT SOME THINGS TO DO...
...THEN THERE'S GONNA BE A JAILBREAK!
I'LL, UM... I'LL TAKE THE ELEVATOR.
AWRIGHT! THIS IS IT!
THIS IS WHAT?
KRIK
AMAZING... SHE'S AMAZING...

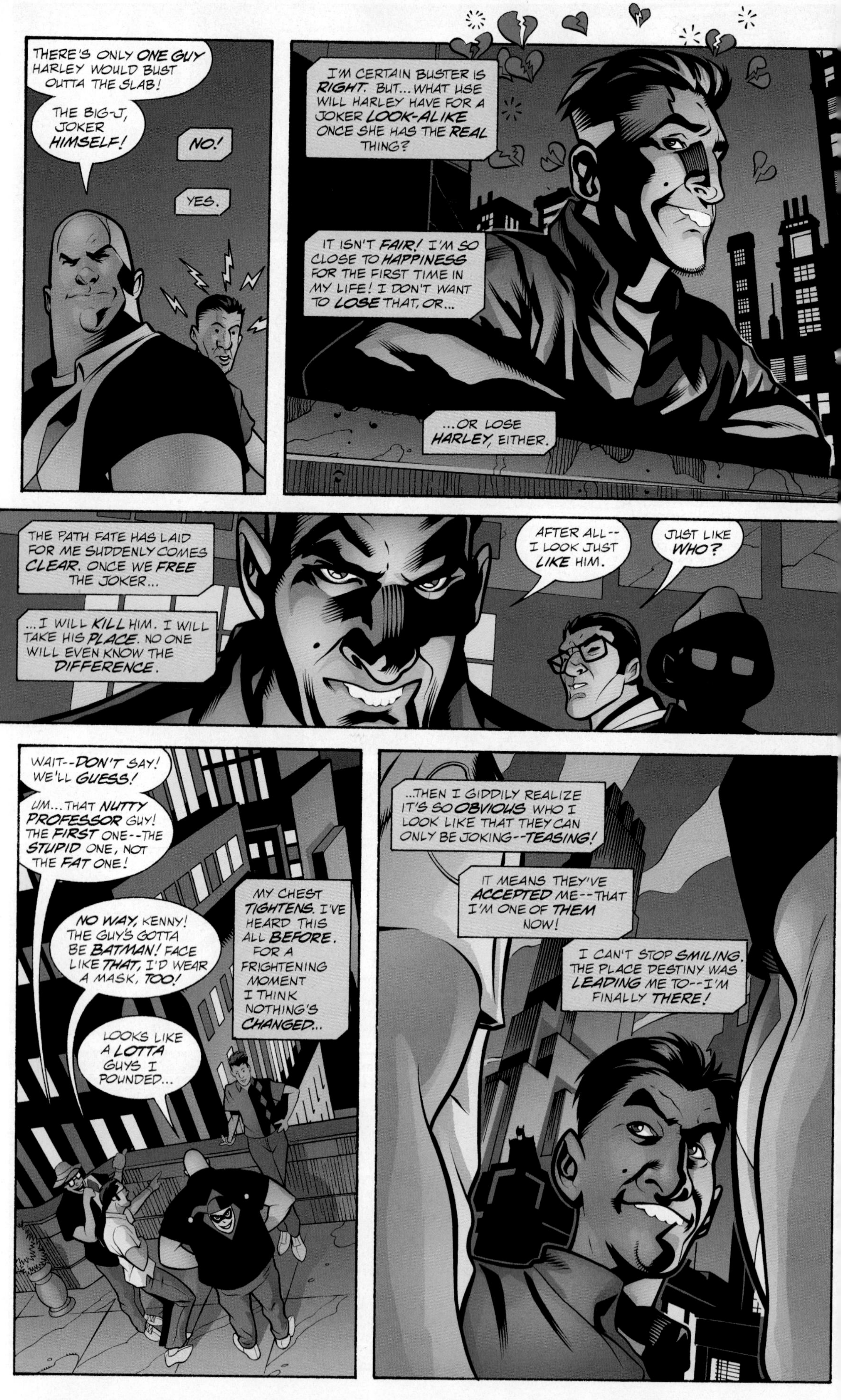
THERE'S ONLY ONE GUY HARLEY WOULD BUST OUTTA THE SLAB!
THE BIG-J, JOKER HIMSELF!
NO!
YES.
I'M CERTAIN BUSTER IS RIGHT. BUT... WHAT USE WILL HARLEY HAVE FOR A JOKER LOOK-ALIKE ONCE SHE HAS THE REAL THING?
IT ISN'T FAIR! I'M SO CLOSE TO HAPPINESS FOR THE FIRST TIME IN MY LIFE! I DON'T WANT TO LOSE THAT, OR...
...OR LOSE HARLEY, EITHER.
THE PATH FATE HAS LAID FOR ME SUDDENLY COMES CLEAR. ONCE WE FREE THE JOKER...
...I WILL KILL HIM. I WILL TAKE HIS PLACE. NO ONE WILL EVEN KNOW THE DIFFERENCE.
AFTER ALL-- I LOOK JUST LIKE HIM.
JUST LIKE WHO?
WAIT--DON'T SAY! WE'LL GUESS!
UM... THAT NUTTY PROFESSOR GUY! THE FIRST ONE--THE STUPID ONE, NOT THE FAT ONE!
NO WAY, KENNY! THE GUY'S GOTTA BE BATMAN! FACE LIKE THAT, I'D WEAR A MASK, TOO!
LOOKS LIKE A LOTTA GUYS I POUNDED...
MY CHEST TIGHTENS. I'VE HEARD THIS ALL BEFORE. FOR A FRIGHTENING MOMENT I THINK NOTHING'S CHANGED...
...THEN I GIDDILY REALIZE IT'S SO OBVIOUS WHO I LOOK LIKE THAT THEY CAN ONLY BE JOKING--TEASING!
IT MEANS THEY'VE ACCEPTED ME--THAT I'M ONE OF THEM NOW!
I CAN'T STOP SMILING. THE PLACE DESTINY WAS LEADING ME TO--I'M FINALLY THERE!

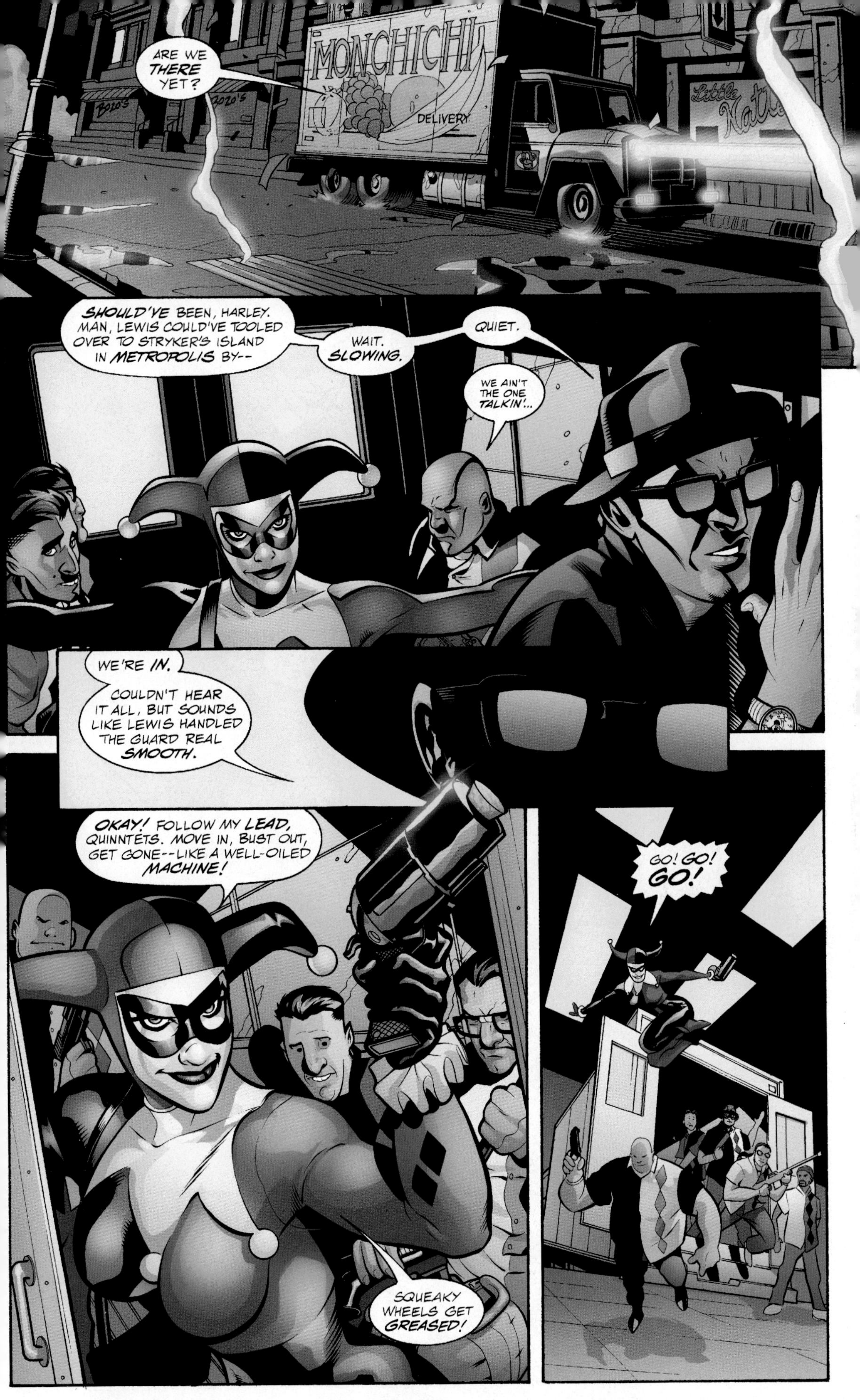
MONCHICHI
DELIVERY
BOZO'S
BOZO'S
Little Natty
ARE WE THERE YET?
SHOULD'VE BEEN, HARLEY. MAN, LEWIS COULD'VE TOOLED OVER TO STRYKER'S ISLAND IN METROPOLIS BY--
WAIT. SLOWING.
QUIET.
WE AIN'T THE ONE TALKIN'...
WE'RE IN.
COULDN'T HEAR IT ALL, BUT SOUNDS LIKE LEWIS HANDLED THE GUARD REAL SMOOTH.
OKAY! FOLLOW MY LEAD, QUINNTETS. MOVE IN, BUST OUT, GET GONE--LIKE A WELL-OILED MACHINE!
SQUEAKY WHEELS GET GREASED!
GO! GO! GO!

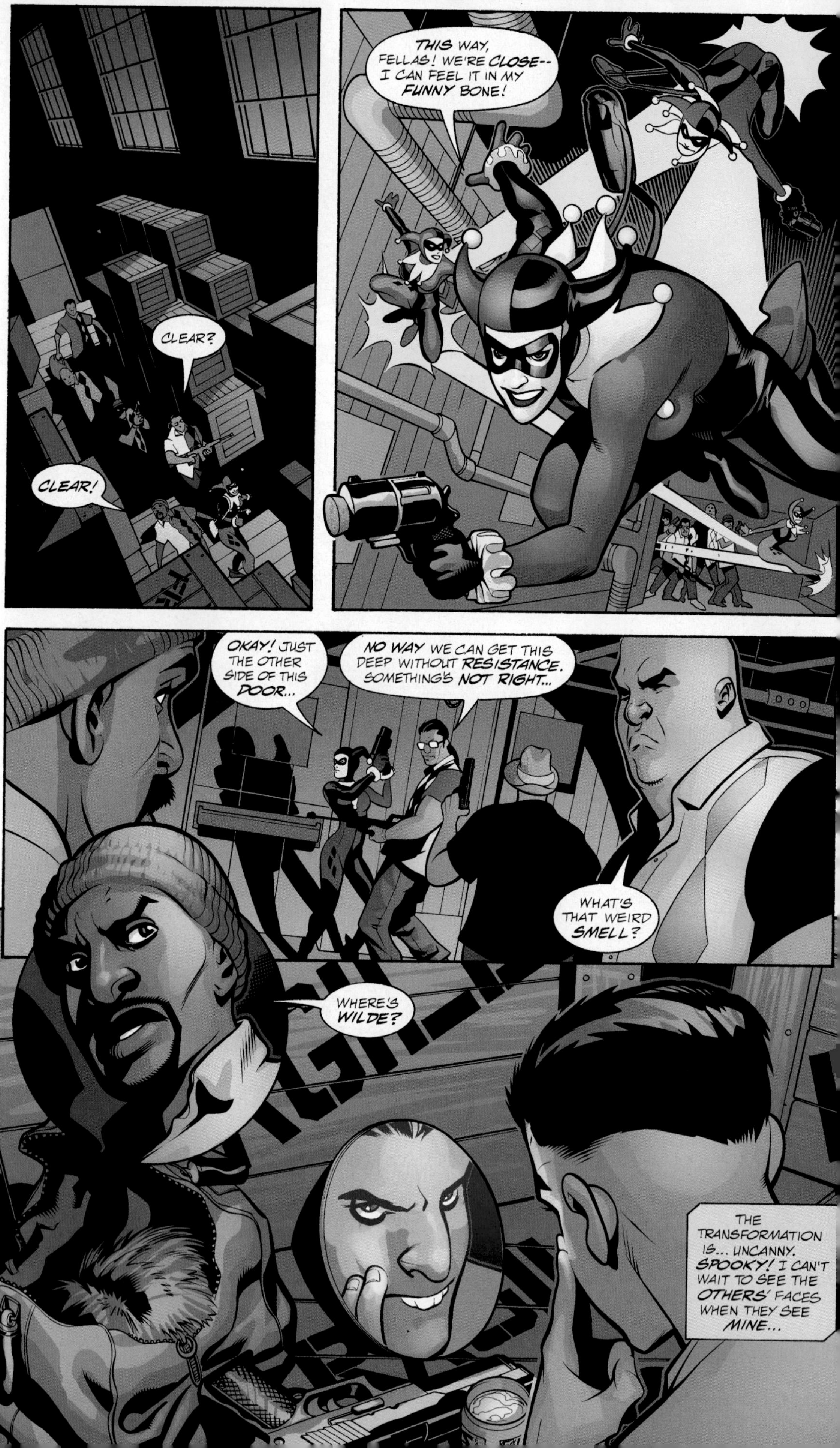
CLEAR?
CLEAR!
THIS WAY, FELLAS! WE'RE CLOSE-- I CAN FEEL IT IN MY FUNNY BONE!
OKAY! JUST THE OTHER SIDE OF THIS DOOR...
NO WAY WE CAN GET THIS DEEP WITHOUT RESISTANCE. SOMETHING'S NOT RIGHT...
WHAT'S THAT WEIRD SMELL?
WHERE'S WILDE?
THE TRANSFORMATION IS... UNCANNY. SPOOKY! I CAN'T WAIT TO SEE THE OTHERS' FACES WHEN THEY SEE MINE...

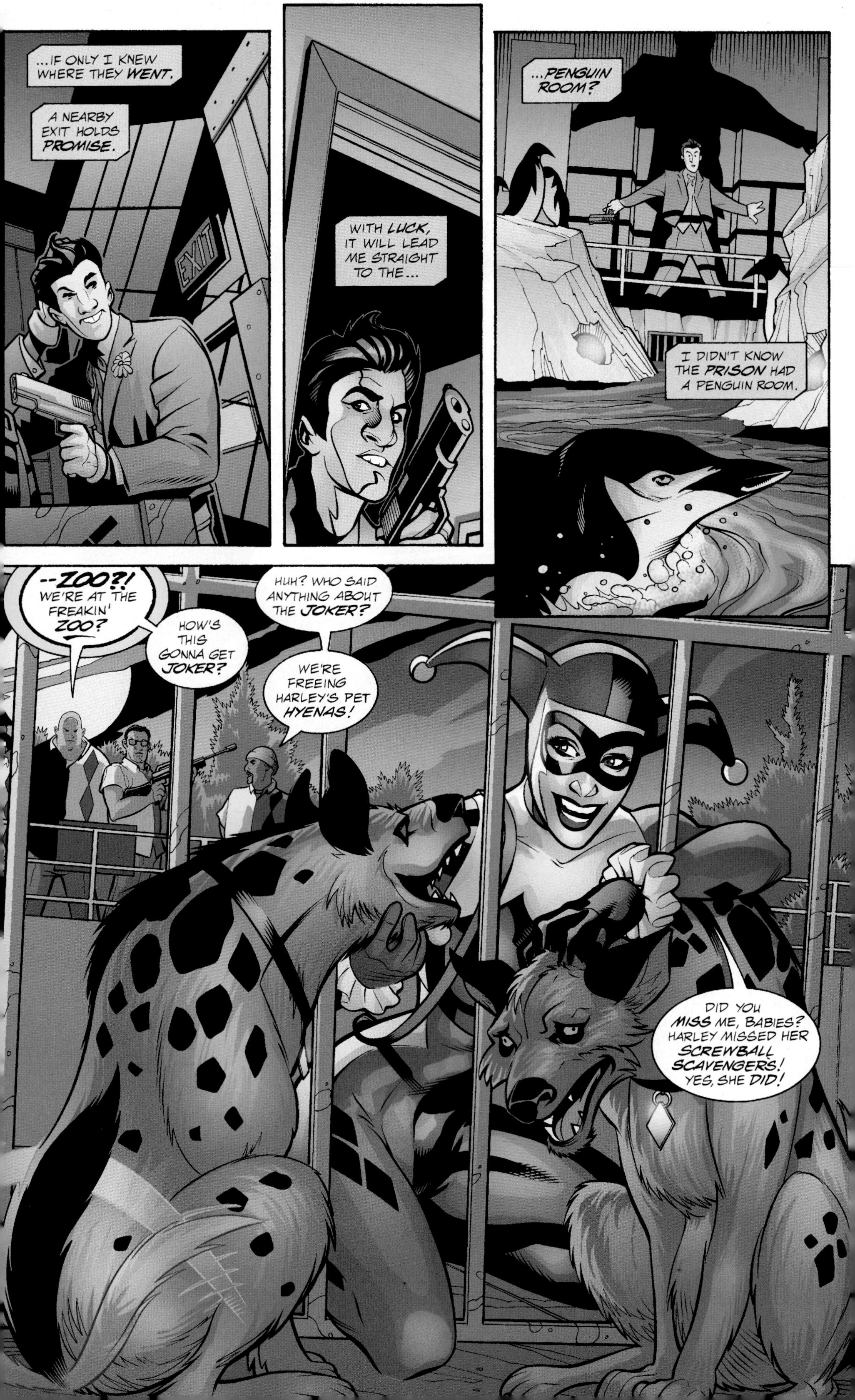
...IF ONLY I KNEW WHERE THEY WENT.
A NEARBY EXIT HOLDS PROMISE.
EXIT
WITH LUCK, IT WILL LEAD ME STRAIGHT TO THE...
...PENGUIN ROOM?
I DIDN'T KNOW THE PRISON HAD A PENGUIN ROOM.
--ZOO?! WE'RE AT THE FREAKIN' ZOO?
HOW'S THIS GONNA GET JOKER?
HUH? WHO SAID ANYTHING ABOUT THE JOKER?
WE'RE FREEING HARLEY'S PET HYENAS!
DID YOU MISS ME, BABIES? HARLEY MISSED HER SCREWBALL SCAVENGERS! YES, SHE DID!

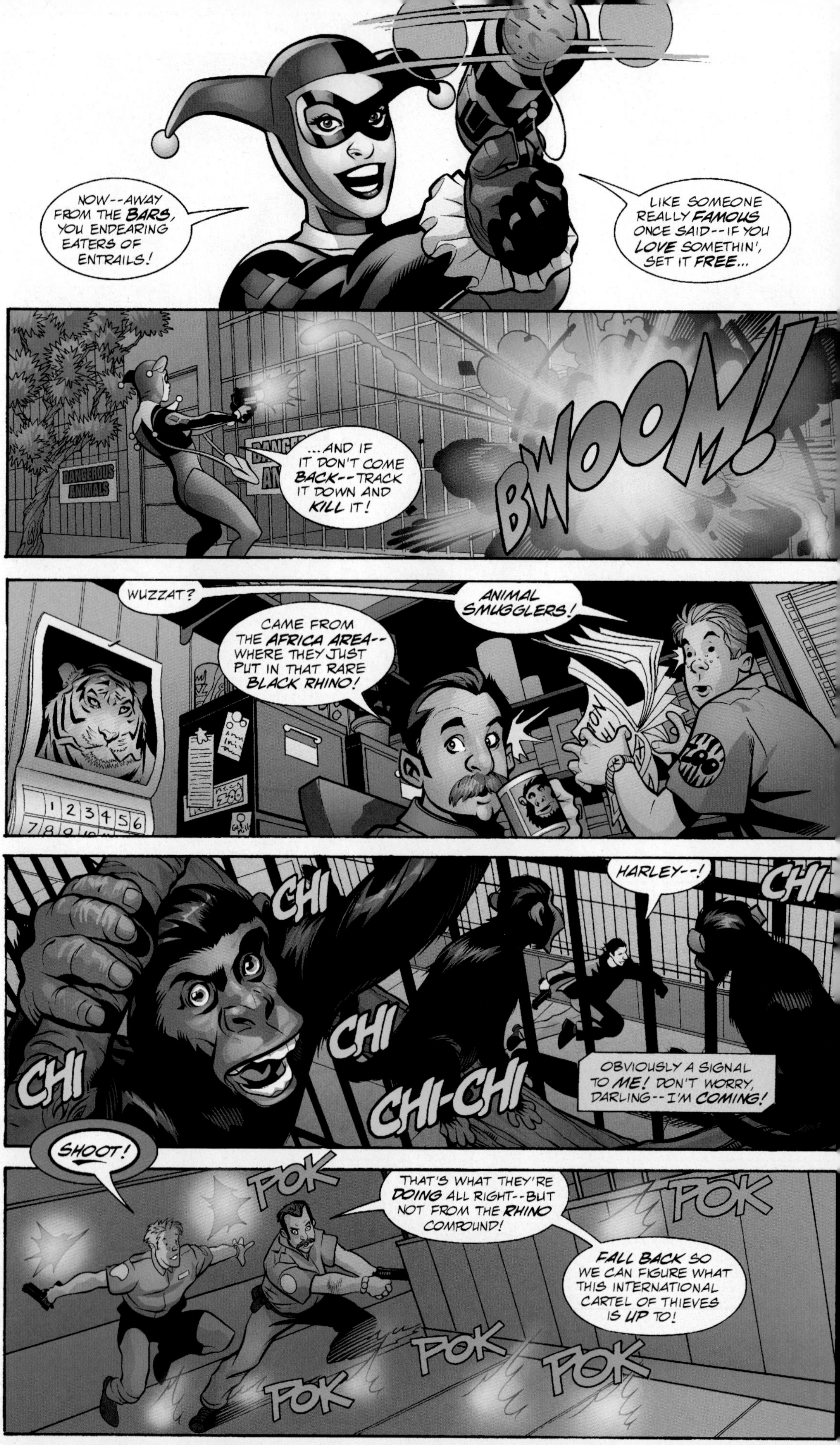

NOW--AWAY FROM THE BARS, YOU ENDEARING EATERS OF ENTRAILS!
LIKE SOMEONE REALLY FAMOUS ONCE SAID--IF YOU LOVE SOMETHIN', SET IT FREE...
DANGEROUS ANIMALS
...AND IF IT DON'T COME BACK--TRACK IT DOWN AND KILL IT!
BWOOOM!
WUZZAT?
ANIMAL SMUGGLERS!
CAME FROM THE AFRICA AREA--WHERE THEY JUST PUT IN THAT RARE BLACK RHINO!
1 2 3 4 5 6
CHI
CHI
CHI
CHI-CHI
HARLEY--!
CHI
OBVIOUSLY A SIGNAL TO ME! DON'T WORRY, DARLING--I'M COMING!
SHOOT!
POK
THAT'S WHAT THEY'RE DOING ALL RIGHT--BUT NOT FROM THE RHINO COMPOUND!
POK
FALL BACK SO WE CAN FIGURE WHAT THIS INTERNATIONAL CARTEL OF THIEVES IS UP TO!
POK
POK
POK

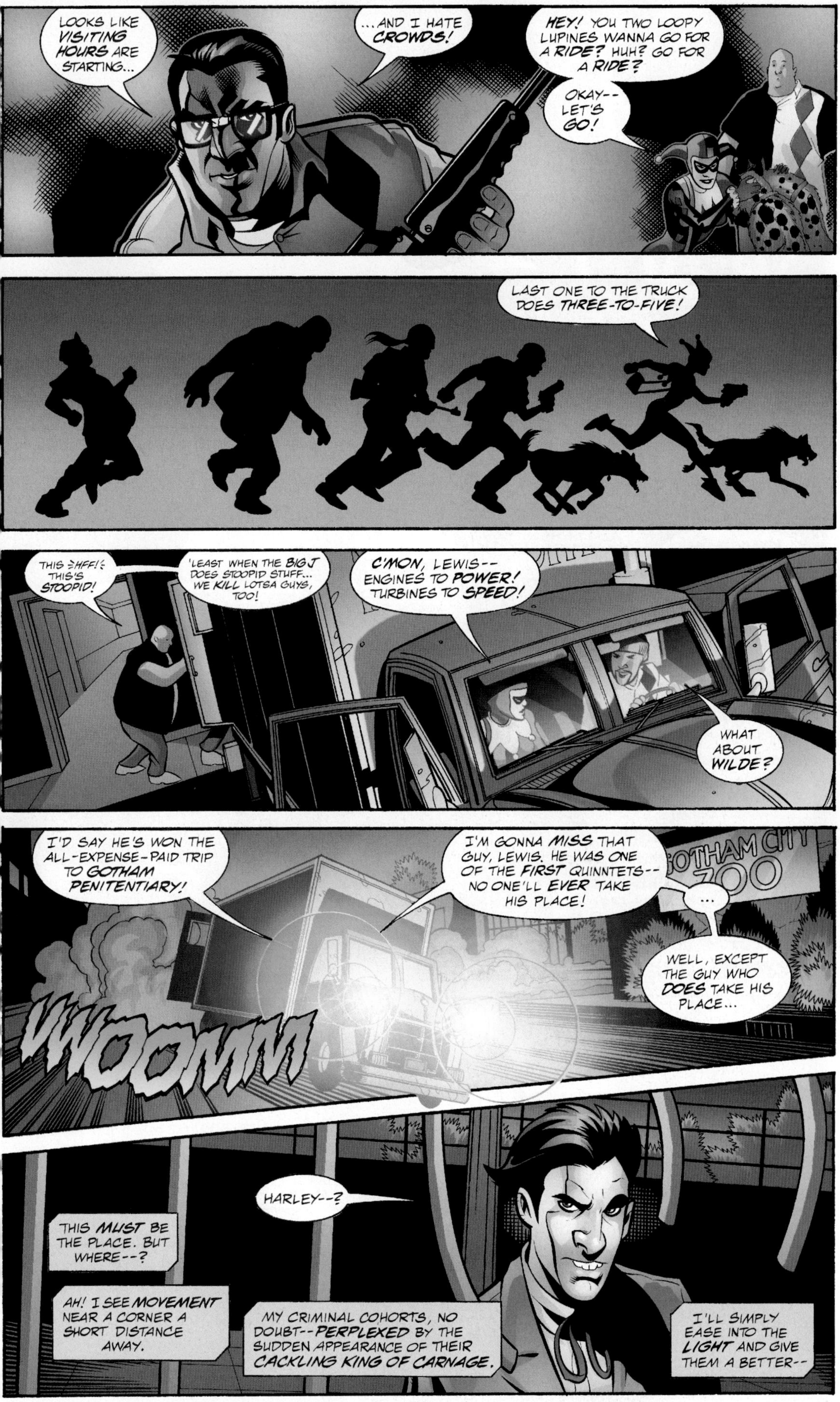
LOOKS LIKE VISITING HOURS ARE STARTING...
...AND I HATE CROWDS!
HEY! YOU TWO LOOPY LUPINES WANNA GO FOR A RIDE? HUH? GO FOR A RIDE?
OKAY-- LET'S GO!
LAST ONE TO THE TRUCK DOES THREE-TO-FIVE!
THIS *HFF!* THIS'S STOOPID!
'LEAST WHEN THE BIG J DOES STOOPID STUFF... WE KILL LOTSA GUYS, TOO!
C'MON, LEWIS-- ENGINES TO POWER! TURBINES TO SPEED!
WHAT ABOUT WILDE?
I'D SAY HE'S WON THE ALL-EXPENSE-PAID TRIP TO GOTHAM PENITENTIARY!
I'M GONNA MISS THAT GUY, LEWIS. HE WAS ONE OF THE FIRST QUINNTETS-- NO ONE'LL EVER TAKE HIS PLACE!
...
WELL, EXCEPT THE GUY WHO DOES TAKE HIS PLACE...
GOTHAM CITY ZOO
VWOOMM
HARLEY--?
THIS MUST BE THE PLACE. BUT WHERE--?
AH! I SEE MOVEMENT NEAR A CORNER A SHORT DISTANCE AWAY.
MY CRIMINAL COHORTS, NO DOUBT--PERPLEXED BY THE SUDDEN APPEARANCE OF THEIR CACKLING KING OF CARNAGE.
I'LL SIMPLY EASE INTO THE LIGHT AND GIVE THEM A BETTER--

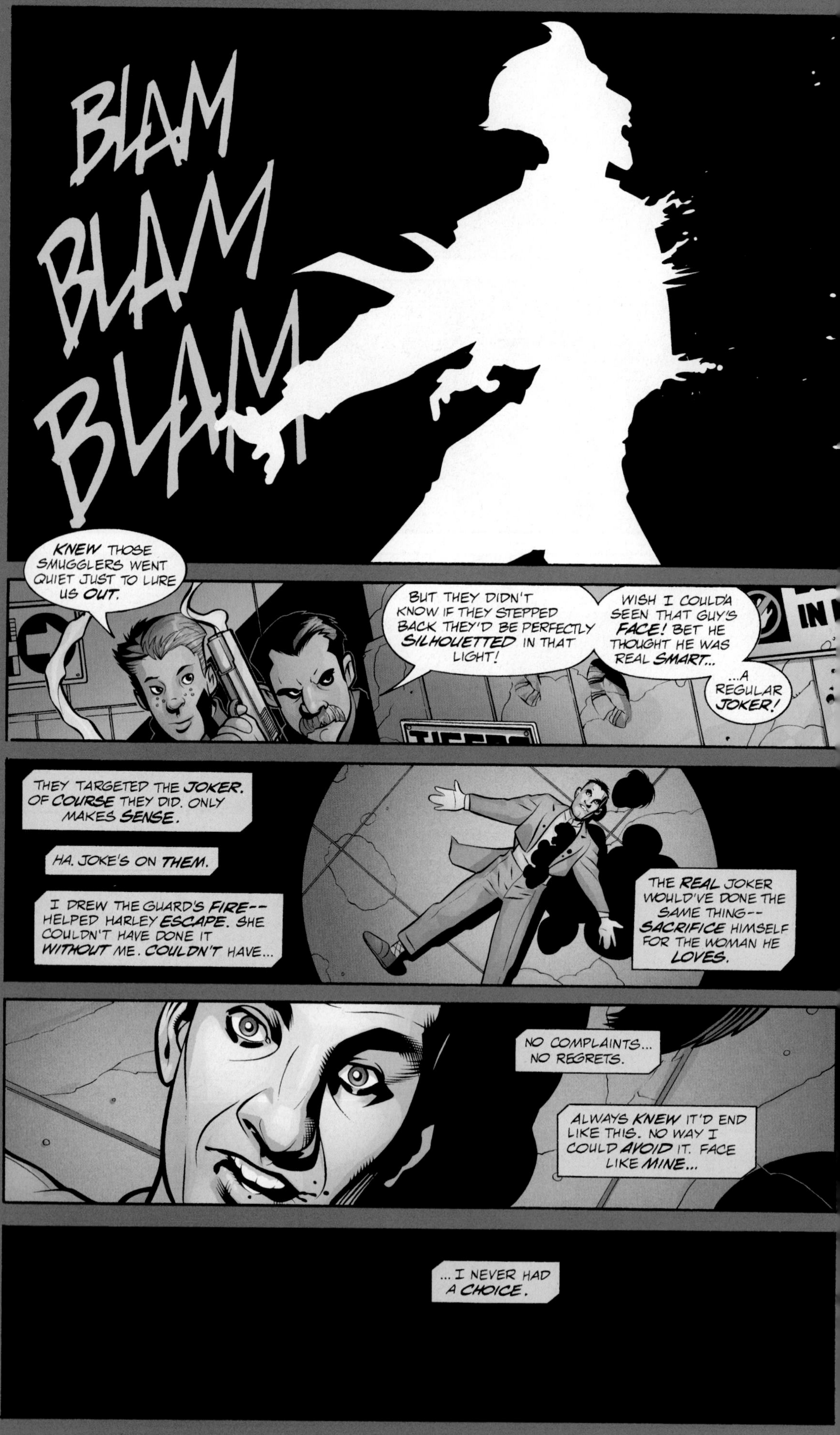
BLAM
BLAM
BLAM
KNEW THOSE SMUGGLERS WENT QUIET JUST TO LURE US OUT.
BUT THEY DIDN'T KNOW IF THEY STEPPED BACK THEY'D BE PERFECTLY SILHOUETTED IN THAT LIGHT!
WISH I COULDA SEEN THAT GUY'S FACE! BET HE THOUGHT HE WAS REAL SMART...
...A REGULAR JOKER!
THEY TARGETED THE JOKER. OF COURSE THEY DID. ONLY MAKES SENSE.
HA. JOKE'S ON THEM.
I DREW THE GUARD'S FIRE--HELPED HARLEY ESCAPE. SHE COULDN'T HAVE DONE IT WITHOUT ME. COULDN'T HAVE...
THE REAL JOKER WOULD'VE DONE THE SAME THING--SACRIFICE HIMSELF FOR THE WOMAN HE LOVES.
NO COMPLAINTS... NO REGRETS.
ALWAYS KNEW IT'D END LIKE THIS. NO WAY I COULD AVOID IT. FACE LIKE MINE...
...I NEVER HAD A CHOICE.

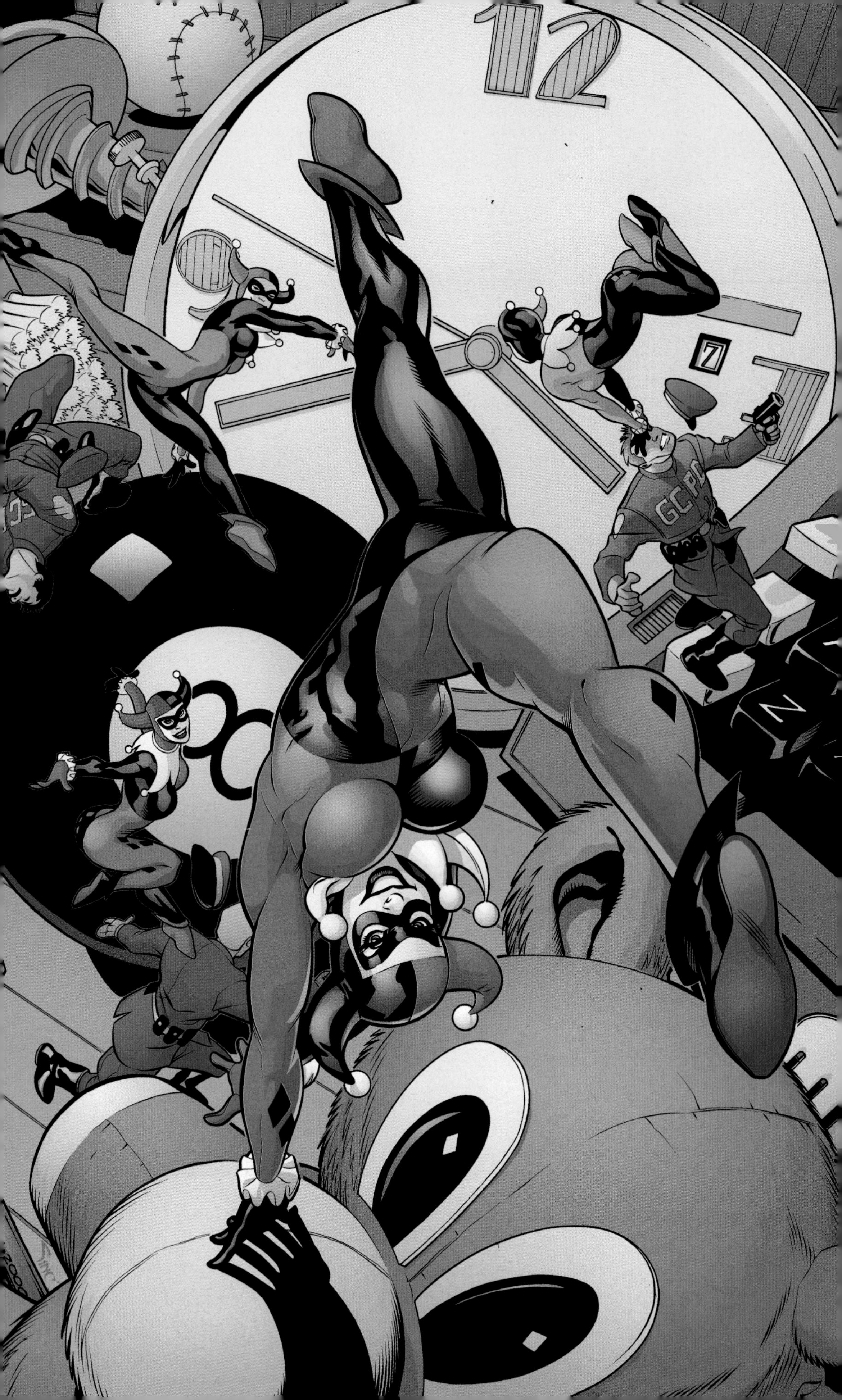
GCPD

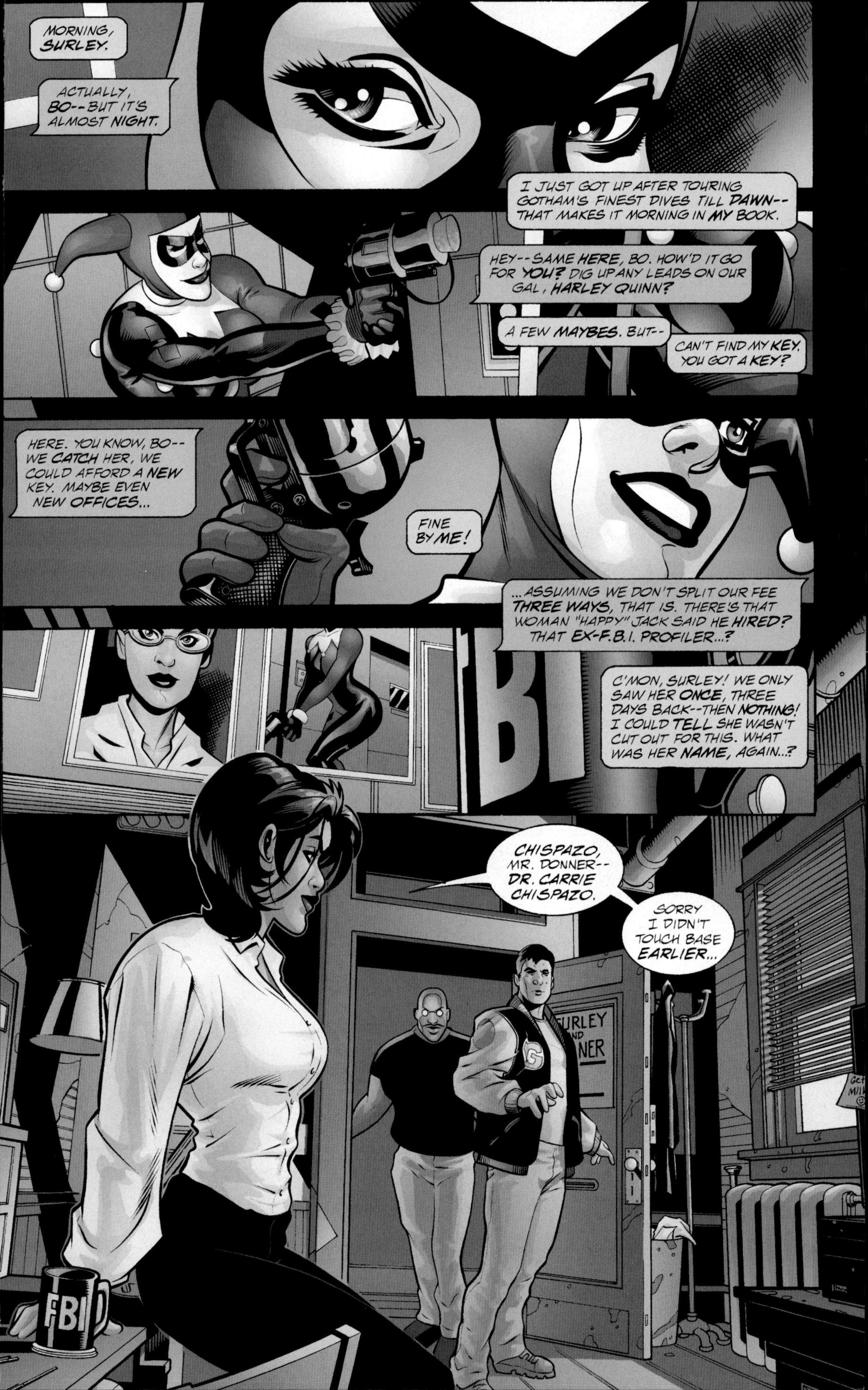
MORNING, SURLEY.
ACTUALLY, BO--BUT IT'S ALMOST NIGHT.
I JUST GOT UP AFTER TOURING GOTHAM'S FINEST DIVES TILL DAWN--THAT MAKES IT MORNING IN MY BOOK.
HEY--SAME HERE, BO. HOW'D IT GO FOR YOU? DIG UP ANY LEADS ON OUR GAL, HARLEY QUINN?
A FEW MAYBES. BUT--
CAN'T FIND MY KEY. YOU GOT A KEY?
HERE. YOU KNOW, BO--WE CATCH HER, WE COULD AFFORD A NEW KEY. MAYBE EVEN NEW OFFICES...
FINE BY ME!
...ASSUMING WE DON'T SPLIT OUR FEE THREE WAYS, THAT IS. THERE'S THAT WOMAN "HAPPY" JACK SAID HE HIRED? THAT EX-F.B.I. PROFILER...?
C'MON, SURLEY! WE ONLY SAW HER ONCE, THREE DAYS BACK--THEN NOTHING! I COULD TELL SHE WASN'T CUT OUT FOR THIS. WHAT WAS HER NAME, AGAIN...?
CHISPAZO, MR. DONNER--DR. CARRIE CHISPAZO.
SORRY I DIDN'T TOUCH BASE EARLIER...
FBI

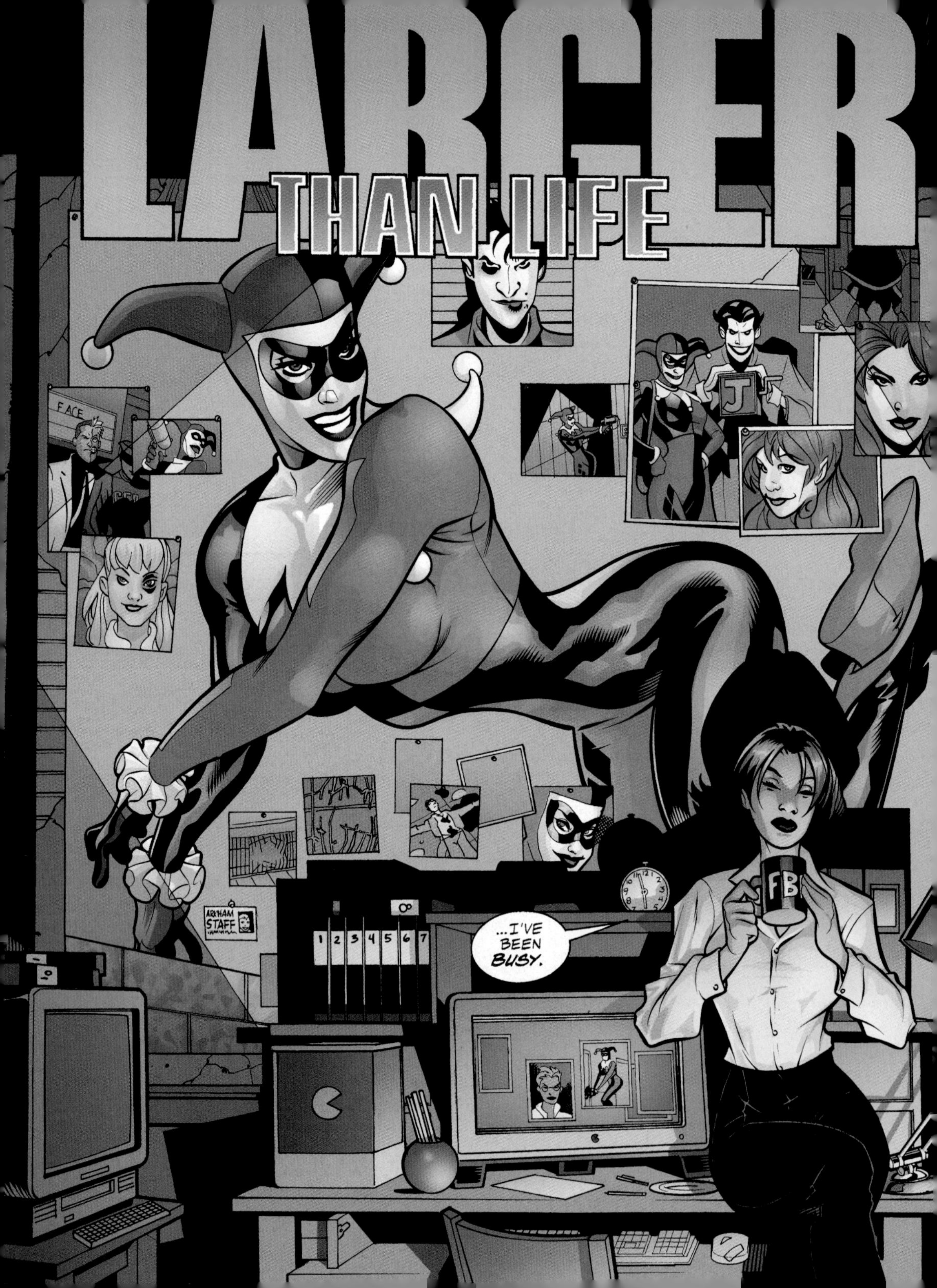
LARGER
THAN LIFE
FACE
ARKHAM STAFF
...I'VE BEEN BUSY.

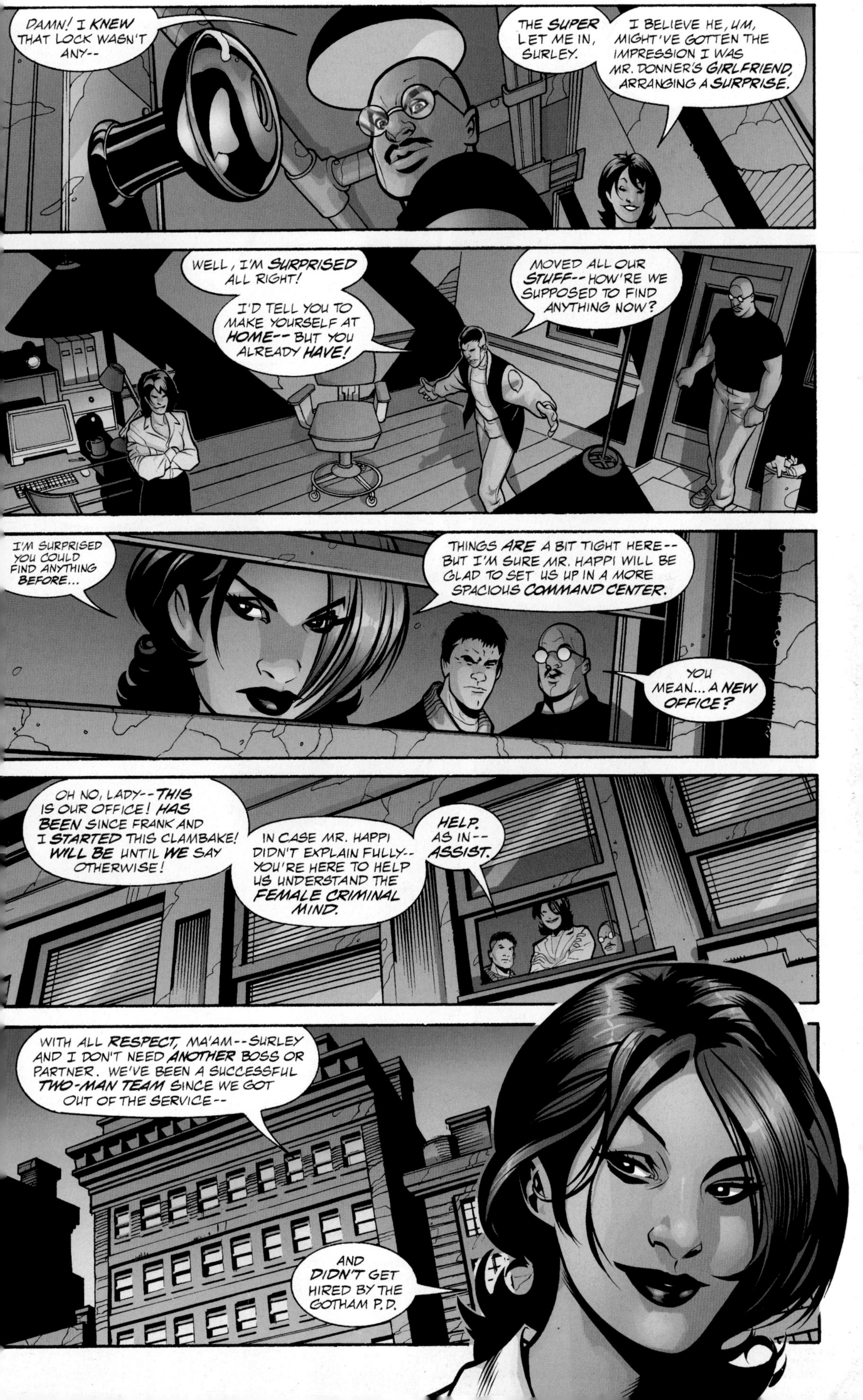
DAMN! I KNEW THAT LOCK WASN'T ANY--
THE SUPER LET ME IN, SURLEY.
I BELIEVE HE, UM, MIGHT'VE GOTTEN THE IMPRESSION I WAS MR. DONNER'S GIRLFRIEND, ARRANGING A SURPRISE.
WELL, I'M SURPRISED ALL RIGHT!
I'D TELL YOU TO MAKE YOURSELF AT HOME-- BUT YOU ALREADY HAVE!
MOVED ALL OUR STUFF-- HOW'RE WE SUPPOSED TO FIND ANYTHING NOW?
I'M SURPRISED YOU COULD FIND ANYTHING BEFORE...
THINGS ARE A BIT TIGHT HERE-- BUT I'M SURE MR. HAPPI WILL BE GLAD TO SET US UP IN A MORE SPACIOUS COMMAND CENTER.
YOU MEAN... A NEW OFFICE?
OH NO, LADY-- THIS IS OUR OFFICE! HAS BEEN SINCE FRANK AND I STARTED THIS CLAMBAKE! WILL BE UNTIL WE SAY OTHERWISE!
IN CASE MR. HAPPI DIDN'T EXPLAIN FULLY-- YOU'RE HERE TO HELP US UNDERSTAND THE FEMALE CRIMINAL MIND.
HELP. AS IN-- ASSIST.
WITH ALL RESPECT, MA'AM-- SURLEY AND I DON'T NEED ANOTHER BOSS OR PARTNER. WE'VE BEEN A SUCCESSFUL TWO-MAN TEAM SINCE WE GOT OUT OF THE SERVICE--
AND DIDN'T GET HIRED BY THE GOTHAM P.D.

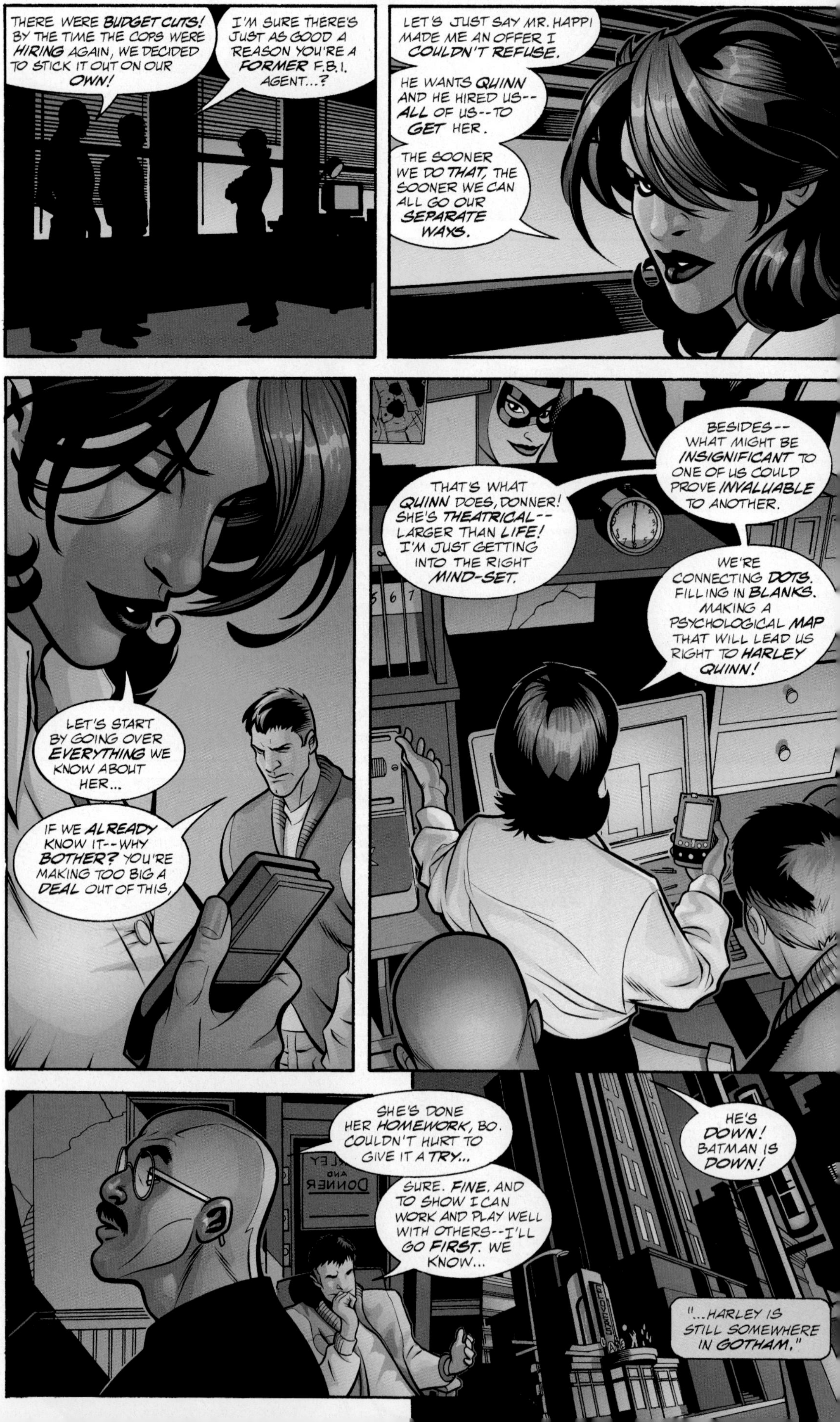
THERE WERE BUDGET CUTS! BY THE TIME THE COPS WERE HIRING AGAIN, WE DECIDED TO STICK IT OUT ON OUR OWN!
I'M SURE THERE'S JUST AS GOOD A REASON YOU'RE A FORMER F.B.I. AGENT...?
LET'S JUST SAY MR. HAPPI MADE ME AN OFFER I COULDN'T REFUSE.
HE WANTS QUINN AND HE HIRED US-- ALL OF US--TO GET HER.
THE SOONER WE DO THAT, THE SOONER WE CAN ALL GO OUR SEPARATE WAYS.
LET'S START BY GOING OVER EVERYTHING WE KNOW ABOUT HER...
IF WE ALREADY KNOW IT--WHY BOTHER? YOU'RE MAKING TOO BIG A DEAL OUT OF THIS,
THAT'S WHAT QUINN DOES, DONNER! SHE'S THEATRICAL-- LARGER THAN LIFE! I'M JUST GETTING INTO THE RIGHT MIND-SET.
BESIDES-- WHAT MIGHT BE INSIGNIFICANT TO ONE OF US COULD PROVE INVALUABLE TO ANOTHER.
WE'RE CONNECTING DOTS. FILLING IN BLANKS. MAKING A PSYCHOLOGICAL MAP THAT WILL LEAD US RIGHT TO HARLEY QUINN!
SHE'S DONE HER HOMEWORK, BO. COULDN'T HURT TO GIVE IT A TRY...
SURE. FINE. AND TO SHOW I CAN WORK AND PLAY WELL WITH OTHERS--I'LL GO FIRST. WE KNOW...
HE'S DOWN! BATMAN IS DOWN!
"...HARLEY IS STILL SOMEWHERE IN GOTHAM."

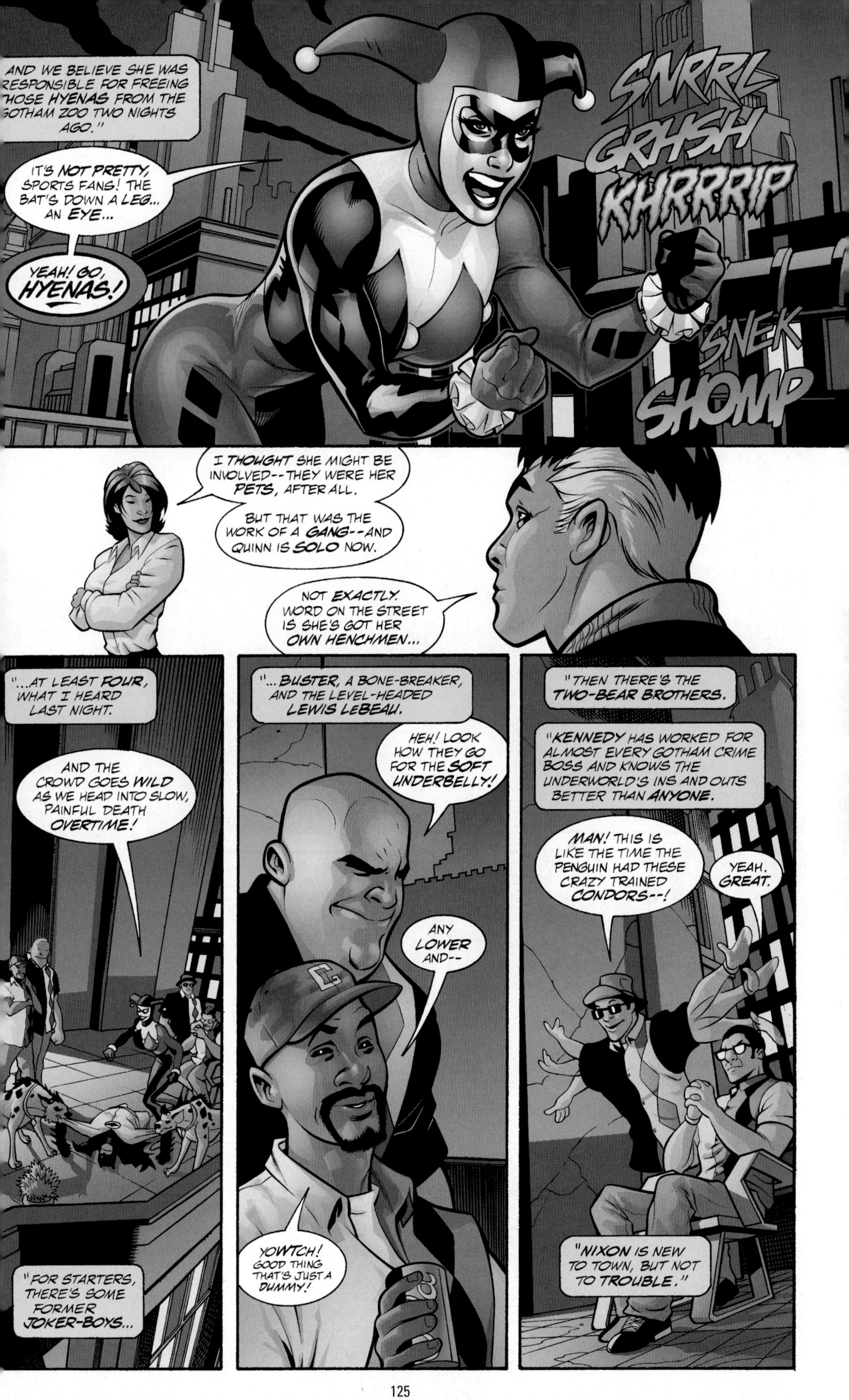

AND WE BELIEVE SHE WAS RESPONSIBLE FOR FREEING THOSE HYENAS FROM THE GOTHAM ZOO TWO NIGHTS AGO."
IT'S NOT PRETTY, SPORTS FANS! THE BAT'S DOWN A LEG... AN EYE...
YEAH! GO, HYENAS!
SNRRL
GRHSH
KHRRRIP
SNEK
SHOMP
I THOUGHT SHE MIGHT BE INVOLVED--THEY WERE HER PETS, AFTER ALL.
BUT THAT WAS THE WORK OF A GANG--AND QUINN IS SOLO NOW.
NOT EXACTLY. WORD ON THE STREET IS SHE'S GOT HER OWN HENCHMEN...
"...AT LEAST FOUR, WHAT I HEARD LAST NIGHT.
AND THE CROWD GOES WILD AS WE HEAD INTO SLOW, PAINFUL DEATH OVERTIME!
"FOR STARTERS, THERE'S SOME FORMER JOKER-BOYS...
"...BUSTER, A BONE-BREAKER, AND THE LEVEL-HEADED LEWIS LeBEAU.
HEH! LOOK HOW THEY GO FOR THE SOFT UNDERBELLY!
ANY LOWER AND--
YOWTCH! GOOD THING THAT'S JUST A DUMMY!
"THEN THERE'S THE TWO-BEAR BROTHERS.
"KENNEDY HAS WORKED FOR ALMOST EVERY GOTHAM CRIME BOSS AND KNOWS THE UNDERWORLD'S INS AND OUTS BETTER THAN ANYONE.
MAN! THIS IS LIKE THE TIME THE PENGUIN HAD THESE CRAZY TRAINED CONDORS--!
YEAH. GREAT.
"NIXON IS NEW TO TOWN, BUT NOT TO TROUBLE."

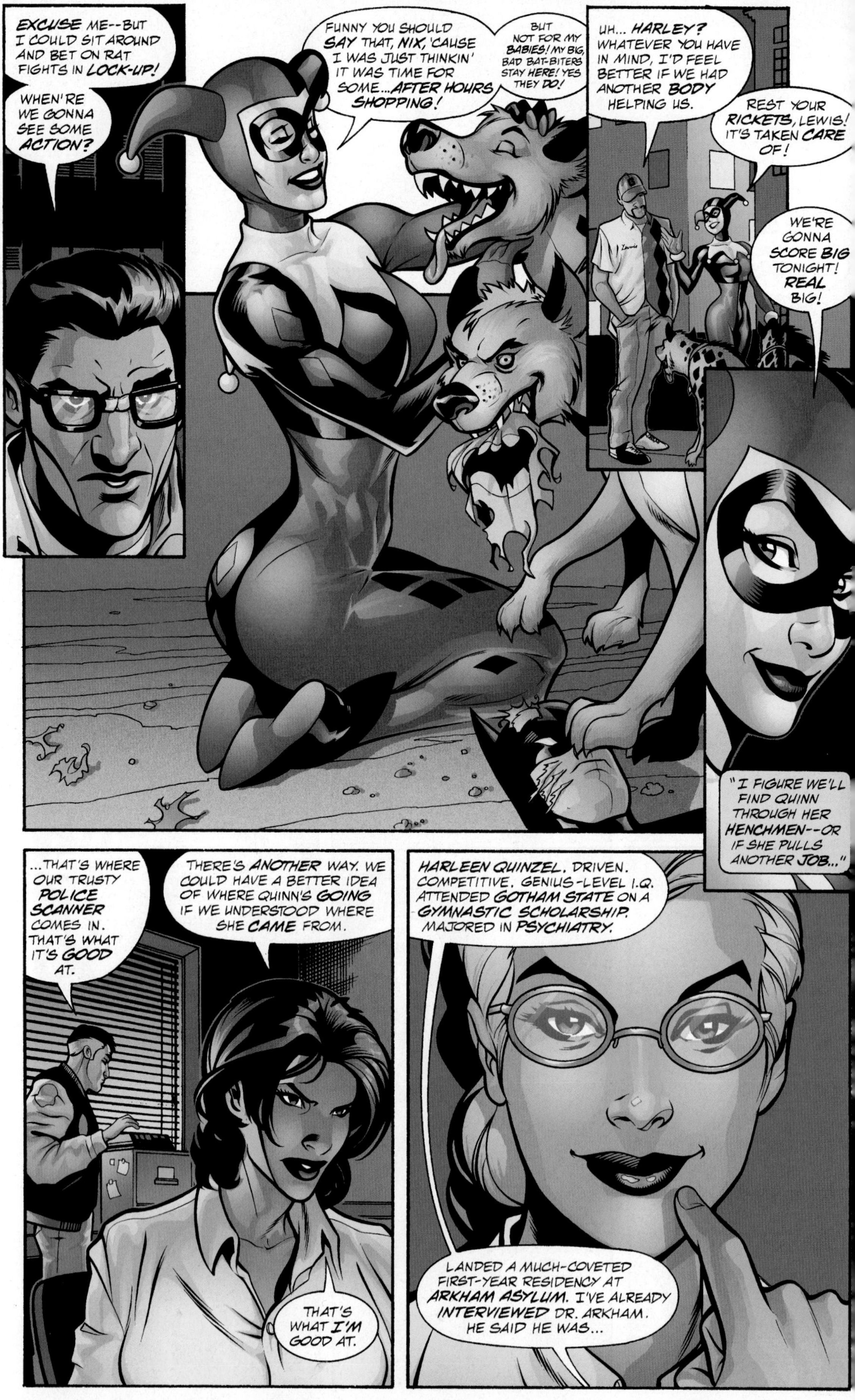

EXCUSE ME--BUT I COULD SIT AROUND AND BET ON RAT FIGHTS IN LOCK-UP!
WHEN'RE WE GONNA SEE SOME ACTION?
FUNNY YOU SHOULD SAY THAT, NIX, 'CAUSE I WAS JUST THINKIN' IT WAS TIME FOR SOME...AFTER HOURS SHOPPING!
BUT NOT FOR MY BABIES! MY BIG, BAD BAT-BITERS STAY HERE! YES THEY DO!
UH... HARLEY? WHATEVER YOU HAVE IN MIND, I'D FEEL BETTER IF WE HAD ANOTHER BODY HELPING US.
REST YOUR RICKETS, LEWIS! IT'S TAKEN CARE OF!
WE'RE GONNA SCORE BIG TONIGHT! REAL BIG!
"I FIGURE WE'LL FIND QUINN THROUGH HER HENCHMEN--OR IF SHE PULLS ANOTHER JOB..."
...THAT'S WHERE OUR TRUSTY POLICE SCANNER COMES IN. THAT'S WHAT IT'S GOOD AT.
THERE'S ANOTHER WAY. WE COULD HAVE A BETTER IDEA OF WHERE QUINN'S GOING IF WE UNDERSTOOD WHERE SHE CAME FROM.
THAT'S WHAT I'M GOOD AT.
HARLEEN QUINZEL. DRIVEN. COMPETITIVE. GENIUS-LEVEL I.Q. ATTENDED GOTHAM STATE ON A GYMNASTIC SCHOLARSHIP. MAJORED IN PSYCHIATRY.
LANDED A MUCH-COVETED FIRST-YEAR RESIDENCY AT ARKHAM ASYLUM. I'VE ALREADY INTERVIEWED DR. ARKHAM. HE SAID HE WAS...

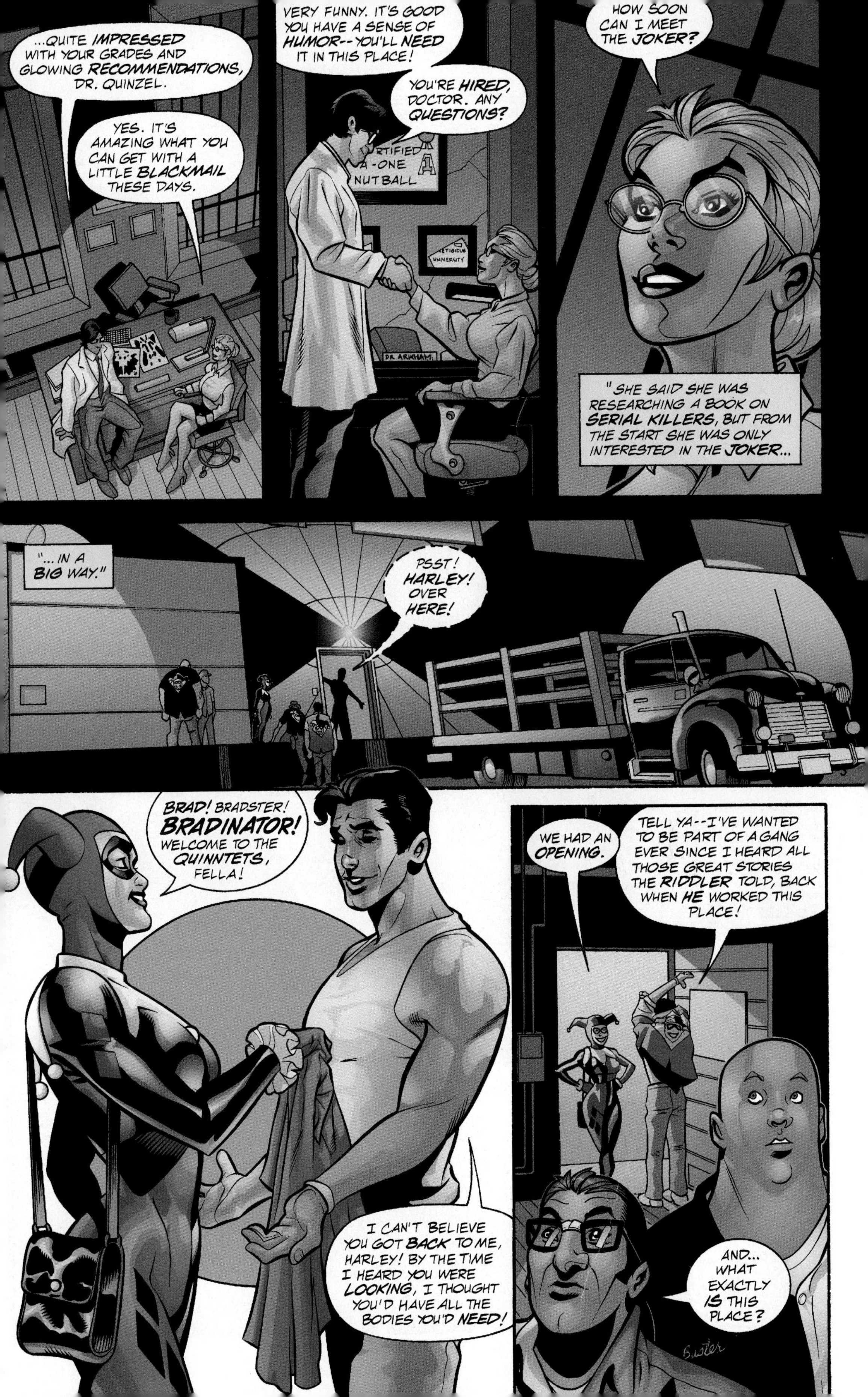
...QUITE IMPRESSED WITH YOUR GRADES AND GLOWING RECOMMENDATIONS, DR. QUINZEL.
YES. IT'S AMAZING WHAT YOU CAN GET WITH A LITTLE BLACKMAIL THESE DAYS.
VERY FUNNY. IT'S GOOD YOU HAVE A SENSE OF HUMOR--YOU'LL NEED IT IN THIS PLACE!
YOU'RE HIRED, DOCTOR. ANY QUESTIONS?
CERTIFIED A-ONE NUTBALL
DR. ARKHAM
HOW SOON CAN I MEET THE JOKER?
"SHE SAID SHE WAS RESEARCHING A BOOK ON SERIAL KILLERS, BUT FROM THE START SHE WAS ONLY INTERESTED IN THE JOKER...
"...IN A BIG WAY."
PSST! HARLEY! OVER HERE!
BRAD! BRADSTER! BRADINATOR! WELCOME TO THE QUINNTETS, FELLA!
I CAN'T BELIEVE YOU GOT BACK TO ME, HARLEY! BY THE TIME I HEARD YOU WERE LOOKING, I THOUGHT YOU'D HAVE ALL THE BODIES YOU'D NEED!
WE HAD AN OPENING.
TELL YA--I'VE WANTED TO BE PART OF A GANG EVER SINCE I HEARD ALL THOSE GREAT STORIES THE RIDDLER TOLD, BACK WHEN HE WORKED THIS PLACE!
AND... WHAT EXACTLY IS THIS PLACE?

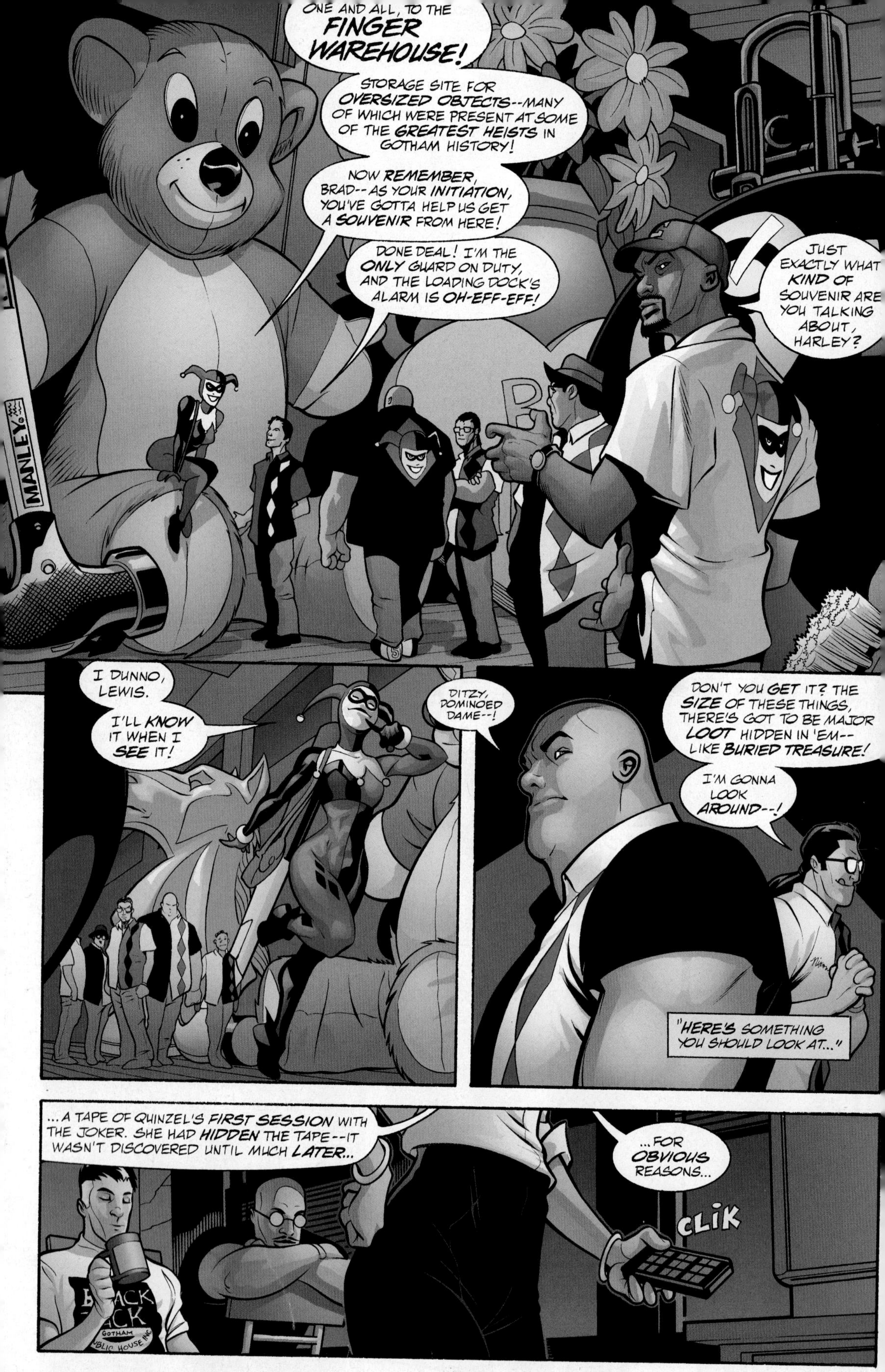

ONE AND ALL, TO THE FINGER WAREHOUSE!
STORAGE SITE FOR OVERSIZED OBJECTS--MANY OF WHICH WERE PRESENT AT SOME OF THE GREATEST HEISTS IN GOTHAM HISTORY!
NOW REMEMBER, BRAD--AS YOUR INITIATION, YOU'VE GOTTA HELP US GET A SOUVENIR FROM HERE!
DONE DEAL! I'M THE ONLY GUARD ON DUTY, AND THE LOADING DOCK'S ALARM IS OH-EFF-EFF!
JUST EXACTLY WHAT KIND OF SOUVENIR ARE YOU TALKING ABOUT, HARLEY?
MANLEY
I DUNNO, LEWIS.
I'LL KNOW IT WHEN I SEE IT!
DITZY, DOMINOED DAME--!
DON'T YOU GET IT? THE SIZE OF THESE THINGS, THERE'S GOT TO BE MAJOR LOOT HIDDEN IN 'EM--LIKE BURIED TREASURE!
I'M GONNA LOOK AROUND--!
"HERE'S SOMETHING YOU SHOULD LOOK AT..."
...A TAPE OF QUINZEL'S FIRST SESSION WITH THE JOKER. SHE HAD HIDDEN THE TAPE--IT WASN'T DISCOVERED UNTIL MUCH LATER...
...FOR OBVIOUS REASONS...
CLIK

--CAN LEAVE US *ALONE* NOW, GUARDS. WE'VE BEEN GUARANTEED *ABSOLUTE PRIVACY.*

DR. ARKHAM *APPROVED* THIS. DO YOU WANT ME TO INTERRUPT HIS BUSY SCHEDULE FOR *VERIFICATION?*

NOW THEN...

MY NAME'S *DR. HARLEEN QUINZEL,* MR. JOKER. I HAVE A FEW *QUESTIONS* I'D LIKE TO ASK YOU.

MR. JOKER?

THAT'S ODD. YOU HAVE A *REPUTATION* FOR BEING EXTREMELY *TALKATIVE.* I THOUGHT YOU'D *ENJOY* THE CHANCE TO--

OH! YOU'RE BEING *FUNNY,* AREN'T YOU?

VERY *CLEVER.*

WELL THEN--I WON'T NEED THESE *QUESTIONS* ANYMORE!

LET'S START OVER. MY NAME'S *DR. QUINZEL.*

DR. *HARLEEN* QUINZEL.

"IN LATER *INTERVIEWS,* QUINZEL INSISTED THE *JOKER* ORIGINALLY TWISTED HER NAME AROUND. BUT..."

BUT YOU CAN CALL ME *HARLEY QUINN*--LIKE *HARLEQUIN?* THE MEDIEVAL *JESTER?*

HAHAHAHA HAHAHAH HAHAHA HA

ARE YOU *FLIRTING* WITH ME, DOC?

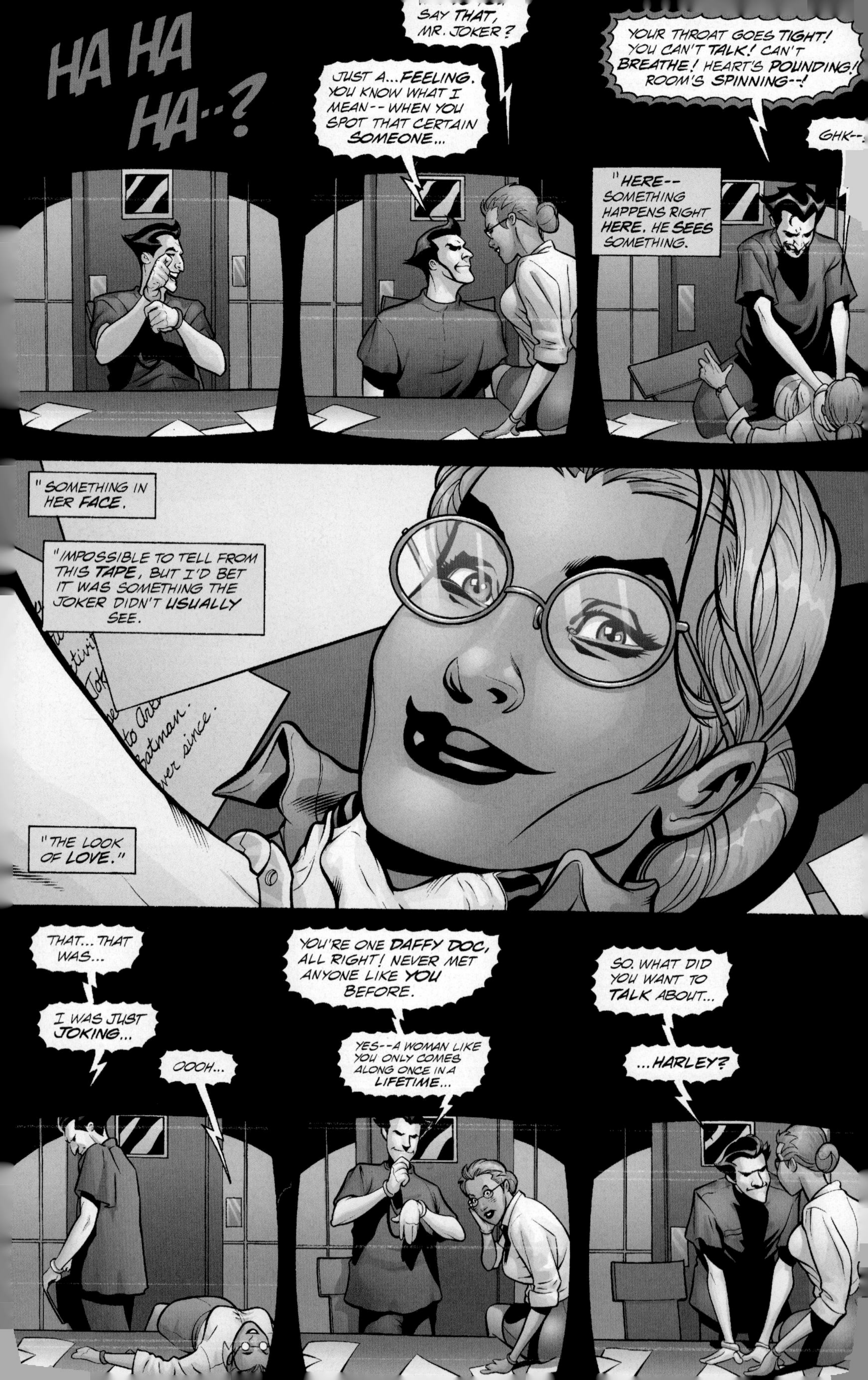
HA HA HA--?
SAY THAT, MR. JOKER?
JUST A...FEELING. YOU KNOW WHAT I MEAN-- WHEN YOU SPOT THAT CERTAIN SOMEONE...
YOUR THROAT GOES TIGHT! YOU CAN'T TALK! CAN'T BREATHE! HEART'S POUNDING! ROOM'S SPINNING--!
GHK--.
"HERE--SOMETHING HAPPENS RIGHT HERE. HE SEES SOMETHING.
"SOMETHING IN HER FACE.
"IMPOSSIBLE TO TELL FROM THIS TAPE, BUT I'D BET IT WAS SOMETHING THE JOKER DIDN'T USUALLY SEE.
"THE LOOK OF LOVE."
THAT... THAT WAS...
I WAS JUST JOKING...
OOOH...
YOU'RE ONE DAFFY DOC, ALL RIGHT! NEVER MET ANYONE LIKE YOU BEFORE.
YES--A WOMAN LIKE YOU ONLY COMES ALONG ONCE IN A LIFETIME...
SO. WHAT DID YOU WANT TO TALK ABOUT...
...HARLEY?

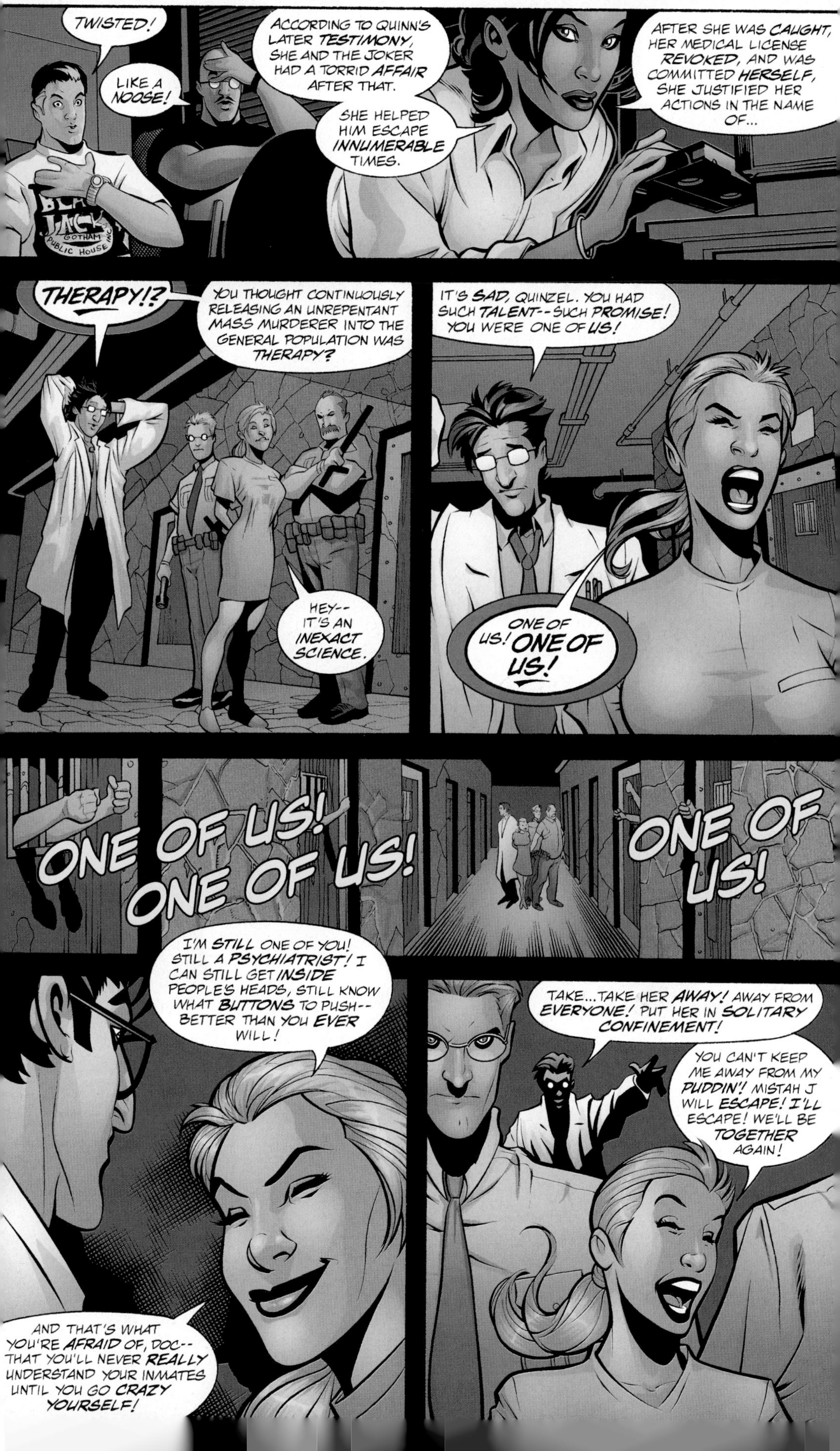
TWISTED!
LIKE A NOOSE!
ACCORDING TO QUINN'S LATER TESTIMONY, SHE AND THE JOKER HAD A TORRID AFFAIR AFTER THAT.
SHE HELPED HIM ESCAPE INNUMERABLE TIMES.
AFTER SHE WAS CAUGHT, HER MEDICAL LICENSE REVOKED, AND WAS COMMITTED HERSELF, SHE JUSTIFIED HER ACTIONS IN THE NAME OF...
BLACK JACK GOTHAM PUBLIC HOUSE INC.
THERAPY!?
YOU THOUGHT CONTINUOUSLY RELEASING AN UNREPENTANT MASS MURDERER INTO THE GENERAL POPULATION WAS THERAPY?
HEY-- IT'S AN INEXACT SCIENCE.
IT'S SAD, QUINZEL. YOU HAD SUCH TALENT--SUCH PROMISE! YOU WERE ONE OF US!
ONE OF US! ONE OF US!
ONE OF US! ONE OF US!
ONE OF US!
I'M STILL ONE OF YOU! STILL A PSYCHIATRIST! I CAN STILL GET INSIDE PEOPLE'S HEADS, STILL KNOW WHAT BUTTONS TO PUSH-- BETTER THAN YOU EVER WILL!
AND THAT'S WHAT YOU'RE AFRAID OF, DOC-- THAT YOU'LL NEVER REALLY UNDERSTAND YOUR INMATES UNTIL YOU GO CRAZY YOURSELF!
TAKE...TAKE HER AWAY! AWAY FROM EVERYONE! PUT HER IN SOLITARY CONFINEMENT!
YOU CAN'T KEEP ME AWAY FROM MY PUDDIN'! MISTAH J WILL ESCAPE! I'LL ESCAPE! WE'LL BE TOGETHER AGAIN!

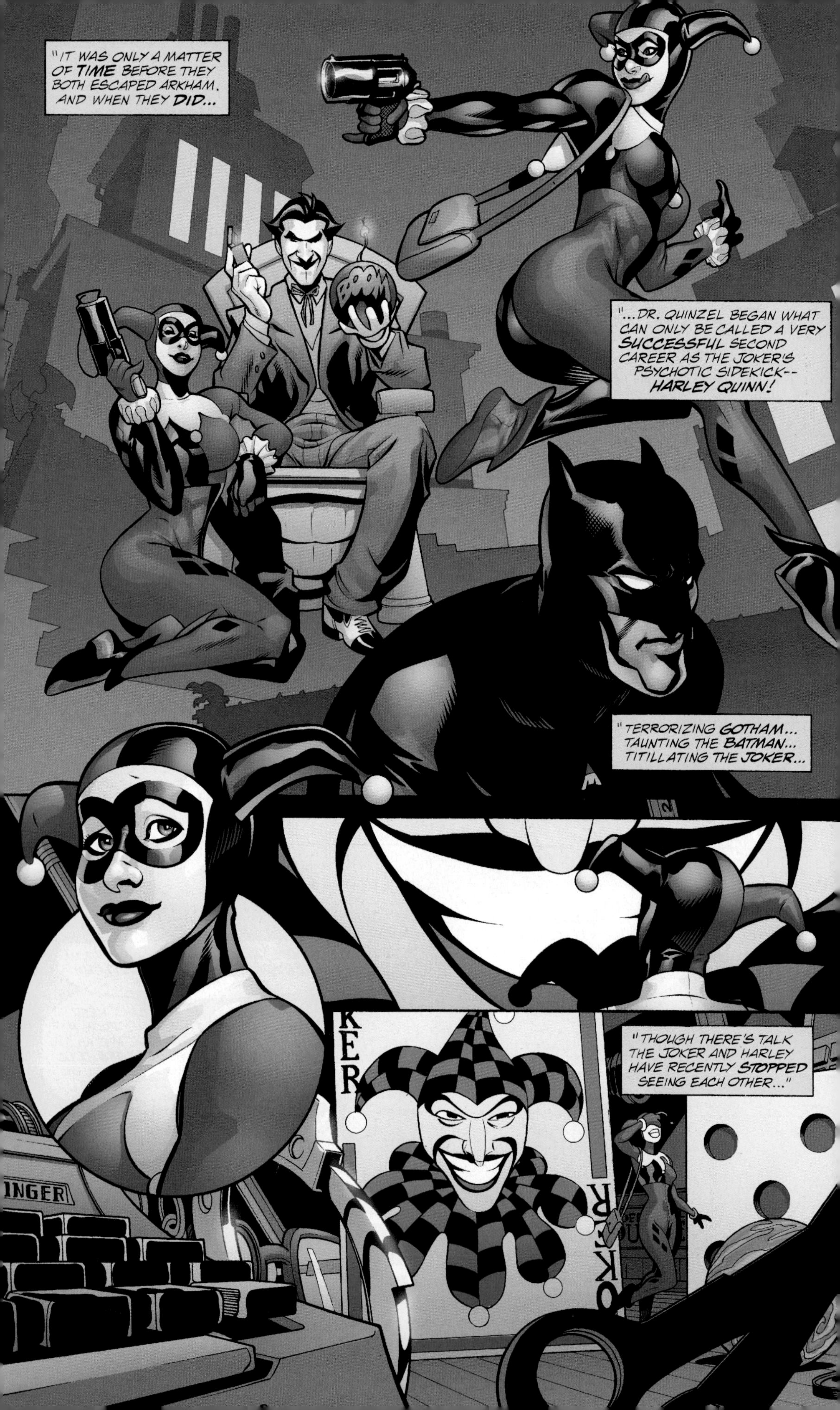
"IT WAS ONLY A MATTER OF TIME BEFORE THEY BOTH ESCAPED ARKHAM. AND WHEN THEY DID...
BOOM
"...DR. QUINZEL BEGAN WHAT CAN ONLY BE CALLED A VERY SUCCESSFUL SECOND CAREER AS THE JOKER'S PSYCHOTIC SIDEKICK-- HARLEY QUINN!
"TERRORIZING GOTHAM... TAUNTING THE BATMAN... TITILLATING THE JOKER...
"THOUGH THERE'S TALK THE JOKER AND HARLEY HAVE RECENTLY STOPPED SEEING EACH OTHER..."
KER
INGER

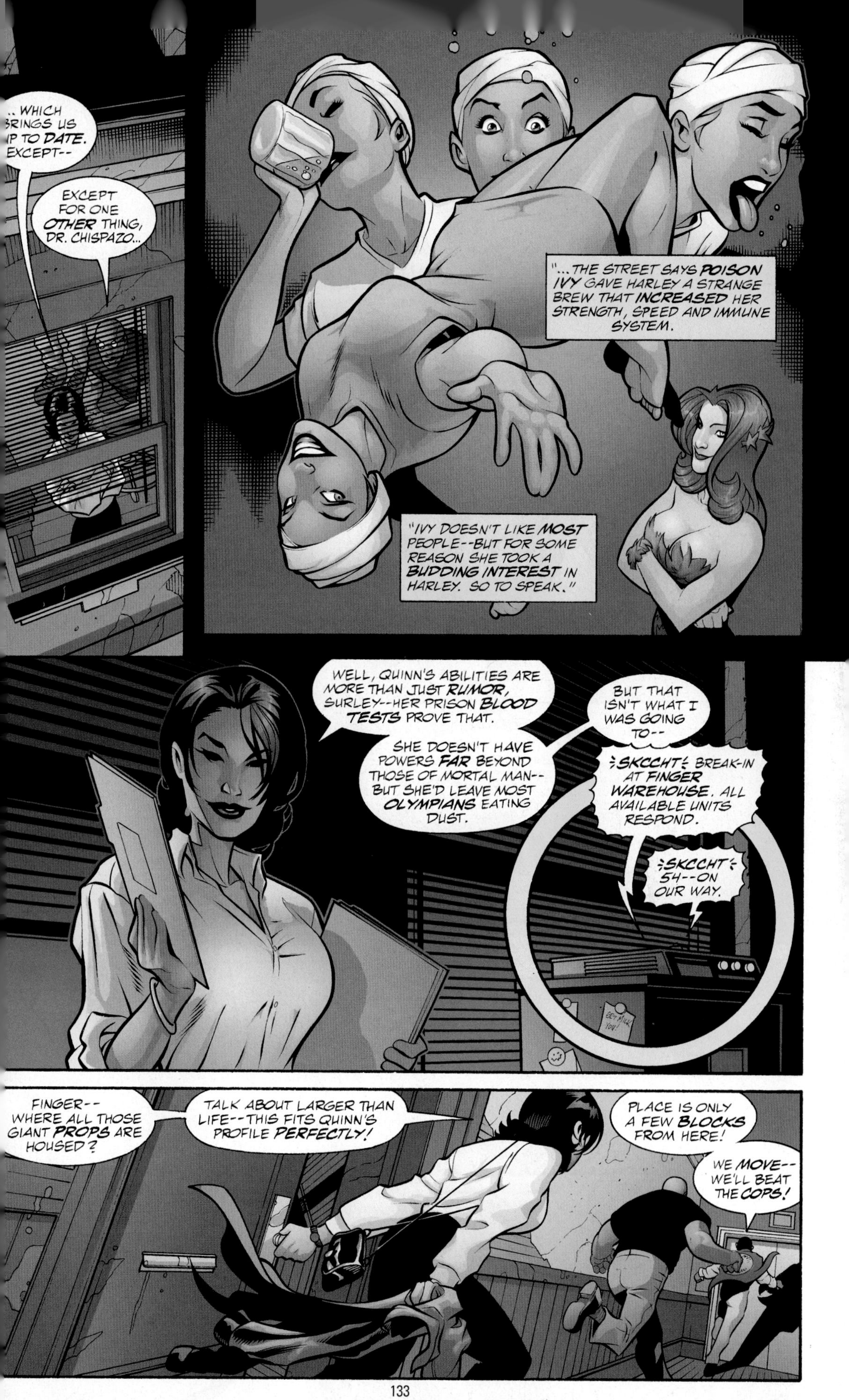

..WHICH BRINGS US UP TO DATE. EXCEPT--
EXCEPT FOR ONE OTHER THING, DR. CHISPAZO...
"...THE STREET SAYS POISON IVY GAVE HARLEY A STRANGE BREW THAT INCREASED HER STRENGTH, SPEED AND IMMUNE SYSTEM.
"IVY DOESN'T LIKE MOST PEOPLE--BUT FOR SOME REASON SHE TOOK A BUDDING INTEREST IN HARLEY. SO TO SPEAK."
WELL, QUINN'S ABILITIES ARE MORE THAN JUST RUMOR, SURLEY--HER PRISON BLOOD TESTS PROVE THAT.
SHE DOESN'T HAVE POWERS FAR BEYOND THOSE OF MORTAL MAN--BUT SHE'D LEAVE MOST OLYMPIANS EATING DUST.
BUT THAT ISN'T WHAT I WAS GOING TO--
SKCCHT BREAK-IN AT FINGER WAREHOUSE. ALL AVAILABLE UNITS RESPOND.
SKCCHT 54--ON OUR WAY.
FINGER--WHERE ALL THOSE GIANT PROPS ARE HOUSED?
TALK ABOUT LARGER THAN LIFE--THIS FITS QUINN'S PROFILE PERFECTLY!
PLACE IS ONLY A FEW BLOCKS FROM HERE!
WE MOVE--WE'LL BEAT THE COPS!

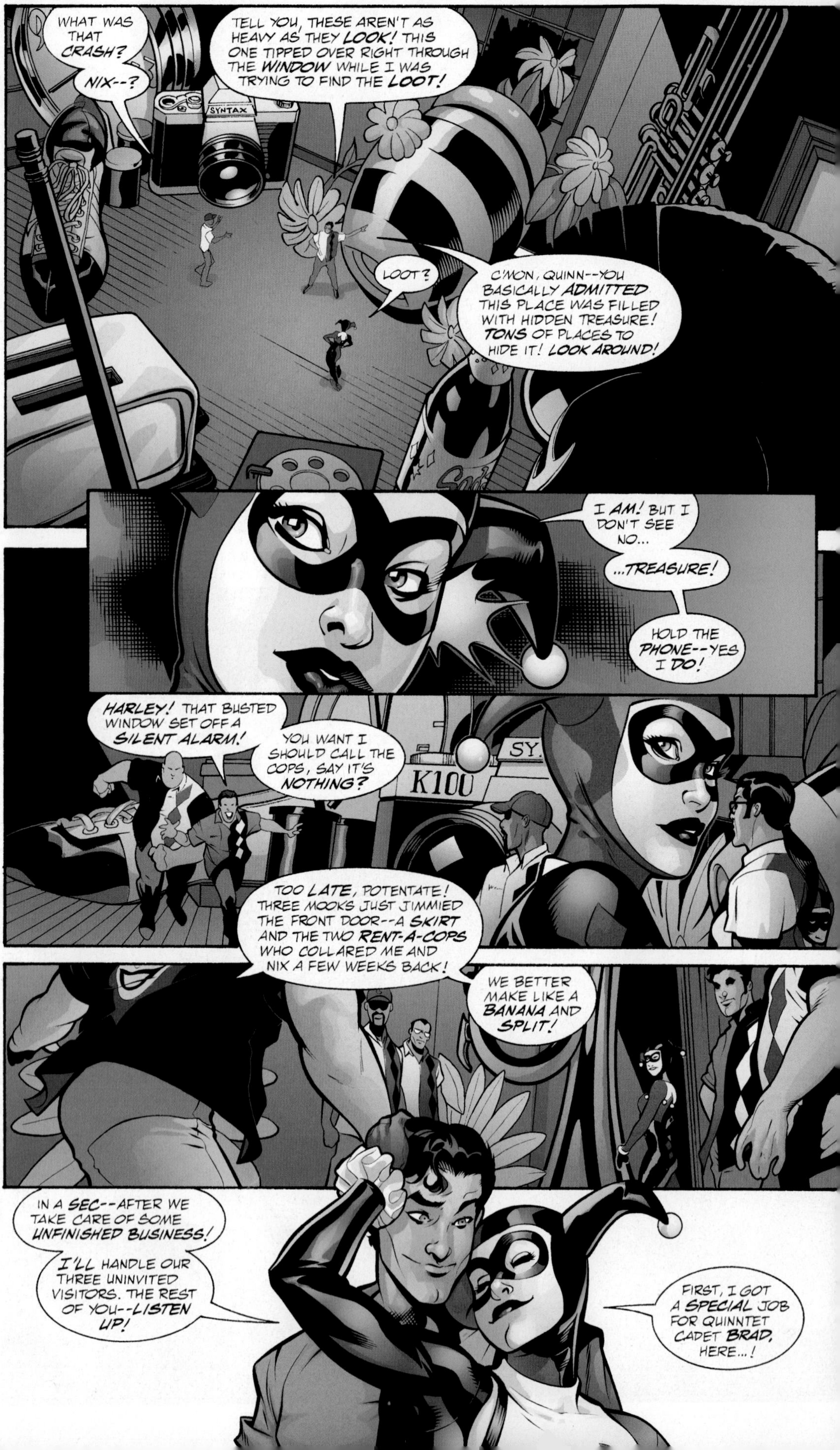

WHAT WAS THAT CRASH?
NIX--?
TELL YOU, THESE AREN'T AS HEAVY AS THEY LOOK! THIS ONE TIPPED OVER RIGHT THROUGH THE WINDOW WHILE I WAS TRYING TO FIND THE LOOT!
SYNTAX
LOOT?
C'MON, QUINN--YOU BASICALLY ADMITTED THIS PLACE WAS FILLED WITH HIDDEN TREASURE! TONS OF PLACES TO HIDE IT! LOOK AROUND!
I AM! BUT I DON'T SEE NO...
...TREASURE!
HOLD THE PHONE--YES I DO!
HARLEY! THAT BUSTED WINDOW SET OFF A SILENT ALARM!
YOU WANT I SHOULD CALL THE COPS, SAY IT'S NOTHING?
SY.
K100
TOO LATE, POTENTATE! THREE MOOKS JUST JIMMIED THE FRONT DOOR--A SKIRT AND THE TWO RENT-A-COPS WHO COLLARED ME AND NIX A FEW WEEKS BACK!
WE BETTER MAKE LIKE A BANANA AND SPLIT!
IN A SEC--AFTER WE TAKE CARE OF SOME UNFINISHED BUSINESS!
I'LL HANDLE OUR THREE UNINVITED VISITORS. THE REST OF YOU--LISTEN UP!
FIRST, I GOT A SPECIAL JOB FOR QUINNTET CADET BRAD, HERE...!

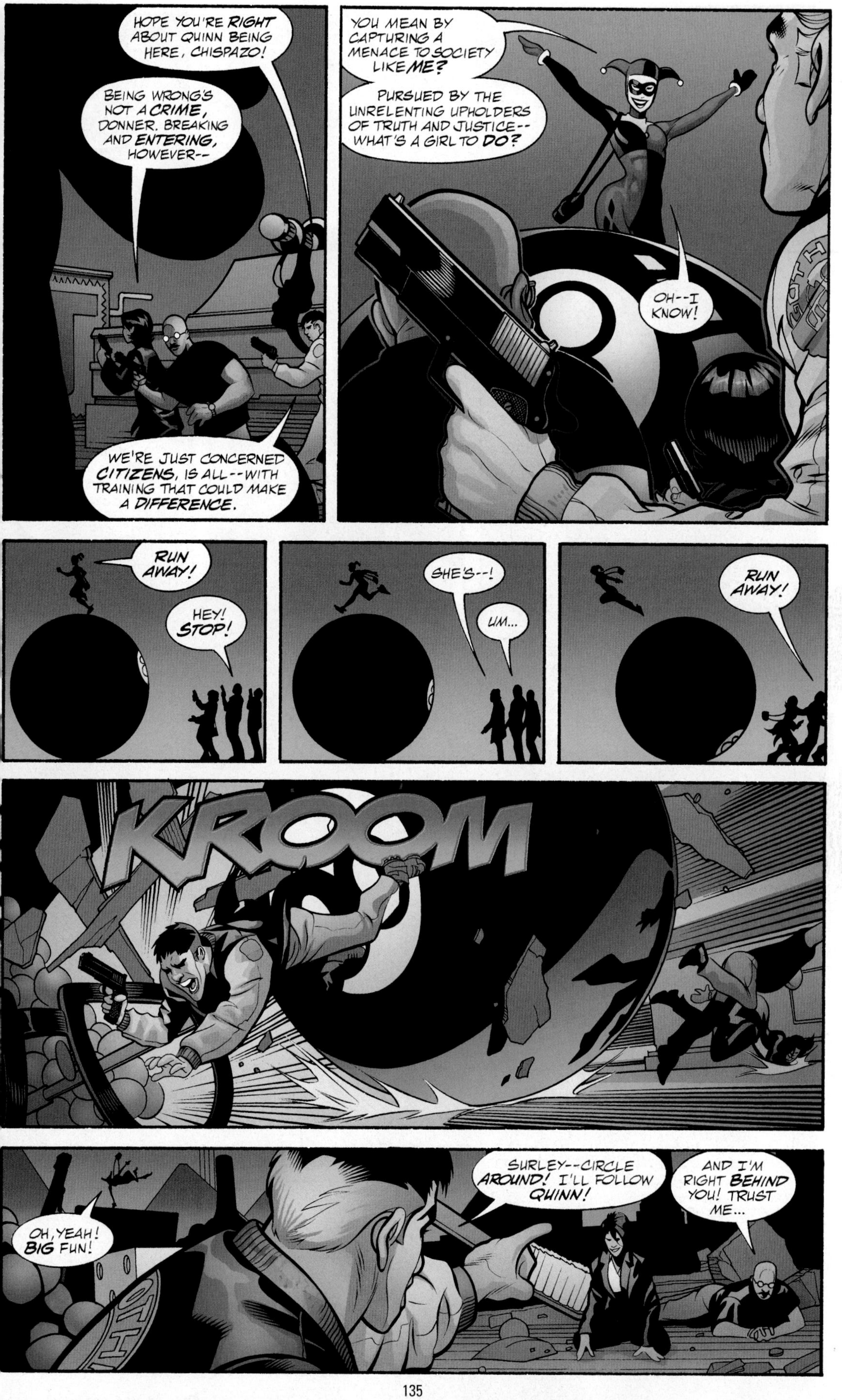
HOPE YOU'RE RIGHT ABOUT QUINN BEING HERE, CHISPAZO!
BEING WRONG'S NOT A CRIME, DONNER. BREAKING AND ENTERING, HOWEVER--
WE'RE JUST CONCERNED CITIZENS, IS ALL--WITH TRAINING THAT COULD MAKE A DIFFERENCE.
YOU MEAN BY CAPTURING A MENACE TO SOCIETY LIKE ME?
PURSUED BY THE UNRELENTING UPHOLDERS OF TRUTH AND JUSTICE--WHAT'S A GIRL TO DO?
OH--I KNOW!
RUN AWAY!
HEY! STOP!
SHE'S--!
UM...
RUN AWAY!
KROOM
OH, YEAH! BIG FUN!
SURLEY--CIRCLE AROUND! I'LL FOLLOW QUINN!
AND I'M RIGHT BEHIND YOU! TRUST ME...

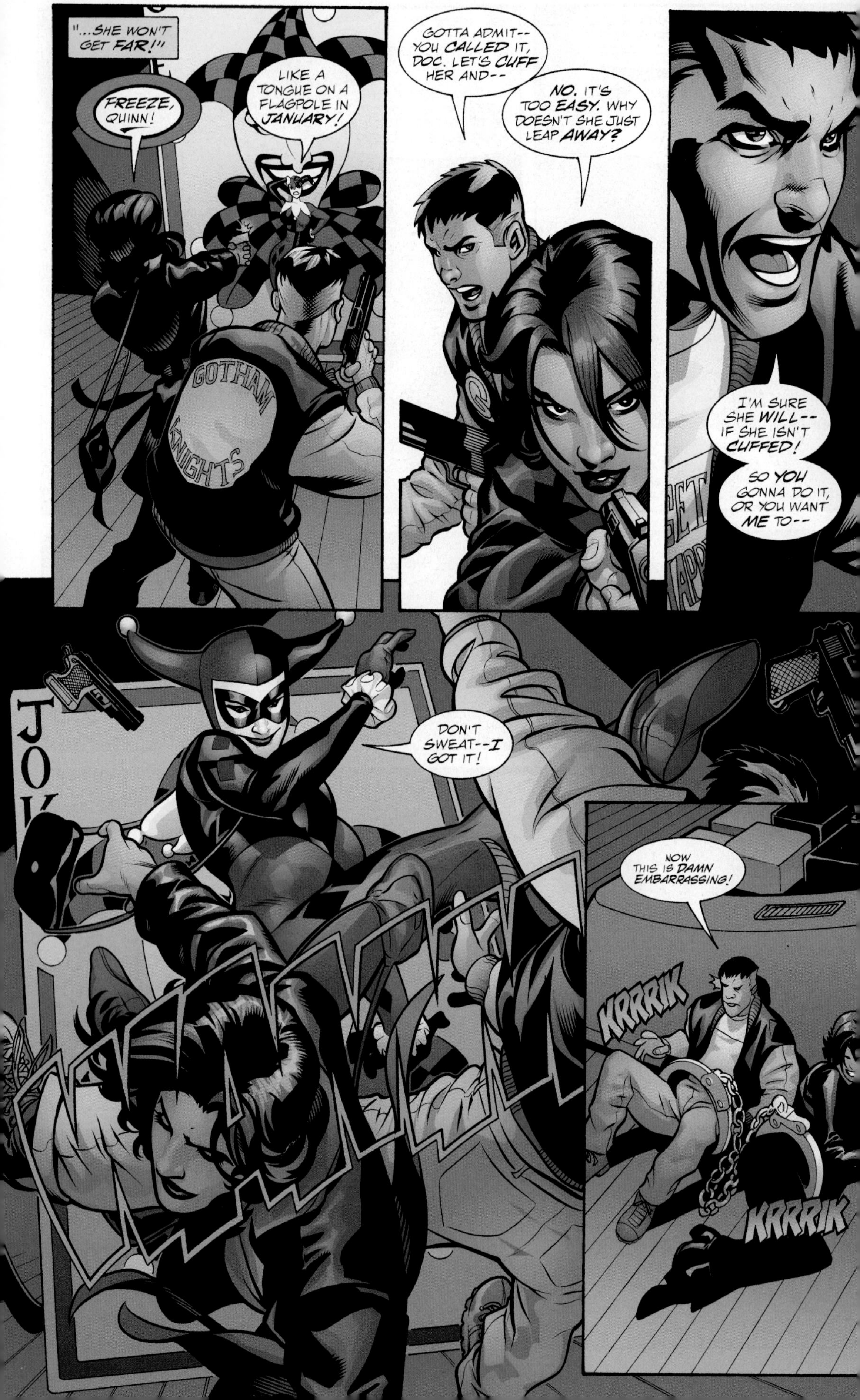
"...SHE WON'T GET FAR!"
FREEZE, QUINN!
LIKE A TONGUE ON A FLAGPOLE IN JANUARY!
GOTHAM KNIGHTS
GOTTA ADMIT--YOU CALLED IT, DOC. LET'S CUFF HER AND--
NO. IT'S TOO EASY. WHY DOESN'T SHE JUST LEAP AWAY?
I'M SURE SHE WILL--IF SHE ISN'T CUFFED!
SO YOU GONNA DO IT, OR YOU WANT ME TO--
DON'T SWEAT--I GOT IT!
NOW THIS IS DAMN EMBARRASSING!
KRRRIK
KRRRIK

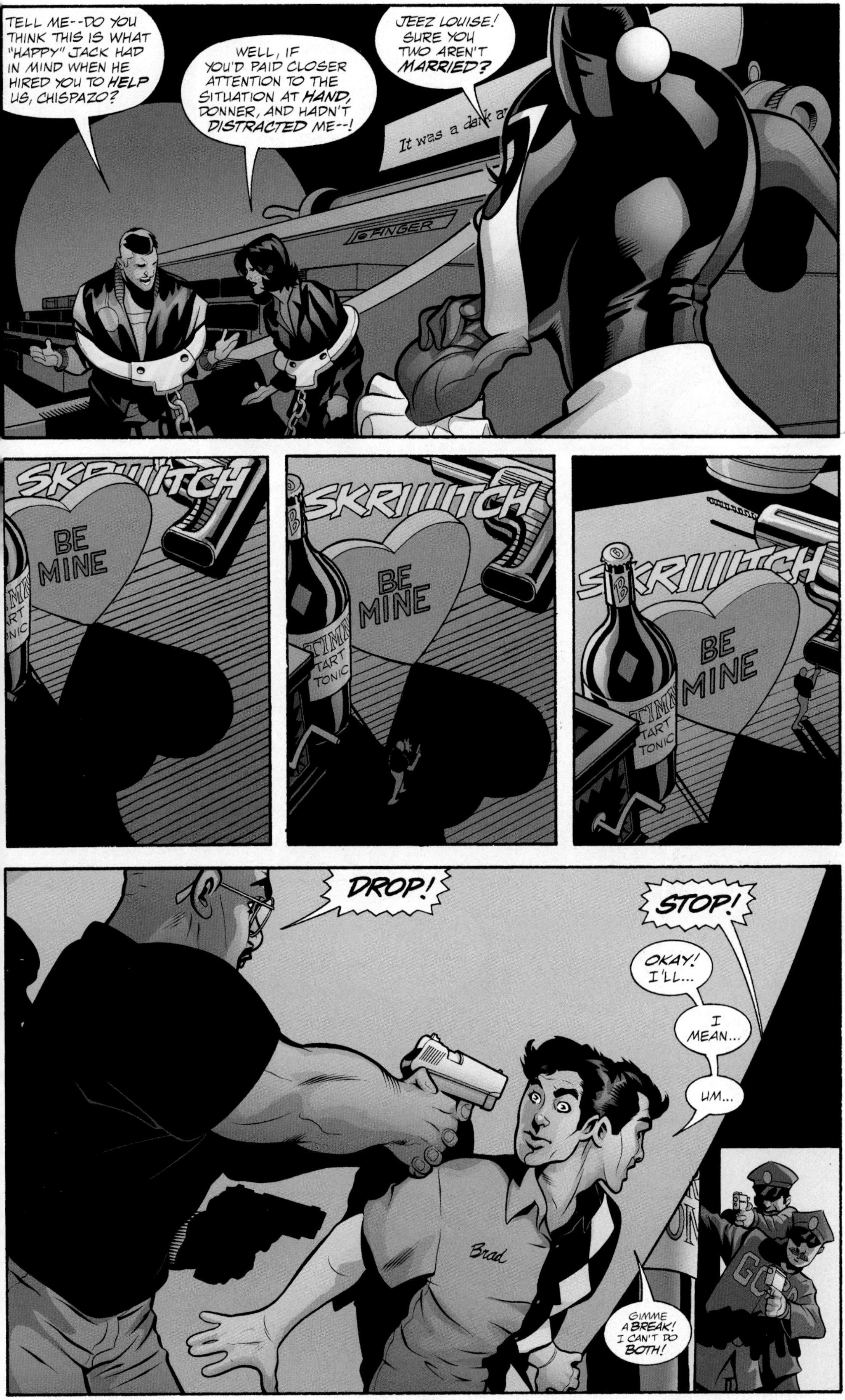
TELL ME--DO YOU THINK THIS IS WHAT "HAPPY" JACK HAD IN MIND WHEN HE HIRED YOU TO HELP US, CHISPAZO?
WELL, IF YOU'D PAID CLOSER ATTENTION TO THE SITUATION AT HAND, DONNER, AND HADN'T DISTRACTED ME--!
JEEZ LOUISE! SURE YOU TWO AREN'T MARRIED?
FINGER
SKRIIIITCH
BE MINE
SKRIIIITCH
BE MINE
TART TONIC
SKRIIIITCH
BE MINE
TART TONIC
DROP!
STOP!
OKAY! I'LL...
I MEAN...
UM...
Brad
GIMME A BREAK! I CAN'T DO BOTH!

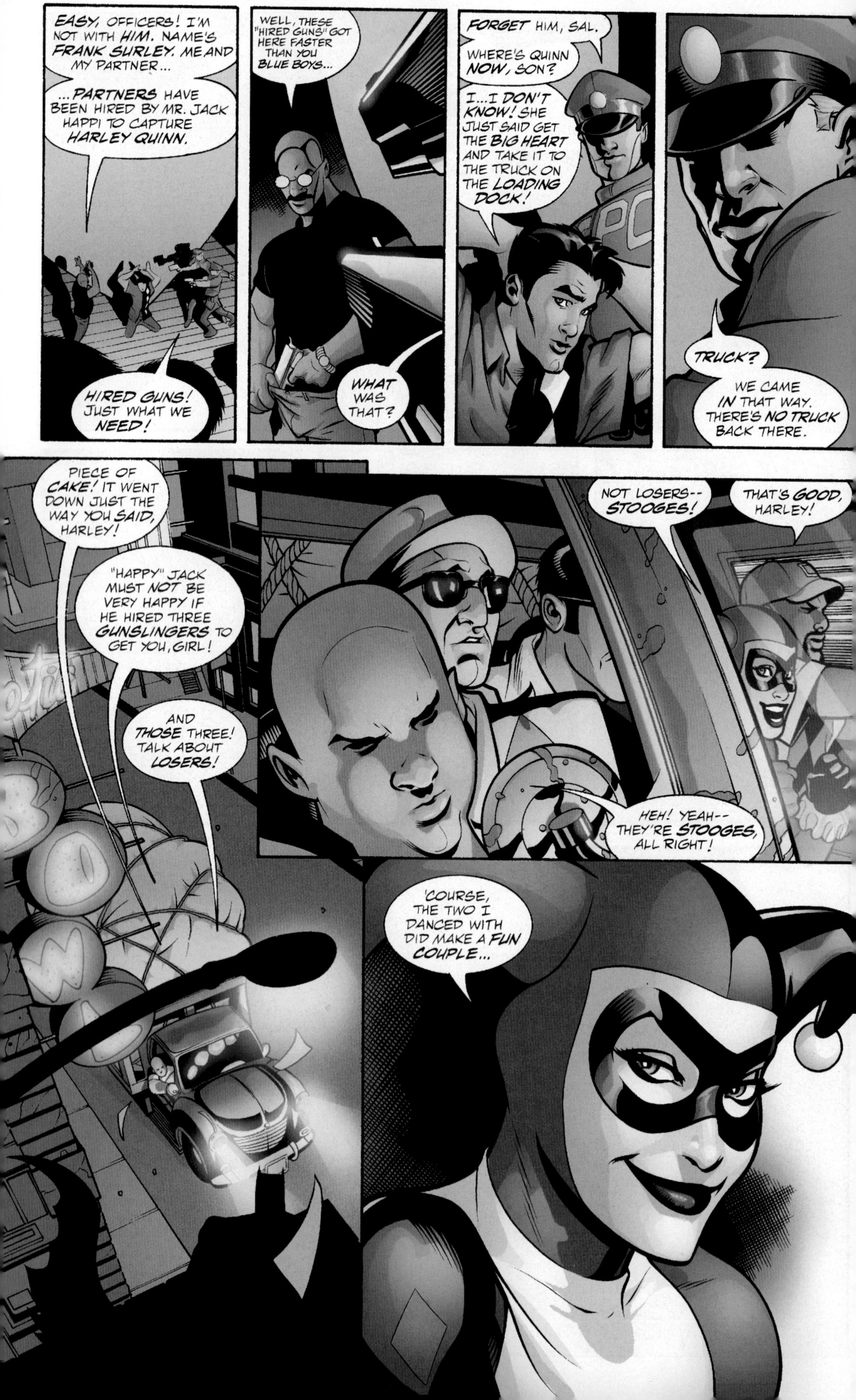

EASY, OFFICERS! I'M NOT WITH HIM. NAME'S FRANK SURLEY. ME AND MY PARTNER...
...PARTNERS HAVE BEEN HIRED BY MR. JACK HAPPI TO CAPTURE HARLEY QUINN.
HIRED GUNS! JUST WHAT WE NEED!
WELL, THESE "HIRED GUNS" GOT HERE FASTER THAN YOU BLUE BOYS...
WHAT WAS THAT?
FORGET HIM, SAL.
WHERE'S QUINN NOW, SON?
I...I DON'T KNOW! SHE JUST SAID GET THE BIG HEART AND TAKE IT TO THE TRUCK ON THE LOADING DOCK!
TRUCK?
WE CAME IN THAT WAY. THERE'S NO TRUCK BACK THERE.
PIECE OF CAKE! IT WENT DOWN JUST THE WAY YOU SAID, HARLEY!
"HAPPY" JACK MUST NOT BE VERY HAPPY IF HE HIRED THREE GUNSLINGERS TO GET YOU, GIRL!
AND THOSE THREE! TALK ABOUT LOSERS!
NOT LOSERS-- STOOGES!
THAT'S GOOD, HARLEY!
HEH! YEAH-- THEY'RE STOOGES, ALL RIGHT!
'COURSE, THE TWO I DANCED WITH DID MAKE A FUN COUPLE...

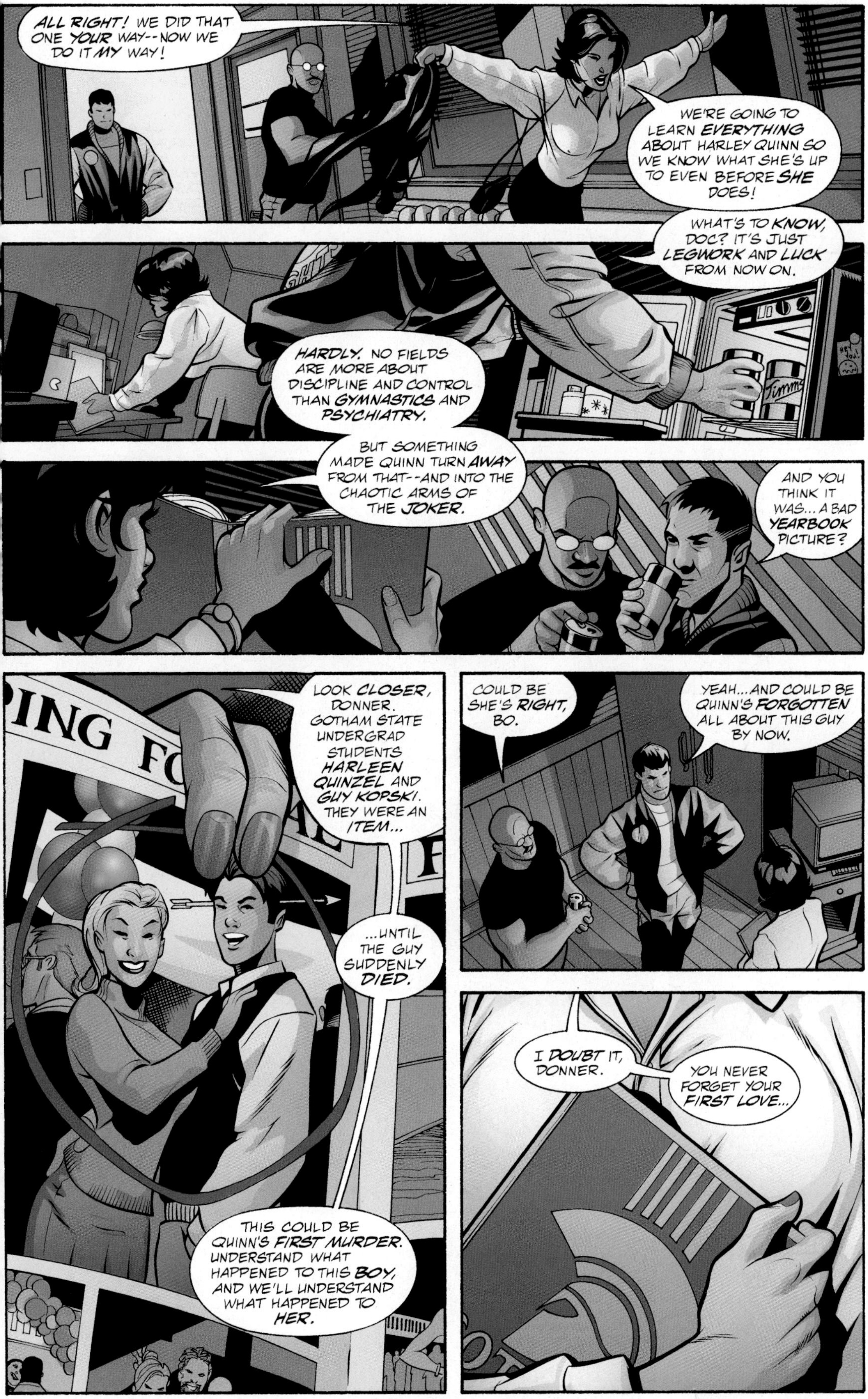
ALL RIGHT! WE DID THAT ONE YOUR WAY--NOW WE DO IT MY WAY!
WE'RE GOING TO LEARN EVERYTHING ABOUT HARLEY QUINN SO WE KNOW WHAT SHE'S UP TO EVEN BEFORE SHE DOES!
WHAT'S TO KNOW, DOC? IT'S JUST LEGWORK AND LUCK FROM NOW ON.
HARDLY. NO FIELDS ARE MORE ABOUT DISCIPLINE AND CONTROL THAN GYMNASTICS AND PSYCHIATRY.
BUT SOMETHING MADE QUINN TURN AWAY FROM THAT--AND INTO THE CHAOTIC ARMS OF THE JOKER.
AND YOU THINK IT WAS... A BAD YEARBOOK PICTURE?
LOOK CLOSER, DONNER. GOTHAM STATE UNDERGRAD STUDENTS HARLEEN QUINZEL AND GUY KOPSKI. THEY WERE AN ITEM...
...UNTIL THE GUY SUDDENLY DIED.
THIS COULD BE QUINN'S FIRST MURDER. UNDERSTAND WHAT HAPPENED TO THIS BOY, AND WE'LL UNDERSTAND WHAT HAPPENED TO HER.
COULD BE SHE'S RIGHT, BO.
YEAH...AND COULD BE QUINN'S FORGOTTEN ALL ABOUT THIS GUY BY NOW.
I DOUBT IT, DONNER.
YOU NEVER FORGET YOUR FIRST LOVE...

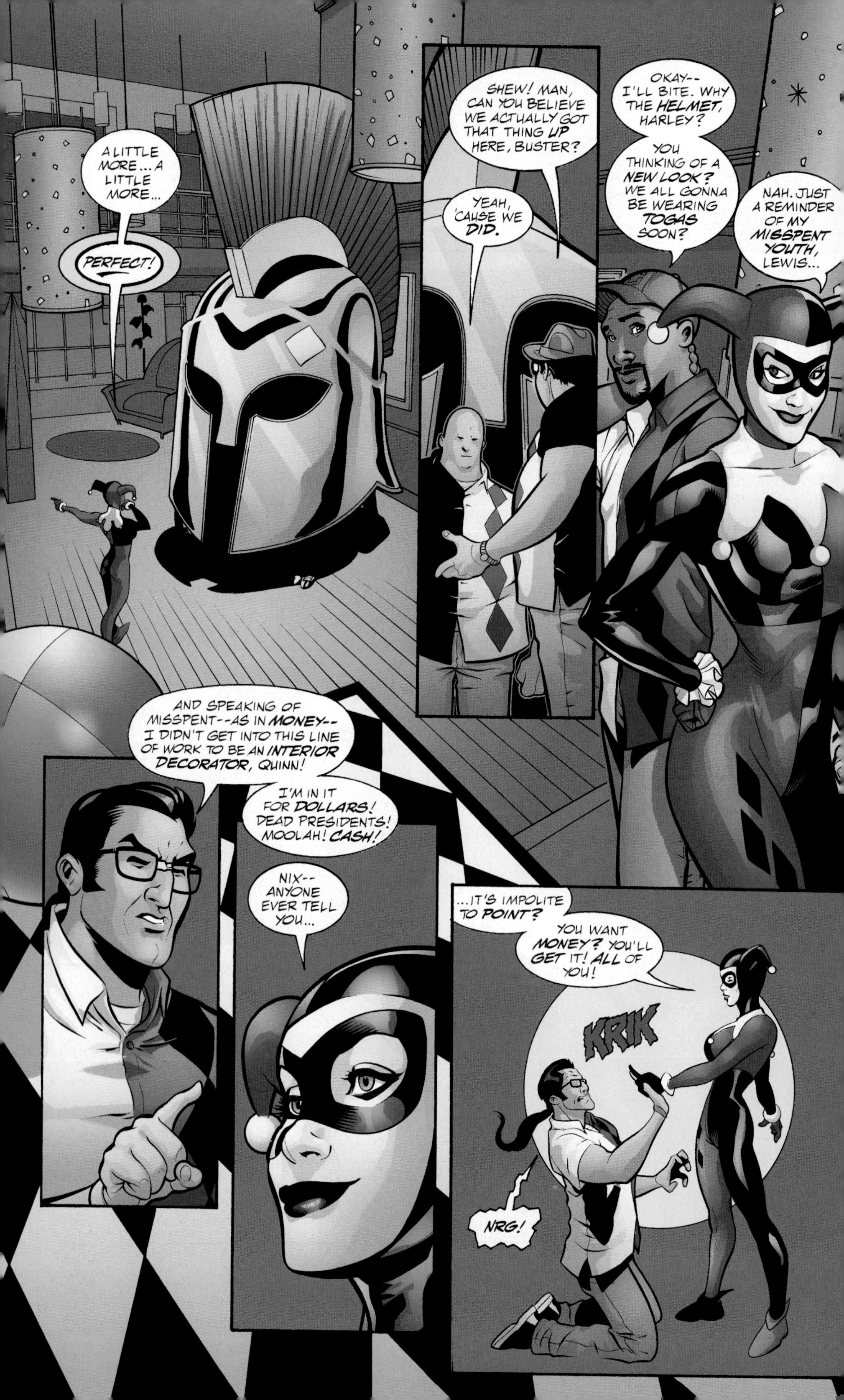
A LITTLE MORE... A LITTLE MORE...
PERFECT!
SHEW! MAN, CAN YOU BELIEVE WE ACTUALLY GOT THAT THING UP HERE, BUSTER?
YEAH, 'CAUSE WE DID.
OKAY-- I'LL BITE. WHY THE HELMET, HARLEY?
YOU THINKING OF A NEW LOOK? WE ALL GONNA BE WEARING TOGAS SOON?
NAH. JUST A REMINDER OF MY MISSPENT YOUTH, LEWIS...
AND SPEAKING OF MISSPENT--AS IN MONEY-- I DIDN'T GET INTO THIS LINE OF WORK TO BE AN INTERIOR DECORATOR, QUINN!
I'M IN IT FOR DOLLARS! DEAD PRESIDENTS! MOOLAH! CASH!
NIX-- ANYONE EVER TELL YOU...
...IT'S IMPOLITE TO POINT?
YOU WANT MONEY? YOU'LL GET IT! ALL OF YOU!
KRIK
NRG!

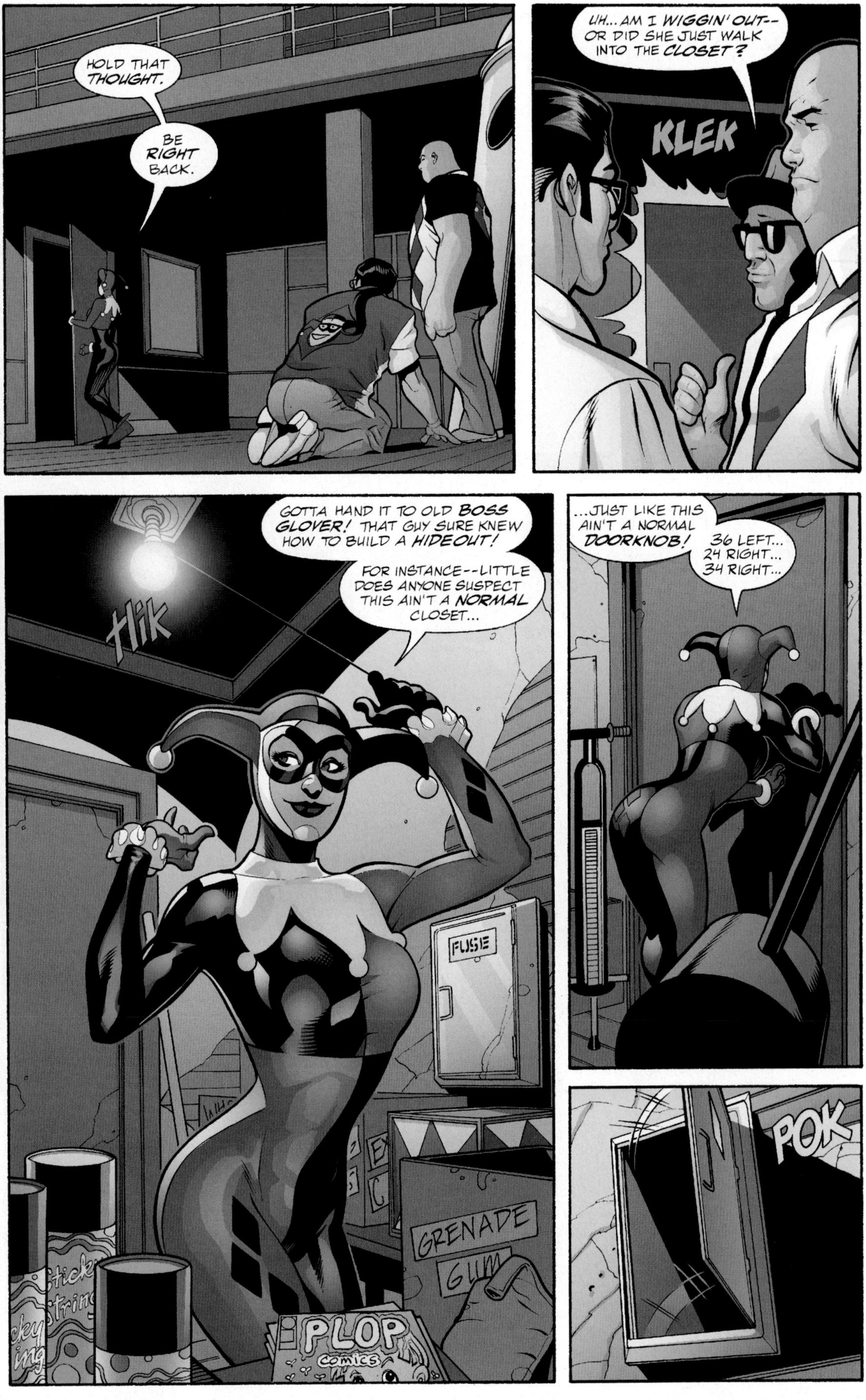
HOLD THAT THOUGHT.
BE RIGHT BACK.
UH... AM I WIGGIN' OUT-- OR DID SHE JUST WALK INTO THE CLOSET?
KLEK
GOTTA HAND IT TO OLD BOSS GLOVER! THAT GUY SURE KNEW HOW TO BUILD A HIDEOUT!
FOR INSTANCE--LITTLE DOES ANYONE SUSPECT THIS AIN'T A NORMAL CLOSET...
tlik
FUSE
GRENADE GUM
PLOP comics
...JUST LIKE THIS AIN'T A NORMAL DOORKNOB!
36 LEFT... 24 RIGHT... 34 RIGHT...
POK

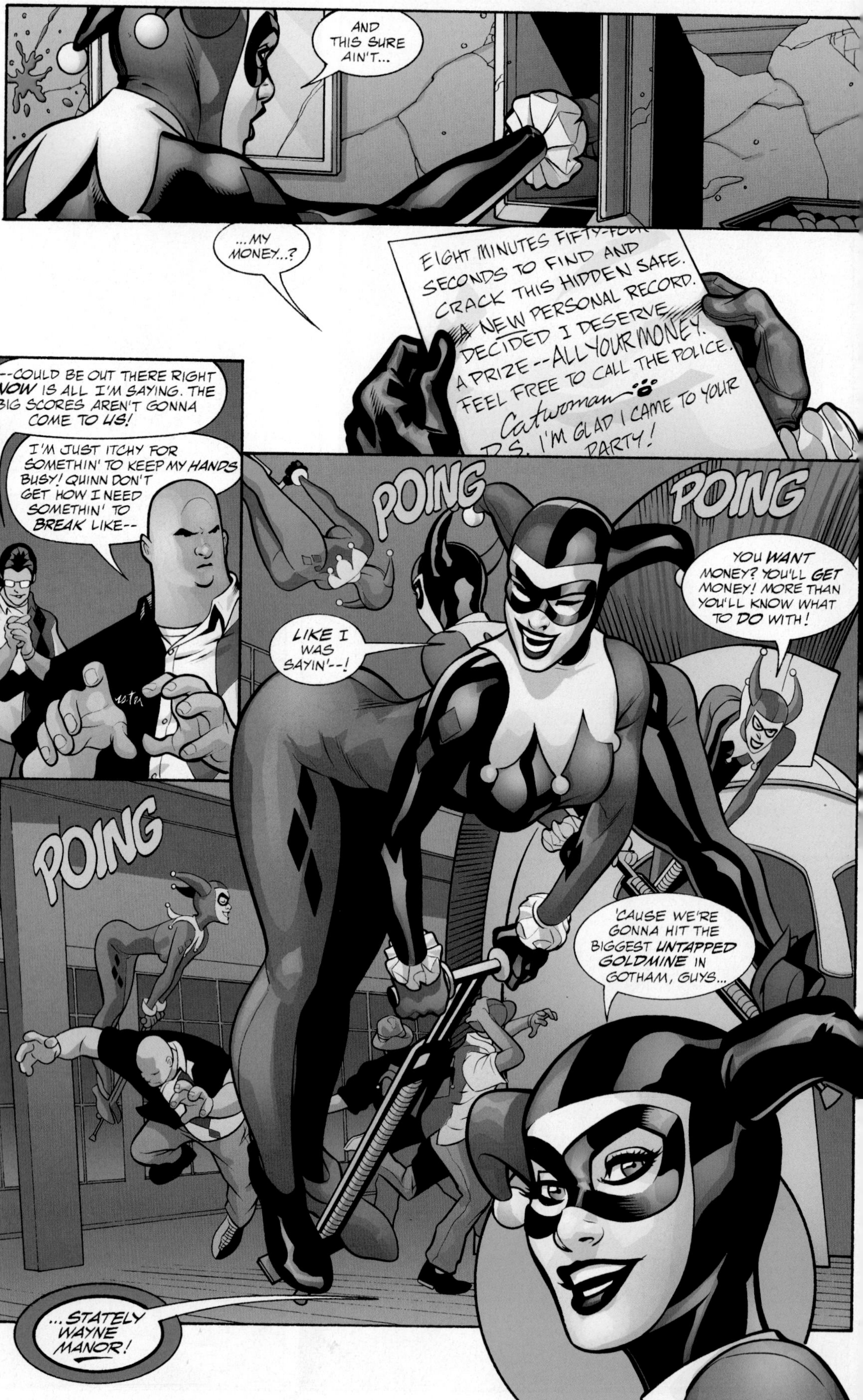
AND THIS SURE AIN'T...
...MY MONEY...?
EIGHT MINUTES FIFTY-FOUR SECONDS TO FIND AND CRACK THIS HIDDEN SAFE. A NEW PERSONAL RECORD. DECIDED I DESERVE A PRIZE--ALL YOUR MONEY. FEEL FREE TO CALL THE POLICE.
Catwoman
P.S. I'M GLAD I CAME TO YOUR PARTY!
--COULD BE OUT THERE RIGHT NOW IS ALL I'M SAYING. THE BIG SCORES AREN'T GONNA COME TO US!
I'M JUST ITCHY FOR SOMETHIN' TO KEEP MY HANDS BUSY! QUINN DON'T GET HOW I NEED SOMETHIN' TO BREAK LIKE--
POING
POING
LIKE I WAS SAYIN'--!
YOU WANT MONEY? YOU'LL GET MONEY! MORE THAN YOU'LL KNOW WHAT TO DO WITH!
POING
'CAUSE WE'RE GONNA HIT THE BIGGEST UNTAPPED GOLDMINE IN GOTHAM, GUYS...
...STATELY WAYNE MANOR!

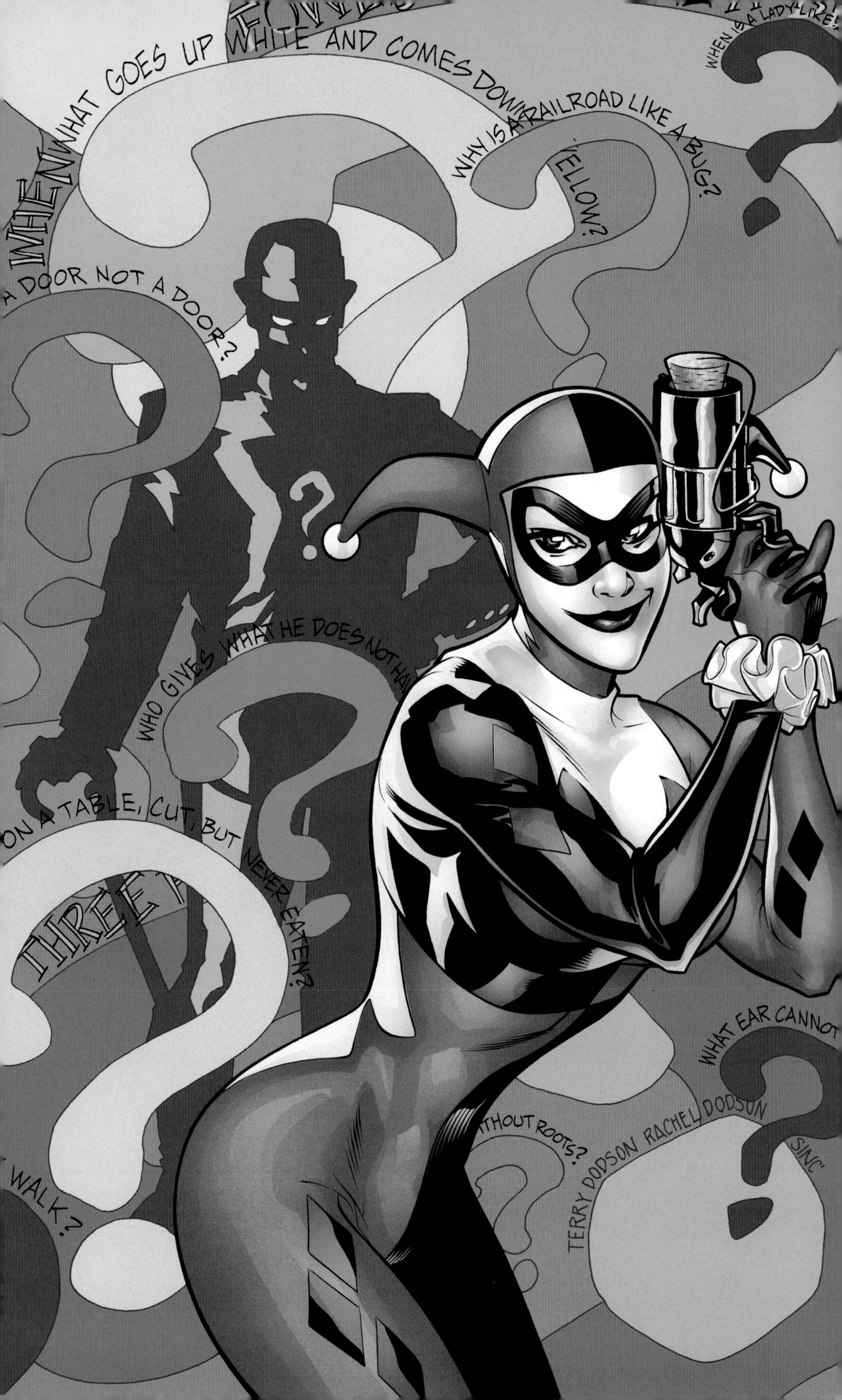

WHEN
WHAT GOES UP WHITE AND COMES DOWN
WHEN IS A LADY LIKE
WHY IS A RAILROAD LIKE A BUG?
YELLOW?
A DOOR NOT A DOOR?
WHO GIVES WHAT HE DOES NOT
ON A TABLE, CUT, BUT NEVER EATEN?
THREE
WALK?
WHAT EAR CANNOT
ROOTS?
TERRY DODSON RACHEL DODSON

This chapter pencils by Terry Dodson and Craig Rousseau
This chapter inks by Rachel Dodson and Wayne Faucher

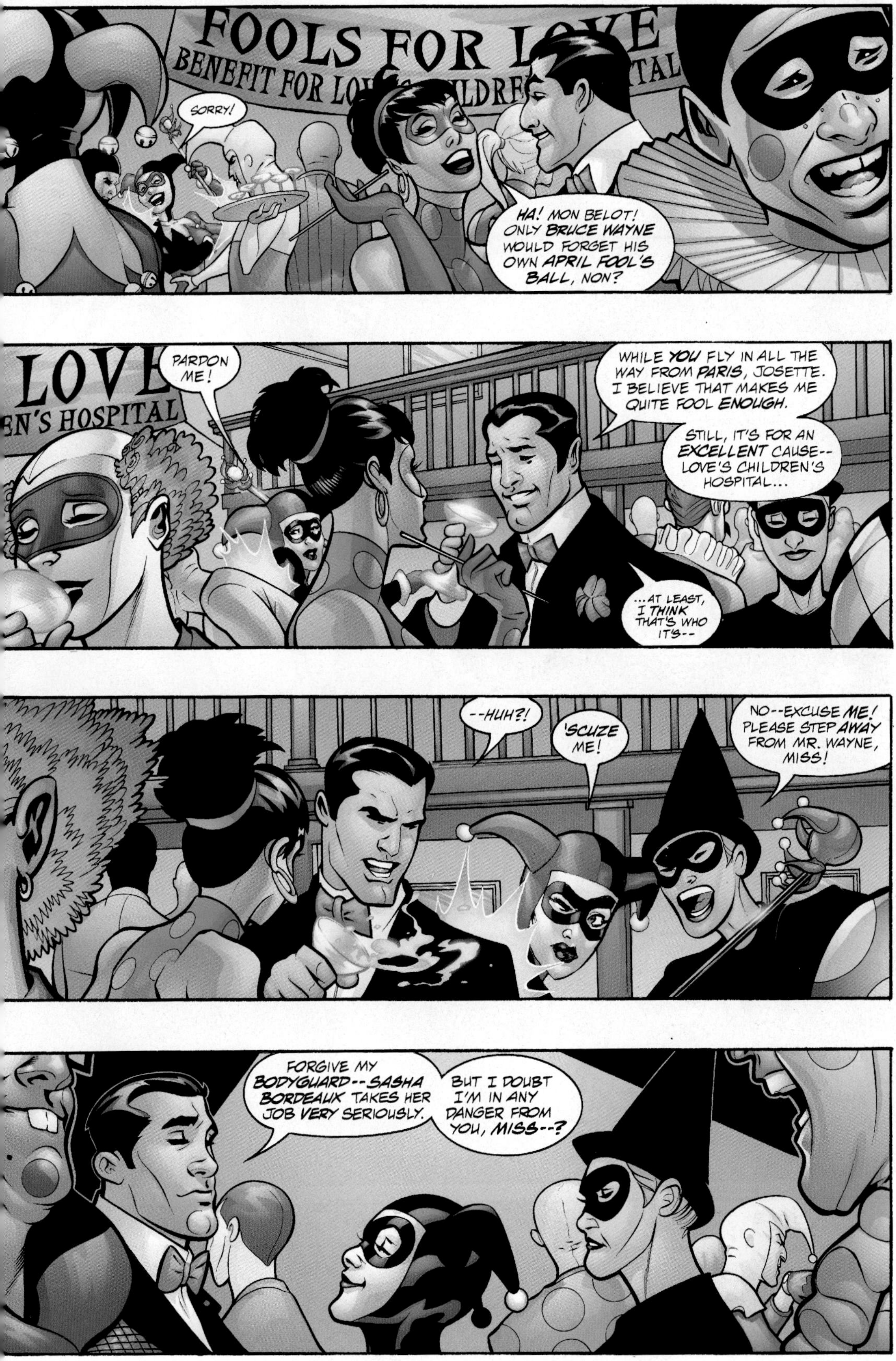
FOOLS FOR LOVE
BENEFIT FOR LOVE'S CHILDREN'S HOSPITAL
SORRY!
HA! MON BELOT! ONLY BRUCE WAYNE WOULD FORGET HIS OWN APRIL FOOL'S BALL, NON?
PARDON ME!
WHILE YOU FLY IN ALL THE WAY FROM PARIS, JOSETTE. I BELIEVE THAT MAKES ME QUITE FOOL ENOUGH.
STILL, IT'S FOR AN EXCELLENT CAUSE-- LOVE'S CHILDREN'S HOSPITAL...
...AT LEAST, I THINK THAT'S WHO IT'S--
--HUH?!
'SCUZE ME!
NO--EXCUSE ME! PLEASE STEP AWAY FROM MR. WAYNE, MISS!
FORGIVE MY BODYGUARD--SASHA BORDEAUX TAKES HER JOB VERY SERIOUSLY.
BUT I DOUBT I'M IN ANY DANGER FROM YOU, MISS--?

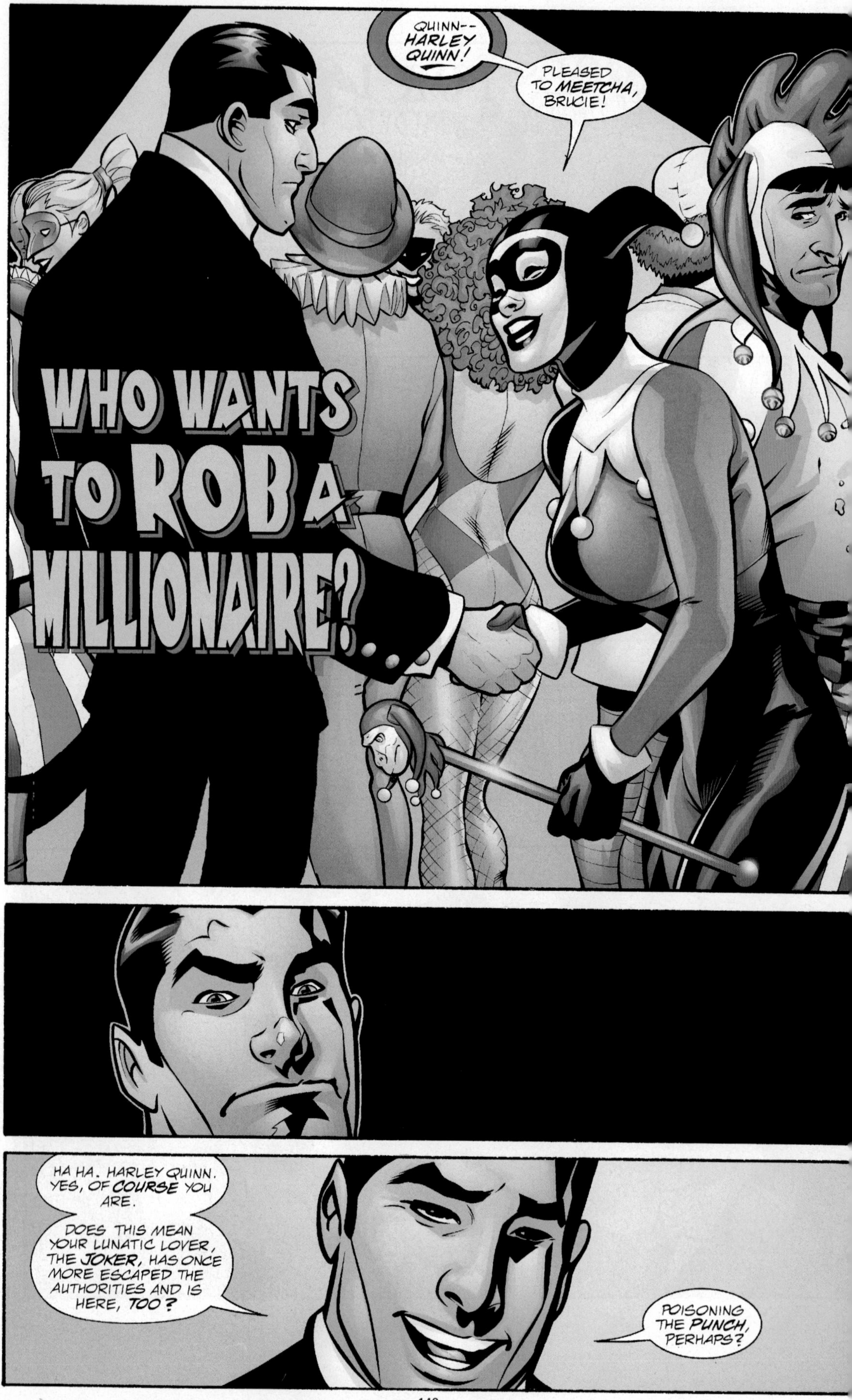
QUINN-- HARLEY QUINN!
PLEASED TO MEETCHA, BRUCIE!
WHO WANTS TO ROB A MILLIONAIRE?
HA HA. HARLEY QUINN. YES, OF COURSE YOU ARE.
DOES THIS MEAN YOUR LUNATIC LOVER, THE JOKER, HAS ONCE MORE ESCAPED THE AUTHORITIES AND IS HERE, TOO?
POISONING THE PUNCH, PERHAPS?

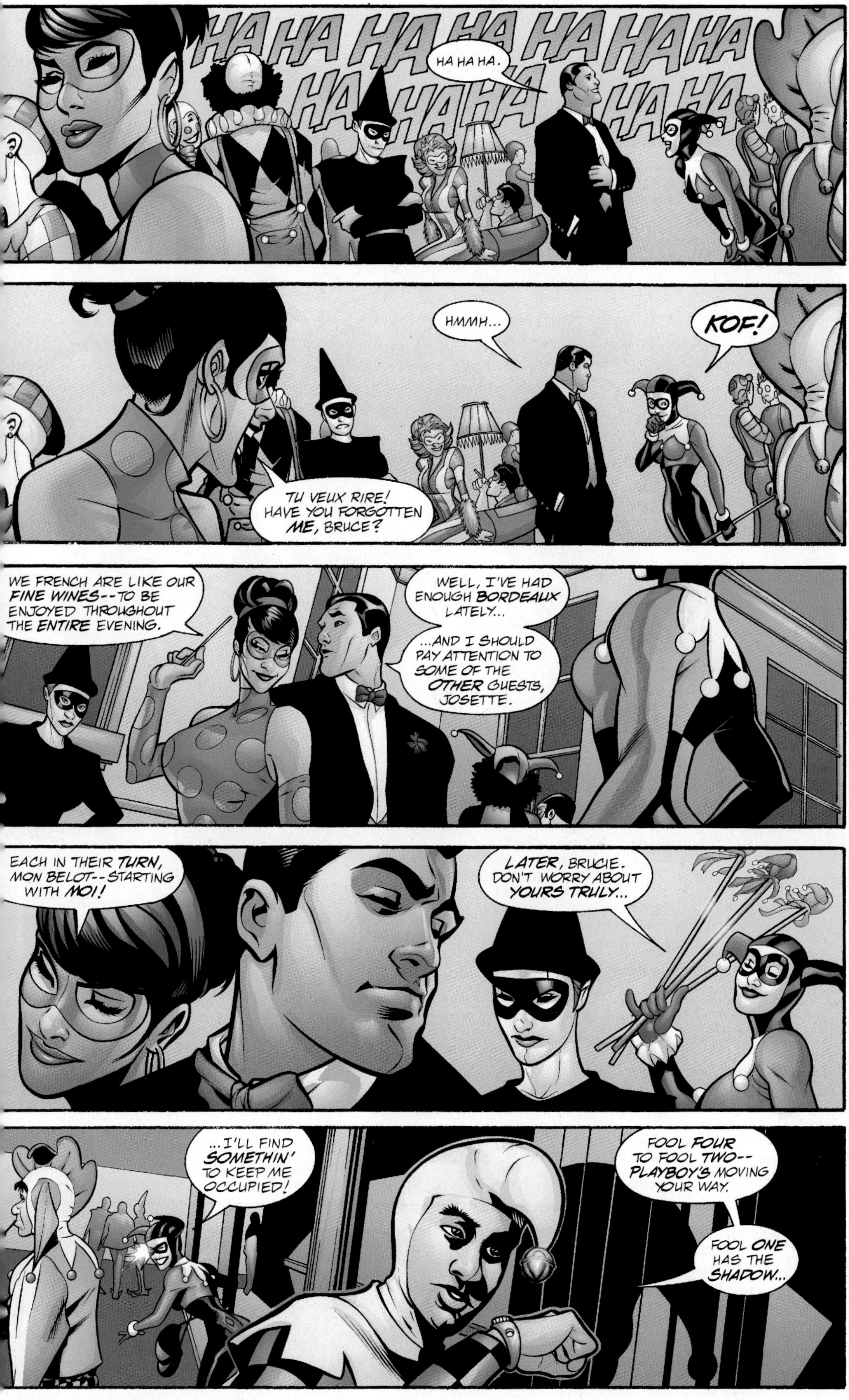
HA HA HA HA HA HA HA HA HA HA HA HA HA HA HA HA HA
HA HA HA.
HMMH...
KOF!
TU VEUX RIRE! HAVE YOU FORGOTTEN ME, BRUCE?
WE FRENCH ARE LIKE OUR FINE WINES--TO BE ENJOYED THROUGHOUT THE ENTIRE EVENING.
WELL, I'VE HAD ENOUGH BORDEAUX LATELY...
...AND I SHOULD PAY ATTENTION TO SOME OF THE OTHER GUESTS, JOSETTE.
EACH IN THEIR TURN, MON BELOT--STARTING WITH MOI!
LATER, BRUCIE. DON'T WORRY ABOUT YOURS TRULY...
...I'LL FIND SOMETHIN' TO KEEP ME OCCUPIED!
FOOL FOUR TO FOOL TWO-- PLAYBOY'S MOVING YOUR WAY.
FOOL ONE HAS THE SHADOW...

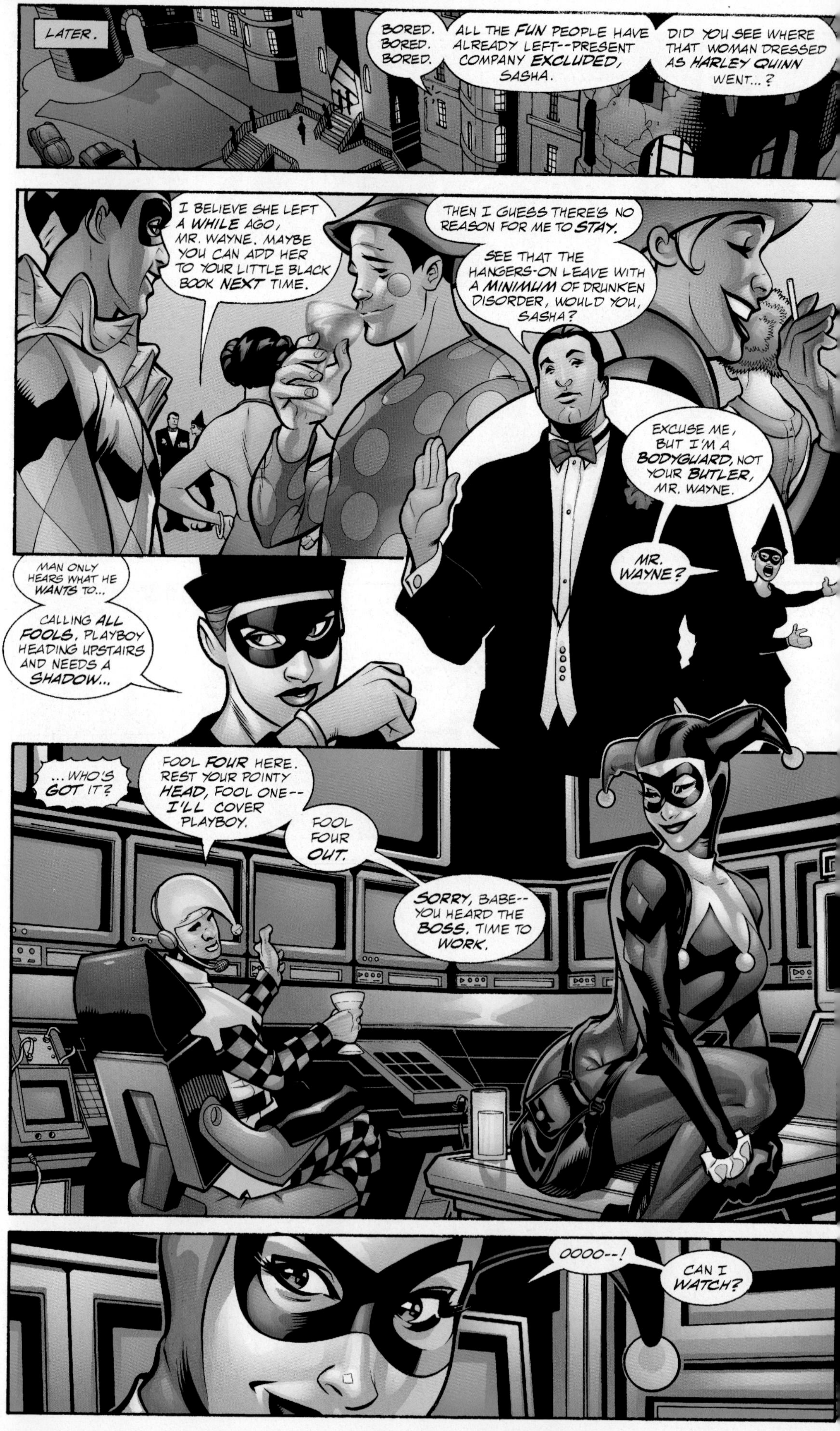
LATER.
BORED. BORED. BORED.
ALL THE FUN PEOPLE HAVE ALREADY LEFT--PRESENT COMPANY EXCLUDED, SASHA.
DID YOU SEE WHERE THAT WOMAN DRESSED AS HARLEY QUINN WENT...?
I BELIEVE SHE LEFT A WHILE AGO, MR. WAYNE. MAYBE YOU CAN ADD HER TO YOUR LITTLE BLACK BOOK NEXT TIME.
THEN I GUESS THERE'S NO REASON FOR ME TO STAY.
SEE THAT THE HANGERS-ON LEAVE WITH A MINIMUM OF DRUNKEN DISORDER, WOULD YOU, SASHA?
EXCUSE ME, BUT I'M A BODYGUARD, NOT YOUR BUTLER, MR. WAYNE.
MR. WAYNE?
MAN ONLY HEARS WHAT HE WANTS TO...
CALLING ALL FOOLS. PLAYBOY HEADING UPSTAIRS AND NEEDS A SHADOW...
...WHO'S GOT IT?
FOOL FOUR HERE. REST YOUR POINTY HEAD, FOOL ONE-- I'LL COVER PLAYBOY.
FOOL FOUR OUT.
SORRY, BABE-- YOU HEARD THE BOSS. TIME TO WORK.
OOOO--!
CAN I WATCH?

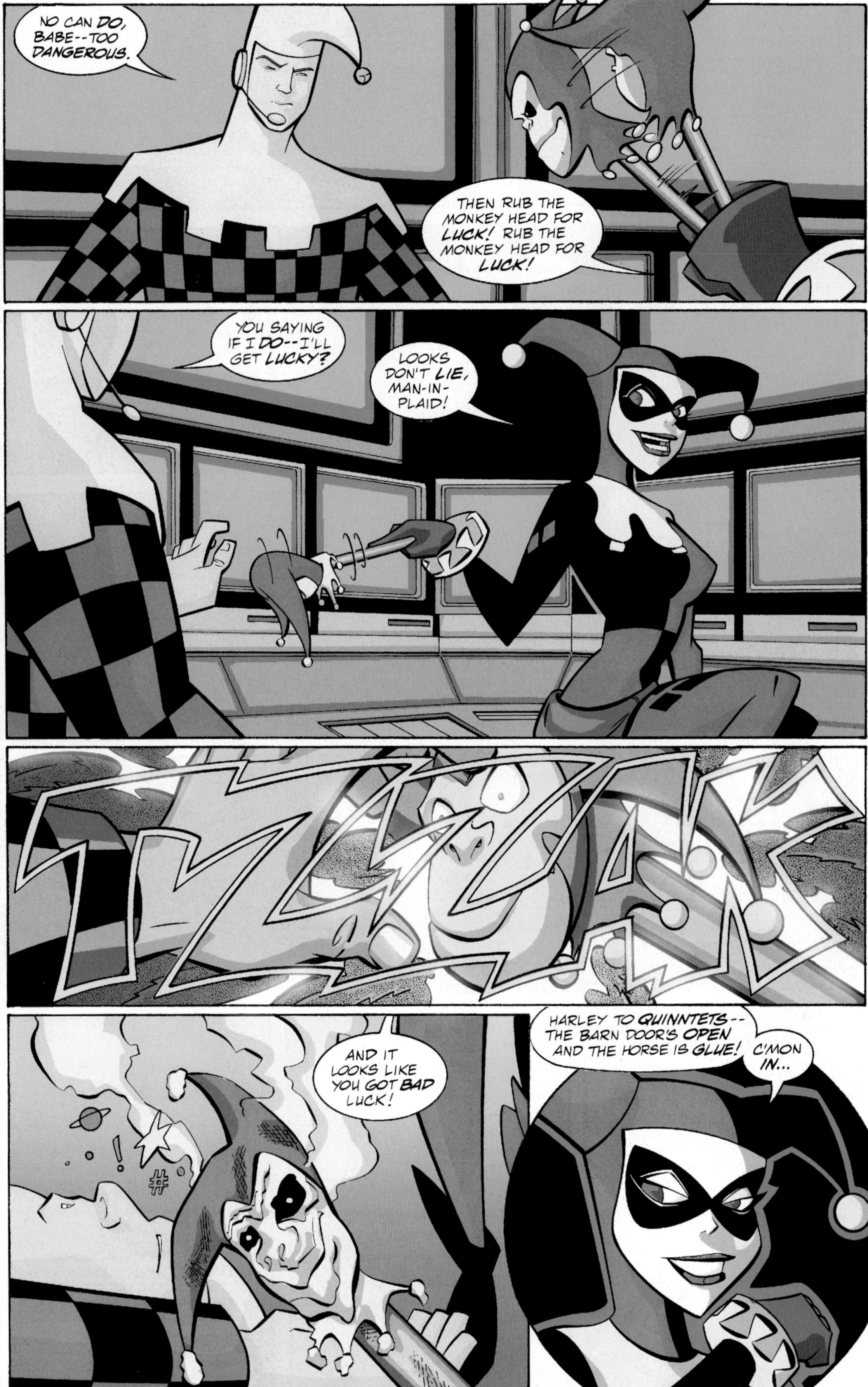
NO CAN DO, BABE--TOO DANGEROUS.
THEN RUB THE MONKEY HEAD FOR LUCK! RUB THE MONKEY HEAD FOR LUCK!
YOU SAYING IF I DO--I'LL GET LUCKY?
LOOKS DON'T LIE, MAN-IN-PLAID!
AND IT LOOKS LIKE YOU GOT BAD LUCK!
HARLEY TO QUINNTETS--THE BARN DOOR'S OPEN AND THE HORSE IS GLUE!
C'MON IN...

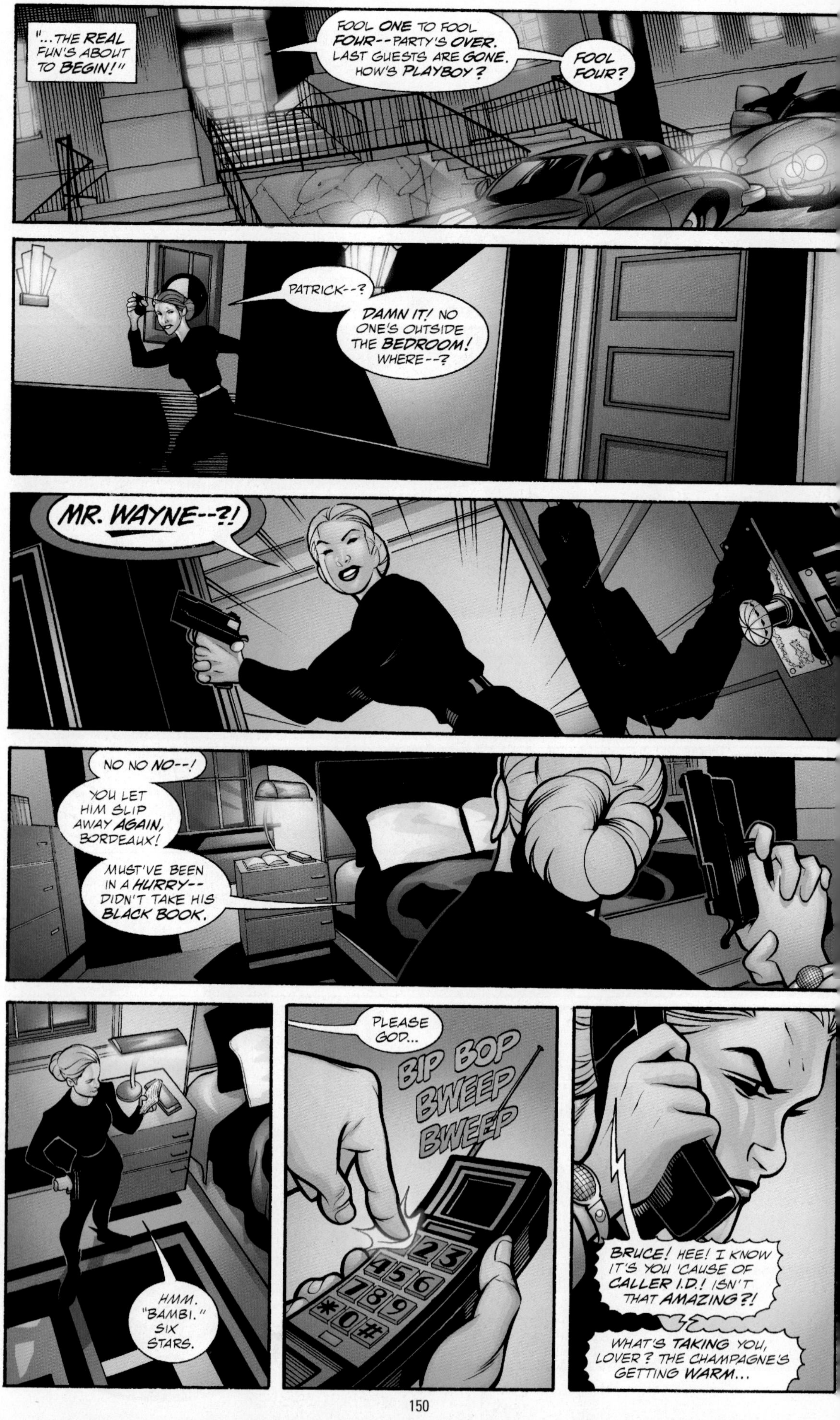
"...THE REAL FUN'S ABOUT TO BEGIN!"
FOOL ONE TO FOOL FOUR--PARTY'S OVER. LAST GUESTS ARE GONE. HOW'S PLAYBOY?
FOOL FOUR?
PATRICK--?
DAMN IT! NO ONE'S OUTSIDE THE BEDROOM! WHERE--?
MR. WAYNE--?!
NO NO NO--!
YOU LET HIM SLIP AWAY AGAIN, BORDEAUX!
MUST'VE BEEN IN A HURRY--DIDN'T TAKE HIS BLACK BOOK.
HMM. "BAMBI." SIX STARS.
PLEASE GOD...
BIP BOP BWEEP BWEEP
BRUCE! HEE! I KNOW IT'S YOU 'CAUSE OF CALLER I.D.! ISN'T THAT AMAZING?!
WHAT'S TAKING YOU, LOVER? THE CHAMPAGNE'S GETTING WARM...

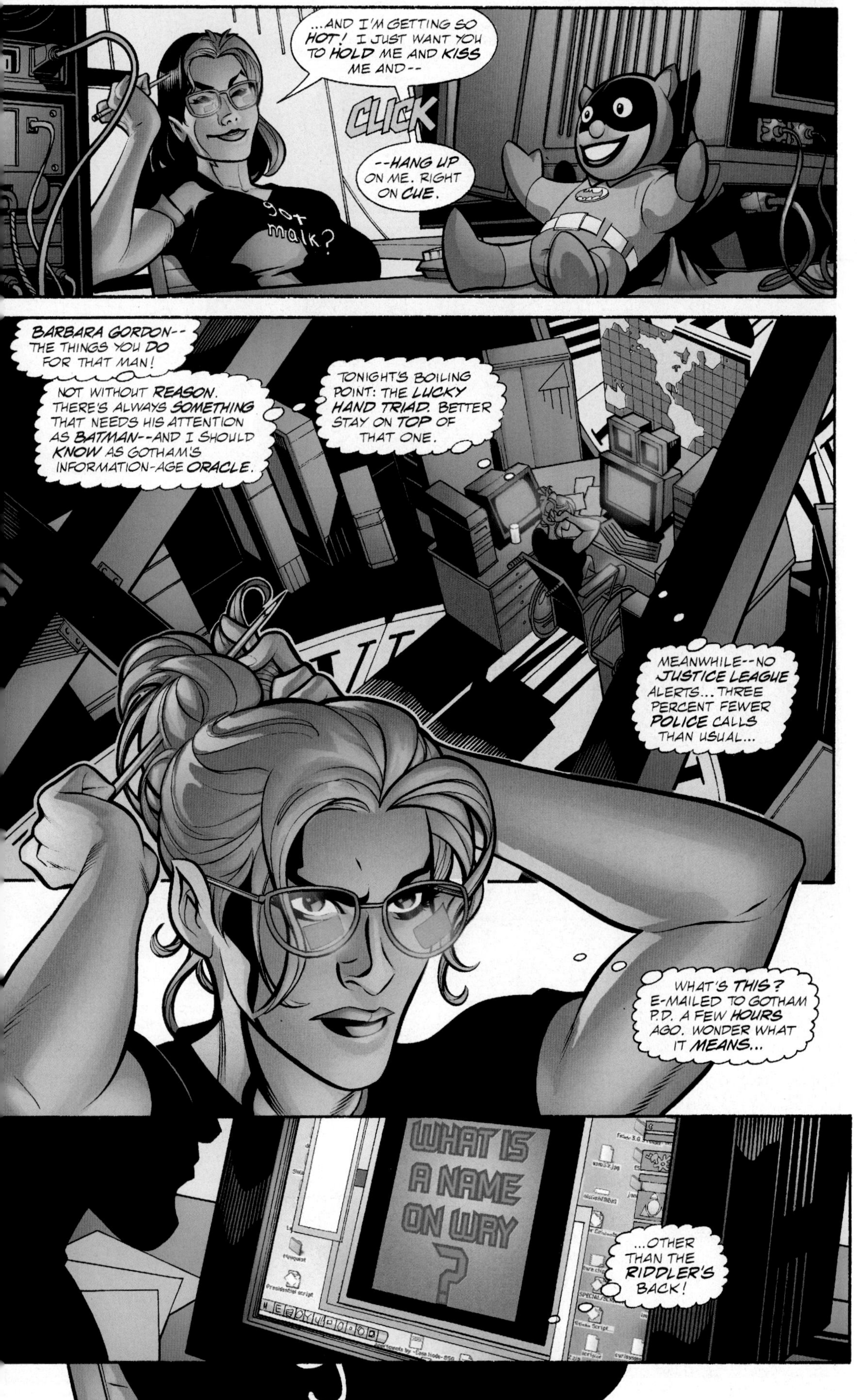
...AND I'M GETTING SO HOT! I JUST WANT YOU TO HOLD ME AND KISS ME AND--
CLICK
--HANG UP ON ME. RIGHT ON CUE.
got malk?
BARBARA GORDON-- THE THINGS YOU DO FOR THAT MAN!
NOT WITHOUT REASON. THERE'S ALWAYS SOMETHING THAT NEEDS HIS ATTENTION AS BATMAN--AND I SHOULD KNOW AS GOTHAM'S INFORMATION-AGE ORACLE.
TONIGHT'S BOILING POINT: THE LUCKY HAND TRIAD. BETTER STAY ON TOP OF THAT ONE.
MEANWHILE--NO JUSTICE LEAGUE ALERTS... THREE PERCENT FEWER POLICE CALLS THAN USUAL...
WHAT'S THIS? E-MAILED TO GOTHAM P.D. A FEW HOURS AGO. WONDER WHAT IT MEANS...
WHAT IS A NAME ON WAY ?
...OTHER THAN THE RIDDLER'S BACK!

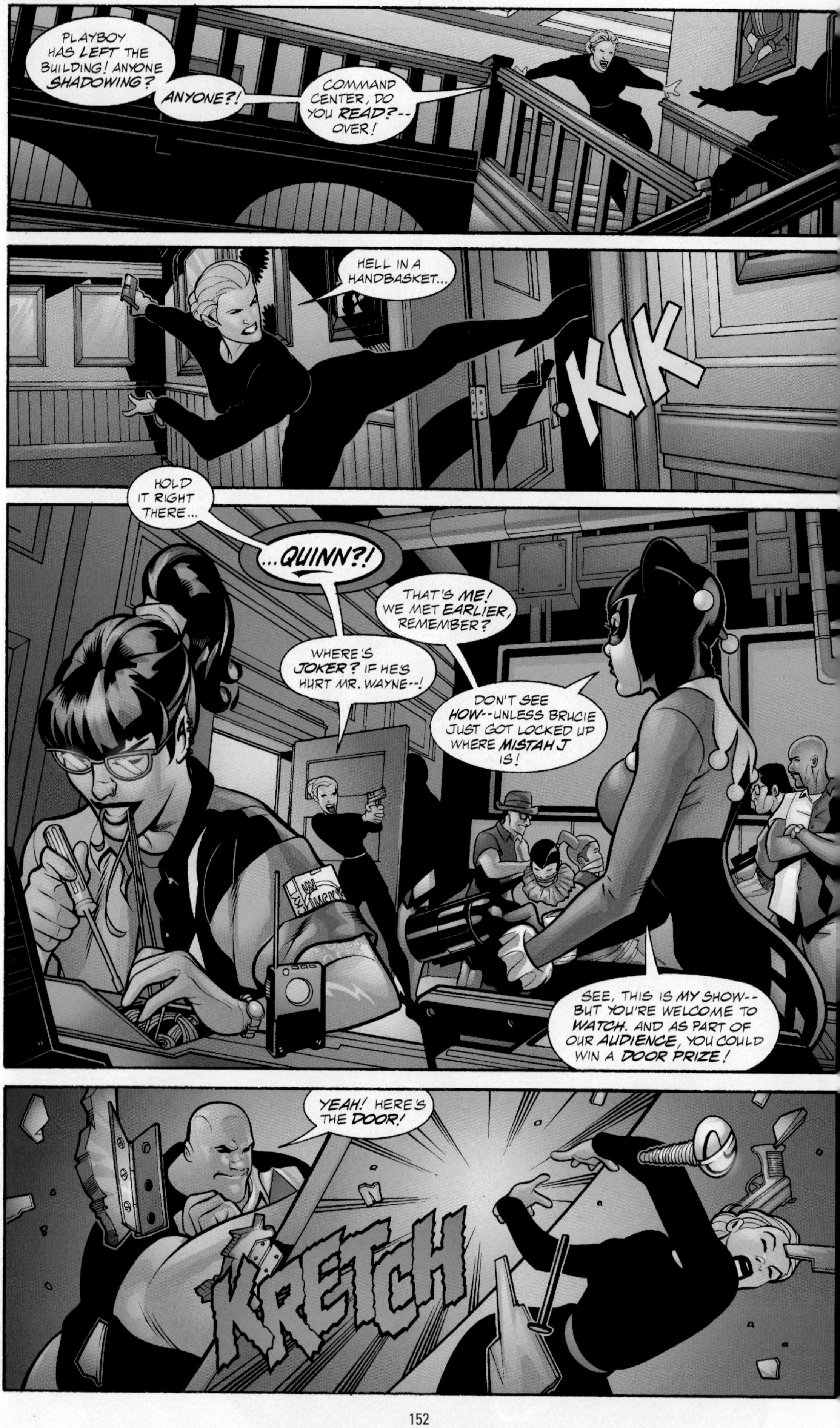

PLAYBOY HAS LEFT THE BUILDING! ANYONE SHADOWING?
ANYONE?!
COMMAND CENTER, DO YOU READ?-- OVER!
HELL IN A HANDBASKET...
KUK
HOLD IT RIGHT THERE...
...QUINN?!
THAT'S ME! WE MET EARLIER, REMEMBER?
WHERE'S JOKER? IF HE'S HURT MR. WAYNE--!
DON'T SEE HOW--UNLESS BRUCIE JUST GOT LOCKED UP WHERE MISTAH J IS!
SEE, THIS IS MY SHOW-- BUT YOU'RE WELCOME TO WATCH. AND AS PART OF OUR AUDIENCE, YOU COULD WIN A DOOR PRIZE!
YEAH! HERE'S THE DOOR!
KRETCH

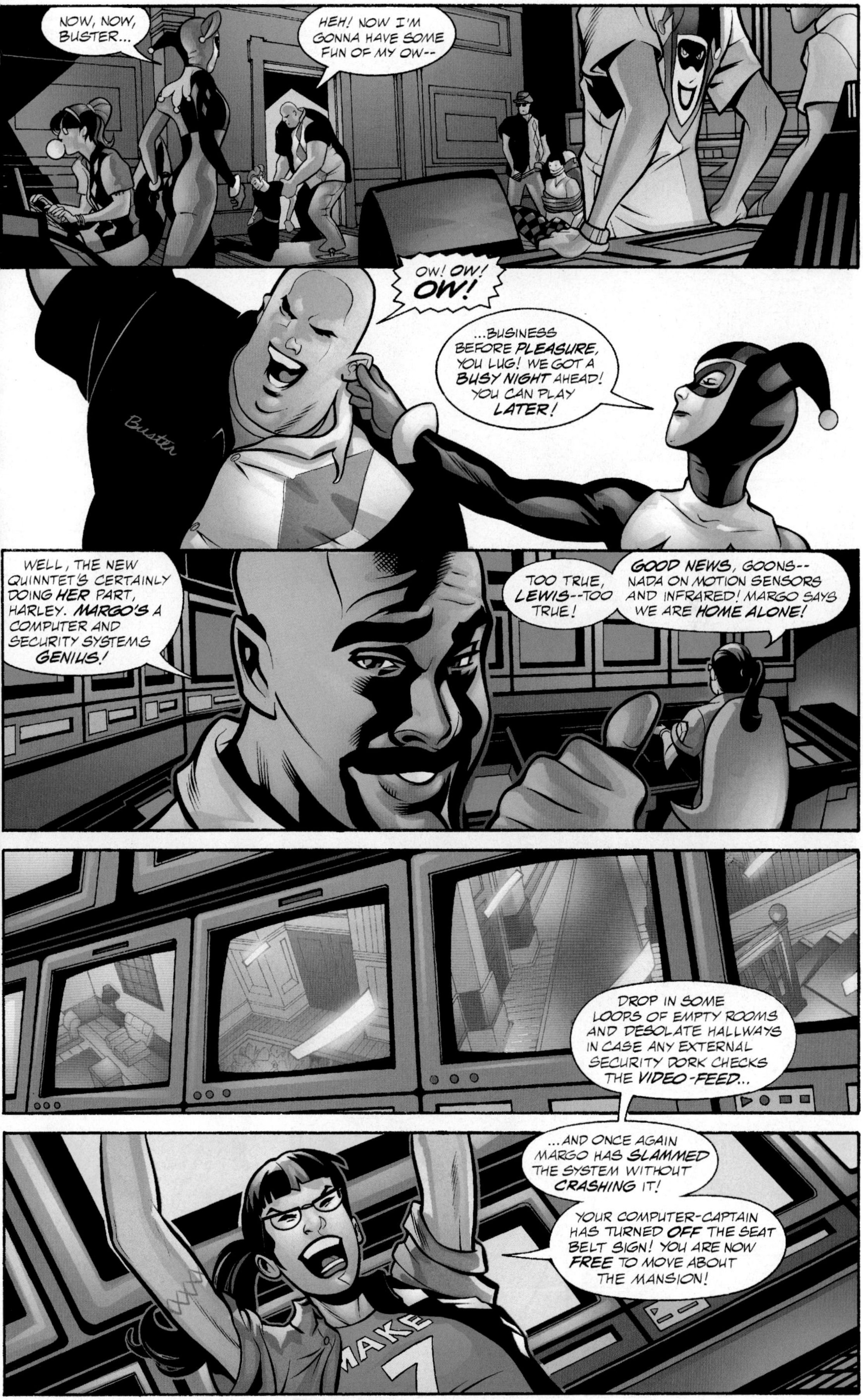
NOW, NOW, BUSTER...
HEH! NOW I'M GONNA HAVE SOME FUN OF MY OW--
OW! OW! OW!
...BUSINESS BEFORE PLEASURE, YOU LUG! WE GOT A BUSY NIGHT AHEAD! YOU CAN PLAY LATER!
Buster
WELL, THE NEW QUINNTET'S CERTAINLY DOING HER PART, HARLEY. MARGO'S A COMPUTER AND SECURITY SYSTEMS GENIUS!
TOO TRUE, LEWIS--TOO TRUE!
GOOD NEWS, GOONS--NADA ON MOTION SENSORS AND INFRARED! MARGO SAYS WE ARE HOME ALONE!
DROP IN SOME LOOPS OF EMPTY ROOMS AND DESOLATE HALLWAYS IN CASE ANY EXTERNAL SECURITY DORK CHECKS THE VIDEO-FEED...
...AND ONCE AGAIN MARGO HAS SLAMMED THE SYSTEM WITHOUT CRASHING IT!
YOUR COMPUTER-CAPTAIN HAS TURNED OFF THE SEAT BELT SIGN! YOU ARE NOW FREE TO MOVE ABOUT THE MANSION!
MAKE
7

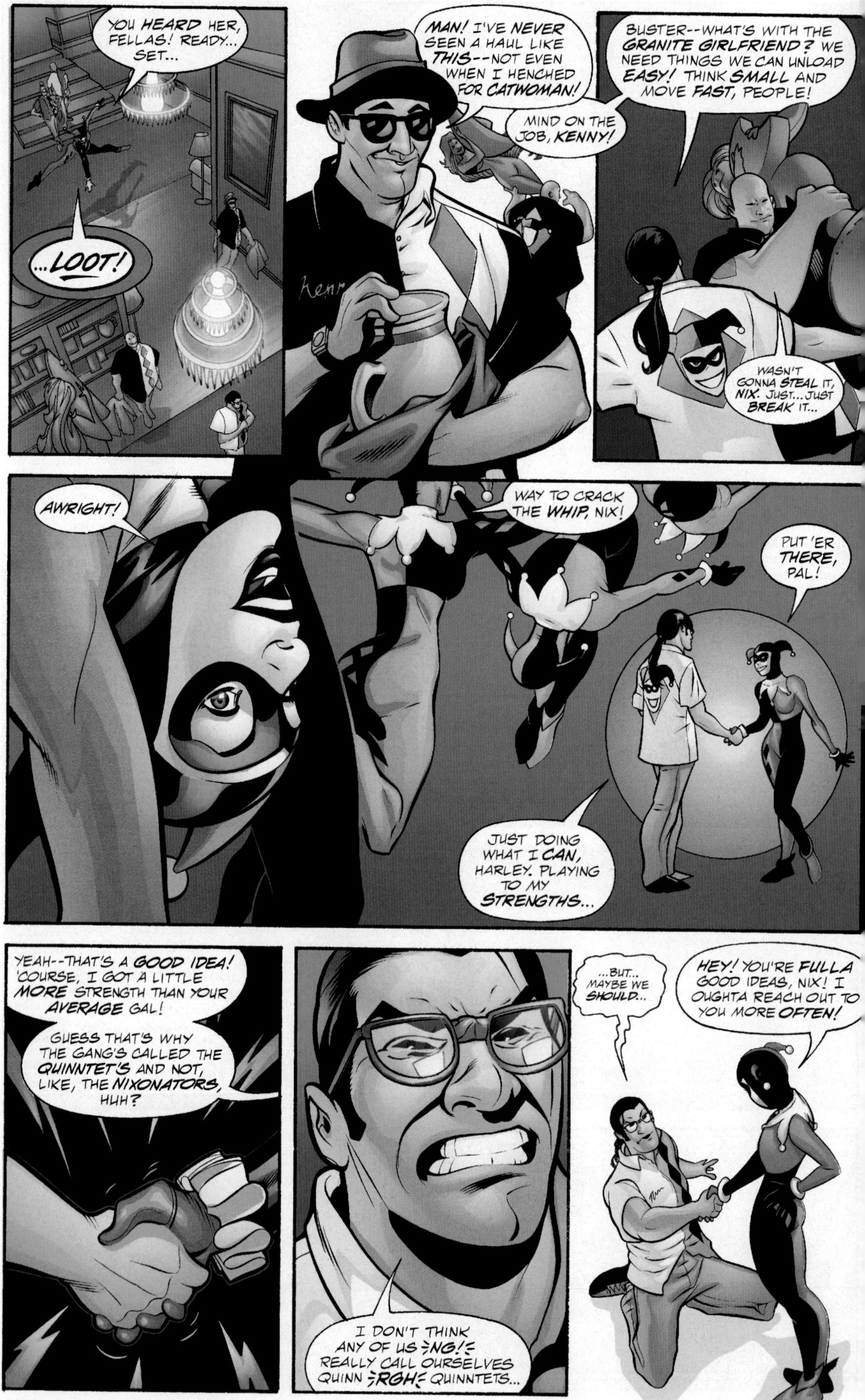

YOU HEARD HER, FELLAS! READY... SET...
...LOOT!
MAN! I'VE NEVER SEEN A HAUL LIKE THIS--NOT EVEN WHEN I HENCHED FOR CATWOMAN!
MIND ON THE JOB, KENNY!
BUSTER--WHAT'S WITH THE GRANITE GIRLFRIEND? WE NEED THINGS WE CAN UNLOAD EASY! THINK SMALL AND MOVE FAST, PEOPLE!
WASN'T GONNA STEAL IT, NIX. JUST... JUST BREAK IT...
AWRIGHT!
WAY TO CRACK THE WHIP, NIX!
PUT 'ER THERE, PAL!
JUST DOING WHAT I CAN, HARLEY. PLAYING TO MY STRENGTHS...
YEAH--THAT'S A GOOD IDEA! 'COURSE, I GOT A LITTLE MORE STRENGTH THAN YOUR AVERAGE GAL!
GUESS THAT'S WHY THE GANG'S CALLED THE QUINNTET'S AND NOT, LIKE, THE NIXONATORS, HUH?
I DON'T THINK ANY OF US NG! REALLY CALL OURSELVES QUINN RGH QUINNTETS...
...BUT... MAYBE WE SHOULD...
HEY! YOU'RE FULLA GOOD IDEAS, NIX! I OUGHTA REACH OUT TO YOU MORE OFTEN!

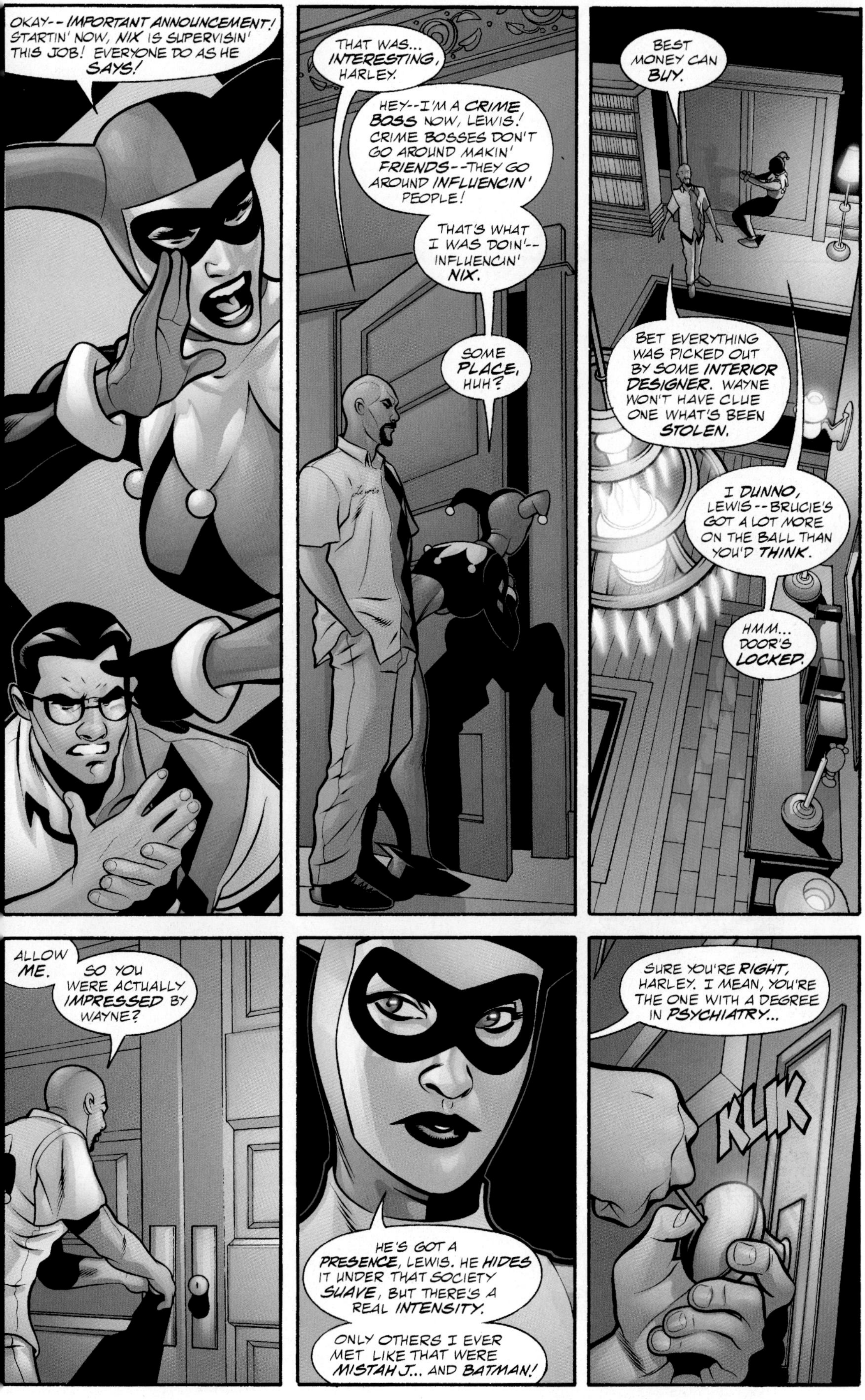
OKAY-- IMPORTANT ANNOUNCEMENT! STARTIN' NOW, NIX IS SUPERVISIN' THIS JOB! EVERYONE DO AS HE SAYS!
THAT WAS... INTERESTING, HARLEY.
HEY--I'M A CRIME BOSS NOW, LEWIS! CRIME BOSSES DON'T GO AROUND MAKIN' FRIENDS--THEY GO AROUND INFLUENCIN' PEOPLE!
THAT'S WHAT I WAS DOIN'-- INFLUENCIN' NIX.
SOME PLACE, HUH?
Lewis
BEST MONEY CAN BUY.
BET EVERYTHING WAS PICKED OUT BY SOME INTERIOR DESIGNER. WAYNE WON'T HAVE CLUE ONE WHAT'S BEEN STOLEN.
I DUNNO, LEWIS--BRUCIE'S GOT A LOT MORE ON THE BALL THAN YOU'D THINK.
HMM... DOOR'S LOCKED.
ALLOW ME.
SO YOU WERE ACTUALLY IMPRESSED BY WAYNE?
HE'S GOT A PRESENCE, LEWIS. HE HIDES IT UNDER THAT SOCIETY SUAVE, BUT THERE'S A REAL INTENSITY.
ONLY OTHERS I EVER MET LIKE THAT WERE MISTAH J... AND BATMAN!
SURE YOU'RE RIGHT, HARLEY. I MEAN, YOU'RE THE ONE WITH A DEGREE IN PSYCHIATRY...
KLIK

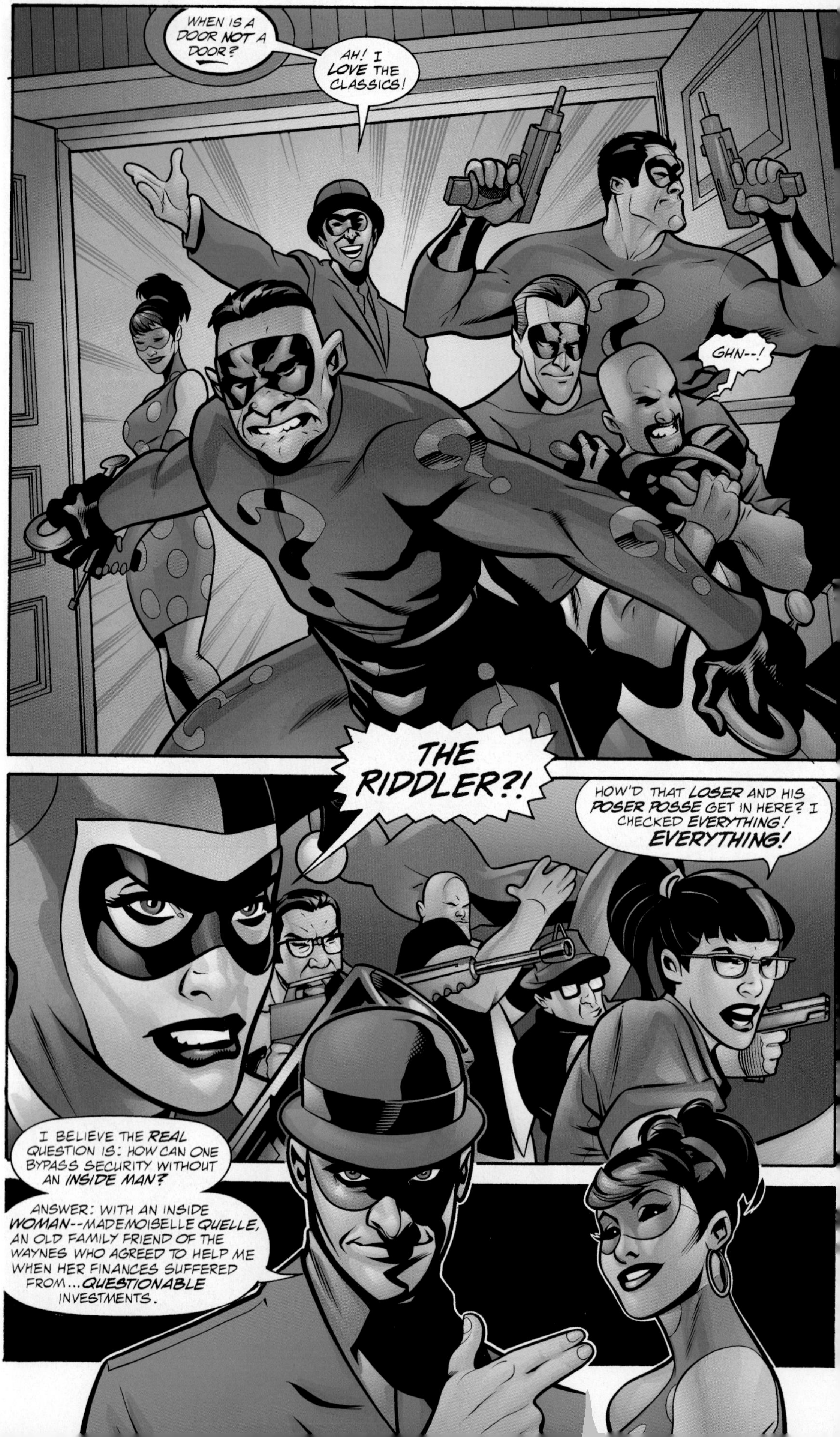

WHEN IS A DOOR NOT A DOOR?
AH! I LOVE THE CLASSICS!
GHN--!
THE RIDDLER?!
HOW'D THAT LOSER AND HIS POSER POSSE GET IN HERE? I CHECKED EVERYTHING! EVERYTHING!
I BELIEVE THE REAL QUESTION IS: HOW CAN ONE BYPASS SECURITY WITHOUT AN INSIDE MAN?
ANSWER: WITH AN INSIDE WOMAN--MADEMOISELLE QUELLE, AN OLD FAMILY FRIEND OF THE WAYNES WHO AGREED TO HELP ME WHEN HER FINANCES SUFFERED FROM...QUESTIONABLE INVESTMENTS.

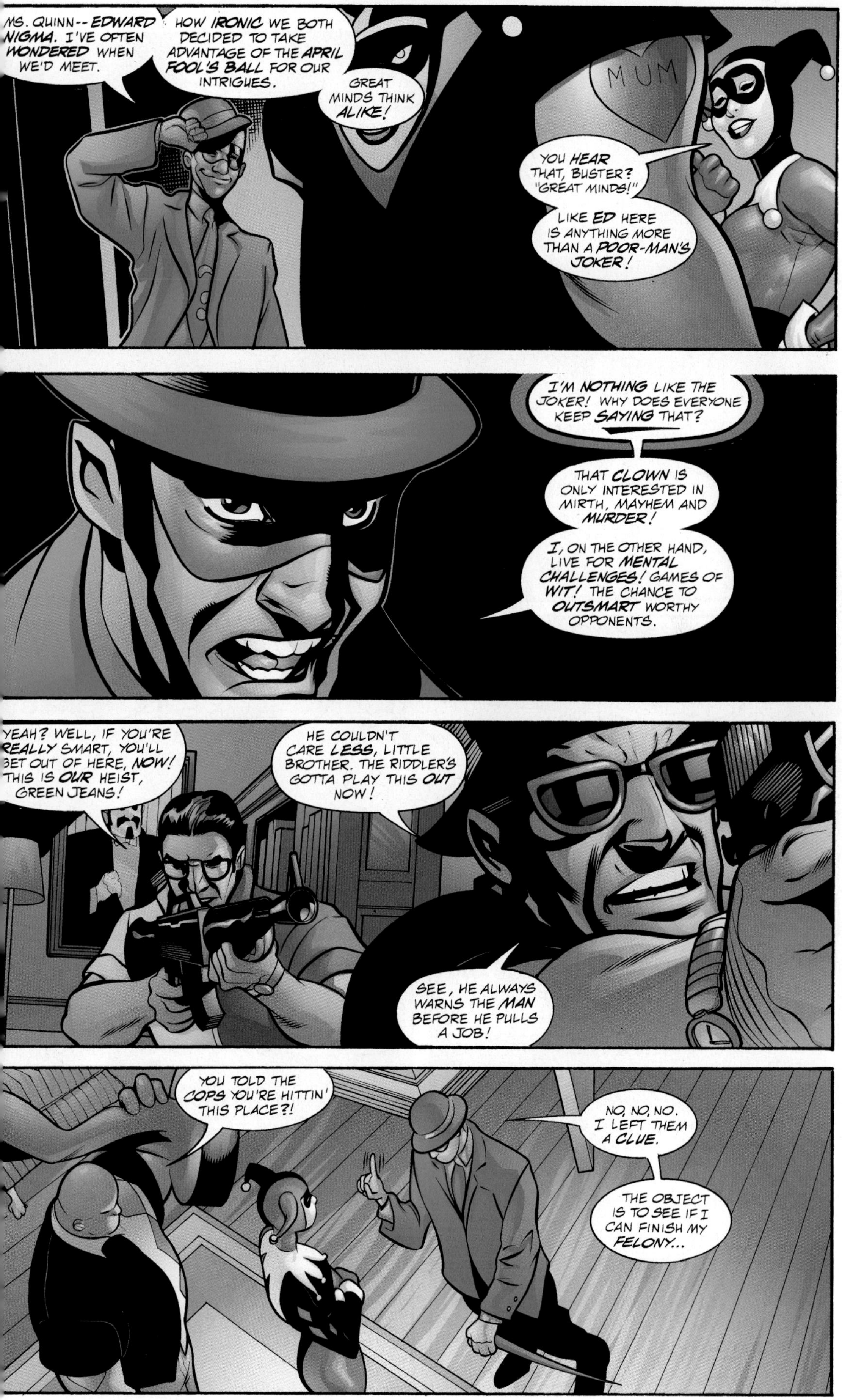
MS. QUINN-- EDWARD NIGMA. I'VE OFTEN WONDERED WHEN WE'D MEET.
HOW IRONIC WE BOTH DECIDED TO TAKE ADVANTAGE OF THE APRIL FOOL'S BALL FOR OUR INTRIGUES.
GREAT MINDS THINK ALIKE!
MUM
YOU HEAR THAT, BUSTER? "GREAT MINDS!"
LIKE ED HERE IS ANYTHING MORE THAN A POOR-MAN'S JOKER!
I'M NOTHING LIKE THE JOKER! WHY DOES EVERYONE KEEP SAYING THAT?
THAT CLOWN IS ONLY INTERESTED IN MIRTH, MAYHEM AND MURDER!
I, ON THE OTHER HAND, LIVE FOR MENTAL CHALLENGES! GAMES OF WIT! THE CHANCE TO OUTSMART WORTHY OPPONENTS.
YEAH? WELL, IF YOU'RE REALLY SMART, YOU'LL GET OUT OF HERE, NOW! THIS IS OUR HEIST, GREEN JEANS!
HE COULDN'T CARE LESS, LITTLE BROTHER. THE RIDDLER'S GOTTA PLAY THIS OUT NOW!
SEE, HE ALWAYS WARNS THE MAN BEFORE HE PULLS A JOB!
YOU TOLD THE COPS YOU'RE HITTIN' THIS PLACE?!
NO, NO, NO. I LEFT THEM A CLUE.
THE OBJECT IS TO SEE IF I CAN FINISH MY FELONY...

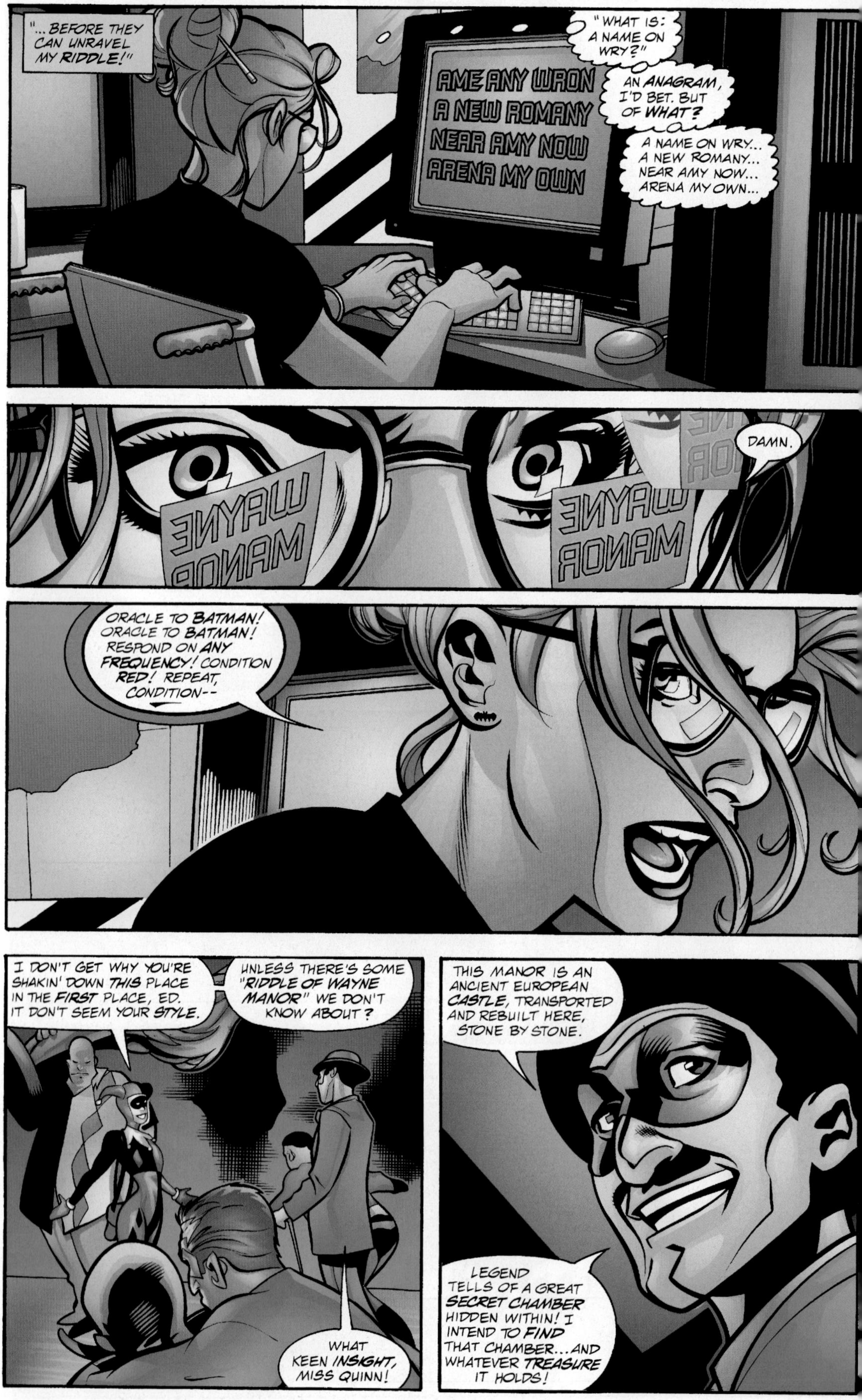
"...BEFORE THEY CAN UNRAVEL MY RIDDLE!"
"WHAT IS: A NAME ON WRY?"
AN ANAGRAM, I'D BET. BUT OF WHAT?
A NAME ON WRY... A NEW ROMANY... NEAR AMY NOW... ARENA MY OWN...
AME ANY WRON
A NEW ROMANY
NEAR AMY NOW
ARENA MY OWN
DAMN.
ORACLE TO BATMAN! ORACLE TO BATMAN! RESPOND ON ANY FREQUENCY! CONDITION RED! REPEAT, CONDITION--
I DON'T GET WHY YOU'RE SHAKIN' DOWN THIS PLACE IN THE FIRST PLACE, ED. IT DON'T SEEM YOUR STYLE.
UNLESS THERE'S SOME "RIDDLE OF WAYNE MANOR" WE DON'T KNOW ABOUT?
WHAT KEEN INSIGHT, MISS QUINN!
THIS MANOR IS AN ANCIENT EUROPEAN CASTLE, TRANSPORTED AND REBUILT HERE, STONE BY STONE.
LEGEND TELLS OF A GREAT SECRET CHAMBER HIDDEN WITHIN! I INTEND TO FIND THAT CHAMBER...AND WHATEVER TREASURE IT HOLDS!

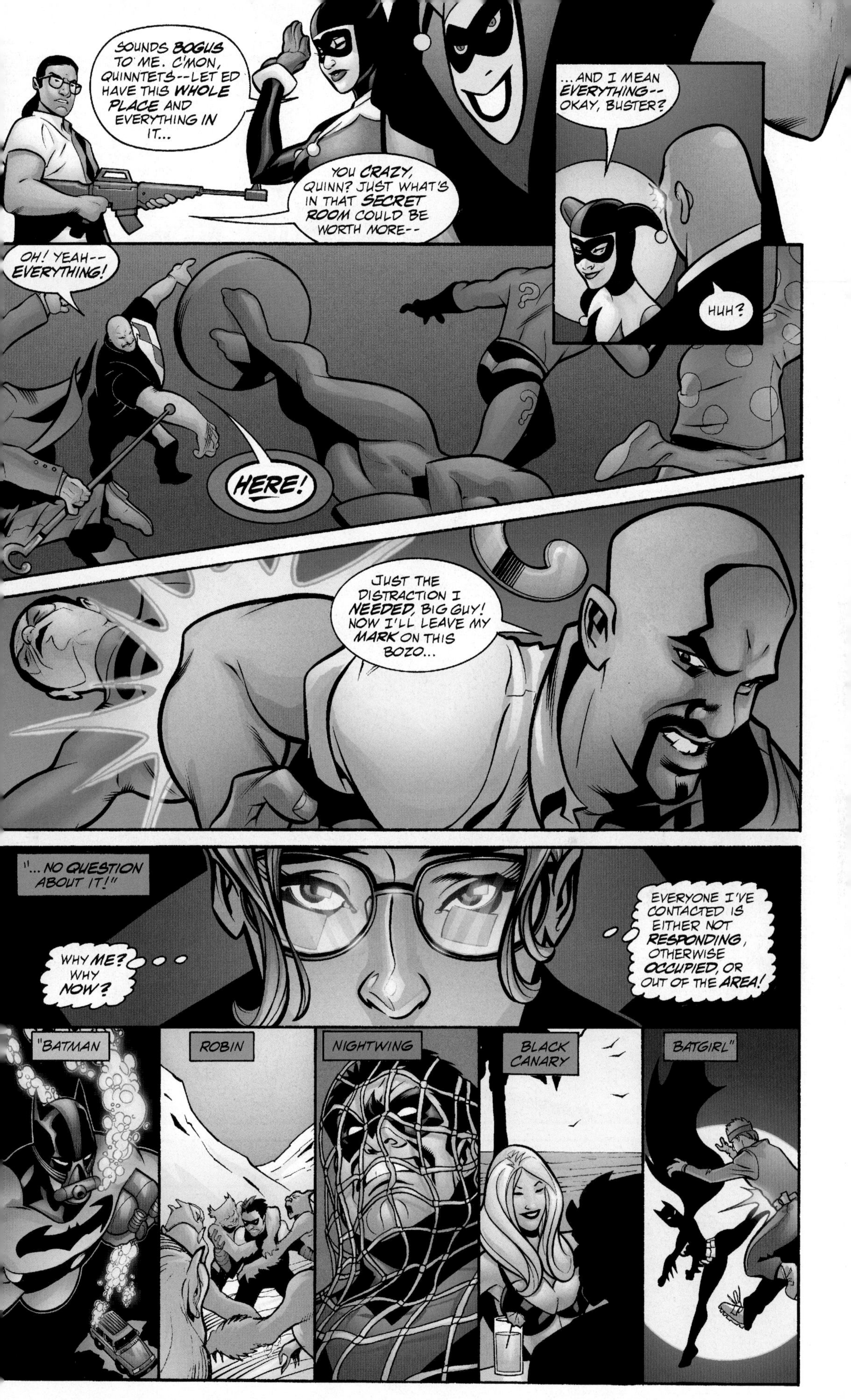
SOUNDS BOGUS TO ME. C'MON, QUINNTETS--LET ED HAVE THIS WHOLE PLACE AND EVERYTHING IN IT...
YOU CRAZY, QUINN? JUST WHAT'S IN THAT SECRET ROOM COULD BE WORTH MORE--
...AND I MEAN EVERYTHING--OKAY, BUSTER?
HUH?
OH! YEAH--EVERYTHING!
HERE!
JUST THE DISTRACTION I NEEDED, BIG GUY! NOW I'LL LEAVE MY MARK ON THIS BOZO...
"...NO QUESTION ABOUT IT!"
WHY ME? WHY NOW?
EVERYONE I'VE CONTACTED IS EITHER NOT RESPONDING, OTHERWISE OCCUPIED, OR OUT OF THE AREA!
"BATMAN
ROBIN
NIGHTWING
BLACK CANARY
BATGIRL"

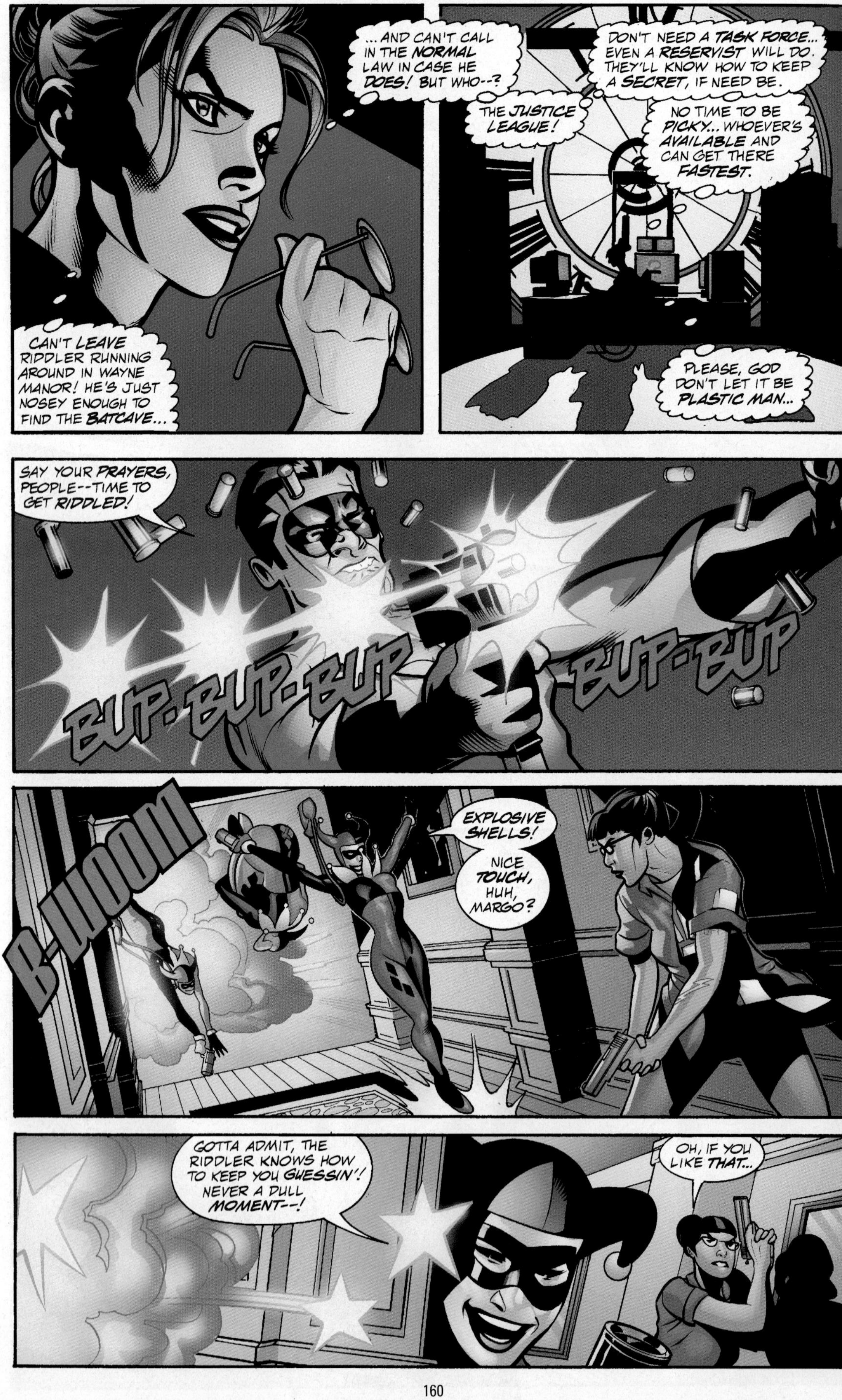
CAN'T LEAVE RIDDLER RUNNING AROUND IN WAYNE MANOR! HE'S JUST NOSEY ENOUGH TO FIND THE BATCAVE...
...AND CAN'T CALL IN THE NORMAL LAW IN CASE HE DOES! BUT WHO--?
THE JUSTICE LEAGUE!
DON'T NEED A TASK FORCE... EVEN A RESERVIST WILL DO. THEY'LL KNOW HOW TO KEEP A SECRET, IF NEED BE.
NO TIME TO BE PICKY... WHOEVER'S AVAILABLE AND CAN GET THERE FASTEST.
PLEASE, GOD DON'T LET IT BE PLASTIC MAN...
SAY YOUR PRAYERS, PEOPLE--TIME TO GET RIDDLED!
BUP-BUP-BUP
BUP-BUP
B-WOOM
EXPLOSIVE SHELLS!
NICE TOUCH, HUH, MARGO?
GOTTA ADMIT, THE RIDDLER KNOWS HOW TO KEEP YOU GUESSIN'! NEVER A DULL MOMENT--!
OH, IF YOU LIKE THAT...

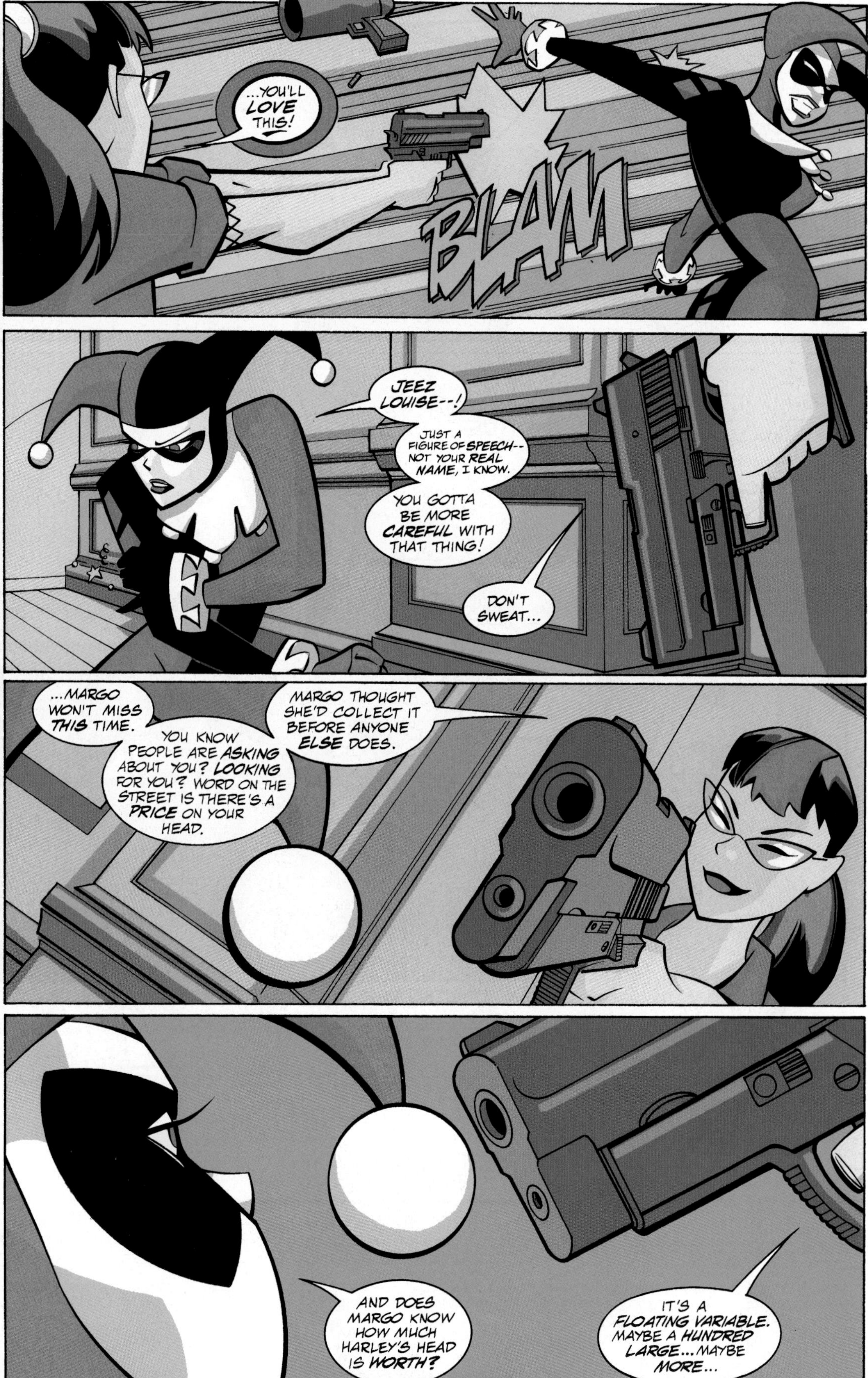
...YOU'LL LOVE THIS!
BLAM
JEEZ LOUISE--!
JUST A FIGURE OF SPEECH-- NOT YOUR REAL NAME, I KNOW.
YOU GOTTA BE MORE CAREFUL WITH THAT THING!
DON'T SWEAT...
...MARGO WON'T MISS THIS TIME.
YOU KNOW PEOPLE ARE ASKING ABOUT YOU? LOOKING FOR YOU? WORD ON THE STREET IS THERE'S A PRICE ON YOUR HEAD.
MARGO THOUGHT SHE'D COLLECT IT BEFORE ANYONE ELSE DOES.
AND DOES MARGO KNOW HOW MUCH HARLEY'S HEAD IS WORTH?
IT'S A FLOATING VARIABLE. MAYBE A HUNDRED LARGE... MAYBE MORE...

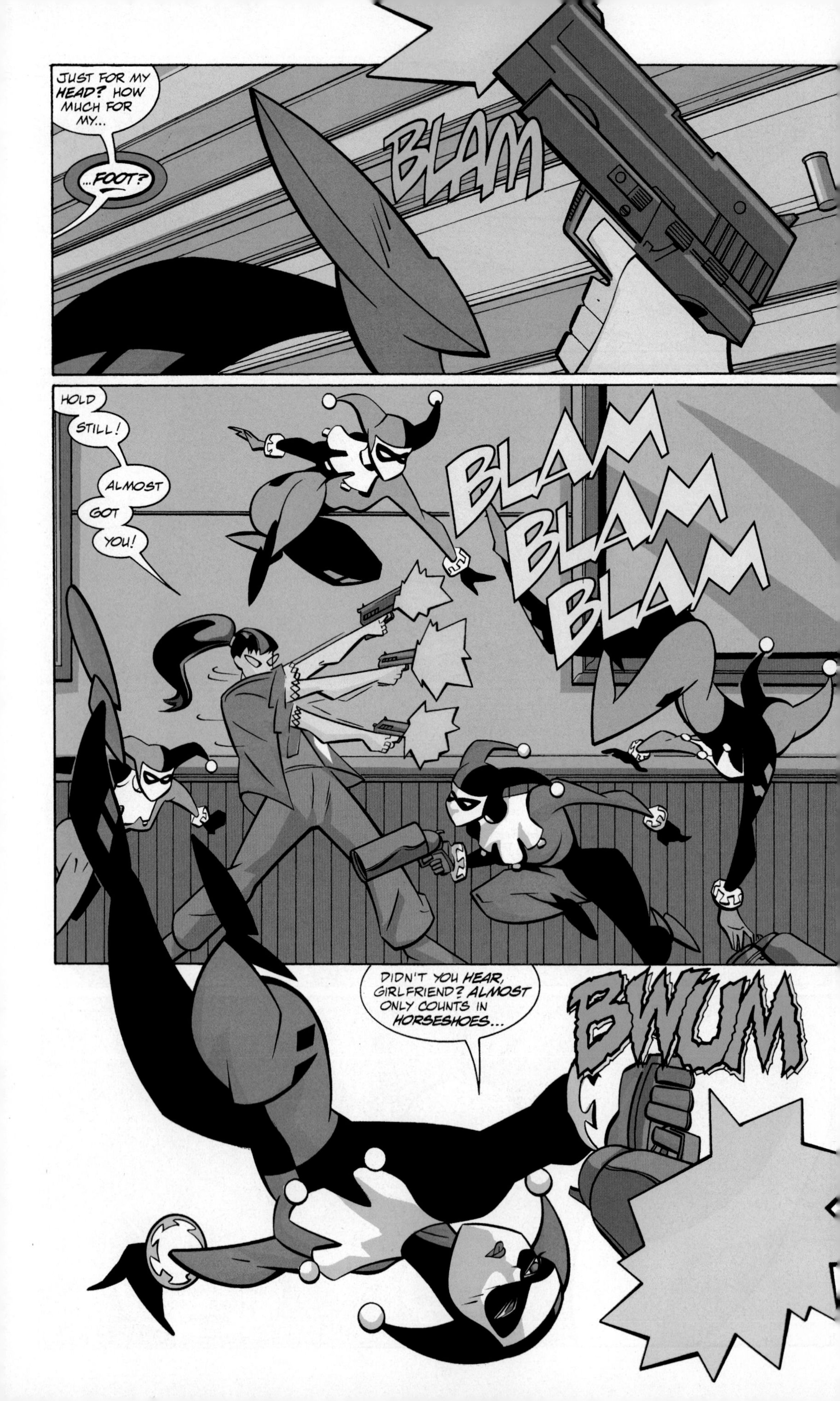
JUST FOR MY HEAD? HOW MUCH FOR MY...
...FOOT?
BLAM
HOLD STILL!
ALMOST GOT YOU!
BLAM BLAM BLAM
DIDN'T YOU HEAR, GIRLFRIEND? ALMOST ONLY COUNTS IN HORSESHOES...
BWUM

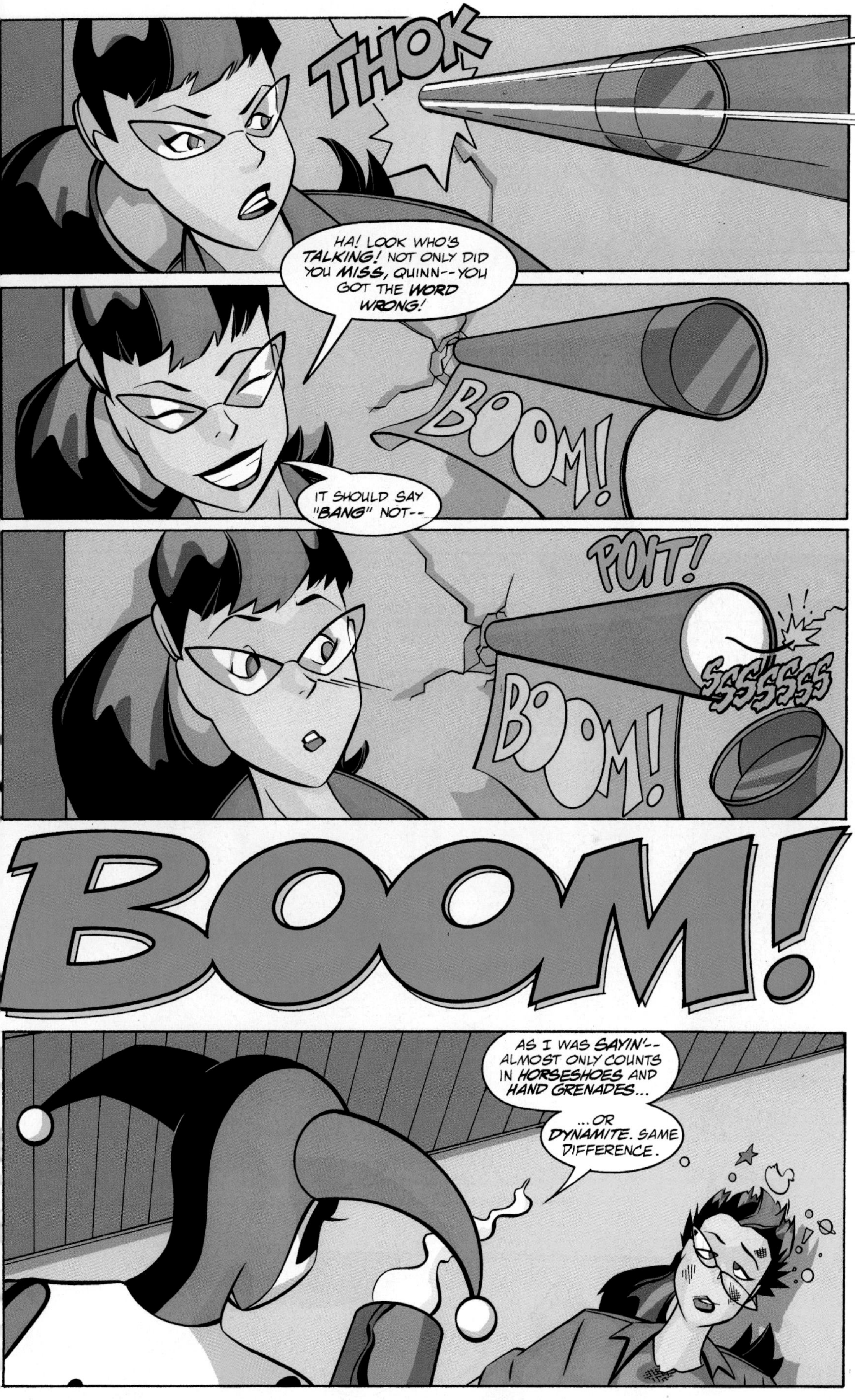
THOK
HA! LOOK WHO'S TALKING! NOT ONLY DID YOU MISS, QUINN--YOU GOT THE WORD WRONG!
BOOM!
IT SHOULD SAY "BANG" NOT--
POIT!
BOOM!
SSSSSSS
BOOM!
AS I WAS SAYIN'-- ALMOST ONLY COUNTS IN HORSESHOES AND HAND GRENADES...
...OR DYNAMITE. SAME DIFFERENCE.

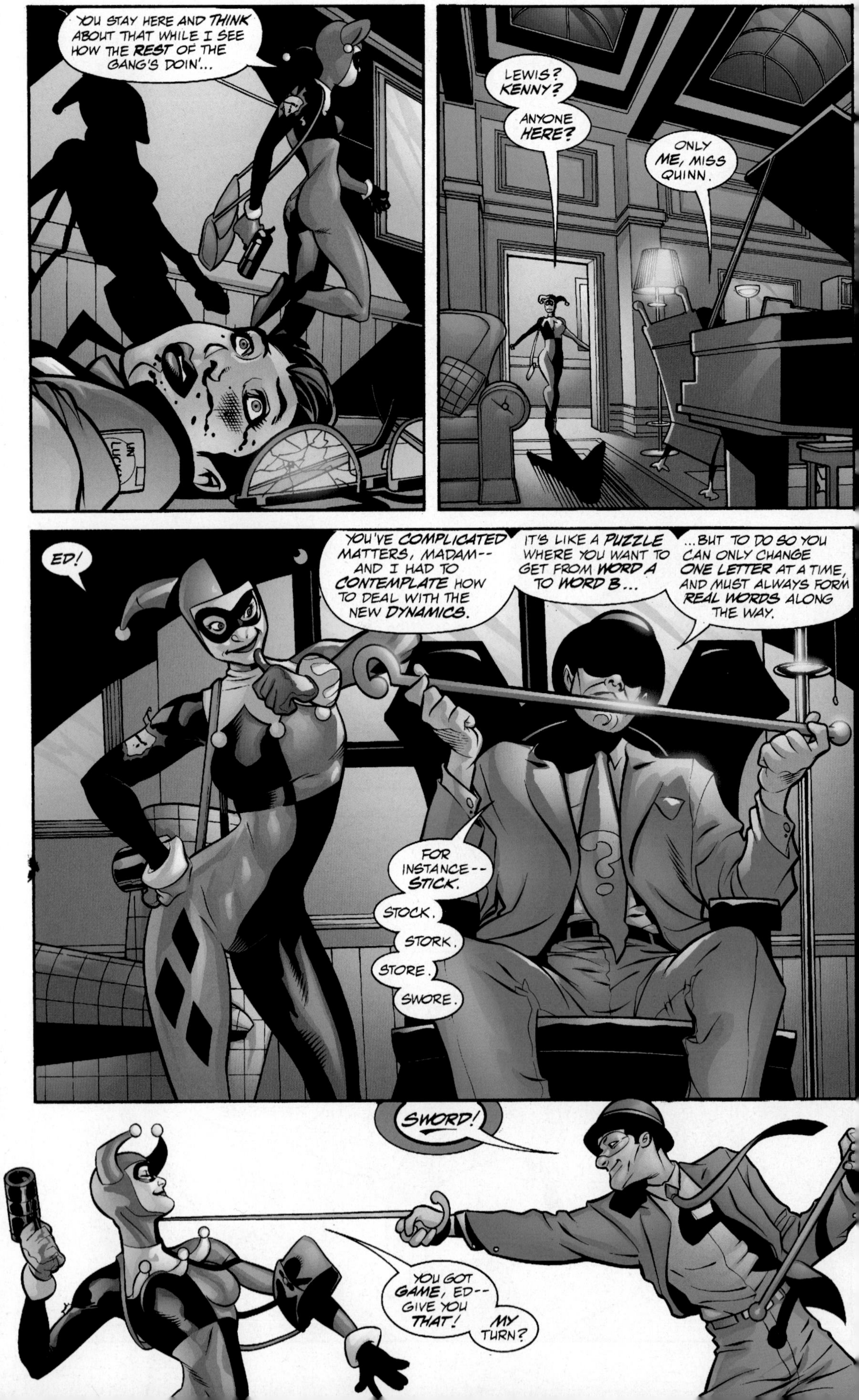

YOU STAY HERE AND THINK ABOUT THAT WHILE I SEE HOW THE REST OF THE GANG'S DOIN'...
LEWIS? KENNY?
ANYONE HERE?
ONLY ME, MISS QUINN.
ED!
YOU'VE COMPLICATED MATTERS, MADAM-- AND I HAD TO CONTEMPLATE HOW TO DEAL WITH THE NEW DYNAMICS.
IT'S LIKE A PUZZLE WHERE YOU WANT TO GET FROM WORD A TO WORD B...
...BUT TO DO SO YOU CAN ONLY CHANGE ONE LETTER AT A TIME, AND MUST ALWAYS FORM REAL WORDS ALONG THE WAY.
FOR INSTANCE-- STICK.
STOCK.
STORK.
STORE.
SWORE.
SWORD!
YOU GOT GAME, ED-- GIVE YOU THAT!
MY TURN?

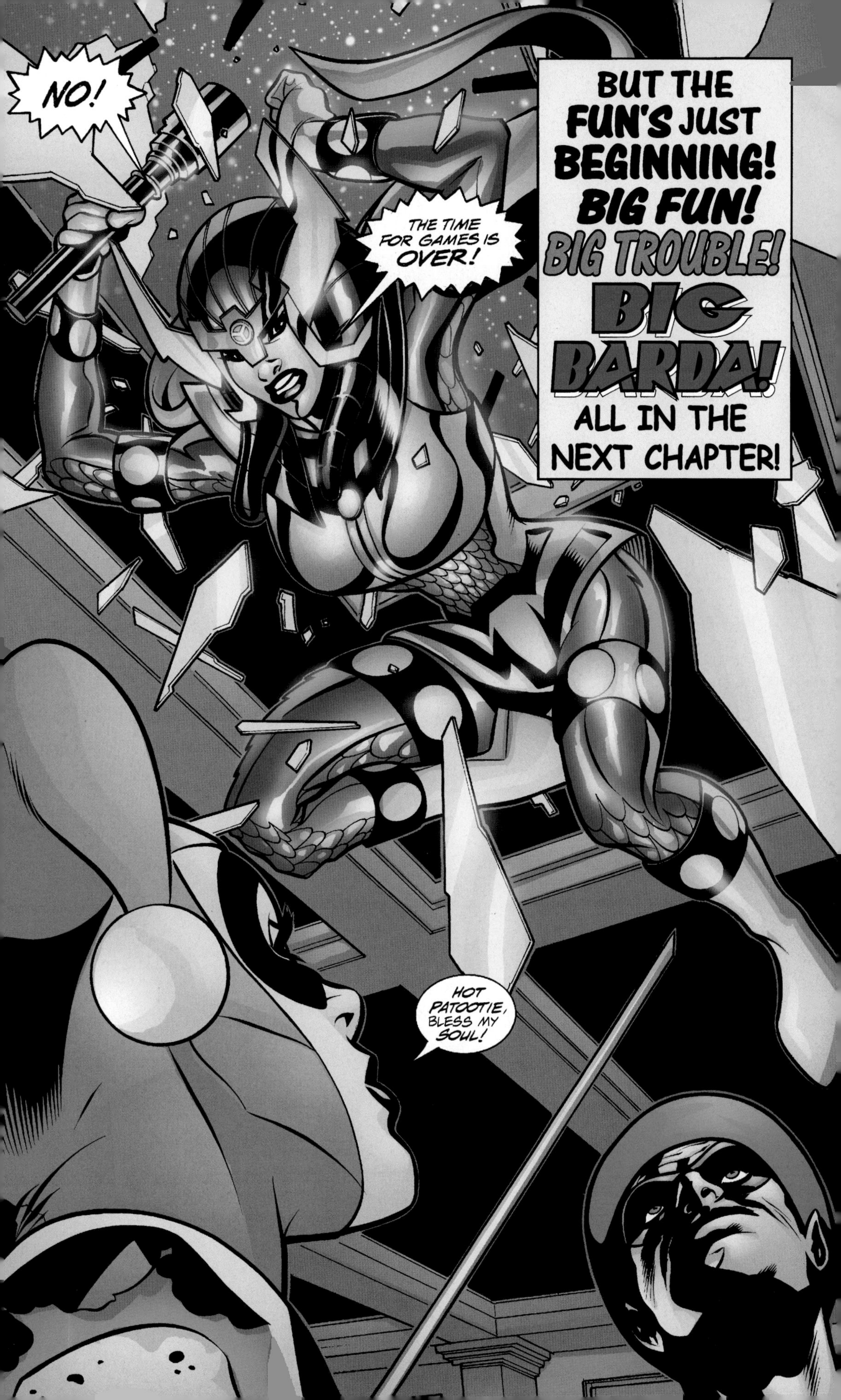
NO!
THE TIME FOR GAMES IS OVER!
BUT THE FUN'S JUST BEGINNING! BIG FUN! BIG TROUBLE! BIG BARDA! ALL IN THE NEXT CHAPTER!
HOT PATOOTIE, BLESS MY SOUL!

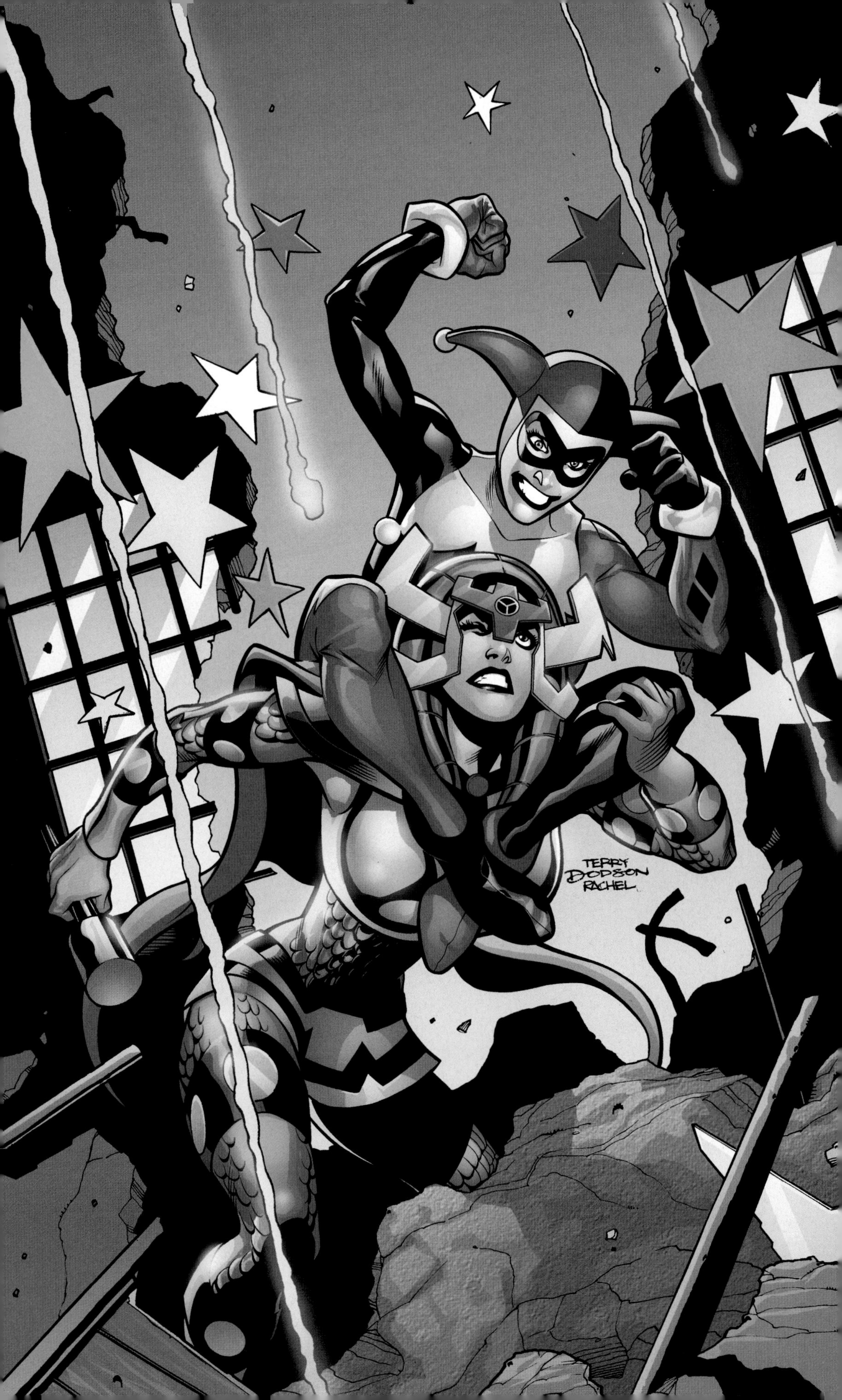
TERRY
DODSON
RACHEL

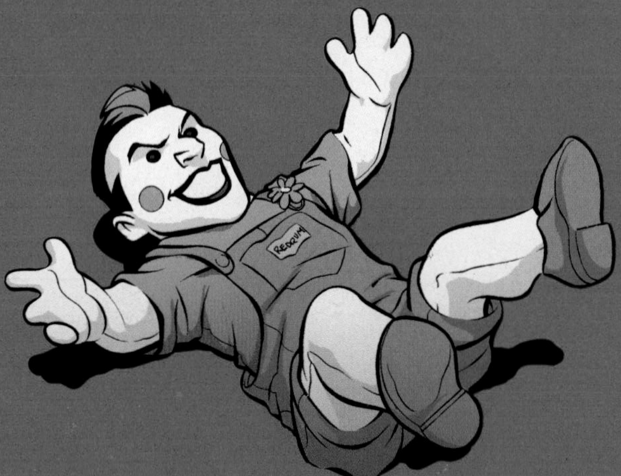
REDRUM

GODS
AND
Mobsters

TALK ABOUT BEIN' BUSTED--!

WHAT--?

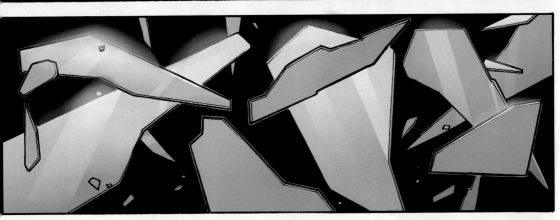

CHOOSE YOUR FATE, LOWLIES! BOW DOWN OR BE--

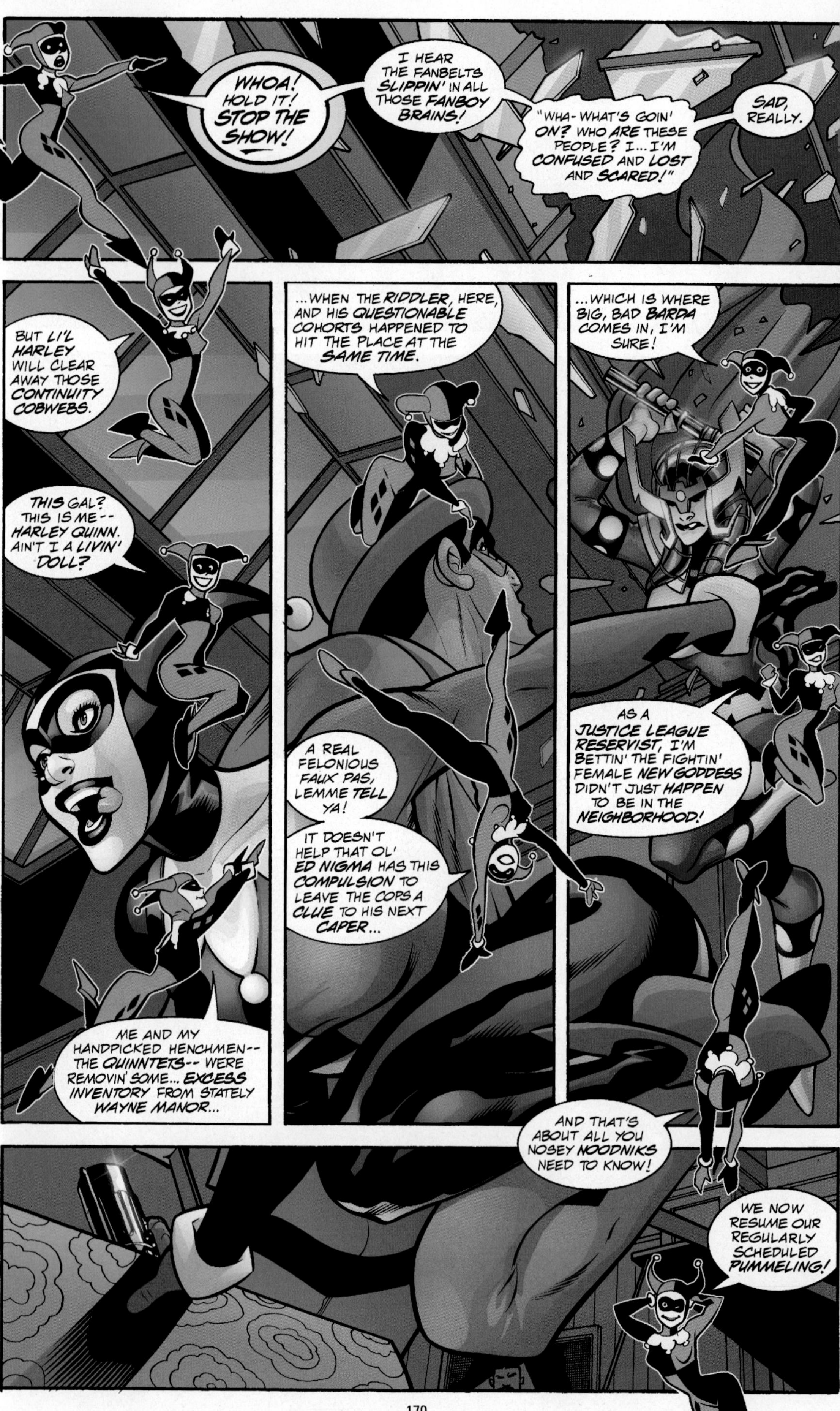
WHOA! HOLD IT! STOP THE SHOW!
I HEAR THE FANBELTS SLIPPIN' IN ALL THOSE FANBOY BRAINS!
"WHA- WHAT'S GOIN' ON? WHO ARE THESE PEOPLE? I... I'M CONFUSED AND LOST AND SCARED!"
SAD, REALLY.
BUT LI'L HARLEY WILL CLEAR AWAY THOSE CONTINUITY COBWEBS.
THIS GAL? THIS IS ME-- HARLEY QUINN. AIN'T I A LIVIN' DOLL?
ME AND MY HANDPICKED HENCHMEN-- THE QUINNTETS-- WERE REMOVIN' SOME... EXCESS INVENTORY FROM STATELY WAYNE MANOR...
...WHEN THE RIDDLER, HERE, AND HIS QUESTIONABLE COHORTS HAPPENED TO HIT THE PLACE AT THE SAME TIME.
A REAL FELONIOUS FAUX PAS, LEMME TELL YA!
IT DOESN'T HELP THAT OL' ED NIGMA HAS THIS COMPULSION TO LEAVE THE COPS A CLUE TO HIS NEXT CAPER...
...WHICH IS WHERE BIG, BAD BARDA COMES IN, I'M SURE!
AS A JUSTICE LEAGUE RESERVIST, I'M BETTIN' THE FIGHTIN' FEMALE NEW GODDESS DIDN'T JUST HAPPEN TO BE IN THE NEIGHBORHOOD!
AND THAT'S ABOUT ALL YOU NOSEY NOODNIKS NEED TO KNOW!
WE NOW RESUME OUR REGULARLY SCHEDULED PUMMELING!

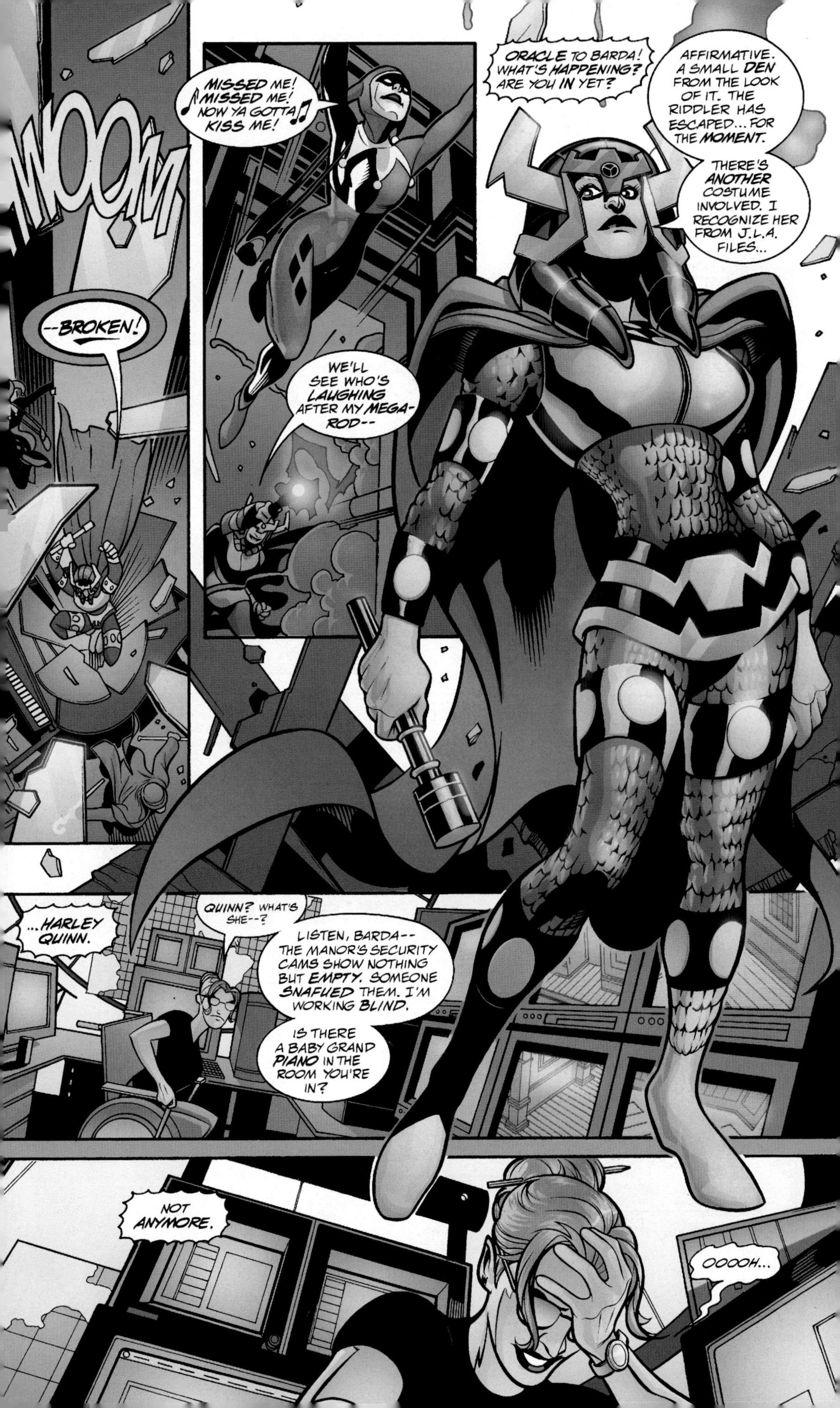
WOOM
MISSED ME! MISSED ME! NOW YA GOTTA KISS ME!
--BROKEN!
WE'LL SEE WHO'S LAUGHING AFTER MY MEGA-ROD--
ORACLE TO BARDA! WHAT'S HAPPENING? ARE YOU IN YET?
AFFIRMATIVE. A SMALL DEN FROM THE LOOK OF IT. THE RIDDLER HAS ESCAPED... FOR THE MOMENT.
THERE'S ANOTHER COSTUME INVOLVED. I RECOGNIZE HER FROM J.L.A. FILES...
...HARLEY QUINN.
QUINN? WHAT'S SHE--?
LISTEN, BARDA-- THE MANOR'S SECURITY CAMS SHOW NOTHING BUT EMPTY. SOMEONE SNAFUED THEM. I'M WORKING BLIND.
IS THERE A BABY GRAND PIANO IN THE ROOM YOU'RE IN?
NOT ANYMORE.
OOOOH...

...'KAY, BARDA--BRUCE WAYNE HAS A LOT OF *PRICELESS* PIECES IN HIS PLACE. LET'S KEEP PROPERTY DAMAGE TO A *MINIMUM.*

YOU SUMMONED ME TO CAPTURE THE *THIEVES*, ORACLE--AND I *VOW* TO DO SO WITH AS *LITTLE* DESTRUCTION AS *NECESSARY.*

IT'S THE "*AS NECESSARY*" PART THAT *WORRIES* ME.

LISTEN, THIS IS *IMPORTANT*--THERE'S A *SECRET PASSAGE* IN THE BUILDING. IT IS *ESSENTIAL* THAT THE THIEVES *NOT* FIND IT.

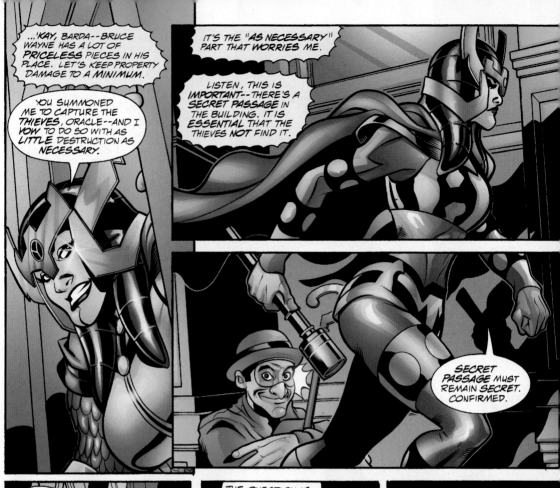

SECRET PASSAGE MUST REMAIN *SECRET.* CONFIRMED.

I *KNEW* IT! I *KNEW* IT! I *KNEW* IT!

THERE IS A *SECRET* TO *WAYNE MANOR!* A *RIDDLE* TO SOLVE! A *SECRET PASSAGE!*

THE QUESTION IS-- *WHERE?*

???

OF COURSE! THE BEST PLACE TO *HIDE* A SECRET PASSAGE IS IN A ROOM *FILLED* WITH PASSAGES...

...THE *LIBRARY!*

GOTTA SAY-- YOU'RE HOURS OF ENDLESS *ENTERTAINMENT,* ED...

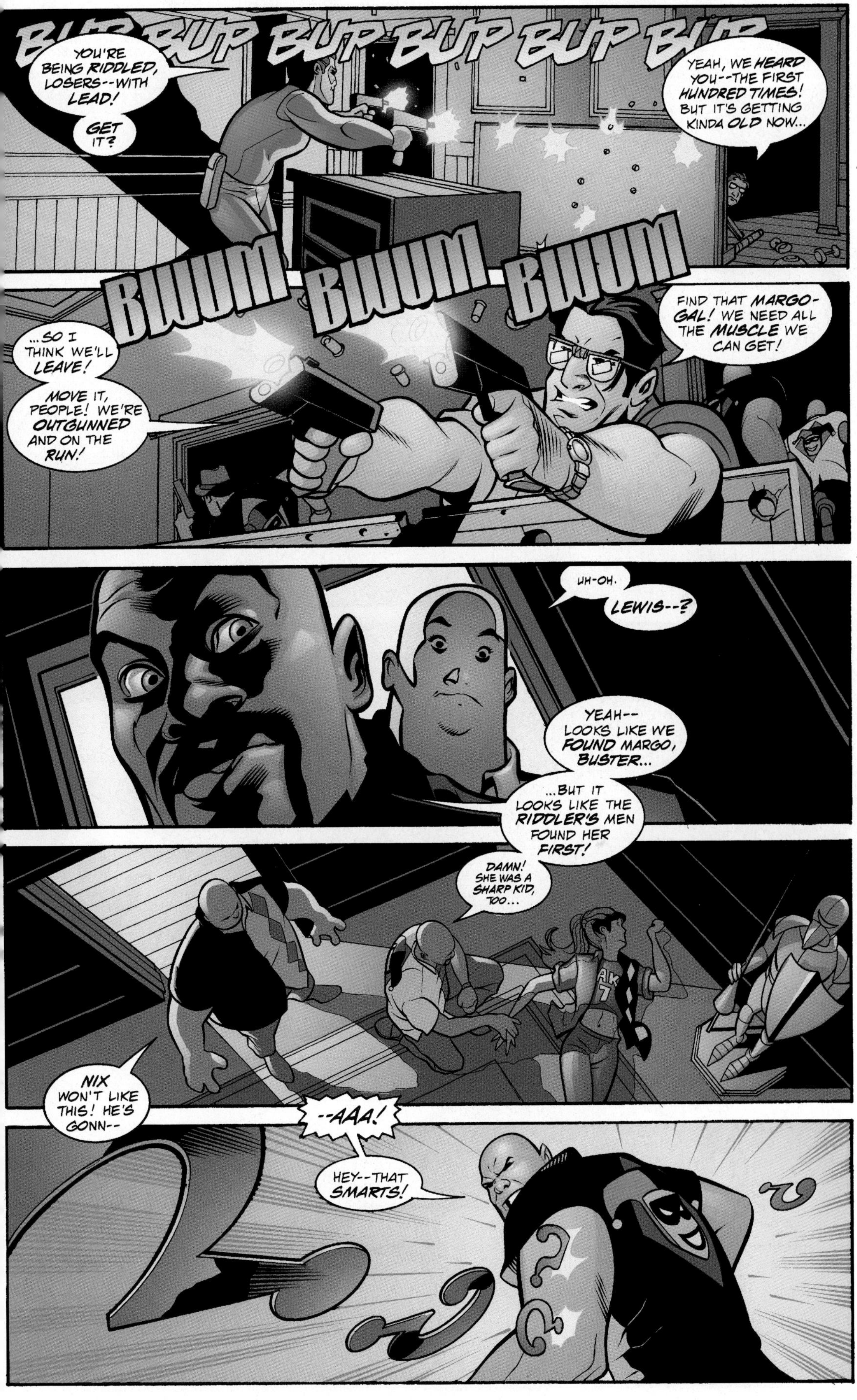

BUP BUP BUP BUP
YOU'RE BEING RIDDLED, LOSERS--WITH LEAD!
GET IT?
YEAH, WE HEARD YOU--THE FIRST HUNDRED TIMES! BUT IT'S GETTING KINDA OLD NOW...
BWUM BWUM BWUM
...SO I THINK WE'LL LEAVE!
MOVE IT, PEOPLE! WE'RE OUTGUNNED AND ON THE RUN!
FIND THAT MARGO-GAL! WE NEED ALL THE MUSCLE WE CAN GET!
UH-OH.
LEWIS--?
YEAH--LOOKS LIKE WE FOUND MARGO, BUSTER...
...BUT IT LOOKS LIKE THE RIDDLER'S MEN FOUND HER FIRST!
DAMN! SHE WAS A SHARP KID, TOO...
AK 7
NIX WON'T LIKE THIS! HE'S GONN--
--AAA!
HEY--THAT SMARTS!

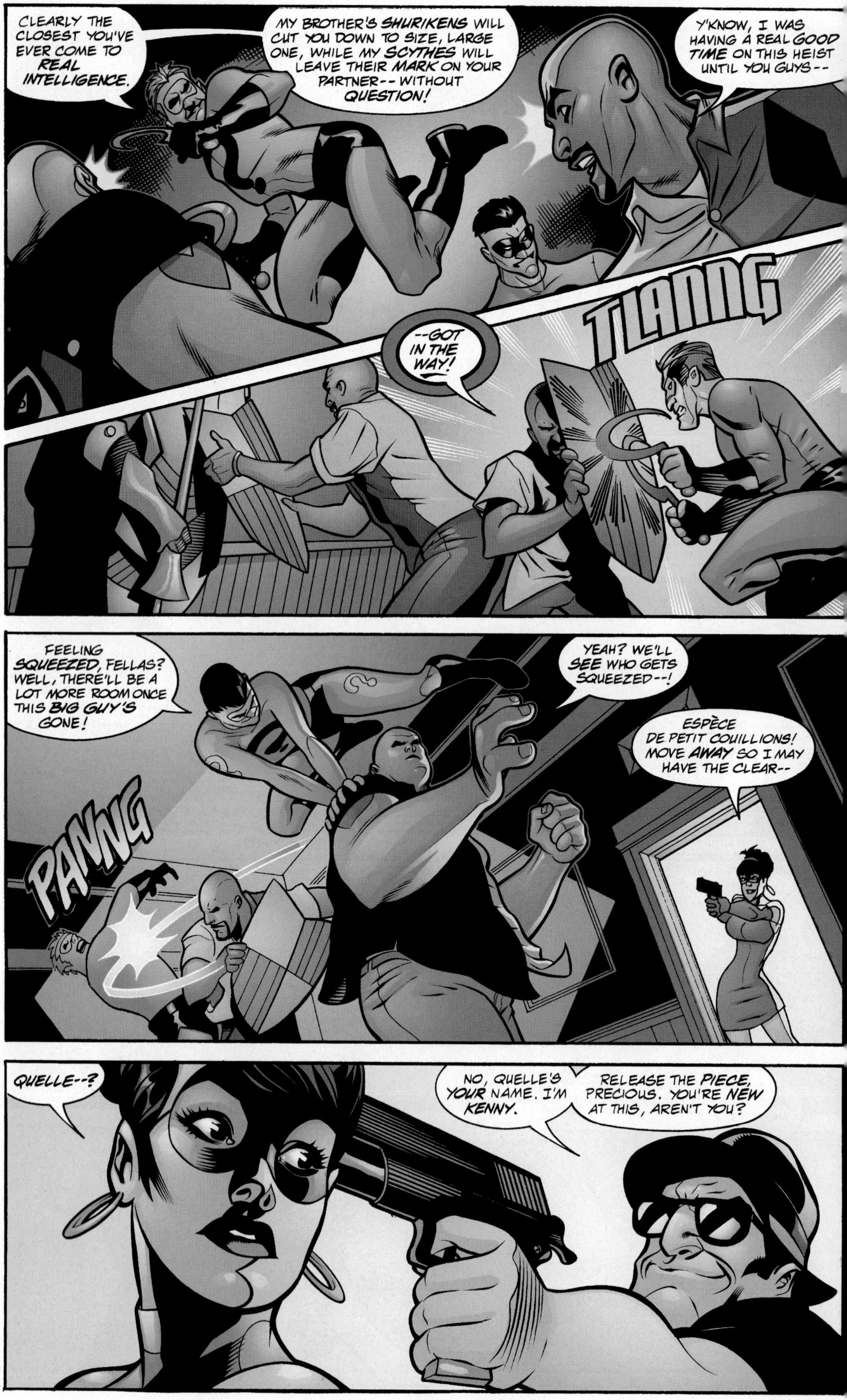
CLEARLY THE CLOSEST YOU'VE EVER COME TO REAL INTELLIGENCE.
MY BROTHER'S SHURIKENS WILL CUT YOU DOWN TO SIZE, LARGE ONE, WHILE MY SCYTHES WILL LEAVE THEIR MARK ON YOUR PARTNER--WITHOUT QUESTION!
Y'KNOW, I WAS HAVING A REAL GOOD TIME ON THIS HEIST UNTIL YOU GUYS--
TLANNG
--GOT IN THE WAY!
FEELING SQUEEZED, FELLAS? WELL, THERE'LL BE A LOT MORE ROOM ONCE THIS BIG GUY'S GONE!
YEAH? WE'LL SEE WHO GETS SQUEEZED--!
ESPÈCE DE PETIT COUILLIONS! MOVE AWAY SO I MAY HAVE THE CLEAR--
PANNG
QUELLE--?
NO, QUELLE'S YOUR NAME. I'M KENNY.
RELEASE THE PIECE, PRECIOUS. YOU'RE NEW AT THIS, AREN'T YOU?

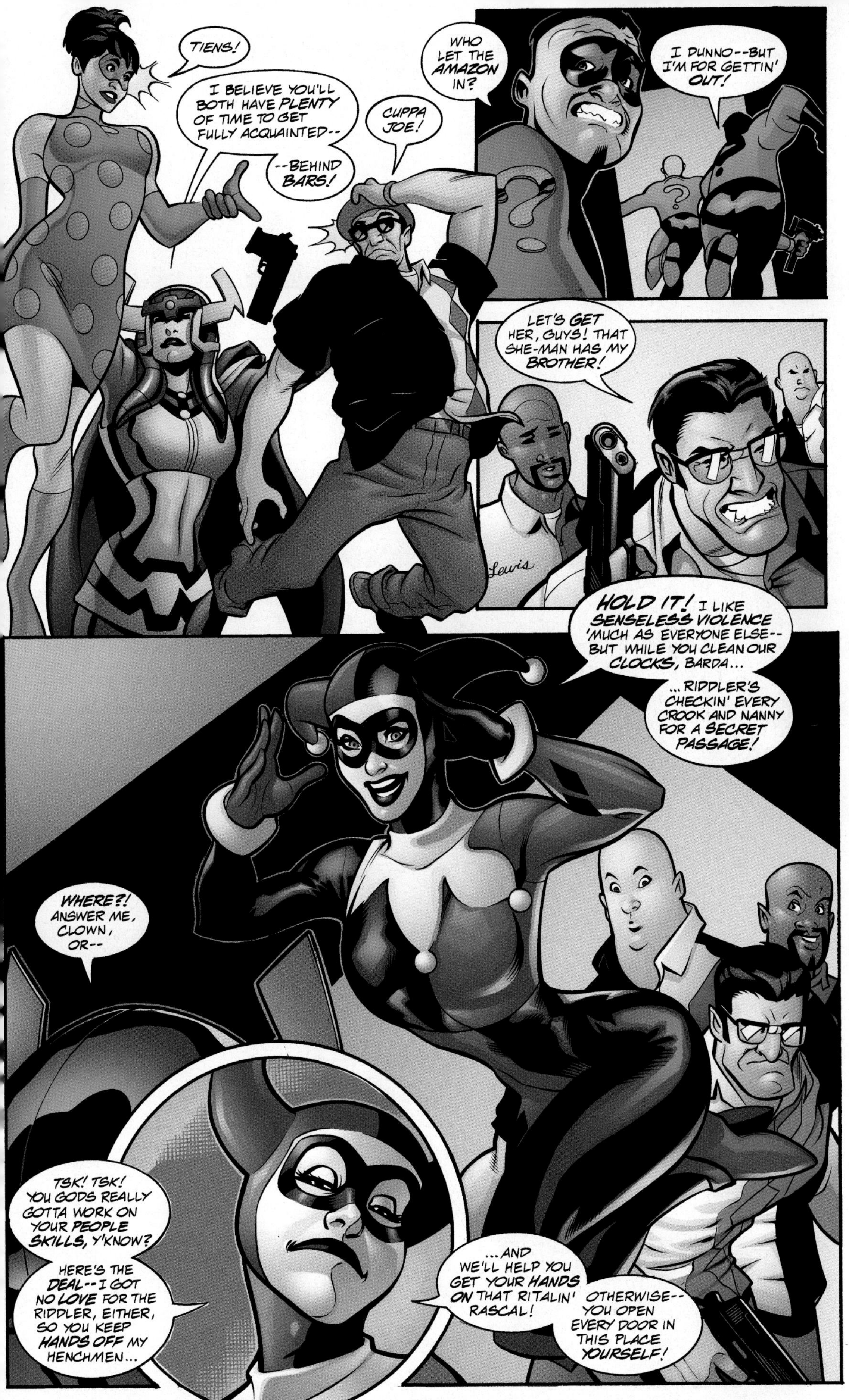
TIENS!
I BELIEVE YOU'LL BOTH HAVE PLENTY OF TIME TO GET FULLY ACQUAINTED--
--BEHIND BARS!
CUPPA JOE!
WHO LET THE AMAZON IN?
I DUNNO--BUT I'M FOR GETTIN' OUT!
LET'S GET HER, GUYS! THAT SHE-MAN HAS MY BROTHER!
Lewis
HOLD IT! I LIKE SENSELESS VIOLENCE 'MUCH AS EVERYONE ELSE-- BUT WHILE YOU CLEAN OUR CLOCKS, BARDA...
...RIDDLER'S CHECKIN' EVERY CROOK AND NANNY FOR A SECRET PASSAGE!
WHERE?! ANSWER ME, CLOWN, OR--
TSK! TSK! YOU GODS REALLY GOTTA WORK ON YOUR PEOPLE SKILLS, Y'KNOW?
HERE'S THE DEAL--I GOT NO LOVE FOR THE RIDDLER, EITHER, SO YOU KEEP HANDS OFF MY HENCHMEN...
...AND WE'LL HELP YOU GET YOUR HANDS ON THAT RITALIN' RASCAL!
OTHERWISE-- YOU OPEN EVERY DOOR IN THIS PLACE YOURSELF!

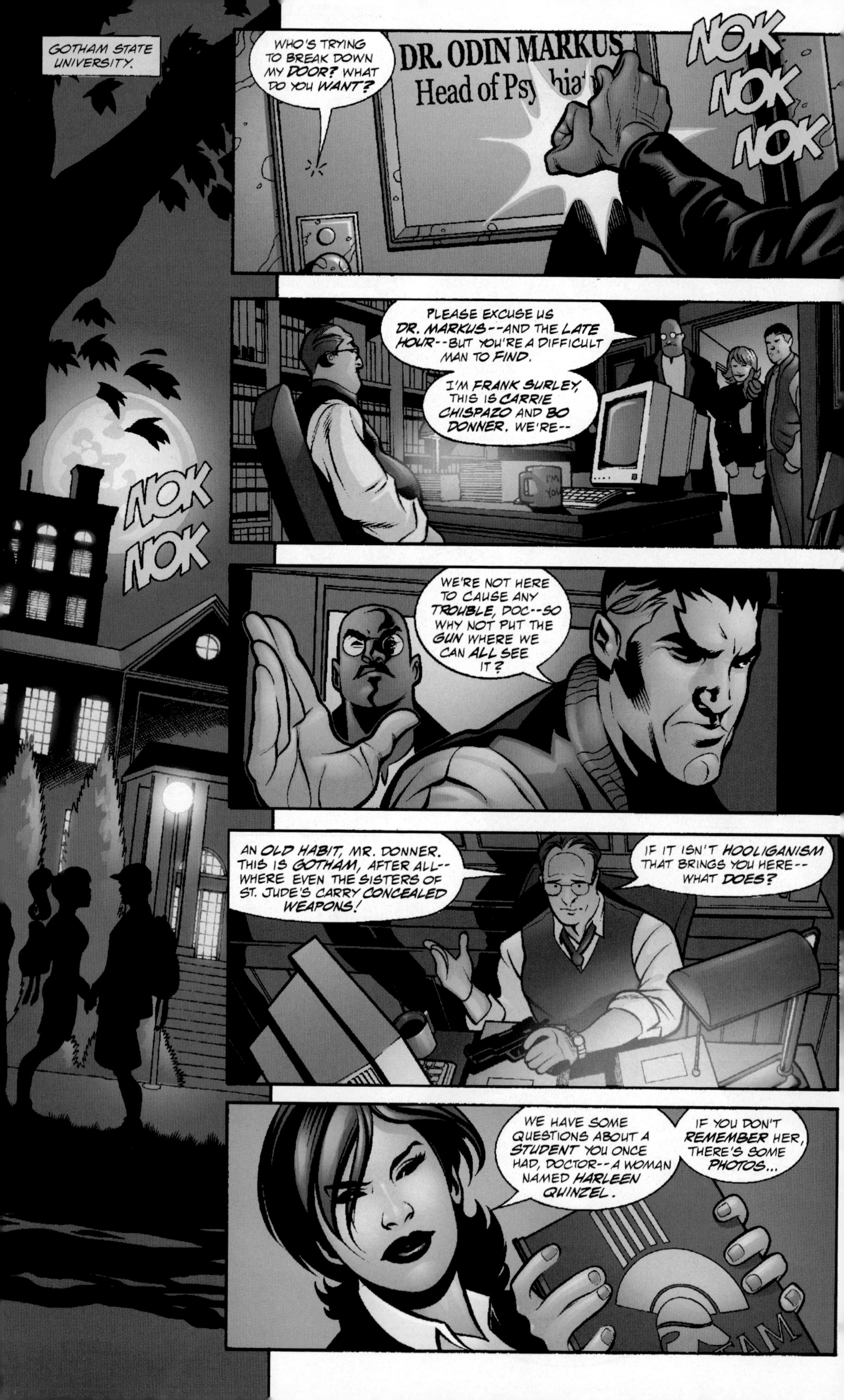
GOTHAM STATE UNIVERSITY.
WHO'S TRYING TO BREAK DOWN MY DOOR? WHAT DO YOU WANT?
DR. ODIN MARKUS
Head of Psy hiat
NOK NOK NOK
NOK NOK
PLEASE EXCUSE US DR. MARKUS--AND THE LATE HOUR--BUT YOU'RE A DIFFICULT MAN TO FIND.
I'M FRANK SURLEY, THIS IS CARRIE CHISPAZO AND BO DONNER. WE'RE--
WE'RE NOT HERE TO CAUSE ANY TROUBLE, DOC--SO WHY NOT PUT THE GUN WHERE WE CAN ALL SEE IT?
AN OLD HABIT, MR. DONNER. THIS IS GOTHAM, AFTER ALL--WHERE EVEN THE SISTERS OF ST. JUDE'S CARRY CONCEALED WEAPONS!
IF IT ISN'T HOOLIGANISM THAT BRINGS YOU HERE--WHAT DOES?
WE HAVE SOME QUESTIONS ABOUT A STUDENT YOU ONCE HAD, DOCTOR--A WOMAN NAMED HARLEEN QUINZEL.
IF YOU DON'T REMEMBER HER, THERE'S SOME PHOTOS...

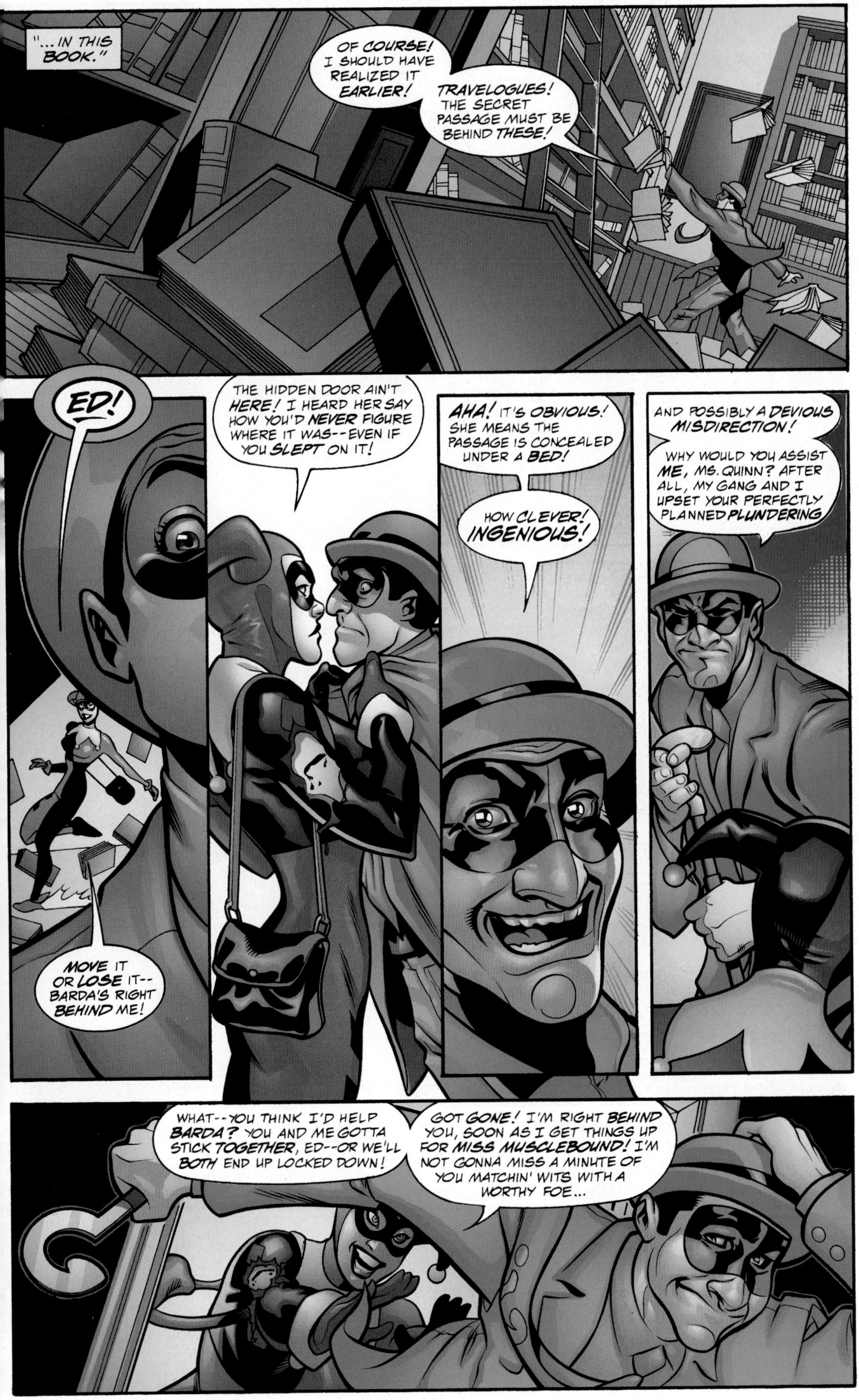

"...IN THIS BOOK."
OF COURSE! I SHOULD HAVE REALIZED IT EARLIER!
TRAVELOGUES! THE SECRET PASSAGE MUST BE BEHIND THESE!
ED!
MOVE IT OR LOSE IT-- BARDA'S RIGHT BEHIND ME!
THE HIDDEN DOOR AIN'T HERE! I HEARD HER SAY HOW YOU'D NEVER FIGURE WHERE IT WAS--EVEN IF YOU SLEPT ON IT!
AHA! IT'S OBVIOUS! SHE MEANS THE PASSAGE IS CONCEALED UNDER A BED!
HOW CLEVER! INGENIOUS!
AND POSSIBLY A DEVIOUS MISDIRECTION!
WHY WOULD YOU ASSIST ME, MS. QUINN? AFTER ALL, MY GANG AND I UPSET YOUR PERFECTLY PLANNED PLUNDERING
WHAT--YOU THINK I'D HELP BARDA? YOU AND ME GOTTA STICK TOGETHER, ED--OR WE'LL BOTH END UP LOCKED DOWN!
GOT GONE! I'M RIGHT BEHIND YOU, SOON AS I GET THINGS UP FOR MISS MUSCLEBOUND! I'M NOT GONNA MISS A MINUTE OF YOU MATCHIN' WITS WITH A WORTHY FOE...

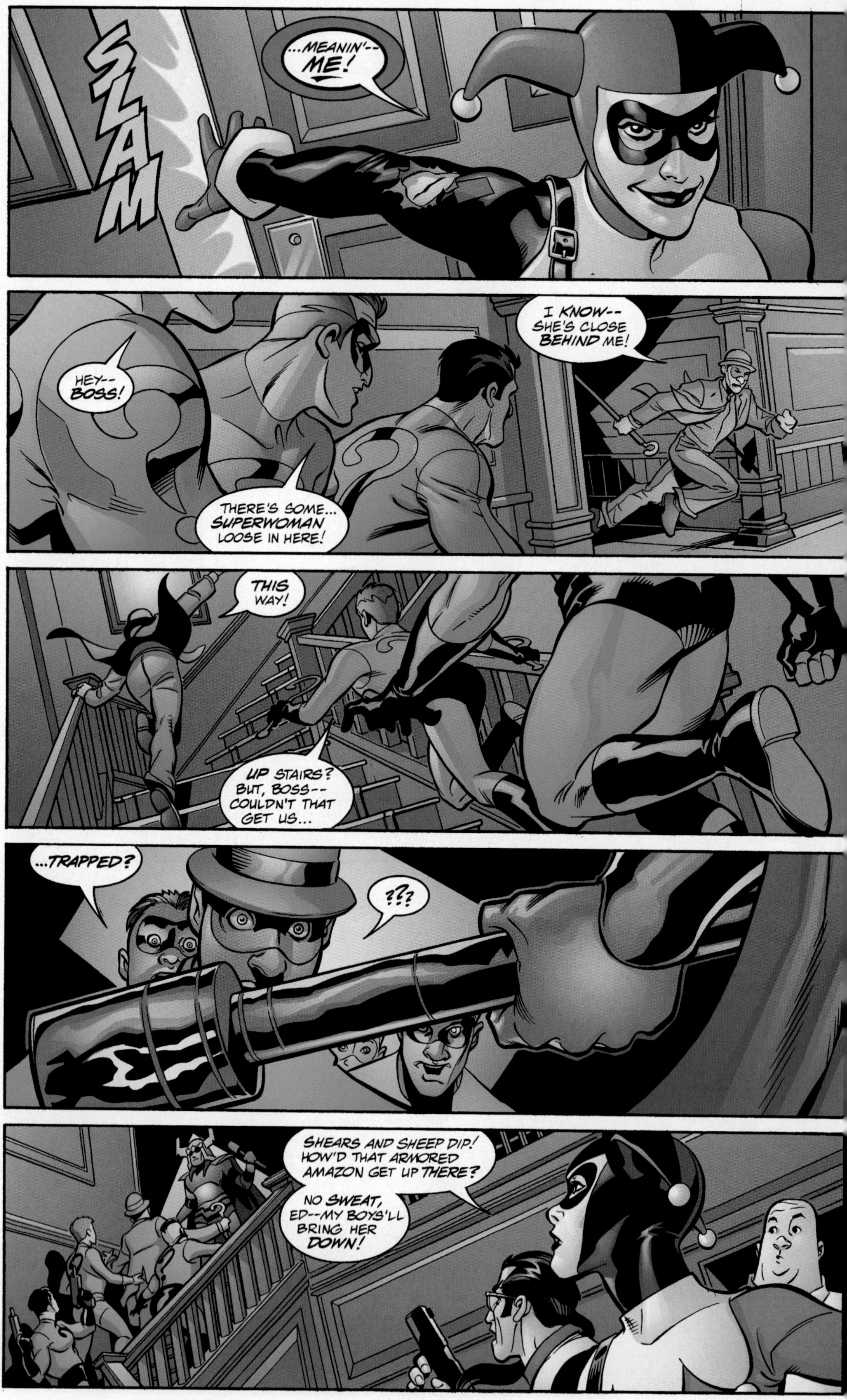

SLAM
...MEANIN'-- ME!
HEY-- BOSS!
THERE'S SOME... SUPERWOMAN LOOSE IN HERE!
I KNOW-- SHE'S CLOSE BEHIND ME!
THIS WAY!
UP STAIRS? BUT, BOSS-- COULDN'T THAT GET US...
...TRAPPED?
???
SHEARS AND SHEEP DIP! HOW'D THAT ARMORED AMAZON GET UP THERE?
NO SWEAT, ED--MY BOYS'LL BRING HER DOWN!

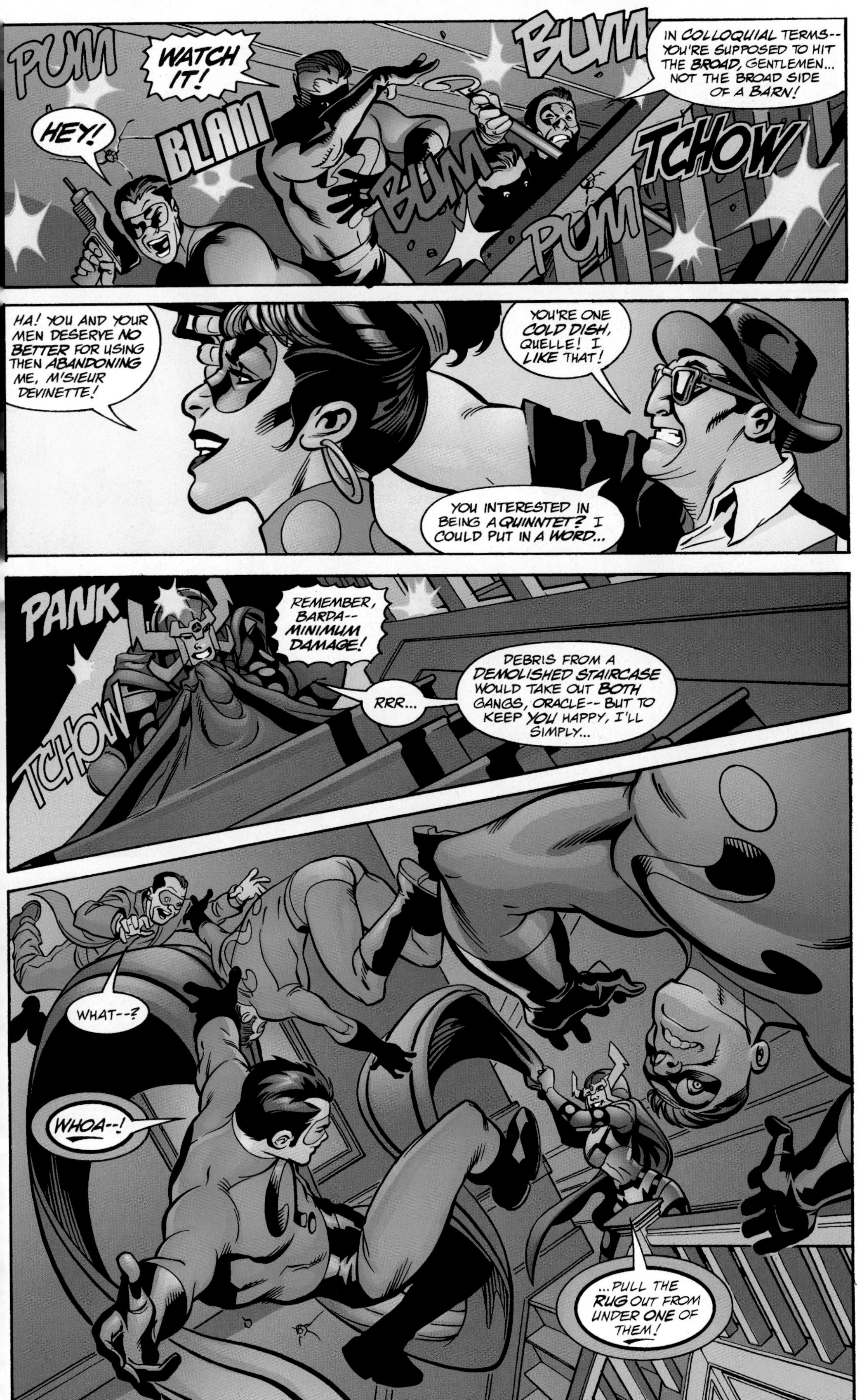
PUM
WATCH IT!
BUM
IN COLLOQUIAL TERMS-- YOU'RE SUPPOSED TO HIT THE BROAD, GENTLEMEN... NOT THE BROAD SIDE OF A BARN!
HEY!
BLAM
BUM
TCHOW
PUM
HA! YOU AND YOUR MEN DESERVE NO BETTER FOR USING THEN ABANDONING ME, M'SIEUR DEVINETTE!
YOU'RE ONE COLD DISH, QUELLE! I LIKE THAT!
YOU INTERESTED IN BEING A QUINNTET? I COULD PUT IN A WORD...
PANK
REMEMBER, BARDA-- MINIMUM DAMAGE!
RRR...
DEBRIS FROM A DEMOLISHED STAIRCASE WOULD TAKE OUT BOTH GANGS, ORACLE-- BUT TO KEEP YOU HAPPY, I'LL SIMPLY...
TCHOW
WHAT--?
WHOA--!
...PULL THE RUG OUT FROM UNDER ONE OF THEM!

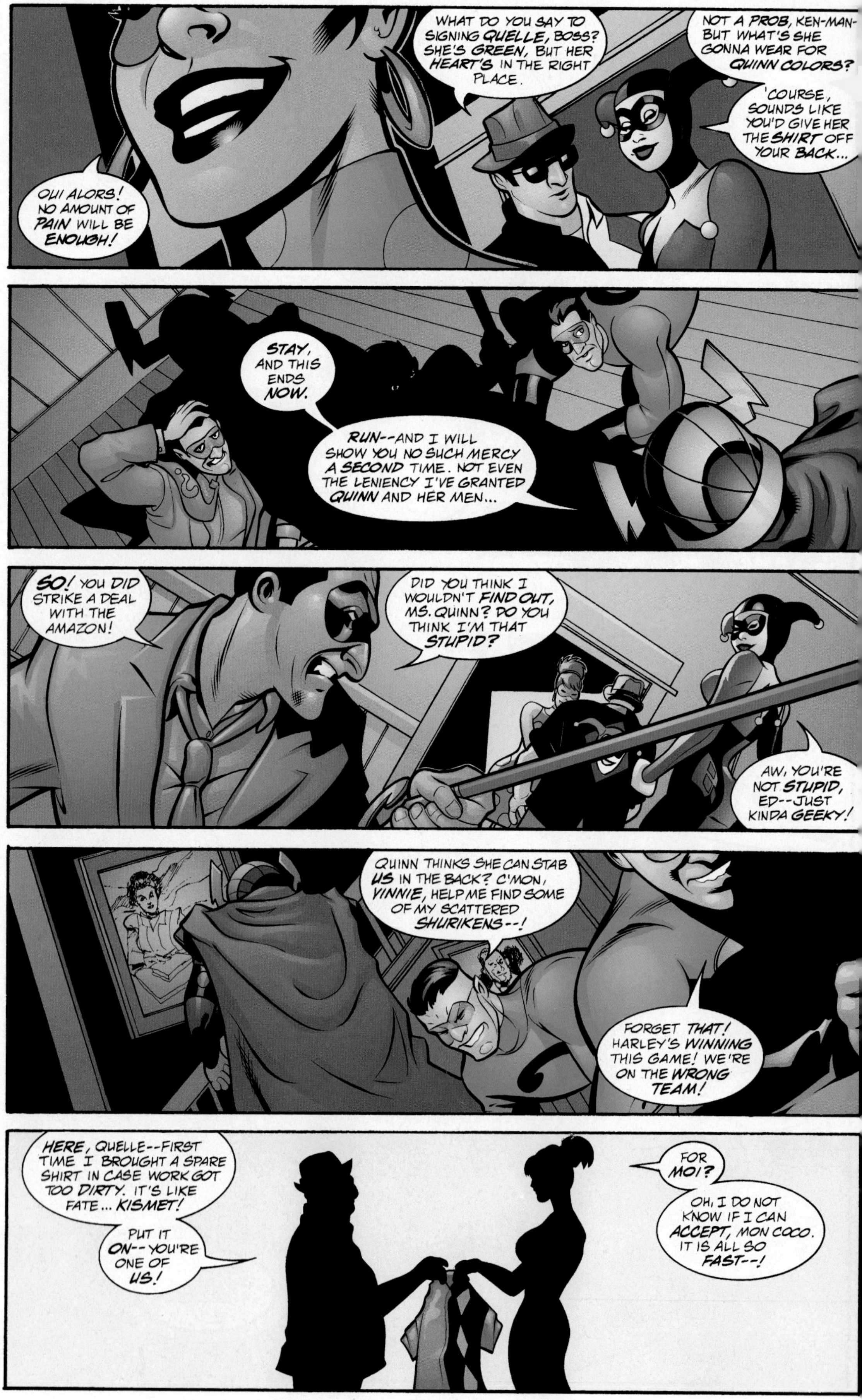
WHAT DO YOU SAY TO SIGNING QUELLE, BOSS? SHE'S GREEN, BUT HER HEART'S IN THE RIGHT PLACE.
NOT A PROB, KEN-MAN-BUT WHAT'S SHE GONNA WEAR FOR QUINN COLORS?
'COURSE, SOUNDS LIKE YOU'D GIVE HER THE SHIRT OFF YOUR BACK...
OUI ALORS! NO AMOUNT OF PAIN WILL BE ENOUGH!
STAY, AND THIS ENDS NOW.
RUN--AND I WILL SHOW YOU NO SUCH MERCY A SECOND TIME. NOT EVEN THE LENIENCY I'VE GRANTED QUINN AND HER MEN...
SO! YOU DID STRIKE A DEAL WITH THE AMAZON!
DID YOU THINK I WOULDN'T FIND OUT, MS. QUINN? DO YOU THINK I'M THAT STUPID?
AW, YOU'RE NOT STUPID, ED--JUST KINDA GEEKY!
QUINN THINKS SHE CAN STAB US IN THE BACK? C'MON, VINNIE, HELP ME FIND SOME OF MY SCATTERED SHURIKENS--!
FORGET THAT! HARLEY'S WINNING THIS GAME! WE'RE ON THE WRONG TEAM!
HERE, QUELLE--FIRST TIME I BROUGHT A SPARE SHIRT IN CASE WORK GOT TOO DIRTY. IT'S LIKE FATE... KISMET!
PUT IT ON--YOU'RE ONE OF US!
FOR MOI?
OH, I DO NOT KNOW IF I CAN ACCEPT, MON COCO. IT IS ALL SO FAST--!

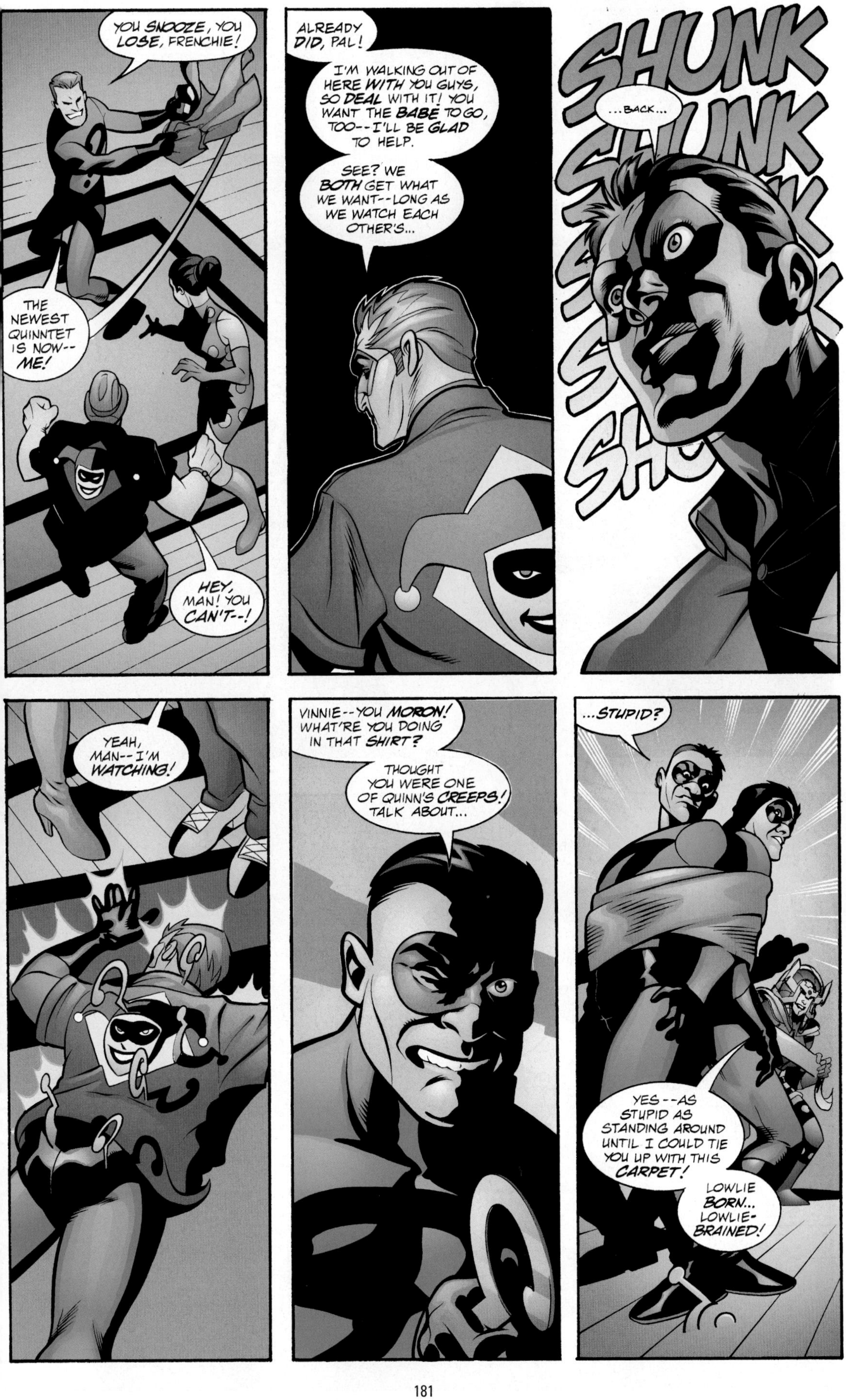
YOU SNOOZE, YOU LOSE, FRENCHIE!
THE NEWEST QUINNTET IS NOW--ME!
HEY, MAN! YOU CAN'T--!
ALREADY DID, PAL!
I'M WALKING OUT OF HERE WITH YOU GUYS, SO DEAL WITH IT! YOU WANT THE BABE TO GO, TOO--I'LL BE GLAD TO HELP.
SEE? WE BOTH GET WHAT WE WANT--LONG AS WE WATCH EACH OTHER'S...
SHUNK
...BACK...
YEAH, MAN--I'M WATCHING!
VINNIE--YOU MORON! WHAT'RE YOU DOING IN THAT SHIRT?
THOUGHT YOU WERE ONE OF QUINN'S CREEPS! TALK ABOUT...
...STUPID?
YES--AS STUPID AS STANDING AROUND UNTIL I COULD TIE YOU UP WITH THIS CARPET!
LOWLIE BORN... LOWLIE-BRAINED!

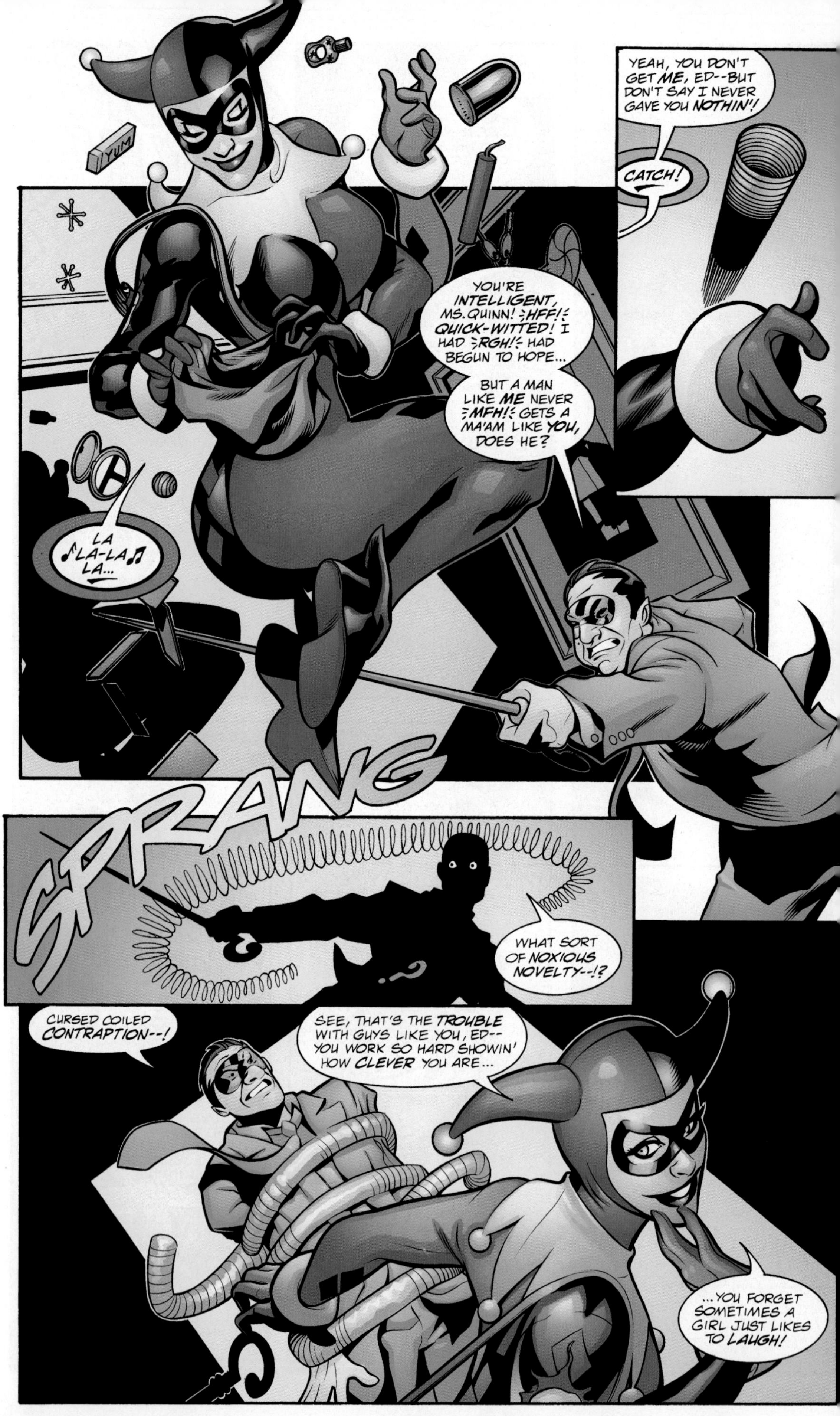
YEAH, YOU DON'T GET ME, ED--BUT DON'T SAY I NEVER GAVE YOU NOTHIN'!
CATCH!
YUM
YOU'RE INTELLIGENT, MS. QUINN! HFF! QUICK-WITTED! I HAD RGH! HAD BEGUN TO HOPE...
BUT A MAN LIKE ME NEVER MFH! GETS A MA'AM LIKE YOU, DOES HE?
LA LA-LA LA...
SPRANG
WHAT SORT OF NOXIOUS NOVELTY--!?
CURSED COILED CONTRAPTION--!
SEE, THAT'S THE TROUBLE WITH GUYS LIKE YOU, ED--YOU WORK SO HARD SHOWIN' HOW CLEVER YOU ARE...
...YOU FORGET SOMETIMES A GIRL JUST LIKES TO LAUGH!

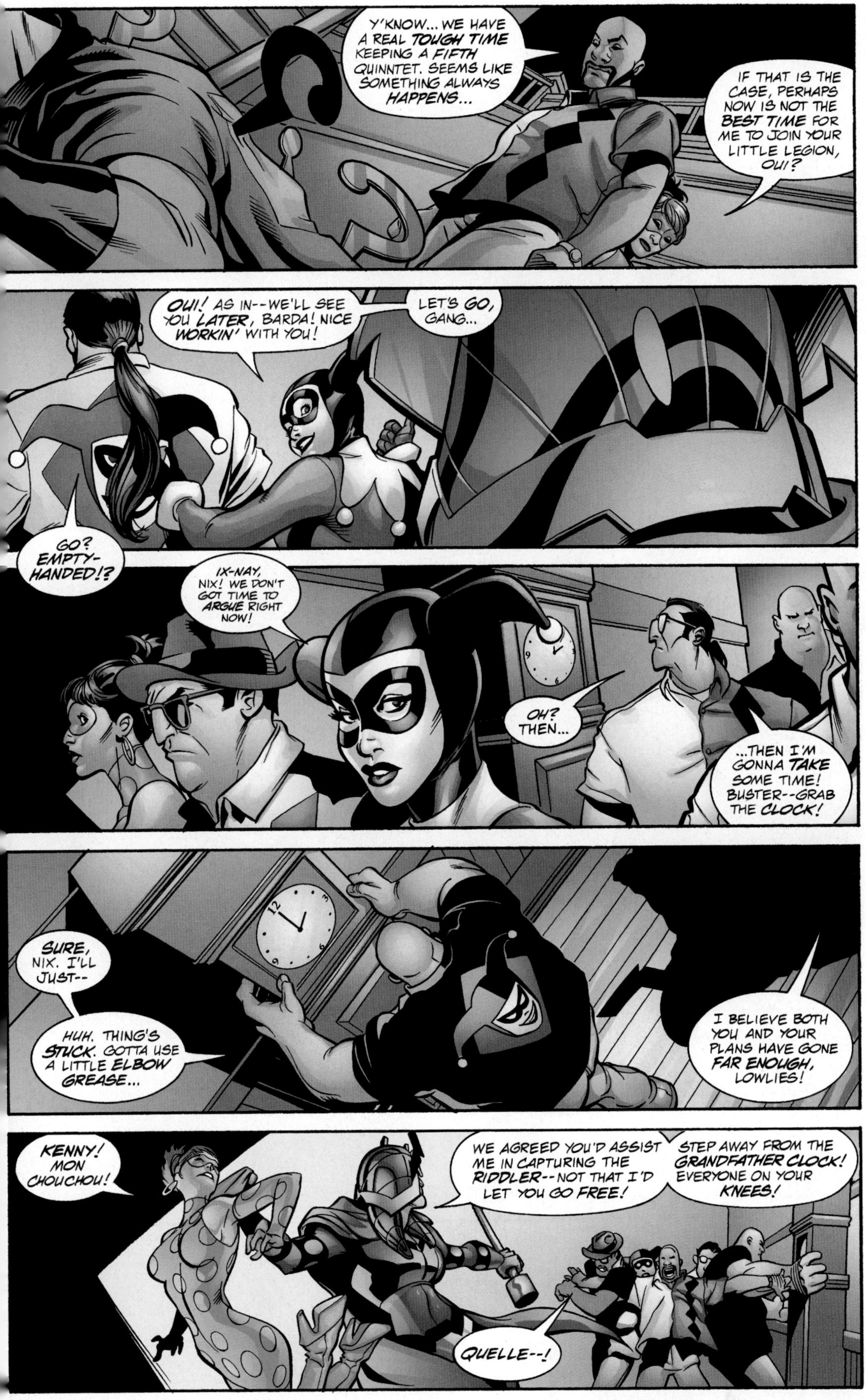
Y'KNOW... WE HAVE A REAL TOUGH TIME KEEPING A FIFTH QUINNTET. SEEMS LIKE SOMETHING ALWAYS HAPPENS...
IF THAT IS THE CASE, PERHAPS NOW IS NOT THE BEST TIME FOR ME TO JOIN YOUR LITTLE LEGION, OUI?
OUI! AS IN--WE'LL SEE YOU LATER, BARDA! NICE WORKIN' WITH YOU!
LET'S GO, GANG...
GO? EMPTY-HANDED!?
IX-NAY, NIX! WE DON'T GOT TIME TO ARGUE RIGHT NOW!
OH? THEN...
...THEN I'M GONNA TAKE SOME TIME! BUSTER--GRAB THE CLOCK!
SURE, NIX. I'LL JUST--
HUH. THING'S STUCK. GOTTA USE A LITTLE ELBOW GREASE...
I BELIEVE BOTH YOU AND YOUR PLANS HAVE GONE FAR ENOUGH, LOWLIES!
KENNY! MON CHOUCHOU!
WE AGREED YOU'D ASSIST ME IN CAPTURING THE RIDDLER--NOT THAT I'D LET YOU GO FREE!
STEP AWAY FROM THE GRANDFATHER CLOCK! EVERYONE ON YOUR KNEES!
QUELLE--!

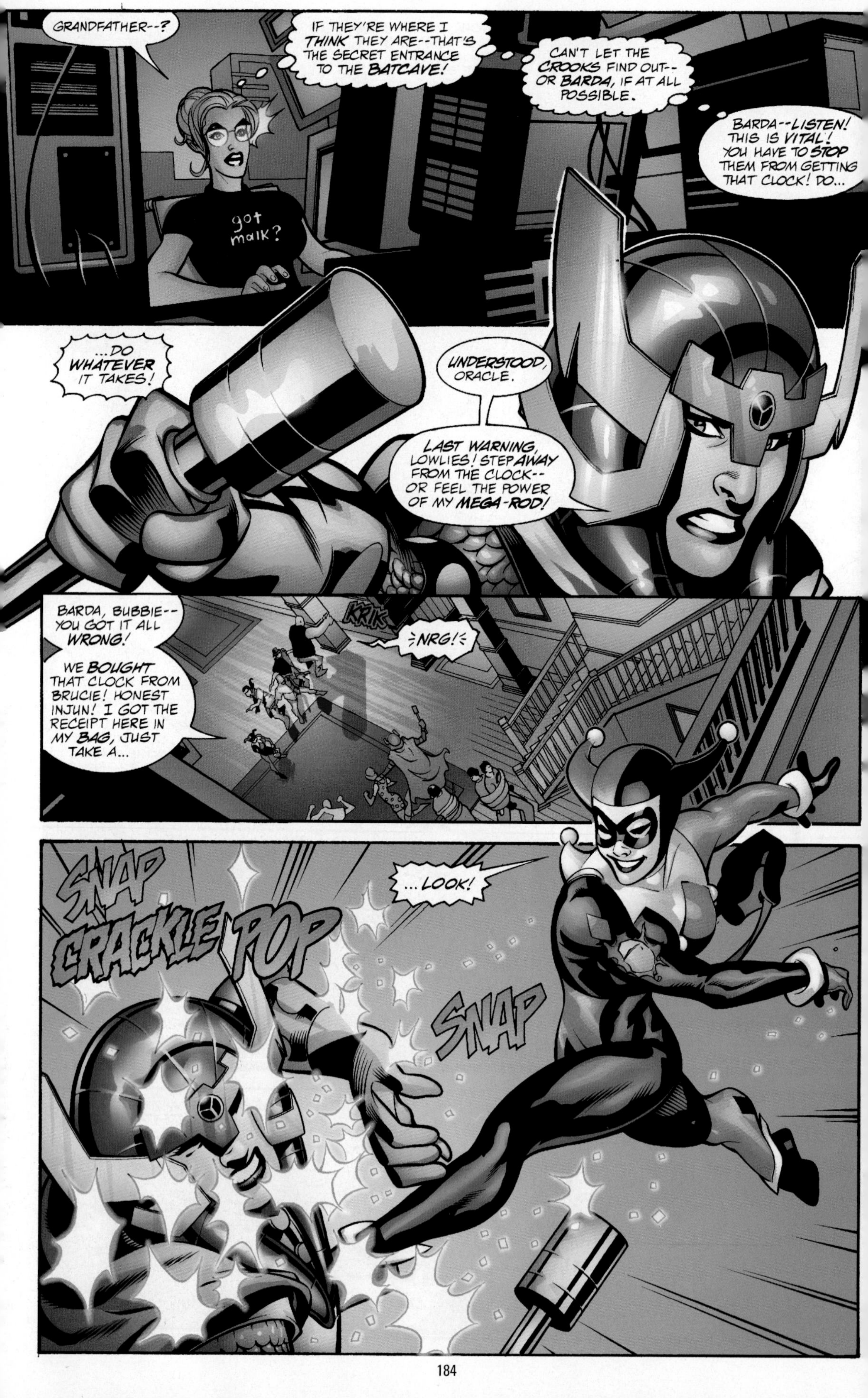
GRANDFATHER--?
IF THEY'RE WHERE I THINK THEY ARE--THAT'S THE SECRET ENTRANCE TO THE BATCAVE!
CAN'T LET THE CROOKS FIND OUT--OR BARDA, IF AT ALL POSSIBLE.
BARDA--LISTEN! THIS IS VITAL! YOU HAVE TO STOP THEM FROM GETTING THAT CLOCK! DO...
got malk?
...DO WHATEVER IT TAKES!
UNDERSTOOD, ORACLE.
LAST WARNING, LOWLIES! STEP AWAY FROM THE CLOCK--OR FEEL THE POWER OF MY MEGA-ROD!
BARDA, BUBBIE--YOU GOT IT ALL WRONG!
WE BOUGHT THAT CLOCK FROM BRUCIE! HONEST INJUN! I GOT THE RECEIPT HERE IN MY BAG, JUST TAKE A...
KRIK
NRG!
...LOOK!
SNAP
CRACKLE POP
SNAP

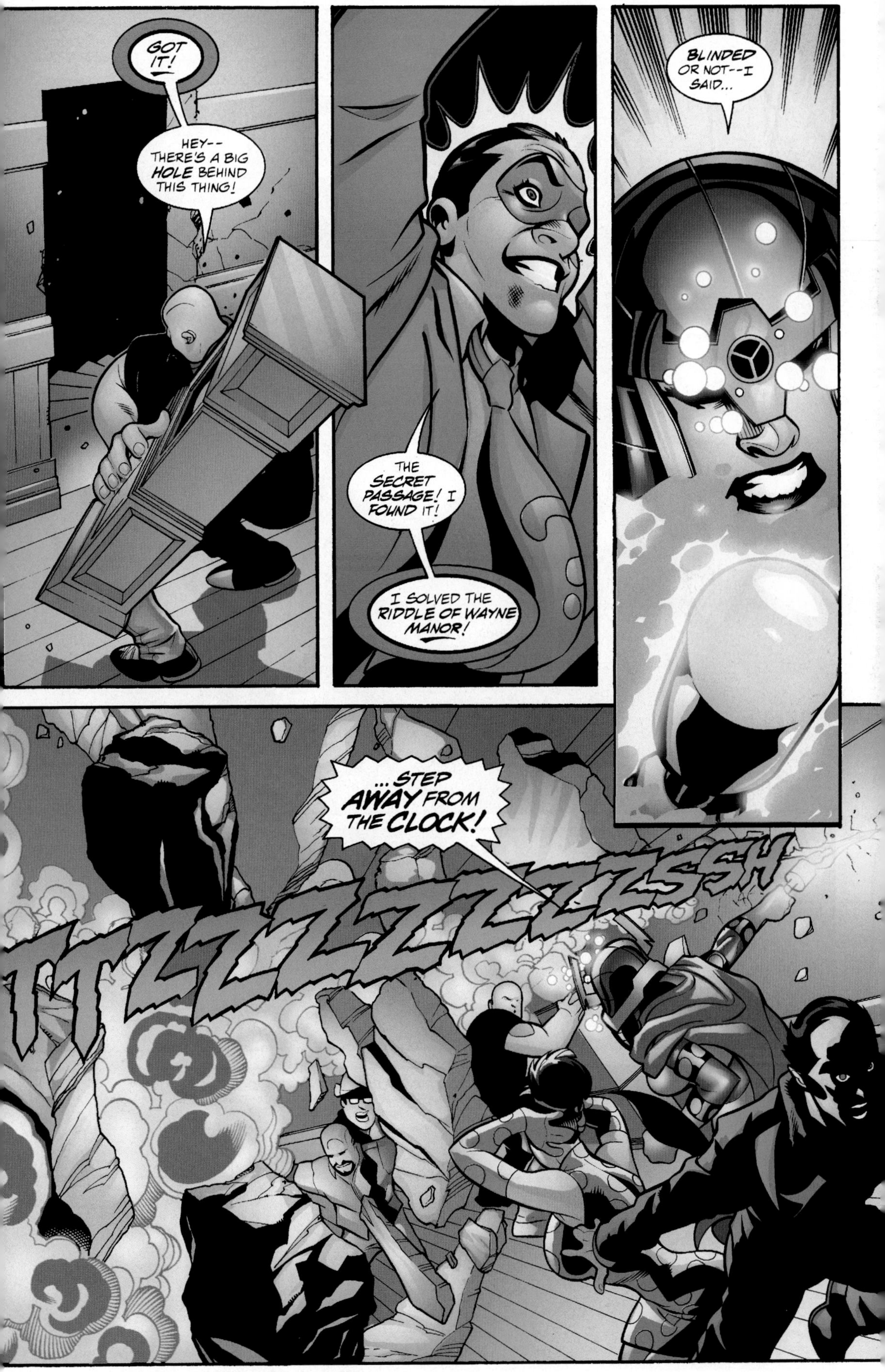

GOT IT!
HEY-- THERE'S A BIG HOLE BEHIND THIS THING!
THE SECRET PASSAGE! I FOUND IT!
I SOLVED THE RIDDLE OF WAYNE MANOR!
BLINDED OR NOT--I SAID...
...STEP AWAY FROM THE CLOCK!
TTZZZZZZZZZZZSSH

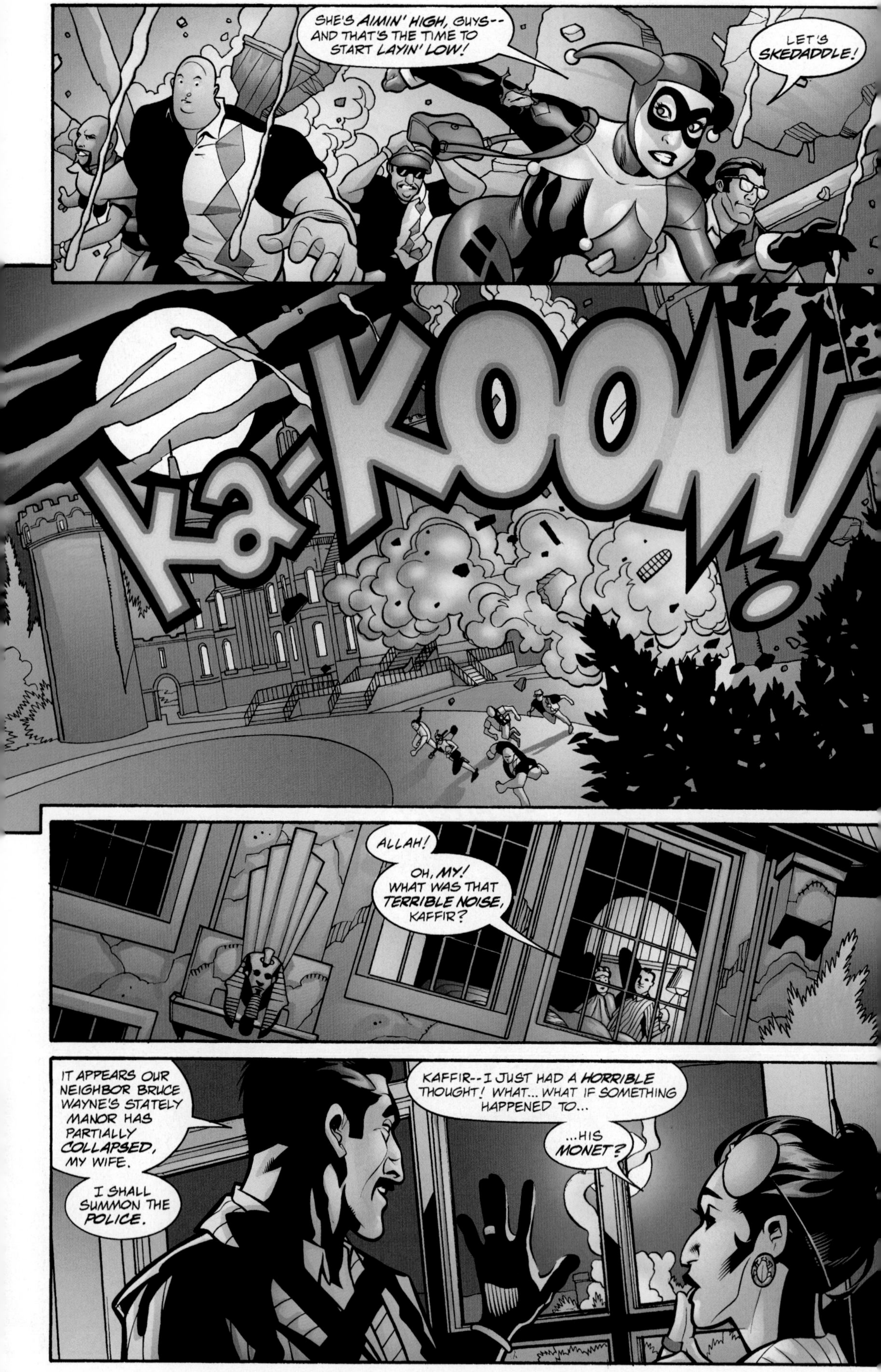
SHE'S AIMIN' HIGH, GUYS-- AND THAT'S THE TIME TO START LAYIN' LOW!
LET'S SKEDADDLE!
KA-KOOM!
ALLAH!
OH, MY! WHAT WAS THAT TERRIBLE NOISE, KAFFIR?
IT APPEARS OUR NEIGHBOR BRUCE WAYNE'S STATELY MANOR HAS PARTIALLY COLLAPSED, MY WIFE.
I SHALL SUMMON THE POLICE.
KAFFIR--I JUST HAD A HORRIBLE THOUGHT! WHAT... WHAT IF SOMETHING HAPPENED TO...
...HIS MONET?

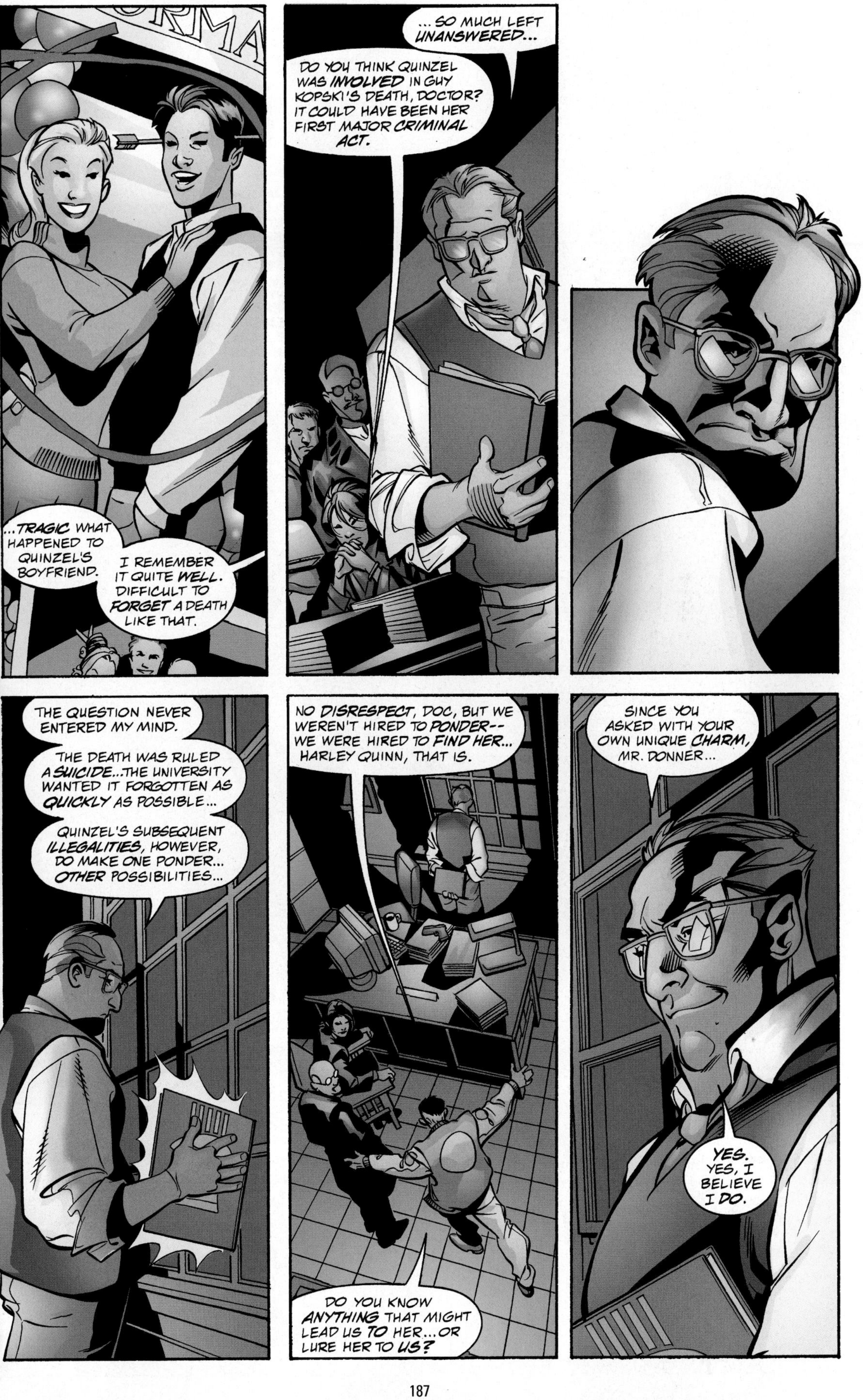
...TRAGIC WHAT HAPPENED TO QUINZEL'S BOYFRIEND.
I REMEMBER IT QUITE WELL. DIFFICULT TO FORGET A DEATH LIKE THAT.
...SO MUCH LEFT UNANSWERED...
DO YOU THINK QUINZEL WAS INVOLVED IN GUY KOPSKI'S DEATH, DOCTOR? IT COULD HAVE BEEN HER FIRST MAJOR CRIMINAL ACT.
THE QUESTION NEVER ENTERED MY MIND.
THE DEATH WAS RULED A SUICIDE...THE UNIVERSITY WANTED IT FORGOTTEN AS QUICKLY AS POSSIBLE...
QUINZEL'S SUBSEQUENT ILLEGALITIES, HOWEVER, DO MAKE ONE PONDER... OTHER POSSIBILITIES...
NO DISRESPECT, DOC, BUT WE WEREN'T HIRED TO PONDER-- WE WERE HIRED TO FIND HER... HARLEY QUINN, THAT IS.
DO YOU KNOW ANYTHING THAT MIGHT LEAD US TO HER...OR LURE HER TO US?
SINCE YOU ASKED WITH YOUR OWN UNIQUE CHARM, MR. DONNER...
YES. YES, I BELIEVE I DO.

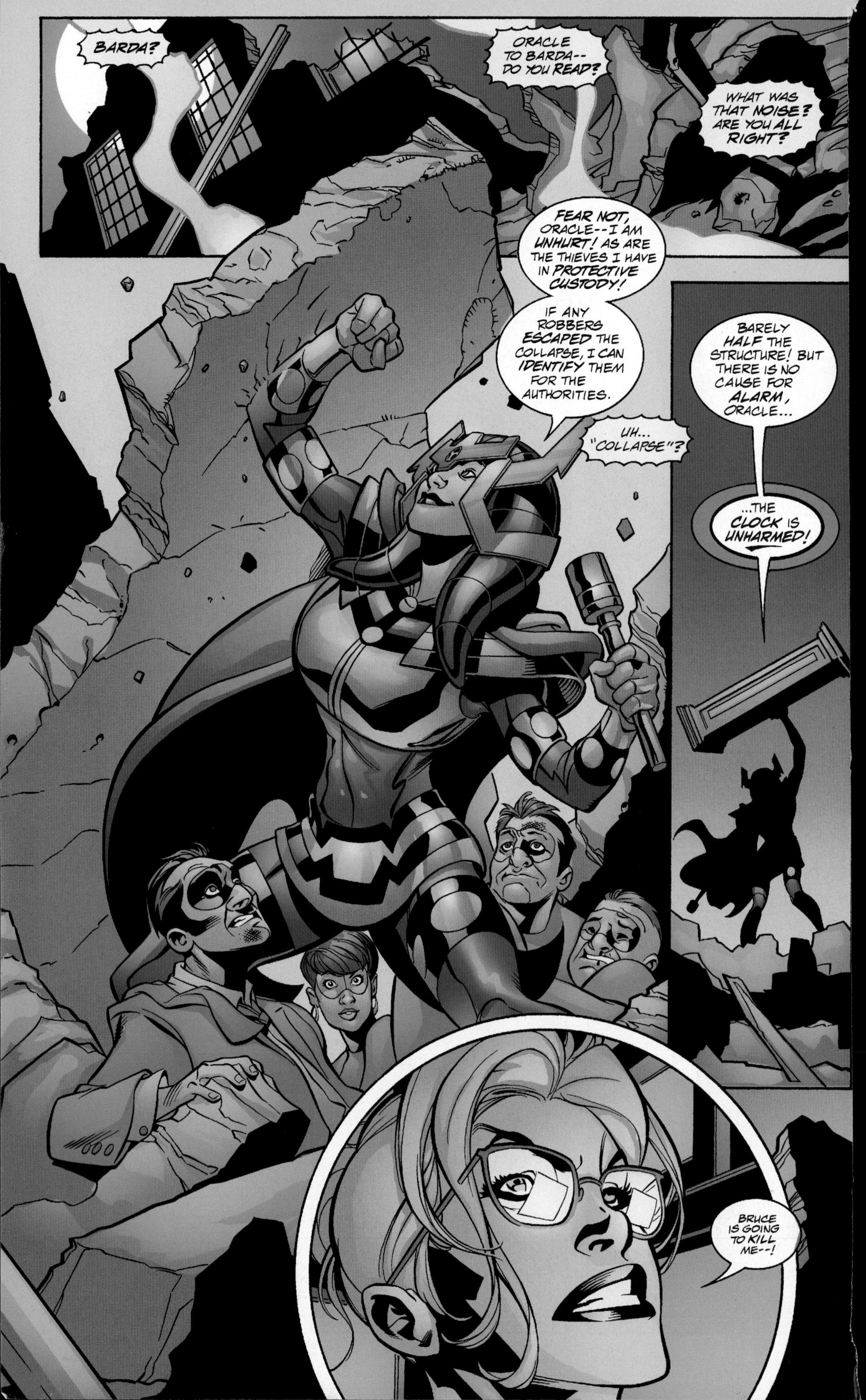
BARDA?
ORACLE TO BARDA-- DO YOU READ?
WHAT WAS THAT NOISE? ARE YOU ALL RIGHT?
FEAR NOT, ORACLE--I AM UNHURT! AS ARE THE THIEVES I HAVE IN PROTECTIVE CUSTODY!
IF ANY ROBBERS ESCAPED THE COLLAPSE, I CAN IDENTIFY THEM FOR THE AUTHORITIES.
UH... "COLLAPSE"?
BARELY HALF THE STRUCTURE! BUT THERE IS NO CAUSE FOR ALARM, ORACLE...
...THE CLOCK IS UNHARMED!
BRUCE IS GOING TO KILL ME--!

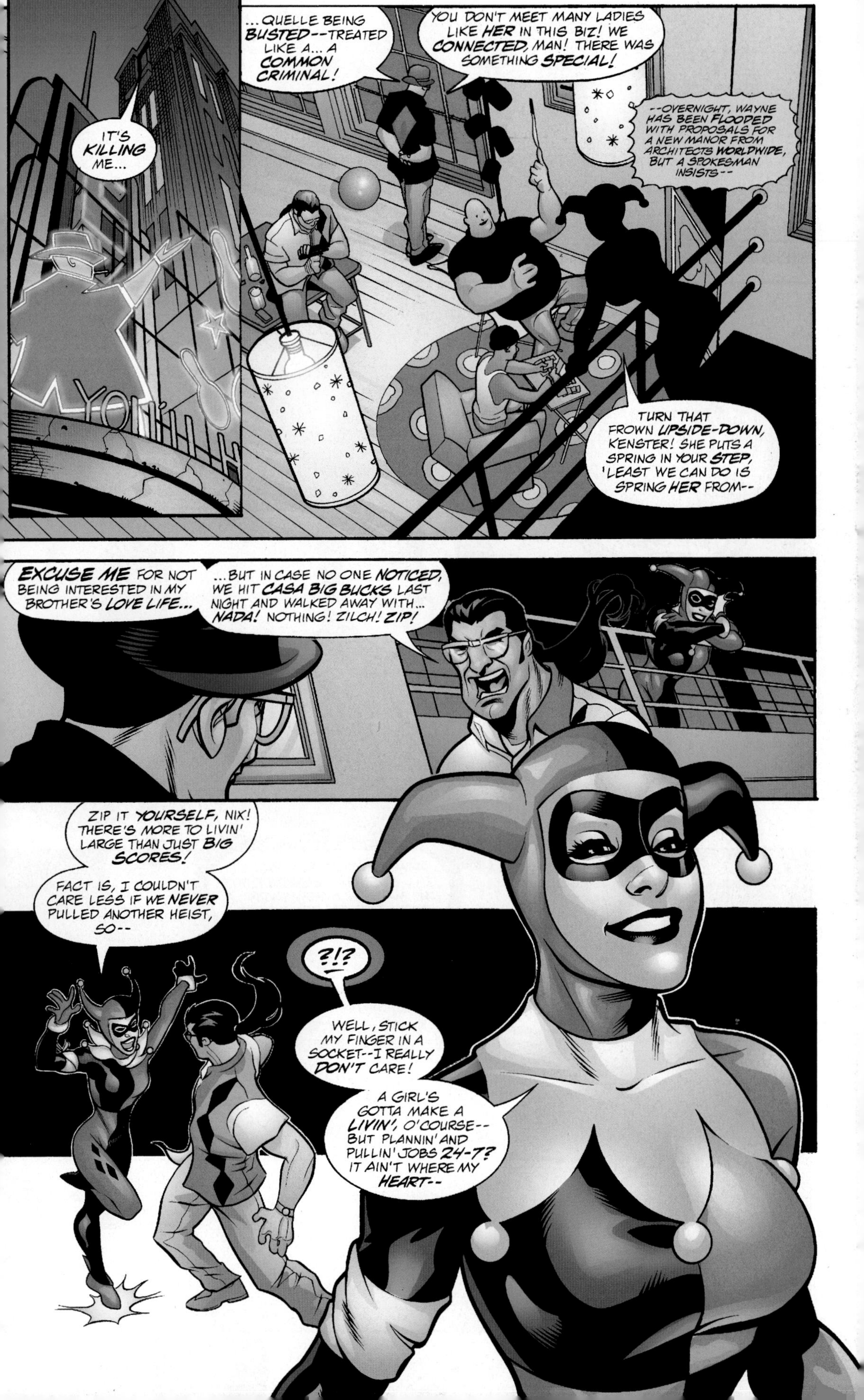
IT'S KILLING ME...
...QUELLE BEING BUSTED--TREATED LIKE A... A COMMON CRIMINAL!
YOU DON'T MEET MANY LADIES LIKE HER IN THIS BIZ! WE CONNECTED, MAN! THERE WAS SOMETHING SPECIAL!
--OVERNIGHT, WAYNE HAS BEEN FLOODED WITH PROPOSALS FOR A NEW MANOR FROM ARCHITECTS WORLDWIDE, BUT A SPOKESMAN INSISTS--
TURN THAT FROWN UPSIDE-DOWN, KENSTER! SHE PUTS A SPRING IN YOUR STEP, 'LEAST WE CAN DO IS SPRING HER FROM--
EXCUSE ME FOR NOT BEING INTERESTED IN MY BROTHER'S LOVE LIFE...
...BUT IN CASE NO ONE NOTICED, WE HIT CASA BIG BUCKS LAST NIGHT AND WALKED AWAY WITH... NADA! NOTHING! ZILCH! ZIP!
ZIP IT YOURSELF, NIX! THERE'S MORE TO LIVIN' LARGE THAN JUST BIG SCORES!
FACT IS, I COULDN'T CARE LESS IF WE NEVER PULLED ANOTHER HEIST, SO--
?!?
WELL, STICK MY FINGER IN A SOCKET--I REALLY DON'T CARE!
A GIRL'S GOTTA MAKE A LIVIN', O'COURSE--BUT PLANNIN' AND PULLIN' JOBS 24-7? IT AIN'T WHERE MY HEART--

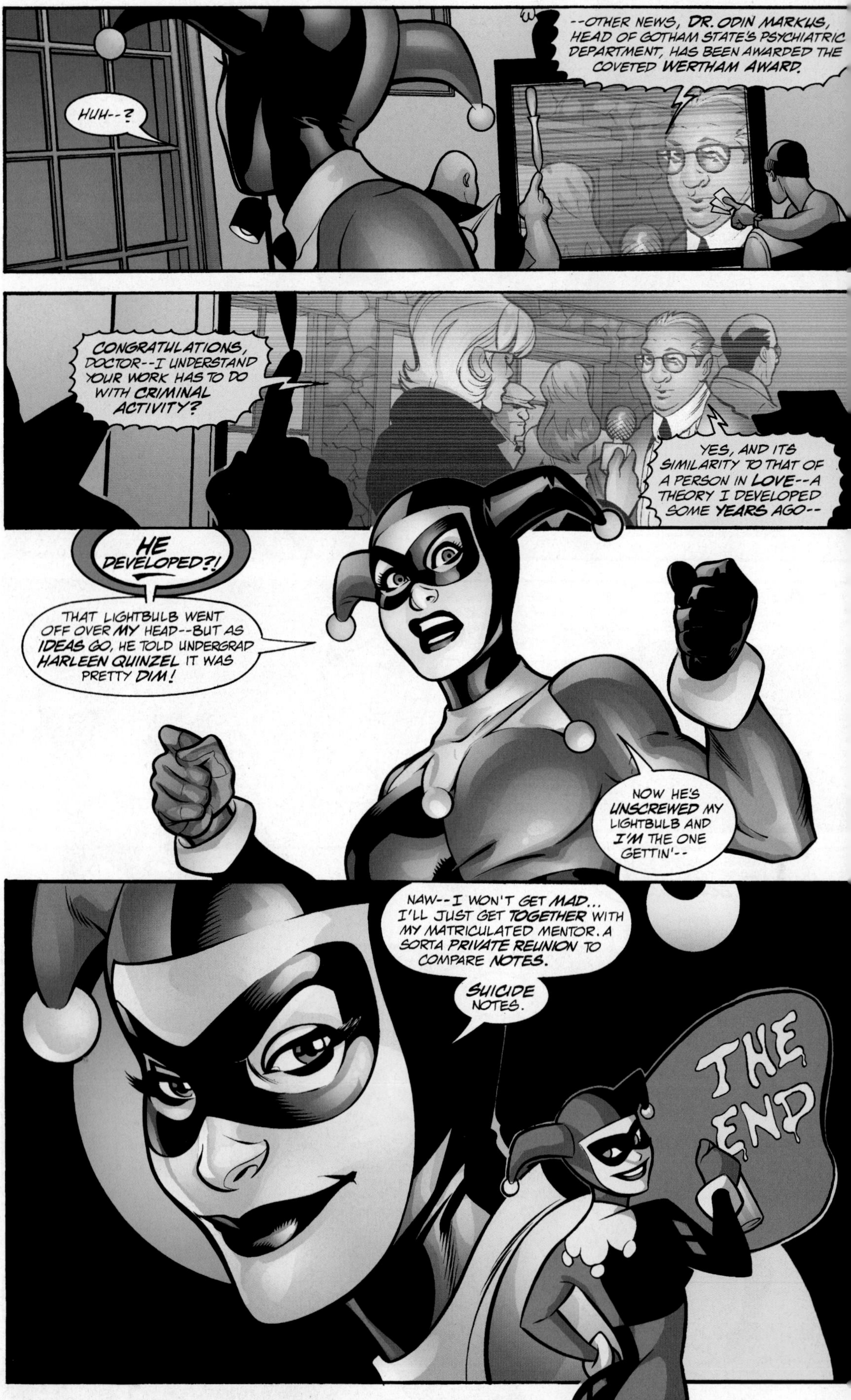

--OTHER NEWS, DR. ODIN MARKUS, HEAD OF GOTHAM STATE'S PSYCHIATRIC DEPARTMENT, HAS BEEN AWARDED THE COVETED WERTHAM AWARD.
HUH--?
CONGRATULATIONS, DOCTOR--I UNDERSTAND YOUR WORK HAS TO DO WITH CRIMINAL ACTIVITY?
YES, AND ITS SIMILARITY TO THAT OF A PERSON IN LOVE--A THEORY I DEVELOPED SOME YEARS AGO--
HE DEVELOPED?!
THAT LIGHTBULB WENT OFF OVER MY HEAD--BUT AS IDEAS GO, HE TOLD UNDERGRAD HARLEEN QUINZEL IT WAS PRETTY DIM!
NOW HE'S UNSCREWED MY LIGHTBULB AND I'M THE ONE GETTIN'--
NAW--I WON'T GET MAD... I'LL JUST GET TOGETHER WITH MY MATRICULATED MENTOR. A SORTA PRIVATE REUNION TO COMPARE NOTES.
SUICIDE NOTES.
THE END

DC COMICS™

FROM THE PAGES OF *BATMAN*

CATWOMAN VOL. 1: TRAIL OF THE CATWOMAN

ED BRUBAKER & DARWYN COOKE

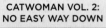

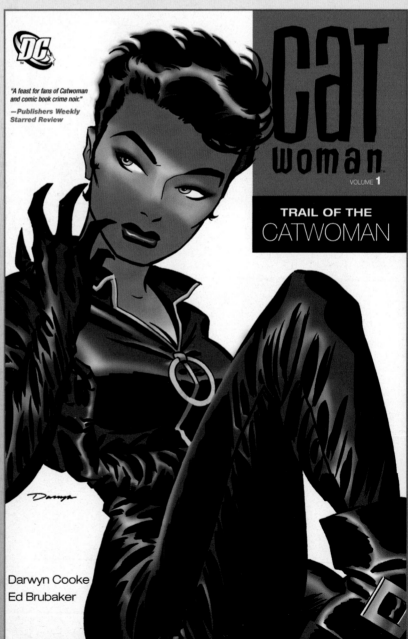

"A feast for fans of Catwoman and comic book crime noir."
—*Publishers Weekly* Starred Review

CAT woman
Volume 1

TRAIL OF THE
CATWOMAN

Darwyn Cooke
Ed Brubaker